REAL ESTATE EDUCATION THROUGHOUT THE WORLD: PAST, PRESENT AND FUTURE

RESEARCH ISSUES IN REAL ESTATE

Sponsored by the
AMERICAN REAL ESTATE SOCIETY

Volume I

APPRAISAL, MARKET ANALYSIS, AND
PUBLIC POLICY IN REAL ESTATE
edited by
James R. DeLisle and J. Sa-Aadu

Volume II

ALTERNATIVE IDEAS IN
REAL ESTATE INVESTMENT
edited by
Arthur L. Schwartz, Jr. and
Stephen D. Kapplin

Volume III

MEGATRENDS IN RETAIL REAL ESTATE
edited by John D. Benjamin

Volume IV

SENIORS HOUSING
edited by
Michael A. Anikeef and
Glenn R. Mueller

Volume V

ETHICS IN REAL ESTATE
edited by
Stephen E. Roulac

Volume VI

ESSAYS IN HONOR OF JAMES A. GRAASKAMP:
TEN YEARS AFTER
edited by
James R. DeLisle
Elaine M. Worzala

REAL ESTATE EDUCATION THROUGHOUT THE WORLD: PAST, PRESENT AND FUTURE

edited by

Karl-Werner Schulte
European Business School
Germany

KLUWER ACADEMIC PUBLISHERS
Boston / Dordrecht / London

Distributors for North, Central and South America:
Kluwer Academic Publishers
101 Philip Drive
Assinippi Park
Norwell, Massachusetts 02061 USA
Telephone (781) 871-6600
Fax (781) 681-9045
E-Mail <kluwer@wkap.com>

Distributors for all other countries:
Kluwer Academic Publishers Group
Distribution Centre
Post Office Box 322
3300 AH Dordrecht, THE NETHERLANDS
Telephone 31 78 6392 392
Fax 31 78 6546 474
E-Mail <services@wkap.nl>

 Electronic Services <http://www.wkap.nl>

Library of Congress Cataloging-in-Publication Data

Real estate education throughout the world : past, present, and future / edited by
Karl-Werner Schulte.
    p.cm.—(Research issues in real estate ; v. 7)
  Includes bibliographical references.
  ISBN 0-7923-7553-X (alk.paper)
    1. Real estate business—Study and teaching (Higher) 2.Real estate business--Study and
       teaching (Higher)—Case studies. I. Schulte, Karl-Werner. II. Series.

HD1381 .R386 2001
333.33'071'1—dc21   2001050373

Printed on acid-free paper.

Printed in the United States of America

The publisher offers discounts on this book for course use and bulk purchases.
For further information, send email to <david.cella@wkap.com>.

2000 American Real Estate Society

President's Council

Appraisal Institute
F. W. Dodge/McGraw-Hill
Fannie Mae Foundation
Fidelity National Title Insurance Company*
John Hancock Real Estate Investment Group
Institutional Real Estate, Inc.
LaSalle Investment Management

Legg Mason
Lend Lease Real Estate Investment
PricewaterhouseCoopers
Prudential Real Estate Investors
Real Estate Evaluation Services*
The Roulac Group
The RREEF Funds

Regents

COMPS Infosystems
Cornerstone Real Estate Advisers
Ferguson Partners*
International Council of Shopping Centers (ICSC)

MIG Realty Advisors
Multifamily Information Solutions
National Association of Real Estate Investment Trusts (NAREIT)

Sponsors

AEW Capital Management
Association of Foreign Investors in U.S. Real Estate (AFIRE)
Bailard, Biehl & Kaiser
BDO Seidman
BOMA International
Boston Financial
C. B. Richard Ellis/Torto Wheaton Research
CIGNA Investments
Citadel Realty
Counselors of Real Estate (CRE)
Dearborn Financial Publishing
The Dorchester Group
Exel Logistics*
Freddie Mac
GE Capital Real Estate
Gorsuch/Prentice Hall
Government of Singapore Investment Corporation (GSIC)
Heitman Capital Management Corporation
International Association of Corporate Real Estate Executives (NACORE)
Irwin/McGraw Hill
Kennedy-Wilson International

Management Reports, Inc.*
Mortgage Banker's Association
National Association of Industrial and Office Properties (NAIOP)
National Association of REALTORS® (NAR)
National Investment Center for the Seniors Housing & Care Industries
National Multi Housing Council
Steven L. Newman Real Estate Institute
New York University Real Estate Institute
Penobscot Group
Real Estate Center at Texas A&M University
Realty One
Research Institute for Housing America*
SNL Securities
Society of Industrial and Office REALTORS® (SIOR)
SSR Realty Advisors
Steven L. Newman Real Estate Institute
UBS Brinson Realty Investors
Urban Land Institute (ULI)
Woods & Poole Economics

*NEW for 2000

2000 Fellows of the American Real Estate Society

Joseph D. Albert
James Madison University

Brent W. Ambrose
University of Kentucky

Michael A. Anikeeff
Johns Hopkins University

John S. Baen
University of North Texas

John D. Benjamin
American University

Roy T. Black
Georgia State University

Donald H. Bleich
California State University–Northridge

Norbert J. T. Bol
GIM Capital Management

Waldo L. Born
Eastern Illinois University

James H. Boykin
Virginia Commonwealth University

Suzanne E. Cannon
DePaul University

Todd A. Canter
ABKB/LaSalle Securities

James Carr
Fannie Mae Foundation

K. W. Chau
University of Hong Kong

Lijian Chen
Lend Lease Real Estate Investments

Ping Cheng
Salisbury State University

James R. Cooper
Georgia State University

Glenn E. Crellin
Washington State University

John A. Dalkowski III
Phoenix Real Estate Advisors

Charles G. Dannis
Crosson Dannis

Karen G. Davidson
Davidson & Associates

James R. DeLisle
Georgia State University

Gene Dilmore
Realty Researchers

Geoffrey Dohrmann
Institutional Real Estate Inc.

Mark G. Dotzour
Texas A&M University

Robert Edelstein
University of California–Berkeley

John T. Emery
Louisiana Tech University

Donald R. Epley
Washington State University

S. Michael Giliberto
J. P. Morgan Investment Management

John L. Glascock
George Washington University

Paul R. Goebel
Texas Tech University

Richard B. Gold
Boston Financial

William C. Goolsby
University of Arkansas–Little Rock

Jacques Gordon
LaSalle Investment Management

G. Hayden Green
University of Alaska–Anchorage

D. Wylie Greig
The RREEF Funds

Terry V. Grissom
Georgia State University

Karl L. Guntermann
Arizona State University

Otis E. Hackett
Otis E. Hackett & Associates

Jun Han
John Hancock Real Estate Investments Group

Richard L. Haney
Texas A&M University

William G. Hardin, III
Mississippi State University

Chao-I Hsieh
National Taipei University

William Hughes
MIG Realty Advisors

Jerome R. Jakubovitz
MAI

Linda L. Johnson
Miller & Johnson

G. Donald Jud
University of North Carolina–Greensboro

Steven D. Kapplin
University of South Florida

George R. Karvel
University of Saint Thomas

James B. Kau
University of Georgia

William N. Kinnard, Jr.
Real Estate Counseling Group of Connecticut

Phillip T. Kolbe
University of Memphis

Paul D. Lapides
Kennesaw State University

Steven P. Laposa
PricewaterhouseCoopers

Youguo Liang
Prudential Real Estate Investors

Frederick Lieblich, SSR
Realty Advisors

2000 Fellows (continued)

Joseph B. Lipscomb
Texas Christian University

Marc A. Louargand
Cornerstone Realty Advisors

Emil Malizia
University of North Carolina–Chapel Hill

Christopher A. Manning
Loyola Marymount University

John F. McDonald
University of Illinois–Chicago Circle

Willard McIntosh
Prudential Real Estate Investors

Isaac Megbolugbe
Fannie Mae Foundation

Ivan J. Miestchovich, Jr.
University of New Orleans

Phillip S. Mitchell*
Mitchell & Associates

Norman G. Miller
University of Cincinnati

Glenn R. Mueller
Johns Hopkins University & Legg Mason

William Mundy
Mundy Jarvis & Associates

F. C. Neil Myer
Cleveland State University

Theron R. Nelson
University of North Dakota

Graeme Newell
University of Western Sydney

Joseph L. Pagliari, Jr.
Citadel Realty

Joseph D. Pasquarella
Joseph D. Pasquarella & Co.

Arnon Perry
Tel Aviv University

Steven A. Pyhrr
Kennedy-Wilson International

R. Malcolm Richards
Texas A&M University

Stephen E. Roulac
The Roulac Group & University of Ulster

Ronald C. Rutherford
University of Texas–San Antonio

Karl-Werner Schulte
European Business School

Arthur L. Schwartz, Jr.
University of South Florida

David Scribner
Scribner & Associates

M. Atef Sharkawy
Texas A&M University

Leon Shilton
Fordham University*

Jong-Wong Shin
Pacific Appraisal Co.

Robert A. Simons
Cleveland State University

C. F. Sirmans
University of Connecticut

Petros Sivitanides
Torto Wheaton Research

C. Ray Smith
University of Virginia

Halbert C. Smith
University of Florida

Rocky Tarantello
Tarantello & Company

Stephen F. Thode
Lehigh University

Grant Thrall
University of Florida

Raymond Torto
Torto Wheaton Research

Raymond Y. C. Tse
Hong Kong Polytechnic

Jorge I. Vallejo
Vallejo & Vallejo

Stephen M. Verba
Realty One

Ko Wang
California State University–Fullerton

James R. Webb
Cleveland State University

R. Bryan Webb
UBS Brinson Realty Investors

John E. Williams
Morehouse College

Larry E. Wofford
C&L Systems Corporation

Marvin Wolverton
Washington State University

Elaine M. Worzala
Colorado State University

Charles H. Wurtzebach
Henderson Properties

Tyler Yang
Freddie Mac

Michael S. Young
The RREEF Funds

Alan J. Ziobrowski
Georgia State University

Leonard V. Zumpano
University of Alabama

*NEW for 2000

Contents

x

VI. Real Estate Education in the Pacific Rim

VII. Real Estate Education in Africa

About the Editor

Karl-Werner Schulte holds an endowed Chair of Business Administration and Real Estate at the EUROPEAN BUSINESS SCHOOL (**ebs**) at Schloss Reichartshausen, in Oestrich-Winkel near Frankfurt, Germany. He is also the Academic Director of the **ebs** REAL ESTATE ACADEMY, which runs postgraduate programmes in Real Estate Management, Corporate Real Estate Management & Facilities Management, and Shopping Centre Development and Management, and of the **ebs** FINANCE ACADEMY, which runs postgraduate programmes in Financial Planning and Estate Planning.

He holds a Dr. rer. pol. (similar to a Ph.D. in Business Administration) (1974) and a Diplom-Kaufmann (1970), the German equivalent to the MBA, from the University of Münster, Germany.

Prior to his current positions, he was Associate Professor of Business Administration at the University of Münster, where he taught mainly Investment Analysis, Accounting and Auditing. In 1986 he took over the position as Chair of Business Administration and Investment & Finance at the EUROPEAN BUSINESS SCHOOL (**ebs**). He was founder and director of the Institute of Financial Management at **ebs** until 1994 when he started fundraising activities to establish the first Chair of Real Estate in Germany, which he took over in the same year.

He initiated the founding of the German Property Databank (1996) and the first German Real Estate Venture Capital Fund (2001).

Karl-Werner Schulte is also a member of the supervisory or advisory boards of a number of property companies and banks.

He published several books and more than 30 articles on Investment Analysis, Accounting and Auditing in the 1970s and 80s. Since he began to concentrate on real estate, he has edited 8 monographs, published numerous articles in German real estate journals and newspapers and has been an active speaker at key industry events. He also has assisted in the review process for some of the major real estate academic journals.

Karl-Werner Schulte is an Honorary Member of the Royal Institution of Chartered Surveyors (HonRICS), Honorary Certified Financial Planner (HonCFP) and an Honorary Member of *immo*ebs, the alumni association of graduates from **ebs** Real Estate Programmes.

Karl-Werner Schulte is an active member of several academic associations and is presently Chairman of the German Society of Property Researchers (gif) and President of the International Real Estate Society (IRES). He was President of the European Real Estate Society (ERES) in 1997/98 and has also served for three years as ERES Executive Director. In 1999 he received the IRES Service Award and in 2001 the ERES Achievement Award.

Preface

In recent years, growing attention has been focussed on real estate education. The objective of this monograph is to document the current status and perspectives of real estate education and the underlying research throughout the world. The intent is to inform students, academicians and practicing professionals about the situation in the widest possible range of countries and to provide a foundation for the future of the real estate discipline.

The editor started work on this monograph in autumn 1998. Some of the authors were found at once, others not until 2000. Some needed 2½ years to deliver their papers, others did so in only 4 weeks. As a result, there are slight differences in effective dates, but it did not seem fair to "punish" those authors who were on time.

The editor advised the authors of this monograph to use the same structure for their contributions, in order to make it easier for the reader to compare the content of the articles and to ensure that all necessary topics were covered.

This collection of papers is unique, in the sense that 50 authors have contributed to the monograph and 37 countries or regions in total are covered. The editor does not know of any comparable book.

The, perhaps ambitious, aim of this book was to give an overview of real estate education in the countries and regions of the world which are of greatest importance economically. For various reasons some areas are missing:

- It seems that most of the Arabian countries do not have any real estate education. There was either no response or a negative reply to letters directed to universities. Internet research was without success.
- The same applies to most countries in Latin America.
- Only a few countries of the ASEAN states are covered as one author did not deliver his paper, but I succeeded in finding authors in some, but not all, countries of Southeast Asia.
- It was difficult to obtain information on real estate education in India, and I was unsuccessful in finding an author in neighbouring Pakistan.

The structure of this monograph follows the organisation of the world-wide network of real estate societies. In Part 1, Stephen E. Roulac sets the framework for the other contributions. Part 2 contains 20 chapters that examine real estate education in Europe. Part 3 consists of two articles covering North America.

Part 4 includes two chapters dealing with Latin America. In Part 5, 8 countries in Asia are examined. Part 6 contains two chapters covering the Pacific Rim. Finally, Part 7 focuses on Africa.

Publishing a monograph with many authors always causes difficulties. For this book, the worst problem arose from the fact that most of the authors were not native English-speakers. Their papers had to be reviewed with respect to correct English. Then I received an email from which the next problem arose:

Alec Evans who checked all the manuscripts wrote:
…there is one very important point that comes from this thought. Some authors prefer "program(me)s" to "courses". This is an American usage, so the point is that we must be careful to use the same system in all the chapters and/or to explain in the introduction exactly what is meant by these terms.

In Britain it is usual to refer to e.g. "a Master's course" or "a university course", meaning the whole 3 (or whatever) year experience. The Americans (and some of our authors) use "course" to refer to what in England would be called a "subject", or alternatively (e.g. for CPD) a "short course".
Irritatingly, the British seem to refer to a collection of short courses (e.g. run in the summer vacation) as a "programme"!

I have done a quick bit of research to confirm my thoughts, please see for example http://www.cam.ac.uk/cambuniv/guide/ugcourses/landecon.html and you will see what I mean.

Although the whole process there is called a "course", it seems to consist of smaller chunks – "subjects", some of which are also called "courses" in the

American manner. Confusing. One thing is however certain – in British English "programme" does NOT mean e.g. a degree "course".

As a contrast, see http://www.fas.harvard.edu/academics/courses/.

To summarise: we have to decide whether to use the British or American terminology.

If it is decided to adopt the American system, we must revert to the American spelling of "program". The problem then is where to stop. My problem with American English is (presumably) the same as yours would be with Schwiezerdeutsch *(the very individual German spoken in Switzerland – ed.)*. I can understand it, but I can't write it correctly – not enough to fool an American anyway.

Alternatively, if we keep everything in British English, we either change "programme" to "course" where appropriate, or (easier) leave it as it is and rely on the introduction to explain. But then "native speaker" chapters have to comply...

Sorry this has become rather long and complicated, but I hope you see what I am driving at (or as the Americans would say, "where I am coming from"). This was also the reason for writing in English!

Best wishes
Alec

And there was one more email:

Prof. Schulte's original instruction was to edit the papers into "Oxford English". This (I assumed) means "British English" – the type I speak- rather than the American variety. The differences are not huge, but are most evident in words like program(me), the American use of *..ize* rather than the British *..ise* on word endings, and the more careful use of articles (a, the etc.) in British English. I mention this because quite a few of the papers (particularly Asian ones) are written in a type of American English, which I have changed. Hope this doesn't upset the authors. If the book is intended for a mainly US audience, we ought to consider changing the words to American, although it may not be quite that easy.

Incidentally, "program" is used in British English, but only for computer software – it keeps its ..me for other purposes (TV or theatre etc.)

Best wishes
Alec

As you will recognise, the editor decided not to use the same system in all chapters. I preferred to explain in the introduction exactly what is meant by these terms (program/programme or course or subject), and that word endings and the use of articles can be different in "British English" and "American English". I hope the reader(s) will find this acceptable.

Finally, I hope this publication will serve as a reference tool and will foster healthy debate among you and your colleagues about the "ideal way" to educate future real estate professionals

Sponsorship for this monograph was provided by the Chair of Business Administration and Real Estate at the EUROPEAN BUSINESS SCHOOL (**ebs**) and by the ebs REAL ESTATE ACADEMY, both in Oestrich-Winkel near Frankfurt, Germany.

The editor would like to thank, first of all, the authors for their contributions, and

- Nico Rottke, MSRE, for his excellent assistance in collating this monograph
- Alec H Evans, FRICS, for his great support in the preparation of this monograph by superbly editing the manuscripts into correct (British) English
- Jim Webb, the former Executive Director of the American Real Estate Society, for his initiative to publish this monograph and for good advice
- and finally my sons Frank-Michael and Sven-Marten for supporting the email conversation with all the authors, and my wife Gisela and my son Kai-Magnus for their understanding.

Dr. Karl-Werner Schulte

Professor of Business Administration and Real Estate
European Business School (**ebs**)
Academic Director
ebs Real Estate Academy

I

REAL ESTATE EDUCATION IN THE GLOBAL CONTEXT

Chapter 1

Requisite Knowledge for Effective Property Involvements in the Global Context

Stephen E. Roulac
The Roulac Group Inc., San Rafael, USA and University of Ulster, Northern Ireland

1.1 Introduction

The requisite knowledge for making effective decisions concerning property involvements in the global context of the 21st century transcends the curriculum content of traditional real estate education. Traditional real estate education, biased towards and reflects a narrow, even restricted interpretation of the dimensions and domain of the discipline, often reflects a limited, culturally narrow, even parochial view of the world. Consequently, graduates of the prevailing programs of real estate study are unlikely to possess the required knowledge for effective property involvements in the global context. The knowledge that is needed to be known for effective property involvements in the global context. is the subject of this paper.

The dynamic forces of change realigning the environments in which the real estate/property professional operates are similar to those occurring within society, the global economic system, and the financial services markets in particular. As a consequence of property having gained substantial acceptance by and recognition within the institutional community, there are more pressures for professionalism on the part of those delivering services and also the need to "bridge" the traditional world of property and the cultures of the new participants. Thus, those who would be effective in their property involvements must blend the traditional with the innovative, the entrepreneurial with the fiduciary, private sector initiative with public sector policy concerns, and the immediacy of specific project focus with the continuity of going concern enterprise and institutional time horizons.

1.2   The Changing Property Discipline

The property discipline today is subjected to extraordinary forces that redefine its attributes and introduce new expectations for those with property involvements. Among the considerations are:

– *Urban Form* — In the United States of American people rate *urban sprawl* and crime as the two greatest societal concerns;
– *Technology Advances* — Advances in telecommunications and information technologies dramatically transform the means and location of work, changing what activities happen in physical spaces and where those physical spaces are located;
– *Environmental Concern* — With more people placing greater emphasis on spirituality and environmental sustainability, considerations of property as a commodity are less and less accepted;
– *Globalization* — With business enterprise expanding the scope of its geographical concerns, drawing resources from distant markets and selling throughout the world, physical proximity no longer is the primary defining guideline or constraint to access labor and customers;
– *Strategic Resource* — Companies increasingly recognize that workplace environment and retail facilities influence their ability to achieve their strategic objectives;
– *Public-Private Concern* — The nature of major urban development, involving linking of public policy objectives and private sector motives, requires partnerships that blend the social and financial attributes of property.

There is need for a cohesive and coherent framework to enable participants to comprehend the overall collection of phenomena, forces and relationships that comprise the property discipline. Further, each player seeks a framework appropriate to their role and purpose in order to rationalize how they perceive and interact with places, spaces, properties, and real estate as well as other players.

Many approaches to the property discipline are overly narrow in focus and limited in scope, thereby being characterized by misplaced emphasis and insufficient attention to critical issues that should be considered. More specifically, too often the traditional approaches are virtually devoid of a strategic orientation, in that they:

- View property involvements primarily from an outmoded deal-making transaction approach, without sufficient consideration of the important policy and portfolio issues;
- Fail to address how large scale political and economic forces generally and capital flows specifically drive markets and therefore property values and returns;
- Ignore the profound implications of advances in information and communication technology concerning how society relates to space and place;
- Pay scant attention to corporate management issues associated with the second largest expense line item on the income statement.

Since strategy involves synthesis and integration, a strategic orientation can provide the unifying approach to the multiple considerations that represent and affect property.

The property industry has moved from a transaction orientation to a strategic orientation. Superior outcomes and rewards result from superior knowledge of the property process and the ability to act on that knowledge. No longer can strategy be an afterthought to a transaction, but rather strategy should be the overriding guide to business decision-making. Effective property involvements follow from comprehending the strategic map of the property industry, identifying key areas of knowledge and the linkages between areas of knowledge.

1.3 Multiple Place Contexts

Fundamental to effective property involvements in the 21st century, then, is appreciation for the importance of the global context. Effective property involvements in the 21st century necessarily embrace multiple geographies and levels of concern, extending from the most intimate and immediate to the most global and expansive. Juxtaposed to the importance of the global orientation is the imperative of sensitivity to and emphasis upon the inherent *localness* of property and real estate. Consequently, to be global but to omit sensitivity to the more localized perspectives can be as perilous as to be local yet innocent of the import of global forces.

The orientation of the majority of participants in property and real estate is predominantly parochial rather than global. Many in approaching property manifest a Ptolemaic orientation, viewing their involvement, function, and role vis-à-vis property as the veritable center of the universe (Roulac, 1998). Such an orientation is increasingly vulnerable to miscalculation, disappointment, financial reversal, if not overt failure, in a time of globalization in which local outcomes are largely influenced by far distant decisions and actions (Friedman, 2000). The Copernican perspective to property champions the perspective not of the property being the center of attention but rather the patterns of society's use of property being the focus of emphasis (Roulac, 1998).

The local-global duality is reconciled by considering that property embraces many discrete segments or levels of involvement, orientation and experience. Effective property involvements derive from consideration of the most macro to the most micro as well as the many intermediate concerns. While many schemes may be employed to describe the multiple levels of location, one framework that has proven useful is to consider that the scale and personalization of where you live can be thought of as comprising sixteen levels, ranging from the continent in which you live to the most meaningful and personal of personal spaces in which you live. An array of these sixteen levels of where you live appears in Exhibit 1. Every property involvement, then, can be considered to consist of these 16 attributes of place and space relationships. Effective property involvement is informed by knowledge of the forces that influence each of these 16 levels, and how each of these 16 levels influence specific property interests, functions, decisions and involvements.

Place embraces the 12 critical elements of continent, country, county, state/providence, region within the state/providence, metropolis, city, region, community, neighborhood, street, and site, which in aggregate are the attributes of *location*. Space embraces the five critical elements of site, building structure, interior design/floor plan, room and *personal space,* which collectively comprise the particulars of the built environment personally experienced. Place and Space intersect at and share site, and each is influenced by the attributes of the other. These key elements of PlaceSpace are visually depicted in Exhibit 1. While all places are defined in these 16 dimensions, the relative priorities that people assign to these different dimensions of where they live can vary dramatically between individuals and, especially significantly, for the same individual between roles.

1.4   Property and Context

Comprehending the relationship of different perspectives of place—property—real estate—facilities is essential to determining what knowledge relates to what level. A curriculum oriented to preparing people to be knowledgeable about considerations relevant to a *facilities* orientation is very different than what would be relevant for a *property* orientation. In the last quarter of the 20th century there emerged a clear schism between the British and American perspectives to education concerning property and real estate. Whereas in earlier times the American approach to higher education embraced property level considerations, over the last couple of decades of the 20th century the emphasis narrowed, resulting in curriculums that championed real estate and a more restricted view of the discipline, its curriculum content and relevant pedagogy. By the end of the 20th century, a disproportionate number of American real estate academics placed a primary emphasis on finance in their approach to the subject, which emphasis is inconsistent with the consideration that the vast majority of real estate academics are either housed in or affiliated with the college of business department of finance (Webb and Albert, 1995). The English approaches continued to reflect a property primacy, with a broader view of the discipline. Whether the dominance of the finance perspective is the appropriate and preferred paradigm for property and real estate involvements has been challenged by a number of thought leaders including Graaskamp (1976), Diaz (1993) and Roulac (1996).

Those who aspire to an impactful professional career in property involvements must exercise self-leadership in designing their academic curriculum and professional training. Presently, where one chooses to pursue graduate study in the property and real estate disciplines will, to a very large degree, determine the education one receives.

If one pursues graduate study in the United States, one most likely will take courses from and study predominantly with professors housed or affiliated with the department of finance in the college of business. Such a curriculum can provide a comprehensive exposure to the multiple disciplines of business, which exposure is all very apropos, for each property is itself a business. Further, as the tenants of non-residential buildings are businesses, the more one knows about business, the more effectively one can interact with those tenants.

Such a business school course of study will, however, omit the learning that could be obtained through a United Kingdom School of the Built Environment, with its heavy emphasis on the classic surveying curriculum, involving an orientation to basic close-to-the-land disciplines. Consequently, strange as it might seem, the majority of graduates of United States real estate program may be blissfully ignorant of the subject of geography, generally, and how it relates to issues of real estate property and place specifically.

If a United Kingdom course of study is chosen, students will have much more exposure to the *real* of real estate, following from the classic surveying tradition. These students in the school of built environment will have much more particular knowledge of the tangible than would their American counterparts. This background better prepares such students for hands on involvement with land and buildings.

The *classic School of the Built Environment* emphasis is disadvantaged, however, because graduates tend to have much reduced exposure to business administration and international context. Lacking the knowledge, perspectives and advanced analytical tool kits that graduates in business administration and law possess, these U.K graduates may be at a big disadvantage in competing with their counterparts who have background in business administration and law. More specifically, the normal survey in education provides only the most limited preparation for such critically relevant professional disciplines as corporate real estate management and real estate investment banking. Without explicit study of the strategic outlook, MBA technical skills, and managerial orientation, the U.K graduates are at a big disadvantage.

Certain real estate education programs in continental Europe seek to bridge the property emphasis of the U.K. and the financial emphasis of the U.S. An interdisciplinary approach, bringing together the multiple perspectives of business management, finance, and the school of the built environment, prospectively offers a more balanced and richer course of preparation.

A typology of the organization perspective and management orientation of the four levels of place, property, real estate and facilities is shown in Exhibit 2. As seen, the dominant American approach to study *real estate* relates to a managerial organization perspective and middle management orientation. Given this orientation, it is not surprising that the majority of leading American business schools possess neither a strong faculty nor offer a credible program of study that is relevant/related to real estate and property. By contrast, the *property* construct relates to strategy and senior management. At the highest level, *place* reflects suprastrategy and the consensus of the CEO and Board.

This larger view of the requisite knowledge for the property discipline is especially significant given the changing composition of those who exert the most influence upon critical decisions concerning the design, creation and use of the built environment. Previously, the property discipline was dominated by real estate people who knew little of business, finance and technology. In the 21st century, by contrast, property and real estate are increasingly dominated by finance and technology people who have only passing familiarity with, much less knowledge of, property and real estate. Indeed, one author describes corporations' space use decisions as dominated by "people who hate real estate" (O'Mara, 1999). Not appreciated sufficiently is that property, rather than being an aggravation or even an irrelevancy, can be the means to achieving extraordinary business outcomes (Roulac, 2000).

The requisite knowledge for effective property involvements in the global context follows from the primacy of property, which, as described above, is a higher level and broader scope approach than real estate per se. Courses of study that are oriented to facilities and real estate would preferably *follow* a foundation course that provides the context of place–property–real estate–facilities. The curriculums of major institutions that aspire to educate people (1) to make informed decisions concerning society and (2) to assume management and leadership positions within society, would do well to have a program that emphasizes property rather than real estate per se. This priority suggests, then, that the higher level orientation of the British system should be emphasized over the lower level orientation of the American system. *Property* is emphasized in this writing, with real estate and facilities being a subset and thereby subsumed within property.

1.5 Societal Spatial Patterns

The how, where, when, which, what and *why* questions of the role of property in society determine the need for property goods and services. Societal spatial patterns are ultimately manifested in the decisions that influence economic regions, property types, investment forms, business strategies, services offers, public services demands, and government fiscal outcomes.

Certain larger level global questions, which have major implications for the property sector, include:

- Where will demand be?
- How does a local-oriented business service a global market?
- What is the location of work and sales?
- What are the implications of the information economy for property demand?
- How will governance forms evolve?
- What are the opportunities and implications of new forms of property ownership?
- Which theory of town development planning will dominate?

The answers to these seven questions reflect new themes of societal spatial patterns (Roulac, 1998).

Collectively, answers to these questions are societal spatial patterns. When societal spatial patterns are consistent and constant, financing practices are relatively consistent and constant. When societal spatial patterns change, financing practices likewise change.

Among the themes redefining societal spatial patterns are:

- New forms of organization;
- New technologies for implementing work and commerce;
- New values, emphasizing spirituality, community and lifestyle balance;
- Demographics including an older population, maturing baby boomers, continuing immigration, cultural diversity, and more lifestyle diversity.

These themes have major implications for property investments and financing practices.

Societal spatial patterns are ultimately manifested in the decisions that influence economic regions, property types, and investment forms. Economic activity is more and more influenced by social values, product concepts and designs, technologies, suppliers, manufacturers, and merchandisers who are located far distant from where goods and services are consumed. A shrinking proportion of goods and services offered by local merchants are produced and delivered by local firms.

Advances in information and telecommunications dramatically increase the economy, portability, power and accessibility of information. These technology advances simultaneously introduce very different patterns of organization, which in turn lead to different physical forms of working, shopping, living, and leisure. There has been a shift of business transactions occurring at the time, place, and convenience of the vendor to the time, place, and convenience of the consumer. At the very time that advances in telecommunications render irrelevant distance as a constraint, travel generally, and especially internationally, is up strongly. These forces have powerful implications for property demand.

With separation of transaction from physical environments as a consequence of non-store shopping as well as redefining the role of corporate headquarters as a consequence of pervasive non-office working arrangements, a very different agenda of location factors are introduced. The combination of sophisticated electronic telecommunications and advance logistics delivery systems dramatically change the proximity parameters of workers and customers to the work place. Information technology advances and social forces of change alter relationships of store purpose to the retail space function.

Although once central to the strategy domain, as reflected in Napoleon's assessment that "strategy is the art of making use of time and space," for much of the 20th century geography has been largely discounted as a primary consideration by those responsible for crafting enterprise strategy. While land-based issues were fundamental to early economic theory, in the form of such important work as that by David Ricardo (1911) concerning land rent and Thomas Malthus (1798) concerning population-productivity interactions, issues of spatial economic geography for much of the last century have been assigned a much-diminished priority. But today, at the same time that there has been a renaissance of big ideas in strategic management, so also are strategic management theorists and economists devoting increasing attention to issues of location and geography.

1.6 Requisite Knowledge for Property Decisions

The capacity to make informed property decisions can metaphorically be viewed as the upstream source that determines the flow that reaches the downstream user. This singular upstream source is the synthesis of theory, history, content, context, process, methodology. The evolution of the property discipline embraces multiple perspectives of licensing, professional designations, university-based education, adult continuing education, applied *how to* courses, theoretical research, applied research, multi-faceted application of theory and learning as well as multiple public interest concerns. The contemporary orientation of the discipline is reflected in the different paradigms employed for considering property, including economics, finance, geography, engineering, highest and best use, city planning, brokerage, legal, corporate decisions, the consumer transaction, and a multi-disciplinary approach.

Effective property involvement employs multiple perspectives and skill sets to address the crucial questions for effective property involvements, and applies the capacity to reframe problems, select appropriate methodologies and tools, gather the requisite information, and be self-educating to learn what one needs to know to address the problems one encounters. Concurrently, it reflects a sense of history of the property discipline, including knowledge of forces that have shaped contemporary places, spaces and urban form as well as the thought leaders of the discipline, including Graaskamp, Ratcliff, Wendt and Zeckendorf plus select individuals still active today.

An illuminating prescription to guide property education and research is provided by Schulte, who employs a *house of real estate* consisting of a foundation of business administration supported by interdisciplinary studies and economics, law, regional planning, architecture and engineering. The two pillars of (1) property types — commercial properties, residential properties, industrial properties and special properties — and (2) institutions — property developers, property investors, construction companies, financial institutions, consultants, property users and others — support (1) strategic — portfolio management, corporate property/real estate management, public property/real estate management; (2) functional — property analysis, valuation, property investment, property finance, property marketing; and (3) phase specific — development, project management, facilities management — aspects of management (Schulte, 2000).

To be effective in property involvements one must simultaneously be and provide the perspectives of:

- Historian
- Behaviorist
- Global citizen
- Urban planner
- Geographer
- Business strategist
- Futurist
- Political economist
- Information specialist

These perspectives transcend the scope of the majority of undergraduate and graduate property and real estate curriculums. Indeed, few people graduating with a specialization in property or real estate will have had meaningful exposure to these topics.

Since property encompasses the physical structures that house society's personal, commercial, recreational and institutional involvements and interactions, virtually any factor relevant to the human condition is relevant to property. The challenge, then, is to determine what relevant knowledge is but not part of property discipline and what is in fact part of the property discipline.

To be effective, a property participant needs knowledge of such core disciplines as physical sciences, behavior theory, political science, economics and management. Yet these core disciplines, relevant as they are to effective participation in property, are not part of the property discipline per se. Less clear cut is the relationship of certain fundamental disciplines to property. Fundamental disciplines, which can be considered to embrace the tools, theories and concepts one must know as a precondition to effective property involvement, are listed in Exhibit 3. Similarly, certain allied sectors of the economy, whose goods and services are utilized and employed in creating real properties and delivering property services, are integral to but not part of the property discipline per se. These critical, linked but separate, allied sectors are shown in Exhibit 4.

To be effective in the property sector, it is necessary to have an understanding of the environment of the business, its institutional relationships, the technical tools necessary to perform fundamental tasks, and the personal style and attributes necessary for effective performance. This knowledge can be acquired in schools, by personal inquiry, and/or through experience. New entrants into the property business must be sensitive to the issue of the judicious use of the power of the superior newly-acquired analytical skills, including an awareness and knowledge of crucial environmental issues. This is contrasted with those who know the "what" but not he "how" of the decision. More than one long-time property operative can determine the indicated course of action but, if pressed, would be hard put to document or describe explicitly the reasons for his decision. In a sense, this tension was well captured in a memorable scene from *The Music Man*, a highly popular musical comedy by Meredith Wilson. In this telling scene, several travelling salesmen on the train are debating the merits of cash vs. credit terms. The traditionalist argues the advantage of cash, whereas the new proposal is to sell on credit. It is a debate that has existed for some time and has yet to be resolved, yet the underlying refrain, repeated over and over, is, "You gotta know the territory."

The lesson to be learned by the new property professional is that knowledge of the basic business environment — who the players are, how transactions work, the major forces that influence decisions, the fundamentals of the business — is a necessary condition for effective participation. At the same time, superior application of managerial skills and techniques should go hand in hand with such environmental knowledge. The *property professional* who would be successful in the property sector will balance and integrate the following attributes:

- *Environmental Knowledge* — As discussed previously, understanding of the "territory" fundamental to successful participation in any business, is particularly crucial in the property sector.
- *Strategic Outlook* — As rapidly accelerating pace of change within the structure of the property business is causing traditional relationships to crumble and new power alliances to emerge, positioning one's self and one's organization strategically assumes great importance.
- *MBA Technical Skills* — The skills that are developed through the MBA learning experience — particularly the analytical methods for problem solving, systems and procedures to achieve economy of operation and

control of performance, and forecasting techniques to plan future operations and facilitate capital budgeting decisions — have an important role
in the "tool kit" of the property manager.

- *Entrepreneurial Initiative* — The property business is inherently entrepreneurial in that it marshals resources and influences behavior patterns
in settings that are largely unstructured and where precedents may be
few if any. Those who need order, structure, and predictability, and who
are uncomfortable with uncertainty, ambiguity, pressure and volatility,
would do well to apply elsewhere.

- *Institutional Style* — The increasing dominance of the role of capital
control by institutions mean that an important prerequisite for effective
operation in the property sector will be appropriate "presence" in the institutional settings. This requirement is both a departure from past practices and alien to many who are involved in various facets of the property business.

- *Managerial Orientation* — More competitive conditions, larger organizations and higher expectations of more sophisticated participants place
a premium on a managerial orientation to the business. A structured approach emphasizing planning systems and controls is becoming increasingly important.

- *Marketing Flair* — The property business is ultimately concerned with
the merchandising of space in the context of the relationship of supply
and demand. A manager's ability to perceive the unrecognized opportunity, to structure creative purchase terms, and to perform effectively the
many functions involved in the property process determine his capacity
to answer such critical questions as:
  - What do people want?
  - What factors influence decisions?
  - What else is available?
  - How does our space compare to that of the competition?
  - How can we differentiate and merchandise our product it to
    achieve a premium return?

Marketing flair can be instrumental in promoting space and achieving
superior returns.

- *Personal Skills and People Orientation* — While the "people factor" is
important in any number of businesses, it is especially important in
property, given the influence that property decisions have on one's personal and organizational life, as well as the role that emotional factors
play in many property decisions. Thus, creating the appropriate personal
rapport can often be fundamental to achieving good property results. At
the same time, such basic personality traits as creativity, integrity,
persistence, persuasiveness, diligence and attention to detail, are all

sistence, persuasiveness, diligence and attention to detail, are all factors that increase one's likelihood of success in the property business.

These knowledge attributes are fundamental for effective property involvements in the global context.

1.7 Property Discipline Scope

The property discipline — its processes, institutions, players, functions, markets, theories and concepts, paradigms, and rules and regulations — mediates and creates connections between society's values and spatial patterns. The property discipline embraces a multitude of stakeholders in property decisions, beyond the primary decision maker who initiates and controls the decision. While sensitivity to the system consequences of property is of great importance to both the success of a specific transaction and also to society broadly, how stakeholders should incorporate these concerns in their property decisions is too seldom explicitly considered.

A specific societal spatial property pattern can be traced back through the labyrithian matrix and methodological constructs of the property discipline to *value values*, for every property decision that impacts *value* reflects the interpretation of values through the institutions, rules, procedures, players and markets that comprise the property sector broadly defined. Every component element of the property process is informed by core values and ultimately is reflected in societal spatial patterns. The output of the property process is reflected in the *value* of the multiple property interests.

Employing the vocabulary of property, it is useful to think of *values* as representing the *foundation* of the construct of the property discipline, and *societal spatial patterns* as representing the *penthouse* of the property discipline. A penthouse in a multi-story building is achieved through the disciplined and effective application of multiple tasks, involving considerable resources, time, money and materials. As necessary as is the foundation, by no means is the foundation sufficient to construct an edifice that would support the penthouse. Many floors must be added to the foundation, with each floor consisting of multiple components and requiring conscientious coordination and application of high level of skills.

Another perspective concerning the property discipline is to consider that *values* determine the prevailing *world view* that influences *societal spatial patterns* that ultimately determine *property outcomes*. The transition and translation from and between values to property outcomes is aided, abetted, shaped and formed by the collective component elements of the property discipline — institutions, rules, regulations, processes, procedures, players, functions, markets, theories, concepts and paradigms — and by the decisions and actions of a multitude of property initiatives — embracing leading thought, government stimulus and constraint, entrepreneurial initiative, business decisions, household choices, investor preferences, competition for resources and professional practices. Property outcomes are by-products of how the values of society are translated into societal spatial patterns through a multitude of institutions, processes, regulations, practices and players and their decisions. These relationships are conceptually presented in Exhibit 5.

The requisite knowledge for effective property involvements in the global context must necessarily bridge the capacity to address constructively the present, and to prepare for bridging from the present to a future that most probably will reflect profound change. Central to effective property involvements is the capacity to recognize, adapt to and lead change. As society moves into the 21st century, property, as well as all who work within it and are influenced by it, will undergo singular changes. These changes will:

- Modify traditional patterns of space use and the functions performed within types of property;
- Introduce new influences on space locations decisions;
- Redefine the parameters of real estate value;
- Change the basic structural demand, resulting in less, in the aggregate, in different locations and of different types;
- Impact the strategies, structures and systems of organizations serving those involved in and using real estate;
- Create new needs for professional services;
- Elevate to a new standard the requisite knowledge, skills and style of professionals working in the real estate sector; and
- Render obsolete many of yesterday's accepted principles and practics.

Any property curriculum that fails to prepare property professionals for the implications of these change forces is per se, by definition, dysfunctional (Roulac, 1996).

1.8   Roulac Place/Property/Real Estate Body of Knowledge Framework

The 17 elements that comprise the property framework are shown in Exhibit 6, which reflects what can be considered to be an edifice of the property discipline, built floor by floor, starting from values and ultimately leading to societal spatial patterns. Significantly, property outcomes are the by-product of how values are translated into societal spatial patterns through a multitude of institutions, processes, regulations, practices, as reflected in these multiple elements of the property discipline. An alternative approach to these seventeen elements of the *Roulac Place/Property/Real Estate Body of Knowledge Framework*, depicting the connections and interrelationships from a concentric rather than an additive perspective, is shown in Exhibit 7.

An alternative approach to the 17 elements of the property framework described above is to view the connections and interrelationships from a concentric rather than an additive perspective. The additive perspective, presented in exhibit 6, and the concentric perspective, presented in Exhibit 7, are somewhat static, suggesting more linearity and sequentiality than a dynamic, iterative and interactive reality of the property process. Another view of the *property process* that captures and reflects the dynamism of the interactions within and between real property, virtual space, property players, decisions and property functions and markets, all informed by values and political economy, the environmental context, and strategic frameworks and decision tools is show in Exhibit 8.

The requisite knowledge for effective property involvements in the global context follows from competency in certain primary disciplines, as listed in Exhibit 9, for each of the elements of the Roulac Unified Theory. While the traditional real estate subject matter is certainly necessary for effective property involvements in the global context, by no means is that knowledge sufficient. Those who would be effective must know much more than is reflected in contemporary real estate curriculums. As reflected in exhibit 10, which depicts the intersection of elements of Roulac Unified Theory and the primary disciplines, the requisite knowledge for effective property involvement extends way beyond the traditional real estate subject matter.

1.9 Conclusion

The property professional who possesses requisite knowledge for effective property involvements in the global context possess knowledge that informs their every interaction with the real estate process through reverence for the land, respect for the cultural heritage of indigenous peoples, insistence on distinctive design, attention to user needs, excellence in professional practice, superb service, reliable representations, and asking the big questions. The big questions are too seldom asked. These big questions include:

- For any proposed real estate venture, what are the assumptions about why people choose to spend their time and resources at this place and space?
- What motivates people to be at this space and spend their resources here rather than at other spaces?

- How many people are presumed to live, work, shop, learn, play at this space? What alternatives to this space do these people have?
- How much money are customers presumed to spend in this space? Are such expenditures consistent with their resources? Motivations?
- Why do people choose to live where they do?
- How do our values influence the design of the structures in which we live, work, shop, learn and play?
- How does the design of the structures in which we live, work and learn influence our values?
- How do our values influence the place where we choose to live?
- How do the places where we choose to live, work and visit affect our values and our experience of life?
- What is the appropriate strategy to provide access to those who are not from a special place and to preserve that special place so it is not despoiled by those who visit?
- What are the implications of these choices on the place and the people?

The requisite knowledge for effective property involvements in the global context facilitates informed, responsible responses to these questions (Roulac, 1996).

The conceptual framework for the body of knowledge in the property discipline presented here, reflects the evolution of past, present and anticipated future directions of the theory and practice of the property discipline and is intended to further several objectives. This framework is intended to be responsive to and reflective of such significant dominant influences as how technology is redefining space use patterns, regulatory influence and constraint, the role of professional property organizations, the inexorable securitization of property finance, and the uncertain standing of the property discipline in the academy. Further, the conceptual framework is intended to reflect the key property decisions, including those concerning the use of space by households and businesses, financial involvements, public regulatory oversight, and individuals' roles as responsible citizens.

On a most basic level, the body of knowledge conceptual framework is a typology, a classifying scheme to organize a vast, multi-faceted, multi-dimensional, multi-disciplinary field that has long struggled for definition, identity, consensus, focus, and respect. The overarching purpose of this body of knowledge conceptual framework is not merely to provide a way of organizing topics, but to introduce a new strategic paradigm that represents both a vision to guide thinking, teaching and research, and also a pragmatic means to organize information to enhance effective property participation and decisions.

REFERENCES

Diaz, J., Science, "Engineering and the Discipline of Real Estate," *Journal of Real Estate Literature*, 1993, 1:2, 183–95.

Friedman, Thomas L., The Lexus and Olive Tree: Understanding Globalization, New York, Farrar Straus & Giroux, 2000.

Graaskamp, James A., "Redefining the Role of University Education and Real Estate and Urban Land Economics, *Real Estate Appraiser*, March–April 1976, 23.

O'Mara, Martha, *Strategy and Place,* Free Press, New York, 1999.

Roulac, Stephen, "Corporate Property Strategy is Integral to Corporate Business Strategy," forthcoming in *Journal of Real Estate Research*.

———, "Property and Ptolemy, Copernicus and Commerce—Toward a Strategic Perspective for Global Property Involvements," *Journal of Property Valuation & Investment* (Vol. 16, No. 5, 1998): 431–446.

———, "The State of the Discipline: Malaise or Renaissance," *The Journal of Real Estate Research* special issue commemorating the tenth anniversary of the American Real Estate Society (Vol. 12, No. 2, 1996): 111–121.

Schulte, Karl-Werner, "Real Estate Education Throughout the World," paper presented to American Real Estate Conference (Santa Barbara, 2000).

Webb, J. R. and J. D. Albert, "Evaluating the Real Estate Journals: The Mainstream Finance Perspective," *Journal of Real Estate Research* (1995, 10:2, 217–26).

APPENDIX

Exhibit 1: The Place and Space Elements of PlaceSpace

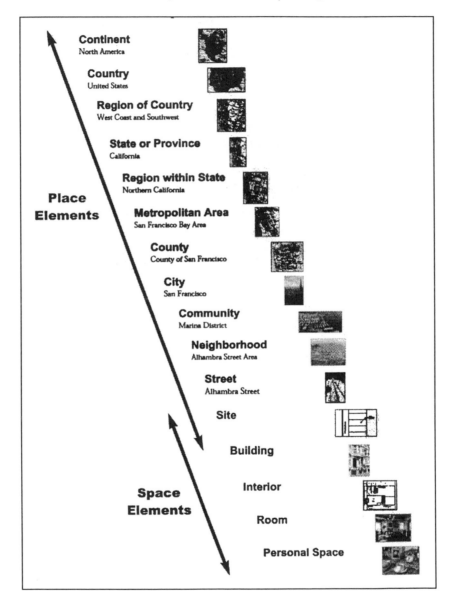

Exhibit 2: Place–Property–Real Estate–Facilities: Perspective & Orientation

	Constructs			
	Facility	**Real Estate**	**Property**	**Place**
Management Orientation	Lower Management	Middle Management	Senior management	CEO/Board
Organization Perspective	Administration	Managerial	Strategy	Suprastrategy
Attention	Physical	Technical	Policy	Concept
Time Horizon	Useful life	Short term	Longer term	Long term
Emphasis	Reliability, suitability	Costs/revenues	Support desired outcome	Profound impacts
Values orientation	Traditional	Modern	Traditional, cultural, & modern	Culture & modern
Measures of Performance	Safety, cleanliness	Revenues, occupancy, cash flow	Customer attraction and satisfaction; employee productivity and satisfaction	Enterprise performance
Evaluation Focus	Costs per person	Rate of return	Business performance	Enterprise value
Attention Focus	Physical element	Deal	Policy	Vision
Tangible Priority	100%	75%	50%	20%
View of the World	Narrow	Limited	Expansive	Expansive
Primary discipline	Engineering	Managerial economics	Strategic management	Social, behavioral, and physical sciences
Geographic Orientation	Specific building	Local market	Multiple markets	Global markets
Level of Concern	Building components	Building and site	Multiple interests in portfolios in context of environment	Multiple levels of place in relationship to society
Attention	Function	Transition	Process	Outcome
Primary Objective	Confirm satisfactory function	Maximize short term measure	Optimize multiple interests over long term	Transform society
Subject of concern	Physical object	Transaction	Process	Contribution to higher purpose

Exhibit 3: Fundamental Disciplines For Real Estate Involvement

Accounting	Investment
Managerial Accounting	Land Economics
Appraisal and Valuation	Landscape
Architecture	Law
Archaeology	Management
Behavioral Economics	Management Science
Computer Science	Marketing
Computer Technology	Philosophy
Construction Management	Planning and Control Systems
Decision Science	Political Science
Decision Theory	Project Management
Ethics	Psychology
Environmental Science	Public Administration
Economics	Quantitative Methods
Managerial Economics	Regional (and Urban) Planning Theory
Engineering	Religious Studies
Finance	Sales
Geography	Science
History	Sociology
History if Design	Spirituality
History of Science	Strategy
Humanities	Statistics
Information Theory	Transportation
Institutional Economics	Urban Land Economics

Exhibit 4: Allied Sectors

Advertising	Hospitality
Agriculture	Insurance
Building materials	Mining
Communications	Security
Energy	Transportation
Equipment and appliances	Timber
Furniture	Utilities
Health care	

Exhibit 5: Property Discipline

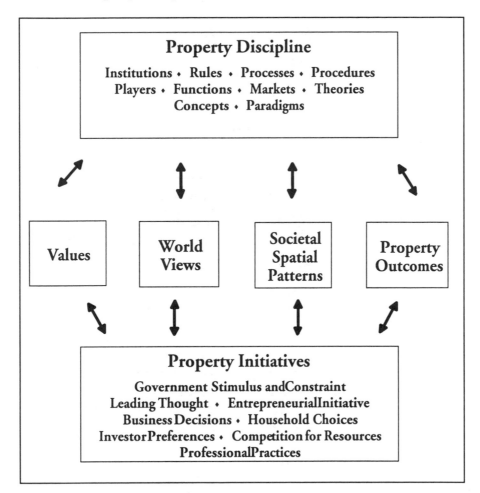

Property Discipline

Institutions • Rules • Processes • Procedures
Players • Functions • Markets • Theories
Concepts • Paradigms

Values

World Views

Societal Spatial Patterns

Property Outcomes

Property Initiatives

Government Stimulus andConstraint
Leading Thought • EntrepreneurialInitiative
Business Decisions • Household Choices
InvestorPreferences • Competition for Resources
ProfessionalPractices

Exhibit 6: The Property Discipline Edifice

Societal Spatial Patterns
Real Property & Virtual Property
Interests in Property
Places & Spaces
Form of the Built Environment
Markets: Property, Services, Regions, Capital, *Market Space*
Property Functions and Decisions
Players & Decision Makers
Information
Theory, Concepts, Tools, Techniques
Paradigms and Framework
Technology
Stakeholders
Environmental Institutional Context
Political Economy
World View
Values

II

REAL ESTATE EDUCATION IN EUROPE

Chapter 2

Austria

Alfons Metzger
Metzger Real Estate Group, MRG Research, Vienna, Austria

2.1 The Property Profession

2.1.1 Legal Framework

In the Austrian real estate industry, two different professions are officially recognised, namely the "Immobilienmakler" (real estate agent) and the "Hausverwalter" (property manager).

Federal law regulates access to both professions, in order to guarantee qualification standards.

Individual entrepreneurs or employees of firms intending to operate in these professional areas must have an authorisation, which may be obtained by passing a standardised examination set by the relevant administrative body.

Persons lacking an authorisation may however work as employees in one of the numerous firms in the sector.

2.1.2   Professional Bodies

Bundesinnung der Immobilien – und Vermögenstreuhänder
(Federal guild of real estate and property trustees)
Schottenfeldgasse 69/4
1070 Wien
Tel: +43 (0)1 522 25 92
Fax: +43 (0)1 522 25 93
http://www.wkimmo.at

Österreichischer Verband der Immobilientreuhänder – ÖVI
(Austrian society of real estate trustees)
President: Dr. Thomas Malloth
Favoritenstraße 24/11
1040 Wien
Tel: +43 (0)1 505 32 50
Fax: +43 (0)1 505 32 50 18
http://www.ovi.at

Hauptverband der allgemein beeideten gerichtlichen Sachverständigen
(Central association of chartered general valuers)
President: Dr. Matthias Rant
Doblhofgasse 3/5
1010 Wien
Tel: +43 (0)1 405 45 460
Fax: +43 (0)1 406 11 56

Vereinigung der gerichtlich beeideten Sachverständigen für das Realitätenwesen
(Association of chartered valuers of real property)
President: Komm. Rat. Peter Frigo
Mariahilferstraße 23-25
1060 Wien
Tel: +43 (0)1 587 71 20
Fax: +43 (0)1 586 89 55

FIABCI Austria
President: Brigitte Jank
Alser Straße 54
1090 Wien
Tel: +43 (0)1 408 78 84
Fax: +43 (0)1 408 78 84 20

Oesterreichischer Verband Chartered Surveyors (OeVCS)
(Austrian association of Chartered Surveyors)
President: Komm.-Rat Alfons Metzger, FRICS, CRE
Administrator: Claudia Wilhelm
Gumpendorferstraße 72
1060 Wien
Tel: +43 (0)1 596 48 50
Fax: +43 (0)1 596 48 54
AMetzger.oevcs@treangeli.at
CWilhelm.oevcs@treangeli.at

2.2 Real Estate Programmes at Universities and Polytechnics

2.2.1 General Overview

So far, there are no courses that focus primarily on real estate economics in Austria. Existing courses, offered by universities or by institutions at a comparable level, only cover real estate economics as part of one of their curriculum's subject areas. Such subjects are not always mandatory.

It is therefore reasonable to conclude that specific courses in the real estate field have not yet been established. The very small number of courses which do exist are either included in, or designed as follow-up education to, courses concentrating predominantly on business administration, economics, law, or technical studies.

Several efforts are currently being made to extend the existing, small range of courses with programmes specialising in real estate economics.

The current possibilities consist of either participating in a postgraduate programme or studying at a Fachhochschule.

The Fachhochschulen offer an alternative choice of higher education from studying at a university. Fachhochschulen mainly emphasise the development of practical skills, in a tightly scheduled programme of studies. They provide a weaker theoretical background than the universities however, with less stress on fostering scientific research.

As a rule, admission to a post-graduate programme requires a university degree. However, appropriate long-term professional experience may often be accepted as a substitute.

The length of both university and Fachhochschule courses varies between four and eight terms. Some course schedules are organised to allow attendance while continuing with a full time job. Some courses are free of admission charge and fees. Most of the courses confer degrees that are recognised throughout Europe.

Apart from the courses mentioned, there are other forms of real estate education in Austria, which are not, however, linked to universities or polytechnics. A training course, which leads to the award of the title Immobilienkaufmann (literally "real estate businessman") has recently been started, but is still in the experimental stage. A few private courses and seminars (usually one- to three-day courses) are also offered, but they are of a extensive character and therefore will not be described in detail.

Further general information and statistical data about real estate and other types of education in Austria can be obtained from the Bundesministerium für Bildung, Wissenschaft und Kultur (Federal ministry of education, science and communication).

Bundesministerium für Bildung, Wissenschaft und Verkehr
Minoritenplatz 5
1010 Wien
Tel: +43 (0)1 531 20 0
http://www.bundeskanzleramt.at

2.2.2   Detailed Description of the Courses

In the following section, all relevant courses in Austria, i.e. courses that are at least related to the field of real estate economics, are listed and concisely described.

As all data were collected by the use of standardised questionnaires, facts and figures concerning e.g. the core curriculum, student numbers, technical equipment, etc. allow direct comparison between courses. Differences in duration, level of the programme, etc., however meant that a conclusive ranking of all programmes could not be established.

The questionnaire used is shown in the Appendix.

2.2.2.1 „Kolleg"

2.2.2.1.1 Facility Management, HTL Wien 16

ZIP-Code:	1160
City:	Wien
Street:	Thaliastraße 125
Telephone number:	++43 (0) 1.49111-410
Telefax number:	++43 (0)
Homepage:	www.wifiwien.at
E-mail:	deimel@htlw16.ac.at
Start of the programme	1998
Location:	Wien
Duration:	four terms
Schedule:	full - time course
Fees:	none
Students / year:	30 (maximum)
Applicants / year:	no statement
Entrance examination:	yes
Drop out ratio:	no statement
Graduates:	no
Prerequisites for admission:	advanced level
Degree/qualification:	no
Educational focus:	technology, economy, law
	- scientific engineering
	- facility planning
	- facility technology and IT
	- business management
	- management & communication
	- economic basics
Group size:	-30
Library:	available
Computer equipment:	available
New media:	yes
Tech. equipment of rooms:	no statement
Lecturers:	no statement
Soft skills:	yes
Applicants:	- basic understanding of technology, economy
	- communication competence
	- creativity
	- willingness to work in teams

Advantages of the programme- strong practical orientation
                                    - versatility
                                    - practitioner teachers

2.2.2.2 „Fachhochschulen"

2.2.2.2.1 „ Facility Management" , Fachhochschule Kufstein – Tirol

ZIP-Code:	6330
City:	Kufstein
Street:	Salurner Straße 57
Telephone number:	++43 (0) 5372 718190
Telefax number:	++43 (0) 5372 718194
Homepage:	www.fh-kufstein.ac.at
E-mail:	info@fh-kufstein.ac.at
Start of the programme	1997
Location:	Tyrol
Duration:	eight terms
Schedule:	full - time course
Fees:	none
Students / year:	50
Applicants / year:	80
Entrance examination:	yes
Drop out ratio:	10%
Graduates:	no
Prerequisites for admission:	academic standard required for programme entrance or long-term experience in an appropriate job.
Degree/qualification:	Dipl. Ing. FH
Educational focus:	technology, economy, law
	- scientific engineering
	- facility planning
	- facility technology and IT
	- business management
	- management & communication
	- economic basics
Mandatory practical training:	1 term
Group size:	5-50
Library:	available
Computer equipment:	available
New media:	yes

Tech. equipment of rooms:	whiteboard, flipchart, video projector, overhead projector
Lecturers:	practitioners, persons related to university
Soft skills:	yes
Applicants:	- basic understanding of technology, economy
	- communication competence
	- creativity
	- willingness to work in teams
Advantages of the programme:	- leading position in the Fachhochschulen concerning facility management
	- strong practical orientation
	- period of practical training
	- versatility
	- practitioner teachers

2.2.2.2.2 „Facility Management und Immobilienwirtschaft" Fachhochschule Kufstein – Tirol

ZIP-Code:	6330
City:	Kufstein
Street:	Salurner Straße 57
Telephone number:	++43 (0) 5372 718190
Telefax number:	++43 (0) 5372 718194
Homepage:	www.fh-kufstein.ac.at
E-mail:	info@fh-kufstein.ac.at

This programme is still in the planning stage. If confirmed, it will start 2000 / 2001

2.2.2.2.3 „ Wirtschaftsberatende Berufe" (Business Advisory Professions)

Fachhochschule Wiener Neustadt

ZIP Code:	2700
City:	Wiener Neustadt
Street:	Johann Gutenberg Straße 3
Telephone number:	++43 (0) 2622 890840
Fax Number:	++43 (0) 2622 8908499
Homepage:	www.fhwn.ac.at

E-mail:	office@fhpost.fhwn.ac.at
Start of the programme	1994
Location:	Lower Austria
Duration:	eight terms
Schedule:	available as full-time course and in addition to full time job
Fees:	no
Students / year:	180
Applicants / year:	550
Entrance examination:	yes
Drop out ratio:	25%
Graduates:	yes
Prerequisites for admission:	academic standard required for entrance or long-term experience in an appropriate job.
Degree/qualification:	Mag. FH
Educational focus:	economics, law

- economics
- revision
- soft skill subjects
- marketing & sales
- information technology
- management
- organisation and personal consultation
- real estate management as an optional focus only

Mandatory practical training:	1 term
Group size:	20-180
Library:	available
Computer equipment:	available
New media:	yes
Tech. equipment of rooms:	whiteboard, flipchart, video projector, overhead projector, video
Lecturers:	practitioners, persons related to university
Soft skills:	yes
Applicants:	

- creativity
- willingness to work in teams
- commitment
- staying power
- determination

Advantages of the programme: - first acknowledged Fachhochschule in
Austria
- strong practical orientation
- period of practical training
- largest Fachhochschule in Austria

2.2.2.2.4 „Immobilienwirtschaft"
Fachhochschulen der Wiener Wirtschaft GmbH

ZIP Code:	1180
City:	Wien
Street:	Währinger Gürtel 97
Telephone number:	++43 (0) 1 47677-353
Fax Number:	++43 (0) 1 47677-145
Homepage:	www.fhw.at
E-mail:	bammer@fhw.at
Start of the programme	2001
Location:	Vienna
Duration:	eight terms
Schedule:	available in addition to full time job
Fees:	5.000,- per term
Students / year:	not started
Applicants / year:	not started
Entrance examination:	examination about general and real estate knowledge
Drop out ratio:	no statement
Graduates:	no
Prerequisites for admission:	advanced level required or long-term experience in an appropriate job.
Degree/qualification:	Mag. FH
Educational focus:	economics, law

- economics
- revision
- soft skill subjects
- marketing & sales
- real estate financing and evaluation
- building engineering
- real estate and project management

Lecturers: practitioners, persons related to university

Applicants: - creativity

- willingness to work in teams
- commitment
- staying power
- determination

2.2.2.3   Postgraduate Studies:

2.2.2.3.1   „Facility Management", Donau - Universität Krems

ZIP - Code:	3500
City:	Krems
Street:	Dr.- Karl- Dorrek- Straße 30
Telephone Number:	++43 (0) 2732 893-0
Telefax Number:	++43 (0) 2732 893-4000
Homepage:	www.donau-uni.ac.at
E-mail:	info@donau-uni.ac.at
Start of the programme:	1999
Location:	Lower Austria
Duration:	four terms
Schedule:	additional to full time job
Fees:	ATS 170,000 (ca. EUR 12,354)
Students / year:	25
Applicants / year:	not stated
Entrance examination:	yes
Drop out ratio:	no statement
Graduates:	no
Prerequisites for admission:	university degree required for entrance (or long-term experience in an appropriate job.)
Degree/qualification:	Master Of Advanced Studies for Facility Management
Education focus:	economy, law

- planning, development and controlling of the infrastructure of a building
- communication and IT
- project management
- real estate management
- building and energy requirements

Mandatory practical training:	no
Group size:	25
Library:	available
Computer equipment:	available

New media:	yes
Tech. equipment of rooms:	whiteboard, flipchart, video projector, overhead projector, slide projector
Lecturers:	practitioners, persons related to university
Soft skills:	yes
Applicants:	- basic knowledge of IT
	- ability to act independently
	- practical experience
	- willingness to work in teams
Advantages of the programme:	- personality (the student is seen as a customer)
	- efficient organisation
	- close contact between students and lecturers

2.2.2.3.2 „Technik und Recht im Immobilienmanagement", (Practice and Law of Property Management) **Technische Universität Wien**

ZIP - Code:	1040
Place:	Vienna
Street:	Karlsplatz 13
Telephone Number:	++43 (0) 1 5880141616
Telefax Number:	++43 (0) 1 5880141699
Homepage:	www.tuwien.ac.at
E-mail:	hanne.gruber@tuwien.ac.at
Start of the programme:	1997
Location:	Vienna
Duration:	four terms
Schedule:	additional to full time job
Fees:	ATS 195,000 (ca. EUR 14,171)
Students / year:	20
Applicants / year:	15
Entrance examination:	yes
Drop out ratio:	20%
Graduates:	yes
Prerequisites for admission:	university degree required for entrance (or long-term experience in an appropriate job.)
Degree/qualification:	Master Of Advanced Studies for Real Estate and Facility Management)

Education focus: technology, economy, law
                                    - facility management
                                    - basics of law and real estate law
                                    - basics of economy and real estate
                                      management
                                    - technology and surveying
                                    - management & communication
                                    - economic basics
Mandatory practical training: no
Group size: 10-50
Library: available
Computer equipment   available
New media: not focused on
Tech. equipment of rooms: whiteboard, flipchart, video projector, over-
                                 head projector
Lecturers: practitioners, persons related to university
Soft skills: no
Applicants: - network abilities
                                 - communication competence
                                 - commitment
                                 - willingness to work in teams
Advantages of the programme: - programme has been filed for registration
                                   with RICS
                                    - parts available as correspondence degree
                                      course
                                    - strong practical orientation

2.2.2.3.3 „Immobilienmanagement und Bewertung"
   (Property Management and Valuation)
   Technische Universität Wien

ZIP - Code: 1040
Place: Vienna
Street: Karlsplatz 13
Telephone Number: ++43 (0) 1 5880141616
Telefax Number: ++43 (0) 1 5880141699
Homepage: www.tuwien.ac.at
E-mail: hanne.gruber@tuwien.ac.at
Start of the programme   1999/2000
Location: Vienna
Duration: four terms

Schedule:	additional to full time job
Fees:	ATS 150,000 (ca. EUR 10,901)
Students / year:	no information available at this stage
Applicants / year:	no information available at this stage
Entrance examination:	yes
Drop out ratio:	no statement
Graduates:	no
Prerequisites for admission:	university degree required for entrance (or long-term experience in an appropriate job.)
Degree/qualification:	Master of Advanced Studies – Real Estate – Investment and Valuation
Education focus:	economics, law

- basics of law and real estate law
- basics of economy and real estate management
- technology and surveying
- Real estate management
- Real estate finance
- Investment & valuation

Mandatory practical training:	no
Group size:	10-50
Library:	available
Computer equipment:	available
New media:	not focused on
Tech. equipment of rooms:	whiteboard, flipchart, video projector, overhead projector
Lecturers:	practitioners, persons related to university
Soft skills:	no
Applicants:	- network abilities

- communication competence
- commitment
- willingness to work in teams

Advantages of the programme:
- programme has been filed for registration with RICS
- parts available as correspondence degree course
- strong practical orientation
- accredited by Royal Institution of Chartered Surveyors (RICS)

2.2.2.4   University Courses

2.2.2.4.1   „Immobilienberatung & Liegenschaftsmanagement"
(Property consultancy and investment management)
Technische Universität Wien

ZIP - Code:	1040
Place:	Vienna
Street:	Karlsplatz 13
Telephone Number:	++43 (0) 1 5880141616
Telefax Number:	++43 (0) 1 5880141699
Homepage:	www.tuwien.ac.at
E-mail:	hanne.gruber@tuwien.ac.at
Start of the programme	1989
Location:	Vienna
Duration:	four terms
Schedule:	additional to full time job
Fees:	ATS 118,000 (ca. EUR 8,575)
Students / year:	50
Applicants / year:	30
Entrance examination:	yes
Drop out ratio:	20%
Graduates:	yes
Prerequisites for admission:	academic standard required (or long-term experience in an appropriate job.)
Degree/qualification:	Academic real estate adviser and real estate manager
Education focus:	technology, economics, law
	- basics of law and real estate law
	- basics of economy and real estate management
	- technology and surveying
	- Real estate management
Mandatory practical training:	no
Group size:	10-50
Library:	available
Computer equipment:	available
New media:	not focused on
Tech. equipment of rooms:	whiteboard, flipchart, video projector, over-head projector
Lecturers:	practitioners, persons related to university

Soft skills:	not focused on
Applicants:	- network abilities
	- communication competence
	- commitment
	- willingness to work in teams
Advantages of the programme:	- correspondence degree course available
	- strong practical orientation

2.3 Real Estate Research and Research Approaches

Research currently being undertaken in real estate concentrates on the core competence of valuation.

Topics covered comprise primarily price and market research and tendency analyses as well as developing, modifying and improving valuation standards.

The research institutions involved are listed in the following section.

2.4 Real Estate Research Societies

Österreichisches Institut zur Förderung der Immobilienbewertung und Bewertungsstandards
(Austrian Institute for the advancement of property valuation and valuation standards)

President: Komm. Rat Alfons Metzger, FRICS, CRE
Gumpendorfer Straße 72
1060 Wien
Tel: +43 (0)1 596 48 50
Fax: +43 (0)1 596 48 54

Österreichisches Institut für Immobilienwirtschaft
(Austrian Institute of property economics)

President: Komm. Rat Alfons Metzger, FRICS, CRE
Gumpendorfer Straße 72
1060 Wien
Tel: +43 (0)1 596 48 50
Fax: +43 (0)1 596 48 54

Institut für Stadt – und Regionalforschung,

(Institute for urban and regional research)
Technical University of Vienna

Head: Prof. Feilmayr
Karlsplatz 13
1040 Wien
Tel: 0043 1 58801 26631
Fax: 0043 1 58801 26699
Homepage: www.immobilien.at/homepages/srf
e-mail: feil@esrnt1.tuwien.ac.at

2.5   Real Estate Journals

There are only a small number of Austrian real estate journals. The most important publications in the field are:

immolex
Der Entscheidungs- und Informationsdienst für neues Miet- und Wohnrecht.
(Decision and information service for new rental and occupation laws)
Manzsche Verlags und Universitätsbuchhandlung
1010 Wien

Österreichische Immobilienzeitung
Offizielles Organ der Immobilien- und Vermögenstreuhänder
(official publication for real estate and investment trustees)
Verlag Lorenz
1010 Wien

Facility Management
International, Österreich
Technopress
3403 Klosterneuburg

Immobilien Magazin
Immobilienverlag GmbH
1100 Wien

APPENDIX

Real Estate Course Questionnaire

- ZIP-Code:
- City:
- Street:
- Telephone number:
- Telefax number:
- Homepage: Institution's internet homepage which often provides further information about the programme
- E-mail: Institution's e-mail address
- Start of the programme: In which year did the programme start the first time?
- Location: Location where the programme is held
- Duration: Duration of the programme
- Schedule: Is it a full-time programme or does the schedule allow attendance of the courses in addition to a full time job? Is the schedule optional?
- Fees: Course fees (Expenses for literature, excursions, etc. are not included)
- Students/year: Number of students per year
- Applicants/year: Number of applicants per year
- Entrance examination: Yes/No
- Drop-out ratio: Percentage (without citing reasons)
- Graduates: Have any participants yet completed the course (Yes/No)
- Prerequisites for admission: Qualifications or professional experience required?
- Degree/qualification awarded: Does the programme confer a degree or other qualification?
- Educational focus: On which areas is the programme's main emphasis put? (business, economics, law, a combination of subjects, etc.)
- Mandatory practical training: Does the programme include mandatory practical training?
- Group size: Number of people in class
- Library: Yes/No
- Computer equipment: Yes/No

- New media: Will the Internet and other new media be
                                          used for educational purposes?
- Technical equipment of rooms: What kind of technical equipment is
                                          available for presentations etc.?
- Lecturers: In which fields and professions do the
                                          Lecturers work?
- Soft skills: Is a training in soft skills, e.g. teamwork,
                                          rhetoric, communication, and presen-
                                          tation techniques part of the programme?
- Applicants: What kind of qualities and skills are
                                          expected from applicants?
- Advantages of the programme: What are the advantages of the pro-
                                          gramme from the Lecturers' point of
                                          view?

Chapter 3

The Baltic States

Henn Elmet
Estonian Agricultural University, Tartu, Estonia

Kaarel Sahk
Tartu University, Tartu, Estonia

3.1 Introduction

In the early 1990s, ownership reforms commenced in all three Baltic States (Estonia, Latvia and Lithuania), following the rebirth of their independence and the foundation of a new democracy.

During the ownership reforms large numbers of ownership rights were restored, and properties were returned to their former owners. In addition, many people became property owners for the first time as a result of the privatisation of dwellings and state property. These processes all added to the growing need for qualified, specialised real estate professionals, of whom there were none in the market.

This overview describes real estate education, past and present, in the Baltic States. It is based mainly on experiences in Estonia but also makes comparisons with Latvia and Lithuania.

3.2   Economic and legal framework

The independence process in all three Baltic States (Estonia, Latvia and Lithuania) began in the mid-1980s as a result of the new Soviet policies of *Perestroika* (reconstruction) and *Glasnost* (openness) led by Mikhail Gorbachov, the former general secretary of the Soviet Communist Party. These two policies liberalised almost all aspects of life throughout the Soviet Union.

The independence movement in the Baltic States started in August 1991, after the August putsch in Moscow and the shock of the collapse that followed. Immediately after their independence and return to statehood, the Baltic States began the process of restitution of the rights of former owners whose land, buildings and other property had been nationalised, as a result of the incorporation of the Baltic States into the Soviet Union, in 1940. The systems of ownership reform decided on by the Baltic parliaments in the early 1990s will play the most important role in the structure and modelling of real estate education. The system will include the following aspects, which substantially change the local legal environment (Appendix 1):

- The concept of land reform;
- The concept of restitution of real property;
- The concept of privatisation, containing also the two named main ideas;

The restitution of real properties is based on the land reform laws and involves three separate stages, which follow each other, each having different legal influences:
- The legitimisation of former owners or their lawful heirs;
- The restitution of buildings and facilities;
- The restitution of the land on which buildings are situated;

The second, and no less important, part of the ownership reform is the privatisation of properties and real estate that are still in state ownership. There are four constituent parts of the privatisation process:

- The privatisation of dwellings. (Appendix 2);
- The privatisation of state property;

- The transfer of properties (land and buildings) from the state into the ownership of local authorities (municipalities);
- The registration of property which is or will be required for government purposes and which will remain in government ownership.

In addition to ownership reform processes and restoration of possessions in the Baltic States, the status of property owners as a social group was also restored. The spectrum of property owners includes a distinct subgroup, the "forced owners". These are persons who become property owners as a result of the privatisation of dwellings but who are unable, for whatever reason, to assume the responsibilities of ownership. There is also a subgroup of "forced tenants", living in apartments or houses which have been returned to their former owners and who, as a result of the restitution procedures, have not been able to take part in the ownership reform.

Property owners in general, including these two special groups, are exerting major influence on the present situation as well as on the development of real estate education and its future trends.

In addition, the government sectors of all three countries have a continuing shortage of qualified real estate specialists at both levels, i.e. national government and local authorities. During the Soviet period, there was no mechanism for the education or training of property specialists to higher-education standards. As a result, there is neither a historical tradition nor a fund of real estate experience.

The circumstances mentioned, coupled with social and political pressures from the whole of society to complete the reforms, mean that the current difficulties can hardly be exaggerated.

The second important influence on real estate education is the legal and economic environment of the real estate market and its players, together with the gradually growing role and impact of local and international professional bodies on the real estate environment. The Estonian real estate market (Appendix 3) may be regarded as typical of the situation in all the Baltic States at the local level. All legal and governmental bodies concerned in the real estate market are currently considering the content and the restrictions of the package of laws that came into force at the time of independence, together with subsequent amendments. All the procedures involved in real estate transactions, including construction of buildings, must be certified by government bodies (the Ministry of Economic Affairs and the Ministry of Environment) and are controlled and registered by local authorities. A number of bodies are, however, able to work without special legal restrictions and are subject to supervision only at governmental level. Examples of these bodies are:

- The Chamber of Real Estate Brokers;
- The Chamber of Real Estate Managers;
- The Real Estate Appraisers Society;

The effect of the geographical location of the three states is important. They have Finland, Sweden and Russia on one side and continental Europe on the other. This location affects first of all the real estate market and legislative procedures and, through them, the basic requirements and curricula for real estate education. The planning of real estate education and the design of courses must have regard to existing market trends in countries neighbouring the Baltic States, i.e. both the educational and real estate markets. The developing trends of the Baltic market, long-term Scandinavian traditions and the fast-developing Russian emerging market, with its special national eccentricities, all need to be considered. In the near future Baltic real estate education will certainly also have to take into account trends in the development of real estate education in the European Union and must harmonise with international standards and methods.

3.3   Real estate education and professional bodies

The three institutions of real estate professionals mentioned in chapter 1 have the main influence on real estate education and on the organisation of courses. The leader in this field is the Estonian Society of Real Estate Appraisers (EKHÜ) (8), established in 1995, which was the first society of professionals in the real estate market to standardise the operations of the market and to establish educational requirements. In 1998, the Estonian Society of Real Estate Appraisers established the requirement for basic education, in accordance with the TEGoVA regulations, for certified appraisers. The Society also compiled a list of the universities whose courses and curricula it would accredit.

Up to 1998 the requirement was for technical or economical applied higher education only, but since then a Bachelor's degree has been required before a certificate of basic education can be granted to an attested (certified) appraiser. The Estonian Banking Association has had considerable influence: commercial banks are only prepared to accept appraisers attested by the Estonian Society of Real Estate Appraisers. Currently 40 members of the Appraisers' society are attested, out of a total membership of 87. The Estonian Chamber of Commerce and Industry has also had considerable impact since it is, at present, accredited and authorised by the Government to lead the attestation process. In the future the Chamber of Commerce will act under the Statute of Professional Law as an accrediting body for vocational certification.

The Chamber of Real Estate Brokers, established in 1997, has made similar preparations. The first accreditation according to the standards and curricula of this institution took place in January 2001. Its standards also set fixed requirements for education and list acceptable universities.

The third and the youngest institution in the local real estate market, the Union of Real Estate Managers and Administrators, established in 1998, has also made progress in this area. Its first accreditation is planned for May 2001.

The educational activities of the last two mentioned institutions are carried out in connection with two organisations of the Third Sector[1]: the Apartment Ownership Societies, established in 1996, and the Estonian Union of Real Estate Firms, established in 1994, as well as the Estonian Housing Agency, which undertakes the Government's housing policy.

An overview of the programmes prepared by these professional societies for appraisers, brokers and managers shows that there is no suitable undergraduate course in Estonia or in the Baltic States generally. The closest to these generalised standards is the programme of the Estonian Agricultural University.

3.4   Trends in the development of higher education

The former state universities, academies and institutes are active in the field of higher education, in accordance with legal requirements and their own revised regulations. Laws passed by the respective governments control the higher education systems in all three Baltic States.

– In Estonia, the Statute of University Law (1996) (5);
– In Latvia, the Law of Higher Education Establishments (1995)(6);
– In Lithuania, the Law of Research and Higher Education (1991) (7);

However, some higher education establishments may operate subject to separate, special acts of parliament (e.g. Tartu University).

The Ministry of Education has ordered the constitution of a special governmental institution (council), which will work under its auspices. According to the law, the Council for the Evaluation of Higher Education is responsible for the accreditation of the following areas of higher education:

– The universities
– The universities' courses
– Programmes of Master's studies
– Programmes of Doctorate studies

During the accreditation process, the organisation and management of a university and its academic programmes and courses are analysed. The balance of resources (financial and human, i.e. the relative numbers of students, assistants, professors etc.) must also be analysed by the accrediting body. Courses are accredited by taking into account their overall organisation, practical and research experience and quality in general. The accrediting organisation, the Council for the Evaluation of Higher Education, evaluates, with the help of foreign experts, the adequacy of a university. If it satisfied, the council issues a training licence. An individual curriculum is issued with a speciality code on accreditation.

In Latvia the procedure is called "regulation of higher educational establishments", in Lithuania it is called an "assessment of rules of quality of institutions of research and higher education". According to the law, courses can only be accredited if they have been in operation for at least 4+2 years (at which point it is possible to assess the economic and professional behaviour of its graduates during the two years after graduation). An important feature in all three Baltic States is the existence of a special government requirement, called "the state order", for graduate specialists (teachers, doctors and nurses, lawyers, etc).

The time needed to complete an accredited course varies between the Baltic States. For a Bachelor's degree, for example, it is:

- 4 years in Estonia
- 3 to 3.5 years in Latvia (depending on the speciality)
- 4 to 5 years in Lithuania (depending on the speciality)

Because of the requirement for a course to be taught for at least 4+2 years, no real estate courses have yet been accredited in Estonia. In Latvia and Lithuania there are no specific real estate university courses. However, in all three countries, a student majoring in e.g. Financial Management, Banking and Financing or Business Management can attend additional courses such as Real Estate Economics, Real Estate Financing etc.

In the permanently changing economic situation and financial environment of the Baltic States and the small size of their domestic markets, it appears that there is a glaring absence of a long term perspective, whether to delineate and work out development plans for higher education itself or specific, specialised courses. The Government is responsible for the harmonisation and unification of higher education standards and principles under the Luganos` Principles and European Union requirements. A stabilisation of both the real estate markets and the higher education system, which in this field are interdependent, is unlikely before the European Commission makes the decision to incorporate the Baltic States into the European Union.

3.5 Bachelor and diploma studies in real estate

Having explored the organisation of real estate education in Baltic universities, it can be seen that the development of real estate courses is very uneven across the three states. There are only two universities, in Estonia, which have special courses in real estate at undergraduate or diploma levels. Each offers the possibility to proceed to a Master's degree or Doctorate. Both courses have been established to take the interests of all market institutions and property types into account. (3).

3.5.1 The speciality of Real Estate Management

The speciality of Real Estate Management (4) has been taught at Tallinn Technical University (Faculty of Construction) since 1998. The nominal period of study is 4 years, during which time a student must successfully complete 160 credit points (CP) as follows:

Studies	Credit points
1. Mayor studies	16.5 CP
2. Basic Studies	27.5 CP
Common studies module	44 CP
3. Special Studies	54 CP
4. Main Studies	32 CP
Main studies module	86 CP
5. Liberal Studies	5 CP
6. Professional Practice	12 CP
7. Diploma Thesis	13 CP

It is important to note that the sub-programmes, e.g. special studies, main studies etc include the possibility to choose between many special courses. During the first stage students acquire knowledge about basic construction matters. "Main Studies" concentrate on real estate and construction management disciplines such as:

- Real Estate Investment Planning
- Real Estate Management
- Real Estate and Housing Economics
- Construction Management
- Reconstruction of Buildings and Facilities

"Special studies" includes the following compulsory subjects: Principles of Urban Planning, Management, Economics, Real Estate Appraisal, and

Construction Cost Planning. The courses in facilities and utilities construction and management must also be passed.

A lack of the current curriculum is a too scant legal content (construction law, contract law, etc.). In the near future it will also be necessary to give more weight to the topics of energy saving and integrated life cycle design issues of buildings. Specialised practice experience for students, in real estate management and development firms, is organised by Technical University, under a bilateral agreement with the Union of Real Estate Firms and Construction Enterprises Society. Property practitioners can also join this course provided that they hold an accepted academic qualification or have passed the special diploma course at the Open University. As a rule, long-term professional experience alone is not sufficient for admission: evidence of complementary studies is also required.

3.5.2   The speciality of Real Estate Planning and Appraisal

The speciality of Real Estate Planning and Appraisal (1) is a new course, which opened at the Estonian Agricultural University as recently as 1999. The course is part of the Agricultural Engineering Faculty. This course is covered by a state order in the same way as the speciality of Real Estate Management mentioned above. During their studies, students must also complete 160 Credit Points, which in this case are divided as follows:

- Common Studies   30.5 CP
- Main Studies   30.0 CP
- Special Studies   76.5 CP

Students must also complete their choice of electives to a total value of 13 CP. The appraised value of a Bachelor thesis is 10 CP. All optional courses that are not included in the Main Studies and Special Studies package may be completed at other Estonian universities, subject to agreement with the university concerned. It is significant that the Tallinn Technical University and the Estonian Agricultural University have signed many contracts with Finnish and Swedish universities that give students the possibility to study for the optional credit points abroad. While the course in Real Estate Planning and Appraisal is largely based on the study of land use, planning and surveying disciplines, the Real Estate Management course concentrates on the study of basic construction disciplines (i.e. construction technologies, house-building and surveying etc.).

To ensure a balanced development of real estate education, even in the short term more attention needs to be given to organising courses concentrating on the business- and service-related aspects of real estate.

The main problem affecting the courses described above is the short time for which they have been in existence on the real estate landscape. Their newness makes it extremely difficult for them to gain international acceptance through the accrediting body and its foreign consultants. The forecast requirements for real estate specialists with higher education qualifications, based on the local real estate market analysis, make it quite difficult for universities to draw up long term, stable plans for the development of courses in this field. Any planned changes to courses will need to take into account the Scandinavian experience, with its well-modelled professional real estate education at both levels - vocational and higher education.

There are two main ways in which the current situation can be improved. 1. The governments of the Baltic States should support the professional bodies more actively on the parliamentary level, e.g. In Estonia by passing the statute of Professional Law. 2. The professional bodies involved in the real estate market need to give clear details about courses, standards and their requirements for membership and associate membership to all persons active in both real estate and higher education.

The development of real estate education will have a major influence over the progress of the real estate profession, its status on local employment markets and its potential to enter the international market. It also has a strong and increasing influence on the development of the whole real estate market.

NOTES

[1] Commonly in the Baltic States the non profit organisations and the formal civil institutions are called the Third Sector.

REFERENCES

[1] Estonian Agricultural University. The Statement of Curriculum and Specialities. (Tartu, 1999).

[2] Hedwall, K.; Leiwo, K.; Challenges of Vocational and higher–level Real Estate Education in Finland. (ERES conference report, Bordeaux, 2000).

[3] Schulte, K-W.; Schulte-Daxbök, G.; Real Estate Education Throughout the World. (ERES conference report, Bordeaux, 2000).

[4] Tallinn Technical University. The Statement of Courses and Specialities. (Tallinn, 2000).

[5] The education System in Estonia. http:// www.hm.ee.

[6] The Education System in Latvia. Latvian ENIC/NARIC. http://www.aic.lv.

[7] The Education System in Lithuania. http://www.is.lt/klausimas3.html.

[8] The Estonian Real Estate Appraisers Society. http://www.ekhy.ee.

APPENDIX

Appendix 1

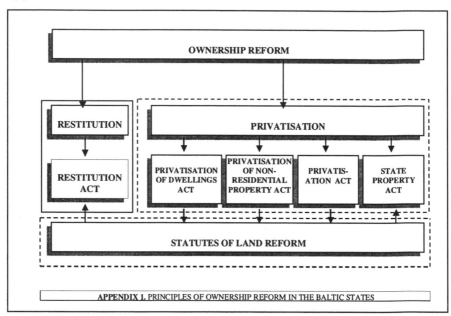

APPENDIX 1. PRINCIPLES OF OWNERSHIP REFORM IN THE BALTIC STATES

Appendix 2

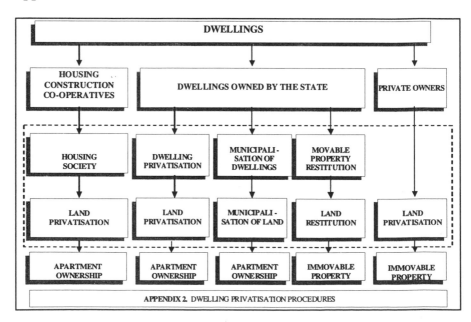

APPENDIX 2. DWELLING PRIVATISATION PROCEDURES

Appendix 3

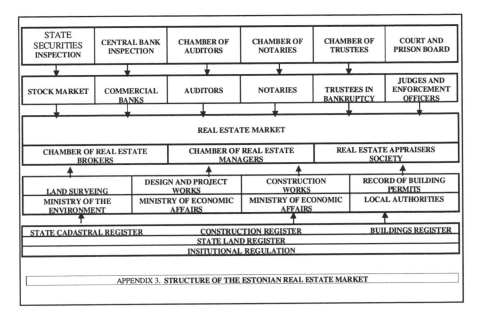

STATE SECURITIES INSPECTION	CENTRAL BANK INSPECTION	CHAMBER OF AUDITORS	CHAMBER OF NOTARIES	CHAMBER OF TRUSTEES	COURT AND PRISON BOARD
STOCK MARKET	COMMERCIAL BANKS	AUDITORS	NOTARIES	TRUSTEES IN BANKRUPTCY	JUDGES AND ENFORCEMENT OFFICERS

REAL ESTATE MARKET

CHAMBER OF REAL ESTATE BROKERS	CHAMBER OF REAL ESTATE MANAGERS	REAL ESTATE APPRAISERS SOCIETY

LAND SURVEING	DESIGN AND PROJECT WORKS	CONSTRUCTION WORKS	RECORD OF BUILDING PERMITS
MINISTRY OF THE ENVIRONMENT	MINISTRY OF ECONOMIC AFFAIRS	MINISTRY OF ECONOMIC AFFAIRS	LOCAL AUTHORITIES

STATE CADASTRAL REGISTER	CONSTRUCTION REGISTER	BUILDINGS REGISTER

STATE LAND REGISTER

INSITUTIONAL REGULATION

APPENDIX 3. **STRUCTURE OF THE ESTONIAN REAL ESTATE MARKET**

Chapter 4

Belgium

Paul Kohnstamm
Stichting voor Beleggings- en Vastgoedkunde, Centre for Investment and Real Estate, Amsterdam, Netherlands

4.1 Introduction

In Belgium, real estate programmes at graduate or postgraduate level only began about five years ago. To date, there are two postgraduate programmes in the Flemish part of the country. No programmes have been started in the French-speaking part of the country. Some institutes are planning a programme, but the Belgian market is probably too small.

4.2 Real Estate Programmes

The existing programmes in Belgium to date are listed in Table 1.

Leuven organises occasional updates for alumni of its programme. These updates take up one afternoon and deal with a number of current issues, although they have mainly been concerned with real estate law.

There is no real estate education in the French speaking part of the country, apart from the CMO, which teaches a real estate course. CMO stands for Centre for Retail Education. It is a night school, where people can obtain a licence to set up a business. These licences are necessary to enter the regulated retail professions. The academic level is low, in both the Flemish-speaking and French-speaking parts of the country.

The Higher Technical Education course is especially aimed at the profession of real estate agent. It also has a rather low academic level. In terms of content, it cannot be compared with academic studies.

Table 1: Existing programmes in Belgium (July 2001)

Institution	Pro-gramme name	Faculty	Spe-cialisa-tion	Programme description	Number of graduates /yr.	Location
University						
KUL Leuven*	Real Estate Studies	department campus KU-LAK (Kortrijk)	none	See website Kulak	±40	Leuven
	Real Estate Law	department campus KU-LAK (Kortrijk)	Real Estate Law		±40	Kortrijk
UFSIA Antwerpen	Real estate Management	IPO management school	none	See website Ufsia	±40	Antwerpen
Polytechnic						
Polytechnic Sint-Lieven	Real Estate	Construction	none	Brochure on request	n/a; variable	Campus Aalst
Polytechnic Gent	Real Estate	Construction	none	Brochure on request	n/a; variable	Campus Gent
Polytechnic Antwerpen	Real Estate	Construction	none	Brochure on request	n/a; variable	Campus Mechelen

* this programme has been accredited by the RICS in 2000

4.3 Real Estate Research in Belgium

There are no foundations or organisations for real estate research in Belgium, which are comparable with, for instance, the SPR in the UK. There are also no magazines or newsletters in this area.

4.4   Real Estate Publications in Belgium

The only representative real estate publication is the fortnightly newsletter *Expertise*, which is published both in Dutch and French. The publishing company is A-linea.

However, *Immotrends*, an appendix to *Trends*, the financial economic weekly, is also published in both Dutch and French.

Most newspapers have an appendix on real estate at least once a week. Other publications are predominantly advertising and residential oriented.

Chapter 5

Central and Eastern European Countries

Nikolai Trifonov
Belarusian Society of Valuers, Minsk, Belarus

5.1   Introduction

First of all, it is necessary to be precise concerning the geographical coverage of this chapter. European countries with transition economies are situated in Central and Eastern Europe and include Albania, Armenia, Azerbaijan, Belarus, Bosnia Herzegovina, Bulgaria, Croatia, the Czech Republic, Estonia, Georgia, Hungary, Kazakhstan, Kyrgyzia, Latvia, Lithuania, Macedonia, Moldova, Poland, Romania, Russia, Slovakia, Slovenia, Tajikistan, Turkmenistan, the Ukraine, Uzbekistan and Yugoslavia. All of these countries, which are based on the ruins of former socialist systems that collapsed in the early 1990s, are now undergoing a transition from administrative to market economies. The real estate market has emerged as one of the essential elements of a market economy in those countries. In the Baltic States of Estonia, Latvia, and Lithuania, as well as in Poland and in Slovenia, the traditions of university education and of the market still existed. Real estate education is therefore more developed in those countries and they are not covered in this section, since they have their own chapters in this monograph.

The evolution of real estate education in countries with transition economies is occurring naturally. There were real estate agents even during the period of socialism, although the profession was then illegal. After economic liberalisation, legitimate real estate offices began to be opened. However, some of their owners continued to run their businesses in ways that were neither very transparent nor ethical, as they used to during the previous regimes. Nevertheless, those active in the new field soon began to understand that it is necessary to pursue ethical norms of behaviour for a number of reasons. These are: to enhance mutual co-operation in all areas of real estate; to increase the quality of services; to exert influence on government in order to update the legislative conditions related to real estate activity; to open their activities to the world; and to implement modern management methods. With the emergence of real estate markets, professionals felt the need to be active in the market and to understand its principles. These professionals are real estate agents or brokers, real estate developers, real estate valuers or appraisers, and real estate managers. They have joint professional societies, which have become members of international organisations. In this region, widely recognised international organisations are the European Real Estate Society, ERES, the European Group of Valuers' Associations, TEGoVA, and the International Real Estate Federation, FIABCI.

Subsequently, with the growing need for specialists, a training system for professionals appeared and, as a result of this, the development of real estate education. As a first stage, needs have been met through various educational programmes designed, in general, to re-train economists, engineers, and lawyers.

The next stage was the appearance of university real estate programmes. Society views a real estate professional ideally as a specialist with Master's degree from a technical or economic university. To begin with, Western European programmes (see *e.g. Schulte 1998*) were quickly applied. The requirements of higher education are quite naturally that the professional should be at the equivalent of partner level, or in management in the appropriate departments of economic entities and, especially, of financial institutions. This also applies to work for judges, notaries public, attorneys-at-law, architects and engineers (in court, before building authorities, etc.). Further, a demanding, specialised postgraduate study is required as follow-up to the university qualification. No amount of experience can substitute for a university education: to analogise, "A nurse with ten years' experience cannot do a doctor's work".

However, the introduction of the university real estate specialisation also created the prospect that graduates might have a problem in finding jobs in the industry in the future. This has already happened in some countries, for instance in the case of students who had specialised in insurance and banking. During the last ten years, rapidly developing banking services have attained their threshold of saturation. The introduction of a specialised real estate programme, with the tuition of small groups of students for a limited employment market, makes such a study quite expensive. This brings into question the ideal educational profile for the future real estate specialist. Should he or she receive a very narrow and specialised education, applicable only to the real estate field? Or should it rather involve broader, less specialised knowledge, enabling the graduate to find a future job in an adjacent field where some of his or her learning would still be of relevance?

The globalisation of real estate markets, the weakening role of national states and the European integration processes are the strong forces that will gradually change the existing situation in the countries in review. The universities in the region will probably have to do something about specialised education for real estate professionals. The preparation of the high quality, specialised programmes in real estate will take some time, because it will be necessary to educate professors to teach real estate. There is also the question of available financial resources for the preparation of new programmes. In most of the countries in transition, the present situation of university education is not very favourable to the opening of new specialisations. This is a result of the public finance crisis, when less and less funds flow to the universities. As a result, young people do not want to work as professors, and thus, the average age of university teachers is increasing. For the future of the universities this development is particularly unhealthy. At some stage, we must expect a radical shortage of highly qualified university teachers. At the same time, the increasing average age of university staff means that the academic senates, which are the important part of the university self-government, are also ageing and becoming more conservative. They are therefore less willing to support innovations such as the introduction of new university specialisations. The policy of low wages for professors means that, at the same time, an important part of the universities' staff begin to consider their university employment as being of a secondary nature. As what may actually become their first priority, they try to earn money outside the university. The private universities could play some role in changing these unfavourable trends, although so far their role is only marginal. For the majority of the population, however, they are just too expensive.

This situation is typical for all countries but of course every country has its specific characteristics. In some countries, such as Albania, Bosnia, Macedonia, some regions of Russia, Tajikistan and Yugoslavia, the political situation is unstable and there are even armed conflicts. In these conditions, the real estate market loses its importance and as a result real estate education is decreasing and even disappearing. For these and other reasons, there is no real estate education in Armenia, Azerbaijan, Bosnia, Croatia, Georgia, Kazakhstan, Macedonia, Tajikistan, Turkmenistan, or Yugoslavia. This article therefore does not cover those countries.

Nevertheless, there is real estate education in this region. As a typical example, the situation in Belarus was chosen, not only for its geographically central position in the region, but also for its median position in the development of the real estate market and real estate education. The personal bias of the author has also played a role in the choice. These are the reasons for selecting Belarus as a typical example of real estate education in countries with transitional economies. The major differences between Belarus and the other countries will be discussed later in this article.

5.2   Belarus

5.2.1   Introduction

The real estate market in Belarus is still modest *(Trifonov 1999)*. Prices are relatively low compared with those quoted in the developed economies and in neighbouring Russia. Property transactions are encumbered with many difficulties, as a result of an insufficient legal basis. Transactions are also affected by high levels of inflation, which causes very high interest rates on long-term loans. In Belarus, there are no strict barriers to prevent the inflow of foreign capital. In such cases (e.g. for purchasing land) foreign investors have, in effect, better conditions than domestic investors.

The transition to a market economy and the process of privatisation in Belarus has created the need for professionals in the emerging real estate market. Real estate education began in Belarus in 1995, when short courses for post-graduate students were established and, later, a programme for high school students.

In this article the following issues are covered:

– The real estate profession in Belarus,
– Real estate research in Belarus,

- Real estate programmes in Belarusian universities (degree specialisation, brief programme description, student numbers, teaching methods, ranking, etc.).

5.2.2 The Real Estate Profession and Research in Belarus

With the developing real estate market, a number of real estate professionals have appeared in Belarus. Most of them are members of the Belarusian Real Estate Guild, BREG. BREG is a republican, public, non-government, non-commercial organisation, which was registered with the Ministry of Law of the Republic of Belarus in 1994. Among its founders were representatives of the major bodies which own, manage, and dispose of real estate properties in the republic, e.g. ministries, local municipal authorities, commercial banks, main development organisations, real estate agencies, state and private enterprises as well as individual businessmen. BREG members include all kinds of real estate professionals, such as agents, investors, developers, valuers, owners, managers, constructors and builders, as well as interested foreign investors and property professionals, who may be looking to the Belarus market to increase efficiency and co-operation in all stages of the development process.

Its main aims are:

- to promote marketing instruments for the privatisation of state property,
- to assist in the forming of a modern real estate market in Belarus,
- to carry out consultancy in the real estate fields of renting, selling and buying as well as investing.

BREG is one of the largest public organisations in the Belarus property market. It has about 100 firms and individuals as members. As well as local real estate market players, firms from Russia, Lithuania and Germany have become foreign members of BREG. There are collaboration agreements between BREG and the Ministry of Management of State Property and Privatisation of the Republic of Belarus, the Bulgarian National Real Property Association, the Russian Guild of Realtors, the Association of Real Estate Professionals (Realtors) of Ukraine and the Moscow Association of Realtors. BREG is an institutional member of the European Real Estate Society, ERES. Every year, in autumn, the Belarusian Real Estate Guild, together with government bodies, manages the International Real Estate Fairs of the CIS Countries.

For the last few years, BREG has conducted real estate research in Belarus. From 1997 onwards, the Republican workshop for real estate economics and valuation has been in operation. As a result, different market analyses have appeared. There are no real estate research societies in Belarus. BREG plays a role, as does the Belarusian Society of Valuers, BSV, which analyses the real estate market. In 1999, a system of regular BSV property indices was produced *(Trifonov 2000)*, and from summer 2000, BSV apartment indices have been produced weekly. There is no real estate journal, but some years ago, the first specialised newspaper, *Building and Real Estate*, appeared.

In 2000, state licensing of real estate agents was introduced. The Ministry of Management of State Property and Privatisation issues the licences. The requirements are for applicants to have had higher education in real estate or at least three years' experience.

5.2.3   Real Estate Programmes in Belarusian Universities

5.2.3.1   Overview

In 1995, BREG began the first real estate course in Belarus *(Trifonov, Levkovich, Sapelkin 1999)*. It collaborated with various bodies for the professional training of real estate brokers and, later, real estate valuers. As the result a two-week course for real estate agents aimed at re-training of high school graduates was arranged. It was carried out with support from the Minsk City Employment Service. The course consisted of 58 to 66 hours of lectures. Such courses since have been offered twice a year. A typical time schedule for the course is shown in Table 1. The same programme is applied in the process of state licensing of real estate agents.

Table 1: Typical time schedule

№	Name of subject	Amount of hours
1	Introduction to the speciality	2
2	Real estate market in Belarus	4
3	Apartments as goods	6
4	Legal base of real estate	4
5	Real estate investment	4
6	Technology of real estate agency	4
7	Structure of real estate agency	4
8	Characteristics of exchange transactions	2
9	Characteristics of lease transactions	2
10	Pricing. Base of real estate valuation	6
11	Methods of privatisation of state property	2
12	Psychological base of activity of the real estate agent	2
13	Computer maintenance and technology of real estate transactions	4

№	Name of subject	Amount of hours
14	Law of security of lot house building	4
15	Taxation and income declaration of real estate transactions	4
16	Notarial certification of real estate transactions	4
17	State registration of real estate transactions	6
18	Basics of residential property management	6
19	Examination. Distribution	6

Higher education establishments in Belarus with real estate programmes are the Belarusian State University, BSU, and the Belarusian State Polytechnical University, BSPU. The specialisations are real estate management and, in the BSU only, real estate valuation. The normal duration of a programme is 5 years, following a general secondary education. The concentration of the curriculum on professional aspects ensures a good reception by the profession to the qualification of "Economist-manager of real estate". The total number of students taking such specialisations is about 400, with about 150 new entrants a year (100 at the BSU and 50 at the BSPU). In addition, at the BSU about 60 students each year are awarded the real estate qualification as a second one. The specialisations are new, the first students have been registered in 1995. The fact that they have appeared in the state universities has resulted in the curriculum being very similar to those of the traditional economics or engineering specialities in these universities.

Entry requirements, for the educational level of applicants and the composition of entrance tests are not below the average for full secondary education in the Republic of Belarus. Scholastic subjects on which an entrance test for applicants can be set are:

– Mathematics,
– Physics,
– Belarusian (or Russian) language and literature.

Future subjects for professional specialist activities will include: different forms of property companies; joint ventures; public housing management bodies and services; construction companies and usage of engineering networks of various purposes; hotel facilities and home service systems; management and personnel departments of ministries; enterprises and organisations; centres of professional orientation; courses of employment service; labour exchanges; social insurance services; organs of regional and municipal administration; real estate agencies; real estate development companies; real estate valuation organisations; real estate leasing companies; research and production associations; banks; financial; leasing; insurance companies;

investment and trust funds, as well as other organisations in the real estate market.

The features on which the award of the qualification of economist-manager in real estate is decided are as follows:

The specialist must have a high level of humanitarian, social, scientific, professional and special knowledge, allowing the successful realisation of a professional adaptation for the accumulation of practical skills and providing further creative activity, after the conferring on him of corresponding qualifications or academic degrees.

Having a fundamental scientific and practical education, the specialist must himself take professional decisions with regard to the social and ecological consequences of his activities, continuously renewing his own knowledge, analysing historic and modern problems of the economic and social life of society, knowing his role in professional activity, and the problems and trends of the world's real estate development.

The specialist must also be able to communicate effectively, both orally and in writing, and be able to use at least one foreign language (usually English) in his or her professional activity. He must know the bases of world and domestic culture and be aware of the need for constant professional, cultural and physical self-improvement. The structure of the scholastic plan of the profession is presented in Table 2.

Table 2: Structure of the Scholastic Plan

№	Name of discipline	Total hours	Including auditorium hours
	Cycle of humanitarian and social disciplines	**2100**	**1400**
1	Theory and history of culture	96	80
2	Ethics	48	40
3	History of Belarus	108	90
4	Economic theories	120	100
5	Bases of pedagogy and psychology	86	72
6	Philosophy	120	100
7	Sociology	66	54
8	Politics	86	72
9	Bases of law	48	40
10	Belarusian language (professional lexicon)	72	60
11	Foreign language	520	432
12	Physical education	458	-
13	Additional studies	272	260
	Cycle of scientific and professional disciplines	**2862**	**2117**
1	Higher mathematics	442	324
2	Computer science	368	270
3	Physics	98	72

№	Name of discipline	Total hours	Including auditorium hours
4	Engineering and computer graphics	98	72
5	Ecology	74	54
6	Population protection in extreme situations	98	72
7	Microeconomics	98	72
8	Modern technologies	172	126
9	Statistics	172	126
10	Macroeconomics	122	90
11	Pricing	98	72
12	Economics of enterprise	94	68
13	World economy and international economic relations	70	51
14	Mathematical modelling in economics and management	94	68
15	Accounting and audit	232	170
16	Information technologies in economics and management	70	51
17	Standardisation, certification and quality control	94	68
18	Taxes and taxation	94	68
19	Finance and credit	116	85
20	Protection of labour	70	51
21	Additional studies	88	87
	Cycle of special disciplines	**1840**	**1502**
1	Foreign language in business relations	168	136
2	Organisation of labour and salary	85	68
3	Marketing and market study	126	102
4	Ethics of business relations and culture of speech	106	85
5	Management theory	106	85
6	Economic sociology	85	68
7	Insurance in commercial activity	64	51
8	Psychology of management	85	68
9	Production management	106	85
10	Personal management	85	68
11	Financial management	85	68
12	Study of Conflict	42	34
13	Legal regulation of economic and management activity	85	68
14	Strategic management	126	102
15	Commercial risks and theory of decision making	85	68
16	Administrative management	85	68
17	Innovation and investment management	106	85
18	Foreign economic activity	64	51
19	Additional studies	146	142
	Cycle of disciplines for specialisation	**638**	**578**
1	Real estate market	88	68
2	Construction of buildings	12	102
3	Technical expertise of buildings	85	85
4	Real estate management	102	102
5	Economic valuation of property	88	68
6	Real estate marketing	51	51
7	Legislative base of real estate market	88	68

№	Name of discipline	Total hours	Including auditorium hours
8	Mortgage and credit system	34	34
	Disciplines by student option	75	50

Work experience is a part of the general process of preparing the specialist, continuing the scholastic process in working conditions and is conducted in leading companies and organisations in the field. Work experience is aimed at applying, in working conditions, the knowledge gained in the university on the mastering of production skills, leading technologies and methods of labour and management. Work experience is organised with provision for the profile of the future specialisation. The following types of work experience (total 22 weeks) are stipulated for the award of the qualification of economist-manager in the real estate market:

– sociological (scholastic) work experience,
– economic (production) work experience,
– accounting (production) work experience,
– management (production) work experience,
– graduate work experience.

To give an indication of the flavour of specialised disciplines, programme descriptions of courses which have been organised by the author in Belarus are shown below:

5.2.3.2   Real Estate Market

Aims and tasks of the discipline and its place in the scholastic process:

The course "Real estate market" has the aim of providing, for both theoretical and practical training of engineers-economists in the field, knowledge of the basic performance of the real estate market, study approaches and methods of analysis of the market, its structure and dynamics of development in transition economics. As a complex scholastic discipline, the course "Real estate market" has a relationship with the series of disciplines which includes "Higher mathematics", "Bases of market economics", "Economic valuation of real estate objects". Each topic covered normally has 2 hours of lectures and 2 hours of seminars. The course is concluded by an examination.

Section 1: Introduction
   Theme 1.1. Introduction to the speciality
   Theme 1.2. Real estate and market.
   Theme 1.3. Real estate as goods

Section 2: Sectors of the Real Estate Market
   Theme 2.1. The market for land
   Theme 2.2. Housing market
   Theme 2.3. Market of non-residential real estate

Section 3: Participants in the Real Estate Market
   Theme 3.1. Agents, developers and managers
   Theme 3.2. Real estate valuers

Section 4: Operations in Real Estate
   Theme 4.1. Real estate transactions
   Theme 4.2. Real estate investment
   Theme 4.3. Criminal aspects of the real estate market

Section 5: International Real Estate Markets
   Theme 5.1. Foreign real estate

Section 6: Legal Regulation in the field of Real Estate
   Theme 6.1. Legal system of the Republic of Belarus
   Theme 6.2. Land-legal regulation
   Theme 6.3. Notarial certification and state registration of real estate
         transactions
   Theme 6.4. Protection of judicial rights, in relation to real estate

5.2.3.3 Economic Valuation of Property

Aims and tasks of the discipline and its place in the scholastic process:

The course "Economic valuation of property" provides theoretical and practical education for engineers and economists in the main aspects of property valuation, the study of approaches and the methods of economic motivation used in the appraisal of the market value of property in the conditions of a transition economy. As a complex scholastic discipline the course "Economic valuation of property" has a relationship with disciplines such as "Higher mathematics", "Bases of market economics", "Real estate market", and "Accounting and audit". Each topic covered normally has 2 hours of lectures and 2 hours of seminars. The course is concluded by an examination.

Section 1: Introduction
    Theme 1.1. Completely theoretical and normative bases of valuation
    Theme 1.2. General questions of real estate valuation

Section 2: Time Value of Money
    Theme 2.1. Functions of accumulation
    Theme 2.2. Functions of discounting
    Theme 2.3. Value equation
    Theme 2.4. Constant accumulation model: additional information
    Theme 2.5. Functions of annuities
    Theme 2.6. Six functions of money for model of constant accumulation

Section 3: Income Approach
    Theme 3.1. Principles of the income approach to the real estate
              valuation
    Theme 3.2. Capitalisation when capital value changes
    Theme 3.3. Discounted cash flow analysis

Section 4: Valuation of Land
    Theme 4.1. Valuation of land: legal basis and practice

Section 5: Cost Approach
    Theme 5.1. Principles of cost approach to real estate valuation
    Theme 5.2. Depreciation, its types and methods of determination

Section 6: Comparative Approach
    Theme 6.1. Principles of the comparative approach to real estate
              valuation
    Theme 6.2. Adjustment process

Section 7: Reconciliation of Results and Expert Conclusion
    Theme 7.1. Principles of reconciliation of results of valuation and
              composition of conclusions
    Theme 7.2. Conclusion remarks

The following types of assessment are applied in the award of the qualification of economist-manager in real estate:

–   examinations, differentiated tests and tests on each discipline;

- a certification after studying the main disciplines of the humanitarian-social cycle and the cycle of scientific and whole professional disciplines, after completing a programme of two years of education;
- total state certification by the state professional examination, and defence of the degree project before the state examination commission.

Requirements and conditions of realisation of the main educational programme are as follows:

The duration of the educational programme, five years, is equivalent to 252 weeks, of which there are 157 weeks of theoretical education, 22 weeks of work experience, 15 weeks for preparation and delivery of state examination, and 32 weeks of vacation, including four weeks of post-graduate furlough.

Educational technologies must be employed to ensure the achievement of requirements to an appropriate level.

Requirements of the scholastic plan for the profession:

- the maximum scholastic load on students must not exceed 54 hours a week, including all types of activity;
- obligatory requirements of students must be between 28 and 36 hours a week, which is defined with provision for specifics of building the scholastic process, equipping the scholastic-laboratory base, and the systems of provision of academic literature;
- students' independent work when preparing for examinations is considered as a type of scholastic work related to the subject and is executed within the hours allowed for the subject;
- course projects are carried out within the hours allowed for the particular subject.

Teachers must have a higher education qualification corresponding to the profile of the teaching discipline, or a corresponding scientific qualification in terms of degree or rank. All courses in the scholastic plan must be provided with academic documentation on all types of scholastic occupations.

The laboratories must be equipped to allow the undertaking of laboratory work in:

physics, information science, mathematical modelling in economics and management, accounting and audit, information technologies in the economy and management, population protection in extreme situations, ecology, labour protection, standardisation, certification and quality control, financial and strategic management, commercial risk and theory of decision making, innovation and investment management, as well as in specialised disciplines such as the real estate market, economic valuation of property. Display time must be not less than 50 hours per student per annum.

The curriculum of the programme for real estate valuers differs, with more specialised subjects in the area for which the course "Economic valuation of property" described above serves as a basis. The post-graduate Master's course (2 years) is dedicated to business valuation.

To summarise: we must underline that state higher education establishments in Belarus have many courses for general education but relatively few for specific professional education. This is a peculiarity of real estate education, which is based on the previous state educational system, in countries with transition economies.

5.3   Albania

Albania underwent a transition to a full market economy in 1992. Before that, private land ownership had not been possible and there was no form of real estate market. Within the first few years after the transition, prices for land and buildings greatly increased. This increase was caused mainly by the large numbers of foreigners coming into the country for the first time. As the numbers of foreigners have stabilised, so has the price level. In many parts of the country however, there is still no real estate market. As of a year ago, though, transactions were beginning to occur in the major towns and cities and information was more readily available. In addition, the government has been using indices to set the value for land when it is to be rented or sold, or to settle the compensation claims of former owners. These indices have regard to a town's population, the situation according to zones or in relation to road access, and the development possibilities of the land. The sale value is calculated as ten times the rental value. Other methods, which do not specifically take account of the market, have been developed for privatisation. However changes are being introduced, including the concept of market value.

With the beginning of market liberalisation, the first real estate educators appeared. They began their work with the creation of the Albanian Society of Real Property Valuers. This group now enjoys membership of TEGoVA. The Society organises and administers the system for the licensing of valuers, on behalf of the government. In the last seven years, educational programmes have been established both at the University of Tirana and in a cooperative project between the Ministry of Public Works and the Society. These are the only two courses that have been established in Albania. They provide the basic education required for professionals to apply for the necessary licence to learn the profession of valuer.

There is also an Albanian Real Estate National Association which is a member of the ERES.

Unfortunately, the political situation during the last two years has practically terminated real estate education. Some leading teachers have had to emigrate from the country.

5.4 Bulgaria

In Bulgaria there is a relatively stable real estate market including housing, commercial and industrial real estate. There are many real estate agencies, in the capital Sofia and in other cities, especially those on the Black Sea Coast. The agents have joined the National Real Property Association. Real estate newspapers have also been established.

There are two professional societies of valuers are in Bulgaria, namely the Association of Business Appraisers, ABA, and the Bulgarian Association of Valuers of Real Property, BAVRP. ABA unites *(Parvanov 1996)* the efforts for professional manifestation of valuers of all kinds of assets, regulated by the Ordinance for Appraisal of Projects Envisaged for Privatisation. These include real estate, businesses, rights over industrial and intellectual property, machinery and equipment and works of art. ABA was registered as a legal person in 1992, as a voluntary non-government and independent non-profit organisation. It has more than 750 individual members. ABA is also a TEGoVA member. In the field of real estate education, Bulgaria currently only offers short-term courses, which are organised by the professional societies.

5.5 The Czech Republic

In the Czech Republic, many real estate agencies have joined the Association of Real Estate Offices of Bohemia, Moravia and Silesia. There is also a Chapter of FIABCI. Most valuers are members of the Czech Chamber of Appraisers, which is also a TEGoVA member. The Central European Real Estate network, CEREAN, is based in Prague.

In the Czech Republic, there is a higher education programme in real estate. Within the frame of the University of Economics, Prague, a Valuation Institute BEWERT has been created.

5.6   Kyrgyzia

The shaping of the real estate profession in Kyrgyzia began in spring 2000, following the edict of the President of the Kyrgyzian Republic "On some measures on the further development of the real estate market in the Kyrgyzian Republic". This document states that the all-out development of the real estate market is one of the most important aims of state policy. Development of the market will be based on the free realisation of rights of physical and juridical persons in real estate, and their guaranteed protection, as well as on maximum liberalisation of the currently prohibitive mechanisms of government regulation of the property market. In mid-2000 the Government approved the concept of the development of a real estate market in the Kyrgyzian Republic, which, in particular, includes organisation of:

– Independent and professional valuation activity,
– Realtor activity.

A non-governmental public association "Trustee", which unites property valuers and other independent real estate market specialists has been created.

In the field of real estate research, the Kyrgyzian-Russian Slavonic University is leading work on a market study of urban residential property, with the aim of carrying out rapid valuations and the approval of strategies for mass computer appraisal of urban properties. In autumn 2000 the first scientifically-practical conference on the problems of independent valuation activity covered real estate questions to a considerable extent.

Real estate education started in 1997, when the Kyrgyzian-Russian Slavonic University began enrolment on its programme for the qualification of "Economist-mathematician" with the specialisation "Real Estate valuer". The programme has a curriculum that allows for more than 8,000 hours of lectures over a 5-year course. 15 students are enrolled each year. As well as traditional disciplines in the field of higher mathematics (mathematical analysis; linear algebra; mathematical logic; differential equations; numerical methods; probability theory and mathematical statistics) the curriculum also includes subjects such as: economic modelling; optimal control of economic systems; game theory; mathematical methods of financial analysis; cluster analysis and others, which form a good foundation for the scientific approach to valuation. The specialisation "Real Estate valuation" has more than 600 hours of lectures over a 14-week period. The subjects studied include the following courses: legal basis of the real estate market; valuation; real estate statistics; basis of mortgages; operational research in the real estate market; methods of financing real estate, systems of real estate registration; risks and real estate insurance.

In 1998, the Kyrgyzian State University of Construction, Transport and Architecture began a programme in "the Valuation and management of property". As well as the 5-year higher education programme there is a 2½-year "refresher course" (second higher education). Subjects offered include:

1. Valuation and management of property with specialisation in:
    1.1. Valuation and management of real estate.
    1.2. Valuation of machinery, equipment and transport facilities.
2. Expertise and management of real estate.
3. Management on branches.
4. Information systems in the economy.

5.7 Moldova

The real estate market in Moldova is very weak. In effect, it only exists in the capital of Chisinau. The first professional organisation in the real estate field, the Association of Professionals in Real Estate, was established in 1996. Later, in 1998, the Moldovan Association of Professional Valuers was created and has obtained Associate Membership of TEGoVA. In 1999, these two societies merged to form the National Real Estate Chamber of the Republic of Moldova, CNIRM. The Moldavian membership of TEGoVA was transferred from MAPV to CNIRM. Since the amalgamation, CNIRM has been registered with the Ministry of Justice, together with the Statute, Membership Rules and Regulations and the Code of Professional Ethics. So far there is no real estate education in Moldova.

5.8 Romania

The real estate market in Romania is quite well developed. The country is open for foreign investment. The Association of Romanian Valuers, ANEVAR, is a member of TEGoVA.

5.9 Russia

Education in the field of real estate in Russia, or the Russian Federation (RF), has wholly been inserted in the scheme provided at the beginning of the section on Belarus. However, such a big country, the largest mentioned in our review, requires to be analysed in detail.

The main public bodies in the field of real estate in Russia are the Russian Guild of Realtors, the Moscow Guild of Realtors and the Russian Society of Appraisers. The headquarters of all three organisations are in Moscow.

Originally, real estate education was associated solely with these organisations, within a framework of short courses or seminars organised by means of grants from the World Bank and other international and, principally American, foreign national organisations, such as USAID. From the beginning, short-term courses were established mainly in the major cities such as Moscow and St. Petersburg. Later, such activity was extended as travelling seminars all over Russia, e.g. in Chelyabinsk, Omsk, Kazan, Kaluga, Archangelsk, Ekaterinburg and other cities. The book *Income Property Appraisal and Analysis* by J.P. Friedman and N.J.D. Ordway is the most popular manual used by Russian valuers.

In the last few years, university programmes in real estate have appeared in Moscow and St. Petersburg, mainly on the base of the economic professions. Courses in real estate management and real estate valuation are typical. In Moscow, the courses are run at the Financial Academy of the Russian Federation Government, the Plekhanov Economic Academy, and the Real Estate and Construction Business Institute. In St. Petersburg, the University of Economics and Finance as well as in the Technological University run real estate programmes.

In some universities, a higher level programme in real estate, usually dealing with valuation, has been established. One exists in the Financial Academy in association with the Institute of Professional Valuation, others in the Plehkanov Economic Academy and the Technological University, both in association with the Institute of Qualification Promotion.

In Russia there are legal requirements, such as federal licences for valuation activity. These requirements have an inevitable effect on the curriculum. A typical curriculum for valuation licences is shown below.

The need for licensing is usually explained by the fact that the standards expected from valuers have greatly increased. Licensing has been introduced in four areas: valuation of real estate; valuation of machinery, equipment and transport facilities; valuation of objects of intellectual property and nonmaterial assets; and company valuation. A licence to value companies is general, since this type of valuation activity requires knowledge and skills from all the other types of valuation. Therefore, a company that has a licence for the valuation of businesses is authorised to carry out any type of valuation work.

According to the Federal Law "On valuation activity in the Russian Federation", by not later than 2000, the Ministry of Education, with the participation of Ministry of State Property, must have prepared proposals for educational programmes. Success in these will meet the demands of positions of the Law under federal licensing. The status of the programmes is as professional refresher courses, success in which is confirmed by the issue of a state diploma. The length of the programmes varies from 500 academic hours for

specialisation in onedirection to 800 academic hours for the general specialisation "Valuation of businesses".

Programmes built on the block principle are under development. The first
block includes a range of professional, economic and financial disciplines.
The second covers professional topics, providing general knowledge on the
methodologies of valuation and separate aspects of valuation activity, while
the third is devoted to the chosen specialisation, covering the finer points of
valuation in the chosen subject area.

The programme of qualification for a general federal licence in valuation
it titled "Professional valuation and expertise of objects and ownership on
directions of valuation activity" with the specialisation of "Valuation of enterprises (business) and other types of property". On completing the course,
students are awarded a state diploma, which certifies conformity with the
qualifications on conduct of professional activity in the field of valuation and
expertise of objects and ownership, required for a general federal licence.
This authorises activity in all licensed aspects of valuation work as well as
certifying compliance with the educational level of qualification referred to
as "expert appraiser" (on the guideline of valuation activity) in accordance
with the resolution of the Ministry of Labour.

The programme of the professional refresher course "Professional valuation and expertise of objects and ownership in the spheres: real estate, land
and natural resources; machinery, equipment, transport and auto-transport
facilities; intellectual property and nonmaterial assets; business of enterprises and securities, rights of requirements of obligations; investment projects" is presented below. It includes more than 800 hours, covered in either
three sessions of three weeks or six sessions of 1½ weeks.

№ Session	Name and stages
1.1	Block of complete topic: "Bases of valuation activity"
1.2	Theory and practice of valuation of real estate and bases of valuation of other types of property
1.3	Theory and practice of valuation of machinery, equipment, transport and auto transport facilities
1.4	Theory and practice of valuation of intellectual property and nonma-terial assets
1.5	Theory and practice of valuation of businesses and valuation analysis of enterprise activity
1.6	Special block: "Professional practice of valuation of businesses and other types of property"
1.7	Preparation and delivery of state exam

Real Estate Education in Europe

Below we present the scholastic plan of the programme "Professional valuation of objects and ownership" with the specialisation "Company Valuation of and other types of property".

№	Name of sections and discipline	Amount of hours				Form of control
		Whole	Lectures	Seminars	Private Study	
1	Base discipline					
1.1	Legal ensuring of shaping, turning and valuation of property	20	20			Test
1.2	Micro- and macroeconomic bases of market pricing	20	10	10		Test
1.3	Accounting and audit	36	24	12		Exam
1.4	Economic analysis	20	16	4		Exam
1.5	Taxes and taxation	16	8	8		Test
1.6	Mathematical methods in valuation	28	14	14		Test
1.7	Bases of theory of property valuation	16	8	8		Test
1.8	Organisation and financing of investments	20				Test
	TOTAL	*176*	*100*	*76*		
2	Professional Aspects					
2.1	Theory and practice of real estate valuation and bases of valuation of other types of property					
2.1.1	Theoretical bases of real estate valuation	72	20	18	34	Exam
2.1.2	Pricing in construction	20	16	4		Test
2.1.3	Practice of real estate valuation. Term paper on valuation	52	24	12	16	Test
2.1.4	Valuation of land	32	22	10		
	TOTAL	*176*	*82*	*44*	*50*	
2.2	Theory and practice of valuation of machinery, equipment and transport facilities					
2.2.1	Theoretical bases of valuation of machinery, equipment and transport facilities	50	20	20	10	Test

		Amount of hours			
2.2.2	Pricing in machine build-ing and device building	24	8	8	8 Test
2.2.3	Practice of valuation of machinery, equipment and instruments. Term paper on valuation	40	14	8	8 Test
2.2.4	Valuation of transport facilities and systems	40	20	12	10 Test
	TOTAL	*154*	*60*	*60*	*34*
2.3	Theory and practice of valuation of nonmaterial assets and intellectual property				
2.3.1	Theoretical bases of valuation of nonmaterial assets and intellectual property	50	20	16	14 Test
2.3.2	Intellectual property as a special object of valuation	24	8	8	8 Test
2.3.3	Pricing in intellectual property	32	16	8	8 Test
2.3.4	Practice of valuation of nonmaterial assets. Term paper on valuation	24	8	4	12 Test
2.3.5	Practice of valuation of intellectual property in particular cases	32	16	16	Exam
	TOTAL	*162*	*68*	*52*	*42*
2.4	Theory and practice of valuation of enterprise (business)				
2.4.1	Theoretical bases of valuation of enterprise (business)	72	22	20	30 Exam
2.4.2	Valuation of securities. Term paper on the valua-tion	20	12	8	Test
2.4.3	Practice of valuation of enterprise. Term paper on the valuation	52	24	8	20 Test
2.4.4	Valuation of financial in-	32	18	8	6 Exam

		Amount of hours		
	stitutes. Value management and restructuring of enterprises and financial institutes				
	TOTAL	*176*	*78*	*42*	*56*
3	Attestation work, graduate practice				
4	Preparation and delivery of state exam	12	8	4	Exam
	GRAND TOTAL	*856*	*396*	*278*	*182*

Note also typical courses on aspects of real estate valuation (included for licensing in Moscow).

№	Name of course	Amount of hours
1.1	Valuation of real estate and bases of valuation of other types of property	126
1.1.3	Valuation of land and natural resources, cadastral land value and technology of mass appraisal	120
1.1.4	real estate management, exploitation, deals and commercial usage	126
1.1.5	Evaluations of correspondence of work volumes to realise facilities. Judicial and creditor building expertise	126
1.1.6	Valuation and expertise of objects in course of construction	120
1.3	Valuation of business and value analysis of enterprise activity	120
1.3.1	Valuation of debtor indebtedness, rights of requirement, obligations (debts). Development of plan of liquidation of an enterprise	120
1.6	Valuation of investment projects and conditions of their financing	120
1.7	Value management and restructuring for business and enterprise	120
3.0	Financial analysis and management of business cash flows	126
4.0	Anti-crisis (competition) control	240
6	Expertise of establishment of rights and valuation of ownership and other property rights on the property and separate belongings from the composition of property	120

5.10 Slovakia

Slovakia has a population of five million, but only two towns with more than 200,000 inhabitants. Bratislava, the capital, has 452,000 inhabitants, and Kosice 241,000. There are another nine towns with populations between about 50,000 and 100,000. The real estate market is at present not very well developed, because of a low demand for property, unsolved constitutional issues and a tough monetary policy in the economy, which is in a state of downturn.

Perceived needs led to the establishment of the Union of Real Estate Offices of the Slovak Republic, and the Association of Real Estate Offices of Slovakia in 1992. In 1998, these organisations merged to form the National Association of Real Estate Offices of Slovakia, NARKS, which is now a member of FIABCI and CEREAN. At present, NARKS has 90 members, both individuals and legal bodies, which it is responsible for training. It is trying to develop a new profile for real estate agents in Slovakia, with responsible and ethical attitudes towards society. In practice, however, this is not easy to achieve, since, according to the *Zivnostensky zakon*, a law on individual entrepreneurs, almost anybody can operate in this field, with or without professional knowledge of real estate transactions or formal training. The government's tolerance of low quality real estate services has resulted in the population having a correspondingly low level of trust in the emergent real estate field.

The small size of the real estate market in Slovakia, together with the unclear legislative status of real estate agents mean that specialised university education is not perceived as an important issue by the real estate professionals. One may perhaps think of this as professional myopia, or the excessively short-term perspective of some specialists, nevertheless, the need for specialists is not too high at present. This is not surprising in the context of the low sophistication of the work of real estate professionals in Slovakia, although there are some exceptions. At the same time, only a limited number of persons have specialised knowledge of some professional areas of the real estate business, but in some instances no expertise at all is available. These are the typical characteristics of underdeveloped real estate markets. During the last year, however, we have observed certain changes in this situation in the capital city Bratislava. Some modern methods typically used in mature real estate markets cannot be used in Slovakia, because of the underdeveloped institutional framework. For example: mortgage finance is used, but on a limited scale; underwriting procedures are not standard and differ from practice in Western countries because of the existing regulations; no real estate company is listed on the stock market; there is obsolete legislation in the area of rented housing (which is the reason why there is practically no private housing rental market) etc.

NARKS is trying to improve the level of qualifications of its members by organising short-term real estate courses, where real estate specialists, developers, managers, tax and accounting specialists, psychologists, and lawyers provide the lectures. The programme consists of two parts.

In the first part the following topics are presented:

– Conditions and the legal forms of entrepreneurship,
– Legal transactions and relationships in the real estate office,
– Legal contracts in real estate,
– Creation and registration of legal real estate relationships,
– Construction law,
– Accounting and taxes in real estate,
– Management of real estate offices.

In the second part the following topics are presented:

– International real estate markets, the legal conditions for the foreign entrepreneurs to undertake business in Slovakia,
– Management of real estate,
– Lease and sale of real estate,
– Psychology of sale,
– Ethics and etiquette in the real estate business,
– Real estate investments and development,
– Real estate cadaster.

Each part of the programme includes 24 hours of lectures. The course is concluded by a final test. Successful participants are awarded a certificate that is valid for four years.

Two institutes of legal expertise (*Ustavy sudneho znalectva*) in the University of Zilina and in the Faculty of Civil Engineering in Bratislava are at present responding to some of the needs of real estate education. The main reason for their existence is, however, the provision of the real estate expertise for the courts and public administration.

The Institute of legal expertise in Bratislava trains experts in the fields of construction, and land surveying. The aim of the study is to train the students, who already have a university degree and a minimum of five years' practice experience, in real estate valuation and the provision of expert opinions for the courts. The total length of study is four semesters (360 hours). In the last semester, the students prepare their final thesis.

For example, in the area of Legal Expertise in Construction, the following subjects are taught:

- Basics of the legal expertise,
- Basics of the Civil Law,
- Basics of Commercial Law,
- Basics of Penal Law,
- Construction Law and related legislation,
- Structures of buildings,
- Building materials and testing,
- Real estate cadaster,
- Building physics,
- Building technology,
- Mechanics of soils,
- Static analysis of building structures,
- Methodology of the expert opinion,
- Life of Buildings,
- Valuation of real estate (old and new regulations, restitution, foreign methodologies, etc.),
- Valuation of building works,
- Value of the firm,
- Building diagnostics,
- Special methodologies of legal expertise,
- Automation of expertise,
- Practice in the real estate reviews,
- Transport infrastructure,
- Water infrastructure.

Certain elements of real estate are also taught in the Faculty of National Economy, where there are specialists on development and investment work. There is no specialised real estate course however.

In the construction faculty of the Slovak University of Technology, students can specialise in the area of economics and management of the construction industry during the last two years of a five-year course. The knowledge acquired during the five years provides them with some background for working in the real estate field, although not all the knowledge needed for the work of high-quality real estate agents is included in the course. The objective of the study is not, however, to train real estate agents, but to educate managers for the construction industry.

The students taking the specialisation in Economics and Management of Real Estate receive a solid background in construction technology during the first three years of the course, while in the last two years they take the following subjects:

- 7th semester: Cost estimation and prices in the construction industry, Economy, Operational research, Building Technology, Economic statistics, Accounting.
- 8th semester: Infrastructure and water works, Management information systems, Law 1, Construction of buildings, Financial management 1, Project management 1; Elective courses: Cost estimation 2, Computer accounting, Decision-making analysis, Systems analysis, real estate valuation.
- 9th semester: Law 2, Financial management 2, Project management 2; Transport infrastructure, Strategic management and marketing, Economic project, Special seminar. Elective courses: Application software, Quality management
- 10th semester: Economic project, Thesis seminar, Personnel management, Housing policy, Controlling, Elective courses: Ecology, Value engineering, Ethics, Production management, Territorial marketing. The last semester lasts only 10 weeks: there is no examination in this section apart from the state examinations. During the remaining time students prepare their final theses.

5.11 Ukraine

The situation in the real estate field in the Ukraine is quite well developed. The real estate market there has its peculiarities, namely there are real estate exchanges, which operate together with real estate offices. There are many real estate professionals, who may now join the Association of Real Estate Professionals (Realtors) of Ukraine (URA). In the capital, there is the Union of Real Estate Specialists of Kyiv which has a membership of about 30 firms. Ukrainian valuers have their own professional organisation, the Ukrainian Society of Appraisers, which has founded a FIABCI-Ukraine Chapter and has obtained membership of TEGoVA.

The Co-ordination & Methodical Centre of URA edits the *Ukrainian Real Estate Bulletin*, including an Internet version. A weekly magazine, *Real Estate*, is published in the capital city, Kiev.

Real estate education exists in the form of short-term courses, which are managed by the Fund of State Property of Ukraine, the Ukrainian Society of Appraisers, and the International Centre of Privatisation, Investment and Management. Typical subjects are real estate consulting, valuation of buildings and land, and valuation of businesses.

5.12 Uzbekistan

The real estate market in Uzbekistan is in development. As a result of the privatisation process, more than 20,700 companies have changed the form of their property ownership and management. As at September 1, 1998, on the basis of former state enterprises, 2,916 joint stock companies, 2,966 collective enterprises, 13,544 small private enterprises and 501 joint ventures had been established. The infrastructure for carrying out the privatisation process has been prepared. At present enterprises with privately-owned property comprise 88,2% of the total. They produce 53.3% of gross internal product, including 63.9% of industrial production and 99.3 % of agricultural production. 74 % of the economically active population is employed in the private sector. There is no professional society in the real estate field in Uzbekistan

There are several educational institutions in the Republic of Uzbekistan, such as an Architectural and Constructional Institute as well as a Constructional Faculty under the Technical University, where future potential real estate professionals are trained. However, so far there is no specialisation in real estate there.

Various general periodicals of wide profile are published, which include articles about real estate and advertisements for the purchase and sale of property, but there are no specialised real estate magazines or newspapers.

5.13 Conclusion

In conclusion, we must emphasise that, at present, real estate education in European countries with transition economies has a fragmentary character. The future development of the market economy and the perspective of European integration are however strong driving forces that will increase the need for this specialisation. The preparation of study programmes for real estate requires time, funding and staff. Unfortunately, the overall economic situation, the relatively small numbers and size of real estate transactions, the existing psychological climate and the lack of public finance are all not conducive to the establishment of such specialisations in the universities. This may, however, change with economic development.

The author would like to thank David Allen, Koloman Ivanička, Jr., Sergey Koplus, and Bakhram Musabekov for useful information on the current situation in their countries.

REFERENCES

Friedman J.P. and Ordway N.J.D. (1994) Income Property Appraisal and Analysis, Prentice Hall, Englewood Cliffs.

Parvanov V.R. (1996) Ratification of a New Profession. Bulgarski Ozenitel, #1(1), p.2.

Schulte K.-W. (1998) Immobilienokonomie, Bd. 1, Oldenbourg, München-Wien.

Trifonov N. (2000) The Use of Indices in Valuation in Belarus. In: Baltic Valuation Conference. 28.-30.9.2000. Turku, Finland. Eds. O.Hiekka and H.Raasakka. Capella Oy, Helsinki, p.50.

Trifonov N. (1999) Real Estate Investments: The Case of Belarus, paper delivered at the IRES Conference, Kuala Lumpur.

Trifonov N., Levkovich O. and Sapelkin E. (1999) Real Estate Education in the Republic of Belarus. In: The European Real Estate Society. Sixth European Conference, Athens, Greece 22-25 June 1999. Book of Abstracts, p.27.

Chapter 6

Denmark

Jens Lunde
Department of Finance, Copenhagen Business School, Copenhagen, Denmark

6.1 Introduction

As in many other countries, real estate education in Denmark is undergoing continuing progress and increasing professionalism, mirroring developments in the property and mortgage markets as well as society as a whole.

Traditionally, the fundamental *real estate functions* were organised within specific professions and corporate structures. These structures have now been reorganised. General innovations, the development and expansion of the property markets, increased consumer protection and ever-growing professional knowledge have greatly expanded the requirements for professional competence for real estate practitioners. More formal, full-time education, and not just informal, on-the-job training is necessary to meet the new demands.

Over decades, the educational level of the population in general has been improved and educational requirements for many professions have become more stringent. An education in real estate has become a condition of employment in the field, while on the other hand professional real estate firms must offer competitive educational and employment possibilities in order to attract qualified candidates.

6.2   Real estate main functions

The organisation of property markets, real estate management, real estate brokerage and mortgage financing varies greatly between countries. This is reflected in their different types of real estate education. However, professional tasks can be broken down into basically similar real estate functions in individual countries. It is the differing combination of real estate functions that give each market its distinctive national character. These varying national characters are the reason for the differences in real estate education.

Eigth real estate main functions can be identified:

– property construction
– maintenance, renovation and replacement of the property
– investment in real estate
– real estate brokerage
– property valuation
– real estate finance / mortgage financing
– registration of rights and claims on the property
– management of real estate

Clearly, these main real estate functions could be further broken down into single activities. This paper will however deal with the professionals working in each of these main fields, and their educational backgrounds.

Property construction requires specialised expert knowledge and education, as do the other building activities of maintenance, renovation and replacement of the property. This dimension of real estate education will not be discussed further in this paper.

In principle, anyone can invest in real estate but professional guidance requires economic, legal and technical knowledge, which is supplied by several types of educational programmes.

Sale of real estate is primarily carried out by real estate agents, but lawyers and financial institutions are both potential and active competitors in this field.

Appraisal of a property's market value is carried out by the real estate agent involved in the sale. Similarly, a mortgage or commercial bank values the property as security for loans, while the tax authorities carry out valuations for their purposes. Normally property finance is arranged on purchase, but the removal of mortgage restrictions at the beginning of the 1990s has also allowed mortgage refinancing to be arranged. Specialised educational programmes and courses have been organised for employees in commercial and mortgage banks. The new qualification of Financial Economist combines this field with education in real estate (see below). An important condition for the security of ownership and loans in the property is the public registration of rights and claims on the property, which nowadays is carried out by electronic means.

Real estate agencies in Denmark mostly offer several functions on behalf of sellers of houses, owner-occupied flats (condominiums), farms and other small non-residential properties. The estate agent sets the price to be asked for the property, selects marketing methods, makes proposals for mortgage finance, negotiates the sale contract, ensures the signature of the preliminary contract and carries out parts of the practical and administrative conveyance of the property. The buyer can consult specialists (e.g. a lawyer, another real estate agent, technical specialists and/or a bank) to advise on and to safeguard his interests. In practice, however, buyers only rarely pay for consultancy. After the deal is concluded, the final legal contract is drawn up either by a lawyer, a real estate agent or a non-professional. In most cases a commercial bank will organise the mortgage finance. Ownership, and loans secured on the property, are recorded in the public land register.

Several different types of specialist, depending on the circumstances, carry out the function of managing a property or a portfolio of properties. Owner-occupiers and many firms manage their properties themselves. However it is usually necessary to instruct a specialist, e.g. an economist, real estate agent or lawyer, to undertake professional administration of highly regulated private rented housing and of more market-conforming non-residential properties. Property companies, or investment funds owning properties, are also likely to employ specialists. Another distinct property group is social housing with its own particular administration procedures, which partly follow its own legal accounting principles but also have cost-based rents fixed by separate statutory rules.

The influence of tenants on decision making, whether in properties owned in condominium or by others, presents a specific administrative problem. In such cases substitution of the tenants' own administration by professional administration may occur and the overall management will include an element of partnership between the tenants and the professional administration. So-called democratic management has been developed in different parts of the housing market:

1. In principle, social housing is democratically organised. However, in economic matters concerning the local housing association[1], the administration of the superior (municipality) housing association, representatives of the municipality and the administration of the national housing association hold most of the decision-making power. Social tenure is strongly regulated. Social housing accounts for 19% of the housing stock.
2. Residents in private co-operatives (condominiums) are both tenants in and owners of their property. The owners, i.e. the residents, take economic decisions but also frequently use professional administrators. Private co-operatives amount to 6 % of the housing stock.
3. Owners of owner-occupied flats must create a common association to decide on the administration and maintenance of the building, even though they own their own apartments. Owner-occupied flats comprise 5 % of the housing stock.[2]

Courses are available for residents in all the three of these different types of tenure, to improve their capabilities to decide on matters concerning the administration of the property.

In conclusion it must be said that persons with very varied educational backgrounds - or even without higher or specialised education (only having attended an ordinary school) can carry out most real estate functions.

The following sections therefore only discuss education for real estate agents and real estate administrators, mainly directed towards real estate functions.

6.3   Financial supermarkets - a reorganisation of financial and real estate functions in Denmark

Through the 1980s, an extensive liberalisation of the Danish capital market took place. From the end of that decade, EU directives on capital markets and other financial matters were carried out to create a structural reorganisation of the Danish financial institutions. As part of the structural changes, mortgage banks were allowed to own, indirectly, most of the real estate agents, which were then reorganised into a few franchising chains.

At the same time, six of the biggest commercial and saving banks merged, creating two so-called mega-banks (Danske Bank and Unibank), with between them two thirds of the banking market. The de facto ban on establishing new mortgage banks was removed, with the result that 10 mortgage banks were in existence in 2000 compared with only 4 in 1989. Ownership of the new mortgage banks was closely connected with the commercial banks. They quickly achieved a very high proportion of new mortgages, almost as soon as they had entered the market. Nowadays, bank, mortgage and insurance products are sold side-by-side in financial supermarkets, which are also closely connected with real estate agency operations. In theory, the commercial banks, mortgage banks, insurance companies and real estate agents are independent companies but in practice they tend to be owned by the same holding companies.

In 2000, a new wave of mergers occurred. Unibank entered a Nordic bank merger (with Swedish Nordbanken, Finnish Merita and Norwegian Christiania Bank og Kreditkasse). Danske Bank merged with the third largest bank and the second largest mortgage bank. It is easy to imagine that other important mergers and changes in the structure of financial institutions will occur in the future.

The commercial banks have begun to sell properties directly from bank premises, although legally through a real estate agency subsidiary. At present, however, this appears to account for only a minor part of their turnover. Although the banks could also carry out real estate administration, they only cover a minor part of that market.

The Danish markets for larger residential and for non-residential properties are not well organised. However, the underlying tendency appears to be to towards the establishment of more and bigger housing and non-residential property companies with a portfolio of properties. Until now, such companies' shares have not been frequently traded and are therefore rather illiquid. The pension funds, with their easy access to capital, tend to dominate the market. Their capital is directly invested in properties, with decision-making and management organised by the funds' own property departments.

The tendency to create still bigger financial and property companies must lead to a greater degree of specialisation in real estate functions, which will in turn place more demands on education, both in terms of formal, full-time courses and on-the-job training.

6.4 The "kitchen table" agent - on the job training

It is legal in every sense for a property owner to manage his or her own property and even to sell it. Apparently, many owner-occupiers believe that being able to take all decisions about their house qualifies them to decide whether, e.g. buying a block of flats or a non-residential property would be profitable and subsequently to undertake the management of it. Of course such attitudes are on the decline in modern society.

Management, as well as the selling of properties, has therefore developed from a level of simple operations and part-time employment, without any external quality standards. Professional real estate agents use the term "kitchen table agent" to refer to agents who attempt to sell properties without any professional qualifications or facilities. Despite the new educational requirements (see 6.7 below) people who are already functioning as real estate agents will be allowed to continue.

It can however also be said of lawyers, that although they hold a law degree, they have not had to take any courses in economics, finance or management, which are now regarded as essential for modern real estate administrators and agents.

6.5   On-the-job training and evening studies

Most Danish vocational training gradually developed as a mixture of on-the-job experience combined with evening courses, the latter probably being the only possibility, because employers were not prepared to accept the loss of their young apprentices' working time. Vocational education in Denmark still relies on a high level of on-the-job training. However, it must be borne in mind that school leavers in Denmark have had a minimum of 10 years schooling, while nearly half have had at least 12 years.

Up to the present, the tradition of Danish universities, unlike those in Anglo-Saxon countries, has not included specialised vocational education. Commercial schools, together with other direct vocational schools, are below university level in the Danish educational pyramid.

In general, on-the-job training is decreasing, in favour of formal full-time education, at all levels in Denmark although the change is occurring slowly. The lack of direct experience for students on full-time courses is made up for by practical case-studies and with periods as trainees in firms.

6.6   The new, extended requirements: from planning and regulations to market economics

The strongly increasing demand for education in all parts of society, including the real estate industries, can only lead to the replacement of vocational part-time evening studies by full-time higher education. The electronic revolution has created requirements for several new educational programmes and has also caused major changes in other, existing courses.

The Danish economy is characterised as a market economy with extensive regulation of the borderlines of the markets. In fact the EU has influenced the regulations by creating common rules. Therefore, in a Danish context it is important to note that the increasing legal restrictions, including those affecting real estate administration and brokerage, will bring increasing educational requirements as an inevitable consequence. It also appears that Denmark is in competition with Sweden to achieve the highest tax burden: the tax rules are often complicated. Environmental regulations are rapidly increasing in complexity. The planning legislation must also be taken into account. The rent regulation of dwellings complicates real estate administration. The rules for real estate agencies and property sales include the most far-reaching consumer protection in Danish legislation. For example, the real estate agent remains fully responsible for all mistakes in calculations and payments even though the agent himself did not make the mistake.

Clients make legitimate demands for more qualified guidance, because options and their limitations have been enlarged but have also become much more complex. As an example, the liberalisation of mortgage legislation has made possible innovations in the types of loan available, which, although they may be beneficial to borrowers, also increase the need for more expertise, information and guidance.

An example of the present complete lack of information and guidance is on the family's choice of type of tenure, between owner-occupation, private co-operatives, private renting and social renting. Only after the choice of tenure has been made is information and guidance offered, by the agents active in that market segment, on the different houses and flats available in it.

6.7 Licensing requirements for real estate agents - Member of Dansk Ejendomsmæglerforening

The Law of Sale of Real Property now restricts the selling of property to: agents who fulfil the licensing requirements for real estate agents and are registered at the Ministry of Trade and Industry; to lawyers; and to commercial banks, mortgage banks and insurance companies.

Only licensed real estate agents are allowed to use the title Ejendomsmægler (estate agent). Among the licensing requirements are that a real estate agent must offer financial security (in the form of a guarantee) for clients' deposits and that the agent must not be subject to suspension of payments or be in bankruptcy. In addition, the agent must not be in debt to the tax office, or any other public authority, for more than DDK 50,000 (approximately EUR 6666 / £ 4000). The agent must also be able to "fulfil a defined demand for theoretical knowledge of property sales" and have the required amount of practical experience as defined by the Ministry of Trade and Industry. A licensed real estate agent or a lawyer must be in charge of each of the estate agency's offices.

Most real estate agents are members of Dansk Ejendomsmæglerforening (the Danish Real Estate Agents Association). Traditionally, membership of the nearly 100-year-old association gives both sellers and buyers more confidence and security. A client's legal claims against a real estate agent can be brought before a board of appeal, which is independent of, although financed by, the Association.

6.8   Current educational methods for real estate agents

Up to the present, education leading to qualification as a real estate agent has been reserved for the employees of agents. In order to be admitted to a programme in real estate agency at a commercial school, applicants should have worked full-time for a real estate agency for at least two years. Employment in a similar capacity in a commercial bank, a mortgage bank, a housing association, a law practice or the like may also qualify for admission to the course. The real estate agency programmes follow the Danish tradition for vocational schooling of skilled workers at commercial or technical schools, i.e. a combination of part-time, evening studies and on-the-job training with firms.

Real estate agency courses include four general commercial school subjects: business law (two courses), business economics and macroeconomics. These are taken for two years on half-time basis and must be passed before taking the two special subjects of the course: property law and real estate brokerage. Each of these two courses lasts for a year of half-time (evening) studies.

Property law includes: the basic law of property (property rights, registration of rights and claims, securities, purchase contracts, tenancy agreements, foreclosures etc.); rent regulations (including non-residential properties, owner-occupied flats, private co-operative housing); and property taxation.

Real estate brokerage includes the basic conditions for buying and selling properties (brokerage) and in particular concerning owner-occupied dwellings, private co-operatives, non-residential and agricultural properties. Completion of the property transaction, mortgage finance, insurance and taxation of properties are other important topics. The subject also covers building technology, and the seller's responsibility for mistakes and defects. The course includes a seminar where participants present, and receive a critique of, a report.

After having passed the examination, a successful candidate can obtain a licence as a real estate agent following registration in the Ministry's register.

Subsequently, the real estate agent has the option of taking the course in property valuation, in order to be able to carry out valuations and to qualify for appointment as an appraisal expert by the courts. The Valuation courses includes valuations of property, both to market value and subject to complicated conditions, as well as the legal rules for financing, foreclosures, estates of deceased persons, special easements, etc. Building techniques are also an important element of the course. A criticism of the course is that it appears to lack financial theory, normally used for valuation in the business environment. The property valuation course requires a year of part-time study at a commercial school. Real estate agents who have successfully completed the course may use the title valuar (valuer).

6.9   Education for real estate administration

The course in real estate administration was started only recently. The course closely resembles that for estate agents and is also taken at commercial schools. However it is taught in the daytime and, as half-time studies, can be completed in two years.

The course is targeted mainly at employees with some years' experience of estate administration, in property companies or otherwise. Employees lacking such experience are allowed to attend the school but are required to take additional, particularly rigorous preparations for the lectures. Although the course is less formal than that for real estate agents, knowledge of basic economics and management to commercial school level will undoubtedly give applicants an advantage.

The real estate administration course includes the following subjects: property law; owner-occupied associations and private co-operatives; property accounting; and administration.

Property law gives participants a detailed knowledge of the extensive Danish rent regulation rules, the calculation of rents and the rules for property taxes and duties. The subject of Owner-occupied associations and private co-operatives also covers the housing laws, with maximum prices and other special rules for co-operatives: many owner-occupiers' co-operative aims in such associations call for legal limits.
Property accounting is self-explanatory.

Administration, service, management and techniques gives students an understanding of the provision of service to tenants[3] property management and technical conditions.

The educational programme is not formal in the sense that no degree or other qualification is conferred. Unlike the estate agency programme, it does not give direct access to a particular job or role. However, the course is very highly regarded and is in demand by students who wish to increase their qualifications, in the expectation of higher future earnings.

6.10 A new course: financial economist

As from August 2000, a new two-year full-time course, financial economist, was introduced at commercial schools. As might be expected, the course is aimed at the financial sector. Real estate is covered as part of the basics of the course. The financial economist course is a distinct alternative to the real estate courses described above but it also has good potential to become the education of the future for real estate professionals.

The first one-and-a-half years of the financial economist programme is spent covering compulsory, common courses, while the final half-year is devoted to electives and special courses. In the real estate field, electives include property law and real estate administration or real estate brokerage. A final examination report (thesis) is required.

The first financial economists, some of whom will have specialised in real estate administration and brokerage, will pass in 2002.

The subjects in the compulsory part are: Financial markets and institutions; Personal finance; Client and interpersonal relations; Business economics; Management and communication; Macroeconomics; Business law; and Statistics. The subjects and their relevant weights are shown in the appendix. The course varies somewhat depending on the local study programmes of the five commercial schools that offer it.

The financial economist course is one of a number of two-year full-time courses at commercial schools, which should create theoretical and practical business competence to match the demands of the Danish employment market.

Admission to the financial economist programme requires the applicant to have successfully completed secondary school education or to have a relevant practical office education. A minimum knowledge of maths and English is compulsory. Participants are paid student grants during the course.

In contrast to students on the real estate programmes, financial economist students are not in employment during the course. They must however spend three months as an unpaid trainee in a firm. After completing the programme, financial economist students specialising in real estate must work in a real estate firm for two years. There are two reasons: firstly they may take the part-time diploma course at university level during the period (see below) and secondly to fulfil the requirements to obtain a public licence as a real estate agent. Students will generally need to have been in contact with the firm, in order to arrange their employment, either before starting the course or before the examinations.

6.11 The diploma - a possible supplementary course?

During the reform of real estate education, in the new programme several former subject courses were discontinued. Some critics consider that more courses at higher level are needed. The demand for supplementary real estate education at all levels is strong. The professional courses for real estate administration and brokerage must also be expanded with supplementary education, as a normal part of students' professional abilities.

Such supplementary education is expected to take place at business schools[4]. A first step could be to start a two-year part-time real estate diploma programme. This would be in line with the Danish tradition of specialised part-time diploma courses. In the long term, another possibility could be to organise a three-year full-time bachelor's degree in real estate at a business school. In this way, university level education in real estate could be provided in a way that would be regarded as natural for executive employees and economic specialists in Danish business.

The financial economist course, alone among 13 new vocational academy courses, will be equivalent to, and exempting from, part 1 of the existing business diploma course (HD. 1). Financial economists will therefore be able directly to enter part 2 (the specialised part) of the existing diploma course (HD. 2). The explanation is the similarity between the courses: the business diploma education, part 1, is a two-year part-time, evening course, while the financial economist course is for two years full-time.

It can be assumed that most financial economists who are employed in commercial banks, mortgage banks and insurance companies will specialise in finance for the second part of their diploma education. Similarly, most financial economists from real estate administration and brokerage will want to specialise in real estate at this level, which means that the establishment of a real estate diploma course may be expected. Students, in both the financial and real estate sectors, who wish to specialise in e.g. marketing, accounting, management or logistics, can choose these areas for part 2 of their diploma courses.

A new real estate diploma course (part 2) will have to be developed by 2002 in order to ensure that newly qualified financial economists, who specialised in real estate, will be able to continue their education. The possible content of the course is outside the scope of this paper.

The demand for additional education will encourage the production of new books and other relevant educational materials. At the same time, the introduction of a real estate course at university level will have the important side-effects of generating economic, legal and other research on the topics of housing and real estate. In the long run this will also improve academic standards by providing research-based education, the universities' guarantee of quality.

6.12 Real estate topics as parts of other higher education courses

Architect and engineer are reasonably well-defined courses, all of which are related to specialised areas of the construction process. In Denmark these courses have the appropriate level of quality and are otherwise reasonably comparable with similar courses in other countries. As mentioned, these university courses are not discussed in this paper.

University courses in law and economics are in general suitable for people involved in real estate administration and brokerage. Civil servants active in the governmental and municipal regulation of the real estate market and the activities of organisations mostly hold such qualifications. These courses also cover relevant topics such as property rights, law of mortgage and guarantees, law of rents, property law, real estate economics and real estate finance. In keeping with Danish educational traditions, social science courses are not aimed at specific professions such as real estate administration and brokerage.

The upgrading of real estate courses to university level must lead, in the long run, to more educational and research activity in this area.

6.13 Courses – continuing professional education

Supplementary training and education is of course also important in real estate. For a number of years, the Danish real estate organisations have systematically arranged courses and seminars, for existing members and their employees as well as new entrants. New legislation, new theory and new problems are introduced to the profession in this way. Lectures and conferences are also arranged. The financial conglomerates and the real estate franchising chains also arrange in-house courses on relevant topics, e.g. the housing and real estate markets.

Inspired by activities in other countries, Danish universities and business schools have started to offer supplementary courses and training, although with less relevance for the real estate area. It is expected that new real estate courses at university level will create increased demand for supplementary courses and continuing education in the field.

6.14 Expectations for the future of real estate education

There is considerable scope for improvement in courses covering housing and property, or indeed real estate education of all types. One effect may be to increase market efficiency, so that for instance properties are sold at prices that reflect the similar yields at a given level of risk.

If the Danish housing market were to be liberalised by the reduction or even abolition of rent regulations, private rented dwellings would be a possible investment choice, depending on market conditions. In this case, the consumers' claims and competition would increase the required level of service from real estate administrators. Tenants' wider options will add to the demand for information and guidance. If social housing were to be privatised, using private capital to provide equity as property investments and with rents at market levels, similar demands would be created. All such changes will of themselves force an increase in the requirements for knowledge and education of people working in the real estate sector.

In the real estate field, the development of full-time formal courses has only just started. The most obvious development would be to establish undergraduate (bachelor's degree) courses in real estate at university level. It is likely that the reaction to existing demand can be relatively fast.

Managers and specialists in the real estate industry in a broad sense are expected to have appropriate level of education. In practice, in a modern society this means education at university level. Such educational requirements for managers and specialists will tend to expand and increase the educational requirements for other real estate professionals. Although many people in the real estate sector already have such educational qualifications, the general educational level and the research base for education need to be enhanced. The implementation of such an upgrading of the real estate professions, once decided on, would in the best case require a number of years.

NOTES

[1] The local housing association include the single block of flats or single group of houses, build at same time. In side a municipality the local housing associations are collected in a (municipality-based) housing associations. The nationwide housing associations are unions of municipality housing associations.

[2] 1.1.1999 all owner-occupied dwellings made up to 53 % of the Danish housing stock while private rented dwellings accounted for 18 %.

[3] In a system with rent regulation and where rents are much below the market rents, the "inexpensive" flats are very easy to let out even the tenants receive a poor service from the property. This could affect the staff members' attitudes and moral and make them unsuited for administration of as example business tenures on market conditions.

[4] In Denmark business schools are ranked among the universities.

REFERENCES

Danish legislation.

ACKNOWLEDGEMENTS

The author wishes to thank Bente Naver, Dansk Ejendomsforening, and Lars Langkjær, Ejendomsforeningen Danmark, for valuable comments and suggestions.

APPENDIX

Table 1: Financial economist for real estate agencies and administrations

The course and the official description of the subjects (90 ECTS points for the compulsory part, 30 ECTS points for the optional part)

Financial markets and institutions (24 ECTS-points)
- be able to manage tasks in relation to financial products and guidance services, based on a unified idea of the financial system's function and limiting conditions.

Personal finance (7 ECTS-points)
- evaluate the private client's need for financial products and guidance services.

Client and interpersonal relations (6 ECTS-points)
- be able to apply knowledge of psychological processes and theories in relation to co-operation and sale, and use the knowledge for finance-related tasks.

Business economics (15 ECTS-points)
- be able to use business economic theory and business economic models and methods; further to reach a unified idea of business economic decision processes. The course includes business analysis, investment and finance, and accounting.

Management and communication (6 ECTS-points)
(also referred to as "method")
- be able to analyse a business enterprise and to be able to make proposals for more efficient organisation and management.

Macro economics (10 ECTS-points)
(also referred to as global economics)
- be able to understand important macro economic connections and evaluate the consequences of changing circumstances and conditions for the business enterprise and those involved; to apply

this knowledge in tasks related to decisions and guidance services.

Business law (12 ECTS-points)
- apply relevant legislation on guidance services and on contracts, and be able to decide when other legal advisers and lawyers must be involved.

Statistics (10 ECTS-points)
- use statistical methods for economic descriptions and analysis, evaluate statistical research as regards data sampling, data inquiries, data analysis and conclusions, identify statistical problems and complete the analysis by oneself.

Optional special courses:

Property law (9 ECTS-points)
- knowledge of laws related to real estate agency and to real estate management and administration. The subject includes rent laws in relation to one- and two-family houses, small properties, the law of buying real property, laws on owner-occupied flats and on co-operative housing and on other regulations of real property.

and for real estate specialists, a choice of: special course 1:

Real estate administration (9 ECTS-points)
- use relevant knowledge of property management and administration to understand the administration of blocks or portfolios of properties as social housing as well as private rented dwellings, owner-occupied associations and private co-operatives.

or special course 2:

Real estate brokerage (9 ECTS-points)
- to be able in practice to handle sale of one- and two-family houses, owner-occupied flats and holiday cottages; be able to impart required knowledge about other tenures and special conditions and to recognise these. The course includes real estate agent's investigations and preparing the relevant documents, as well as building laws and rules for small houses, and building technology for one- and two-family houses.

Final thesis / project:

Final examination project (12 ECTS-points)
- based on relevant methods, analyse a complex problem in relation to a specific task in finance.

Chapter 7

Finland

Olli Olkkonen
KTI, The Institute for Real Estate Economics, Helsinki, Finland

Kaisa Leiwo
The Finnish Real Estate Training and Education Institute, Helsinki, Finland

Hanna Kaleva
KTI, The Institute for Real Estate Economics, Helsinki, Finland

7.1 Introduction

Real estate economics (REE) as a field of both research and education has a relatively short tradition in Finland. This is partly because of the special features of the Finnish property market. The construction sector has traditionally had a leading role in the Finnish real estate business, mainly due to the relatively strict regulation and planning process. The real estate business was always considered to be a part of the construction industry, which was the focus of both research and education. Until recently, there have been very few people with a background in economics or business administration in the real estate business. This has naturally influenced academic RE education. Construction management and related topics, together with surveying, dominated real estate education until the 1990's.

7.2   Real estate education in Finland

In Finland, real estate education historically followed the engineering tradition with the focus on the property construction. On the other hand there is also a long tradition of educating land surveyors. Pan-European changes in the property sector have, however, altered the industrial structure of the real estate sector, towards greater business-orientation. This development has major implications for real estate education in Finland. These structural changes are similar to those in most other European countries. In Finland, traditional real estate education is largely based on the study of construction technology, the building process, and surveying. Education is technology-oriented, and the economic and financial aspects have received only minor attention. This is true of vocational education and training as well as of the universities and polytechnics.

Finland experienced a steady growth in its economy during the decades following the Second World War. This growth, although not among the fastest in Europe, continued, with a few exceptions, until the beginning of the 90's. As a result of the extended post-war re-building, the stock of properties in Finland is fairly young. More than 50 per cent of the stock was built after 1980. Thus, it is natural that the real estate profession in Finland has been geared towards the investment and building phases of property life-cycle. This has consequently affected the structure of the educational system.

In this article, an attempt is made to examine the current status of education and research related to real estate economics. As stated above, the field is very young in Finland and thus there are, as yet, no strong educational or research traditions.

7.2.1   University-level education

Currently, education related to real estate economics takes place at four universities: Helsinki University of Technology; Swedish School of Economics and Business Administration; Turku School of Economics and Business Administration; and Tampere University of Technology.

7.2.1.1 Helsinki University of Technology

Helsinki University of Technology (HUT) has run courses related to real estate since the beginning of the 20th century. The major goal of the studies has been the education of surveyors. HUT real estate programmes currently have a strong emphasis on REE and also, recently, Facilities Management, although programmes still lack a coverage of basic economics. The courses can be considered to be quite broad and are still technically oriented, especially if compared with international mainstream REE education. A new Master's programme, entitled Real Estate Economics is scheduled to start in 2001. In this REE programme, students can concentrate on either real estate management or real estate law and technology.

In HUT, there is also a separate Master's programme in Facilities Management, which is organised in co-operation with The Groening Institute of Technology in the Netherlands.

Master's programmes in HUT consist of 180 credits, equivalent to 5 years' full-time studies.

7.2.1.2 Swedish School of Economics and Business Administration (Hanken)

The Swedish School of Economics and Business Administration in Helsinki (Hanken) started its REE-related one-year specialisation programme "Master's programme in Real Estate Finance" in autumn 1999. Although the programme is entitled "Real Estate Finance", it also covers topics like Introduction to real estate and RE development. The programme is targeted at both Master's students and RE practitioners for continuing education or post-graduate purposes. The lecturers are predominantly American professors, who make short visits to Finland to provide one separate module of the programme, which altogether consists of 40 credits (of which 20 credits are given by the Master's thesis).

7.2.1.3 Turku School of Economics and Business Administration

The third university with a course in real estate economics is the Turku School of Economics and Business Administration (TSEBA). Even though it only offers one course in real estate economics (2 credits), since 1990 it has established a strong tradition of real estate economics research. In recent years, TSEBA has been active in producing licentiates. This is partly explained by the close linkage between TSEBA and KTI (The Institute for Real Estate Economics, see below).

7.2.1.4 Tampere University of Technology

The Tampere University of Technology has also been active in developing real estate education in recent years. It has a strong tradition of education

related to construction, architecture and engineering, but recently REE related topics have also been given more attention in the RE course. Students
can choose property management as a main subject and also take some
courses in business economics.

7.2.2   Polytechnic-level education and vocational education

In addition to university-level real estate education, there is also a relatively broad supply of polytechnic-level education for real estate professionals in Finland. Polytechnics are oriented towards practice and base their operations on vocational skill requirements. The real estate education in polytechnics is largely technology-oriented, although there are also some relatively new programmes in facilities or real estate management as well as real
estate economics. In polytechnics, 160 credits are usually required for a degree.

Real estate economics is traditionally not included in initial vocational
education for young people or in additional vocational education for experienced workers. The training is very practical and the focus of studies is on
work methods and practices.

7.2.3   Executive education

7.2.3.1   Real Estate Training and Education Institute

The Finnish Real Estate Training and Education Institute offers continuing education for RE practitioners. Their main programme related to REE,
PGP (post-graduate programme in property management), is targeted at real
estate managers. PGP emphasises real estate economics, which is one of the
main areas in which Finnish real estate managers want to develop their skills
and knowledge. The one-year programme started in 1995 and is normally
considered to be an equivalent of 26 credits. PGP is also a prerequisite for an
application for the status of Certified Real Estate Manager (KJs, see below).

7.2.3.2   Lifelong Learning Institute Dipoli

The Lifelong Learning Institute Dipoli, of the Helsinki University of
Technology organises under- and postgraduate courses, continuing education
and professional development programmes in fields within the expertise of
the university. Courses include subjects such as property management, construction management and property business management.

7.2.3.3   Certification of Real Estate Managers (KJs)

Since 1999, 34 people have achieved the status of Certified Real Estate Manager (KJs) in Finland. Requirements for certification include sufficient basic education, a minimum of 3 years' work experience in the real estate business, a diploma from a post-graduate programme in property management (PGP, see above) and participation in an accepted general business management education programme. An independent board consisting of both academics and practitioners vets the applications.

7.3   Research activities

7.3.1   Research institutes

Real estate economics research in Finland can be divided into three different categories: academic research, applied research and practitioner-oriented research services. Four types of organisations carry out these research activities:

1. Departments of academic institutions (e.g. Helsinki University of Technology, Tampere University of Technology, Swedish School of Economics and Business Administration, Turku School of Economics and Business Administration)
2. State-funded research institutes (e.g. VTT, Motiva)
3. Private research institutes and professional bodies (e.g. KTI and trade organisations)
4. Commercial companies (e.g. Catella Ltd)

The majority of REE research in Finland is in applied research and practitioner-oriented research services. There are several reasons for the paucity of academic research, the main reason being the lack of professors and PhD –level practitioners in the field of real estate economics.

Post-graduate studies in REE are not very popular, for several different reasons, the most important of which are lack of financial support for students, lack of post-graduate education programmes and the unpopularity of REE studies among students (compared with other technical fields like information technology and electronics for example).

7.3.1.1   Helsinki University of Technology (HUT)

In terms of professors, lecturers and researchers, Helsinki University of Technology has the largest resources in Finland. It has also produced the most post-graduate exams in Finland.

The Institute of Real Estate Studies provides research and education in the fields of real estate economics and valuation, real estate management and land management. It is part of the Department of Surveying of HUT.

The Centre for Urban and Regional Studies concentrates on research topics like communicative planning, housing and community development, and city culture. It also co-ordinates the doctoral programme, the Graduate School for Urban and Planning Studies, and provides further education in the field.

7.3.1.2   The Institute for Real Estate Economics (KTI)

The Institute for Real Estate Economics (KTI) is a private, independent research institute, which was originally founded by TSEBA (see above) and two major trade unions in the Finnish real estate sector (RAKLI and SKL, see below) in 1993. KTI provides mainly applied research, and research and information services. It has extensive databases of rents, returns, prices and costs. Another major activity of KTI is research and development projects, which are normally carried out in close co-operation with companies operating in the real estate business. KTI employs 15 full-time researchers, most of which have backgrounds in economics, and several assistants for special projects.

The KTI Property Index measures total returns on property investments in the Finnish property market. 25 major property investors contribute to the KTI index, which covers all the major property types in the largest cities in Finland. The total market value of existing investment properties in the KTI index is over FIM 37 billion. The index covers approximately 20 % of the total Finnish investment property market.

7.3.1.3   Technical Research Centre of Finland (VTT)

VTT (Technical Research Centre of Finland) mainly carries out applied research projects, although not based on real estate economics, but rather a tradition of technical research. VTT is a state-sponsored research organisation with substantial resources. The real estate research department has over 100 employees. Most of the VTT's research activities concentrate on the technical aspects of real estate such as construction, refurbishment and maintenance.

7.3.1.4   Catella Ltd

The only real estate service company offering research services in Finland is Catella Property Consultants Ltd. Catella is a European company, represented in Finland since 1997, when Catella Property consultants Ltd acquired the Finnish company Huoneistomarkkinat.

Catella has a research department which mainly serves the needs of brokerage and valuation, but also runs occasional research projects, usually in co-operation with universities and research institutes. Catella has five researchers, who are also responsible for producing its market reports, which provide regular information on the Finnish property market.

7.3.2 Research programmes

7.3.2.1 RemBrand

A significant contribution to the promotion of real estate-related research in Finland was made by TEKES (The National Technology Agency), which started an extensive research and development programme called RemBrand in 1999. TEKES is a state-owned fund that allocates money to technically oriented research and development activities in Finland. It produces R&D programmes for various, mainly technology-based industries. RemBrand is the first service-oriented technology programme financed by Tekes. It is a five-year programme that aims to enhance and develop the competitiveness and service orientation of the Finnish real estate sector. RemBrand provides two major types of financing: 80 % of the total budget (120 Million FIM) is allocated to company-level R&D projects, the remaining 20% to research projects in universities and state-financed research institutes.

7.3.2.2 Doctoral Programme for RE studies

Currently, the Academy of Finland, TEKES (The National Technology Agency) and RAKLI (The Finnish Association of Building Owners and Construction Clients) are preparing an initiative to set up a doctoral programme for RE studies. This doctoral programme would offer education and guidance as well as financial support for students. Participation in the programme would enable students to acquire the necessary international connections with leading RE research centres around the world.

7.4 Professional bodies

7.4.1 The Finnish Association of Building Owners and Construction Clients (RAKLI)

The Finnish Association of Building Owners and Construction Clients (RAKLI) is an interest group representing the major commercial real estate owners and construction clients in Finland.

The membership base of RAKLI covers a wide range of property owners and occupiers, from listed property companies and pension funds to municipalities and retail companies. The membership consists of over 400 public and private real estate companies and 69 shopping centres. Together they represent over 50 % of all commercial facilities in Finland.

RAKLI is active in promoting the real estate profession and the implementation of modern tools for real estate management. As RAKLI is basically a trade organisation, it also provides recommendations and advice to its members.

RAKLI acts as an initiator of several development programmes in the real estate sector. Approximately 50 % of the annual turnover is allocated to development work. The organisation has six persons involved in R&D activities.

Currently, RAKLI co-ordinates four major R&D projects, which are: the Environmental programme ProGresS, the Management and service programme RemBrand, the Automation systems programme SaMBA and the Healthy Buildings Client Processes programme.

7.4.2   The Finnish Property Federation (SKL)

The Finnish Property Federation (SKL) is the central association of property owners, landlords and builders in Finland and acts also as an employers' association for its members. Housing companies make up 70% of the membership, the remainder being owners of business premises, banks, insurance companies etc.

SKL provides advice to its members on legal, technical, financial and economic matters. It also takes initiatives to change legislation affecting its members interests.

SKL has a research department of three persons involved in R&D projects, related mainly to the residential sector. It has its own research projects and also participates in the management of projects for other parties.

7.4.3   Authorised valuers

The establishment of a procedure for the authorisation of property valuers is a recent attempt to improve the quality and status of the property valuation profession. All valuers applying for authorisation have to possess significant practical experience in the field together with an acceptable educational degree. They also have to pass a special examination arranged by an independent authorisation committee, *Kiinteistöarvioinnin auktorisointiyhdistys ry* (the Association of Authorised Real Estate Valuation). An authorised valuer is allowed to use the title AKA (*auktorisoitu kiinteistöarvioija,* authorised property valuer).

Since 1995, 115 valuers, specialising either in general, commercial, residential or agricultural real estate, have been authorised. Authorised valuers have a professional body, *Auktorisoidut Kiinteistöarvioijat ry* (the Association of Authorised Property Valuers).

7.4.4 Authorised brokers

In Finland, an authorisation is required to offer brokerage services. All authorised brokers have passed an official broker's examination organised by the Ministry of Trade and Industry (in the future this will probably be run by the Chamber of Commerce). An authorised broker, who has passed the broker's examination and is registered in the official record of authorised brokers, is allowed to use the title LKV (*laillistettu kiinteistönvälittäjä,* authorised and registered broker).

Authorised brokers have a professional body, *Suomen Kiinteistönvälittäjäliitto ry* (the Finnish Association of Authorised Brokers). The Association has about 500 member organisations, who are responsible for about 30% of all property transactions made by brokers in Finland. Members are allowed to use the title [A], which indicates an authorised member of the association.

Chapter 8

France

Ingrid Nappi-Choulet
ESSEC Business School, Paris, France

Alain Bechade
Institut de la Construction et de l'Habitat (ICH), Paris, France

8.1 Introduction

The real estate sector in France is undergoing radical transformation. Post-crisis real estate management, the arrival of the Anglo-Saxons on the office market and the appearance of new professions linked to asset- and real estate management have noticeably modified the traditional approach to real estate and the classical methods of real estate expertise. The funding of the real estate sector and the internationalisation of real estate investments have necessitated the emergence of new management training in real estate finance, notably the 3rd Cycle in the business schools. Such education in France was traditionally legal or urbanistic.

New training programmes, more centred on real estate management and finance, have been rapidly developed in France. Since the mid-1990's, new diplomas have been created and new training programmes launched. As a general rule, this training is distinguished by a short or long period of initial training (1st or 3rd Cycle of university) offered by public universities, the private schools or the private *grandes écoles*, or, alternatively, by vocational training or continuing education.

8.2   Higher Education and Initial Training for Real Estate

The French educational system is unique in offering students three different and complementary educational programs after *Baccalaureate* (A level): university degree courses; advanced study programmes in *grandes écoles* (management or engineering schools); and specialised programmes such as art, architecture or design. At the moment, top-level real estate education is offered both by the universities and the management schools (*grandes écoles*)

8.2.1   University Education & 3rd Cycle Training

University studies are organised into three levels or cycles. At the moment, only the third level of French university courses offers real estate education, under the form of **DESS** (*Diplôme d'Etudes Supérieures Spécialisées* - Diploma in Higher Specialised Studies) or **DU** (*Diplôme d'Université*), in the fields of law or management. These professionally oriented DESS courses take in students after a 2nd Cycle diploma such as a Masters or a *Grande École* diploma. The number of DESS in the real estate field has been increasing considerably for some years. However, the great majority of these 3rd Cycle programs still, all too often, concern training dedicated to real estate law and construction. In France, currently around twenty diplomas of the third university cycle predominantly cover law.

On the other hand, DESS openings in real estate finance or economics remain little developed and reflect the all-too-recent development of the new professions in real estate finance and asset management in France. Examples of the courses available are: the DESS in Real Estate Management at ESSEC and Poitiers University; the DESS in Real Estate and Property Holdings Management at Toulon University; the DESS in Real Estate Engineering at the University of Marne-la-Vallée; and the DESS in Real Estate Engineering at the University of Paris XII.

It is evident that most of these professionally-oriented DESS are involved not only in initial training programmes but also in continuing education, to allow for the participation of executives and leaders of companies in the real estate sector.

In some programmes, in particular the DESS ESSEC/Poitiers University, the use of new information technology and multimedia allows participants to pursue their training whilst continuing to work in their respective companies. This experience is new to France in this domain: as part of the training, every participant receives a laptop computer and CD-ROMS on the teaching of basic management. They are connected by network using "groupware" technology (with Lotus Notes software) and hence are able to work collectively in a team.

In addition to the long courses of the 3rd Cycle in university, for some years the national Ministry of Education has been developing short training programs, in conjunction with the professional organizations in the real estate sector. These notably include a **BP** (*Brevet Professionnel*) in Real Estate (a Real Estate Certificate) and a **BTS** (*Brevet de Technicien Supérieur*) in Real Estate (a Higher National Certificate). These short training programs allow students who hold the Baccalaureate to reach the level of real estate or condominium administrator, negotiator or estate agent over a two-year period (cf. 8.2.3).

8.2.2   The Grandes Ecoles

The specialised institutions called *Grandes Ecoles* are a unique feature of the French higher education system. Mostly private, they educate students in three main fields: business and management; engineering; and political sciences.

Some *grandes écoles* of business or engineering propose specialised *Masters* or diploma courses in Real Estate for the 3rd Cycle. Paradoxically, unlike the United States, real estate education is still poorly developed in the majority of business schools in France. The reasons for this are essentially structural and historic (cf. Nappi-Choulet, 1999).

These diplomas generally take a year, following an engineering diploma or a third university cycle. The programmes offered by the engineering high schools, such as the ENPC (National School for Highways Departments) or the ESTP (College for Civil Engineering) in Paris propose Masters courses which tend to be technically oriented, particularly towards contracting and real estate management. Conversely, the business high schools mainly offer Masters courses dedicated to property holdings management, which in essence is real estate management. This is true of the ESCs (Business Schools) of Bordeaux, Marseilles, Nice and Paris.

Only the ESSEC Business School, another business *grande école*, distinguishes itself from this program, by offering not only a 3rd Cycle program and a Masters in real estate management, but also post-graduate training, with marketing and real estate management courses available to the students of the various programmes. In addition, an ESSEC-FNAIM Real Estate Chair was recently created, to offer theoretical and practical training, conferences, etc. to students on the second and third years of the MBA course at ESSEC. Students will be selected for the interest that they show in real estate and in the new professions of real estate management and finance.

8.2.3   Other Institutions offering training

Some private schools, other than those belonging to the *grande école* system, also offer initial training programmes. These are short-duration courses, open to holders of the baccalaureate. The basis of the teaching, which is delivered directly by real estate professionals, (unlike the training presented above in points 8.2.1 and 8.2.2) is generally law. Among the bodies offering initial training programs are ESPI (the Higher College for the Real Estate Professions) and the EFAB (the French School for Real Estate Administrators).

In addition, the ICHs (the Institutes of Housing and Construction), which are public establishments dependent on CNAM (Institute for Engineering Studies) have developed professional courses and continuing education programmes in real estate law and economics, in most of the major French cities. These courses are available to holders of the baccalaureate, or to those who have been carrying out a professional activity for at least three years. The courses generally last for a period of three years and are recognised by a state diploma.

8.3   The Professional Organisations and Continuing Education in France

The professions connected to real estate activity in France can be divided into three categories:

– Property developers, private or public
– Real estate consultants,
– Real estate managers.

To which can be added a fourth professional category, which is gaining in strength: Chartered Surveyors.

8.3.1 Property developers

The private property developers are grouped essentially within the FNPC-*Fédération Nationale des Promoteurs Constructeurs* (National Federation of Property Developers) who have around 360 members distributed among 20 regional associations.

Private real estate development in France represents about 35 % of new house building permits and close to 70 % of offices and business premises. This federation groups together a varied mixture of companies, from the very large subsidiaries of big banking or industrial groups, with thousands of employees, to small firms with only a few workers. Thus there is a substantial heterogeneity in the professions involved in this business in France.

The FNPC has a lobbyist attitude towards the authorities. This concerns particularly the laws and regulations governing the development of new buildings (Perissol or Besson legislation) or the development of office buildings in the Isle de France region (around Paris) where problems can involve *inter alia* obtaining approval for both the building and its use.

The FNPC does not provide training itself. However, it recently concluded agreements with ESPI (an Upper College for the real estate professions). ESPI is not a university: it trains real estate-related staff to the BTS level. The National Federation, or the regional associations, organise occasional conferences, generally in conjunction with public authorities, to discuss the problems of the profession.

8.3.2 Real estate consultants

In France real estate agency is essentially focused within the National Federation of Real Estate (FNAIM - *Fédération Nationale des Agents Immobiliers*). The Federation has some thousands of agents as members and includes very diverse elements: the big international offices, members of the global networks, and all the small district estate agencies, which are mainly oriented toward housing transactions.

A particular law governs the exercise of the profession of real estate agent or property broker in France: the Hoguet legislation of 2nd January 1970, and the application decree of the 20th July 1972. In summary, to exercise this profession, it is necessary to have an authorisation in the form of an official card, called "carte T" issued by the *Préfecture* (administration) of the *Département* where the estate agent plans to operate. To obtain this card, which is essential for the exercise of this profession, it is necessary to possess evidence of professional skills. This could be in terms of diplomas obtained (e.g. Master's degree, business high schools, ICH). However, it is also possible to make a claim on the basis of professional experience: at least 4 years' experience as an executive in an HLM (housing estate) office or with a lawyer, or 10 years non-executive experience is required.

After the identity card is issued, the agent must comply with two other conditions:

– Take out a third party liability insurance policy covering professional activities
– provide financial guarantees for clients' funds

It is therefore recognised that approval to practise as a real estate agent in France requires training in the real estate profession, confirmed by the existence of a relevant diploma or professional experience.

The National Federation of Real Estate Agents frequently organises training sessions, at regional level, for estate agency staff. These seminars are given by speakers from the profession: e.g. lawyers, notaries, financial consultants, on very specific subjects. Some examples are house rents, commercial leasing, and liabilities on sale and purchase instructions.

An idiosyncrasy of France is that the award of the university or *grande école* (High School) degree, on which the granting of authorisation depends, need not have involved any specific training in real estate, but is instead a general university education. This is one of the characteristics of French educational system.

However, some specific real estate diplomas are now accepted for authorisation purposes by the *Préfectures*. Examples are the ICH diploma and the DES of the University of Paris I, both of which are accredited by the Royal Institution of Chartered Surveyors.

8.3.3   Real estate administration - Real estate managers

Real estate administrators are subject to the same conditions as real estate agents, i.e. the Hoguet legislation, in exercising their profession. Even though they have a very different professional role, the law and the application decree, as well as the qualifications required for authorisation, are exactly the same.

However, their real estate managers' professional organisation differs from that of the National Federation of Real Estate Agents. Real estate managers are grouped in either a special section of the National Federation of Real Estate Agents, or within the National Confederacy of Real Estate Managers, a rival professional organisation.

Therefore, there is no single organisation that represents real estate administrators and the real estate managers, no more than there is a single organisation for real-estate agents.

The real estate managers also organise specific conferences related to their work, generally more specifically oriented towards e.g. drawing up leasing agreements, recoverable charges (particularly in housing, for which French law defines the criteria) etc.

8.3.4 Real estate professionals

A peculiarity in France is that there are no legally protected titles for real estate professionals. Only the adjusters of the Appeal Court and the Company of Experts linked to the High Court of Appeal benefit from protection. Thus, in France there are no particular routes, by studies and/or professional experience, which lead directly to qualification as an officially recognised real estate professional. Any real estate agent or manager can easily, and arbitrarily, proclaim themselves to be 'professional'.

It is for this reason that the profession has tried to reorganise, notably by the creation of the *Institut Français de l'Expertise Immobilière* an active member of TEGOVA, a European organisation of property professionals. To be a member of the *Institut Français de l'Expertise Immobilière*, it is necessary to submit a file proving numerous years of experience with one of the major offices, recognised as such, and to justify unquestionable professional qualities.

It must be pointed out that a number of leaders of the profession are also members of the Royal Institution of Chartered Surveyors.

The *Institut Français de l'Expertise Immobilière* is increasingly inspired by the regulations of the Royal Institute of Chartered Surveyors, notably the Surveyor's Charter, largely inspired by the regulations of the RICS "Red Book", and the TEGOVA "Blue Book". The charter is signed in France not only by the members of the *Institut Français de l'Expertise Immobilière*, but also by members of the other associations of property professionals.

Property experts in France are very concerned about training and the recognition of their professional qualifications. They are moving towards the educational standards of the Royal Institution of Chartered Surveyors.

8.3.5 The Chartered Surveyors

The Royal Institution of Chartered Surveyors has a strong presence in France, through the French Association of Chartered Surveyors (AFRACS). Currently, there are nearly 300 FRICS or MRICS qualified professionals practising in France.

The RICS has accredited two specialised courses for the real estate professions, which enable their graduates to qualify as Chartered Surveyors, subject to fulfilling the experience and Assessment of Professional Competence (APC) requirements. The courses are the CNAM (Institute for Engineering Studies) course at ICH in Paris and the DES course of Real Estate and Financial Management at the University of PARIS 1 Panthéon - Sorbonne.

Increasing numbers of young professionals are taking these courses and subsequently presenting themselves as candidates for qualification as Chartered Surveyors. The rules governing the possible routes to the Chartered Surveyor qualification in France are identical with those in the other member countries of the European Union.

In France there are essentially three paths:

– The university path, that is to obtain an accredited diploma, followed by two years' practical experience under a tutorial system, before taking the qualifying examination (APC).
– The second path is for those with an accredited diploma and 5 years of appropriate professional experience. In this case the tutorial period can be reduced to 12 months before the final examination is taken.
– Finally, a third path is available throughout Europe, the path by way of professional qualification. It is then necessary to possess a non-accredited university degree (at least Master's level) and 10 years of professional experience. A tutorial period of one or two years will then be necessary, as well as taking three complementary course modules from the accredited diplomas. After the tutorial period, the final examination (APC) must be taken in the same way as for the other paths.

In summary, it is clear that in France, the professional real estate organisations have not yet taken a leading role in university or professional training. Education and training currently remains very varied, with the French universities continuing to educate graduates in very general terms, not particularly centred on the real estate economy. Graduates must then continue their training within the companies which employ them. However, the situation is changing, as more and more French universities or High Schools establish diplomas, particularly centred on education for the real estate profession, in the 3rd cycle. The RICS has already accredited two courses and is considering the accreditation of four other courses in France. Finally, other French institutional bodies, such as the notaries, are very closely interested in this type of education, in order to obtain the Chartered Surveyor qualification.

Table 1: Initial training for real estate in France (Non-exhaustive)

Initial Training	Diploma/Length of Studies	Entry level	Institutions
Short Program	B.T.S. in Real Estate (2 yrs)	Baccalaureate	▪ Lycées, Institutes and private schools, etc. ▪ EFAB, CEFLU, CEFPI, etc.
Long Program (3ème cycle)	Masters (1 yr)	Diploma in Engineering or 3rd Cycle	▪ Universities ▪ Grandes Ecoles d'ingénieurs : ENPC, ESTP ▪ Grandes Ecoles de commerce : ESC Bordeaux, Nice, Paris, ESSEC, etc.
	D.U. (1 yr)		Universities
	D.E.S.S. (1 yr)	Diploma in Engineering or 2nd Cycle	Universities, ESSEC : — DESS Real Estate Law and Construction — DESS Real Estate Management — DESS Real Estate and Property Holdings Management

Source: ONISEP

REFERENCES

Capitale Editions (1999) "la formation, les écoles, les Universités", *L'année immobilière*.

Nappi-Choulet (1999) "The Recent Emergence of Real Estate Education in French Business Schools: the Paradox of the French Experience", working paper ERES Conference, Athens, May.

Onisep (1997) *les métiers de l'immobilier*, n°167, mai.

Richard Philippe (1999) "Qui formera les hommes de l'immobilier?", *Réflexions immobilières*, n°24, janvier.

L'étudiant, *Annuaire national de l'enseignement supérieur* (2000) Editions l'Etudiant, Paris.

Websites :

www.edufrance.fr

Chapter 9

Germany

Karl-Werner Schulte
Chair of Real Estate at the European Business School (ebs) and Academic Director of ebs Real Estate Academy, Oestrich-Winkel, Germany

9.1 The Property Profession

9.1.1 Legal Framework

Legislation governing the education of property specialists in Germany is divided into two fields: the technical professions and the business-related sector. The technical field, e.g. in architecture, has long-established qualification standards. In contrast, the trade and administration sector, which includes the property field, has neither regulations nor minimum qualification standards for entry.

Virtually anyone who wants to enter the management activities of the property sector can do so without being required to prove his or her expertise. As this is contrary to the conditions in most other European countries, the German property market has lagged behind, both in reputation and in the professional structures required for a more international approach to investment. The lack of regulation has also resulted in the comparatively poor image of the property-related professions in Germany.

There is still no legislation in that field, but the German property sector has itself taken the initiative to implement structures which are comparable to the British example of the Royal Institution of Chartered Surveyors.

The state has made no attempt to encourage professional bodies in the property sector to develop a structured concept of professional and ethical standards. Germany has no tradition like the "Royal Charter" in the UK, by which a professional body is responsible for regulating particular aspects of the economy.

As the European countries become more closely related, not least with the advent of the single currency, which will extinguish exchange rate risks within the European Currency Union, the need for property executives who are able to compete with their European competitors has grown. Professionals who are able to do business on a European scale are particularly in demand. This is because the single currency makes yields in the various markets directly comparable, speeding up the efforts of investors to diversify their portfolios Europe-wide. The demand has been answered in recent years by a growing number of institutions providing education for the business administration sector of the real estate industry.

9.1.2 Professional Bodies

The situation already described led to the existence of a wide variety of professional bodies in the German property industry, as shown by the following list.[1]

- Bundesarchitektenkammer (BAK)
  [Federal Chamber of Architects]
- Bundesfachverband Wohnungsverwalter e.V.[2] (BFW)
  [Federal Professional Association of Residential Housing Administrators]
- Bundesverband Deutscher Immobilien-Manager e.V. (BDIM)
  [Federal Association of German Property Managers]
- Bundesverband Deutscher Wohnungs- und
  Immobilienunternehmen e.V. (GdW)
  [Federal Association of German Residential Property Companies]

- Dachverband Deutscher Hausverwalter e.V. (DDH)
  [Central Association of German Residential Property Administrators]
- Deutscher Städtetag
  [Council of German Cities/MSAs]
- Deutscher Verband der Projektsteuerer (DVP)
  [German Association for Construction Project Managers]
- Deutscher Verband für Facility Management e.V. (GEFMA)
  [German Facility Management Association]
- German Council of Shopping Centers e.V. (GCSC)
- Haus & Grund Deutschland – Zentralverband der Deutschen Haus-,
  Wohnungs- und Grundeigentümer e.V.
  [Association of the German Property and Real Estate Owners]
- International Facility Management Association (IFMA) Deutschland e.V.
- International Development and Research Council (IDRC)
  German Chapter
- National Association of Corporate Real Estate (NACORE),
  German Chapter
- Ring Deutscher Makler (RDM)
  [Society of German Property Agents]
- Urban Land Institute (ULI), German Chapter
- Verband Deutscher Makler (VDM)
  [Association of German Property Agents]
- Deutsches Volksheimstättenwerk e.V. (vhw)
  (Bundesverband für Wohneigentum, Wohnungsbau und
  Stadtentwicklung)
  [German organisation of people's homes]

The only association which claims to represent "the" property profession in Germany, is the *Deutscher Verband Chartered Surveyors* (German Association of Chartered Surveyors; DVCS) founded in 1993, which has 537 members (as at the end of August 2000).

9.1.3 Deutscher Verband Chartered Surveyors (DVCS)

The Deutscher Verband Chartered Surveyors (DVCS) is the professional association for Chartered Surveyors practising or resident in the Federal Republic of Germany. The association is sponsored by the Royal Institution of Chartered Surveyors (RICS) based in London and the European Society of Chartered Surveyors (ESCS) based in Brussels. The association was formally founded in 1993 in Frankfurt at a meeting for this purpose in the city of Frankfurt. The first chairman of the association was John F.W. Morgan.

The DVCS is arranged in a divisional structure on the same lines as the RICS prior to the introduction of the Faculties, the majority of the current membership are part of the General Practice or Quantity Surveying Divisions. General Practice Chartered Surveyors in Germany are generally involved with the valuation, sale, letting and management of commercial and residential properties, Chartered Quantity Surveyors are generally involved with the construction and project management of commercial and residential properties. The association has a single board, which is elected on an annual basis. In addition to the board there is a working party, concerned with the issue of property valuation and a sub-committee dealing with the Assessment of Professional Competence. Members of the Board have actively promoted the growth of the association since its inception, culminating in 1999 with the appointment of a permanent chief executive, Eckhard Lammel and the establishment of offices in Frankfurt. The DVCS currently has a staff of four people working on a full and part time basis. In August 2000 the membership of the DVCS was as described in Table 1.

Table 1: Membership of the DVCS

Status	Designation	Number
Honorary Associates	HonRICS	3
Fellows	FRICS	55
Member	MRICS	213
Probationers	---	198
Students	---	68
Total		**537**

Source: DVCS

Since 1995 a number of regional groups have been established who hold regular meetings for the purposes of continuing professional development and to discuss relevant issues.

Members qualify as Chartered Surveyors via the Assessment of Professional Competence (APC). The APC was set up during the course of 1994 with the first round of assessments taking place in November of the same year. The APC has been structured on the same basis as the APC in the United Kingdom whereby probationer members are required to record the development of relevant professional skills by way of regular written reports over a 24 month minimum period ending with a final assessment comprising an interview with three Chartered Surveyors and a short written examination. As a number of the academic courses that have been accredited by the RICS in Germany are post-graduate diplomas for professionals already practising in property, experienced probationers are able to apply for remission for the 24-month training period prior to final assessment. Applications are decided on a case by case basis and must be supported by all relevant career documentation, letters from two proposers and an interview with two Chartered Surveyors.

Final assessments are held twice a year, in spring and autumn with between 30 and 40 candidates being tested per annum. As course accreditation activity has increased in Germany during the last three years, the number of candidates is expected to grow rapidly with a doubling of assessment capacity currently being actively planned.

Owing to the limited number of qualified Chartered Surveyors the main problem of the APC system was the proper support and preparation of the candidates during the two-year training period and for the final assessment itself. In order to counteract this problem an active regional network of Chartered Surveyors, known as the APC Advisory Team, was established as a point of contact for all APC candidates in search of Counsellors. The APC Advisory Team presently has members in all major locations throughout Germany. In addition the association offers a two-day APC seminar some two months before the final assessment in order to address key issues and offer advice regarding the assessment day itself. The APC seminar has since been made mandatory for all candidates wishing to sit the final assessment.

At the present time the focus of APC is the further education and training for all assessors and to further improve the APC system to be more in line with German property practice. Following the introduction of the professional competencies on the same basis as the UK APC model at the beginning of the year, the first major step has been taken in this direction.

9.2   Real Estate Programmes at Universities

As the German educational system is very diverse, the following chapter provides a short introduction into the organisation of education.

9.2.1   The German Educational System in General

After primary school, German pupils can enter one of two kinds of secondary school, only one of which, the *Gymnasium* (grammar school) leads to the *Abitur* (university entrance level examination). This type of school offers a specialised curriculum during the last three years (10th to 13th classes). The *Abitur* examination is then taken in specialised subjects.

Armed with the *Abitur*, a student is entitled to either enter a university, a lower-level *Fachhochschule* (university of applied sciences) or a *Berufsakademie* (university of co-operative education). These two latter are characterised by a shorter study time and more practice-oriented methods than the universities.

Those who did not attend a *Gymnasium* leave school at the age of 16, normally to start an apprenticeship with a company. Apprenticeships last from 2 to 3½ years and include tuition and exams at a *Berufsschule* (technical college). The final exams are organised by the local chambers of commerce (*Industrie- und Handelskammern* (IHK)) or the chambers of craftsmanship (*Handwerkskammern*) depending on the line of work of the apprentice and his company. All companies in Germany, whether or not they have apprentices, are obligatory members of the local Chambers, which are financed by compulsory membership fees. This system guarantees uniform standards throughout the so-called dual education system in Germany. This organised form of company-based education provides high educational standards at the shop-floor level. In the property sector, most of the courses end with the award of the non-academic diploma *Kaufmann der Grundstücks- und Wohnungswirtschaft* (Qualification in the land and residential business).

Anyone who has completed an apprenticeship can enter the vocational programmes of the *Verwaltungs- und Wirtschaftsakademien* (Academies of Administration and Economy) which are run by the Chambers of Commerce in connection with local government (at the equivalent of county level) and associations of local companies. Admission depends on results in the final exams of the apprenticeship and the employer's willingness to promote the employee concerned. Courses cover mainly practical problems but also give an overview of the main academic topics in the field covered by the course. Most of these programmes end up with the non-academic diploma *Fachwirt der Grundstücks- und Wohnungswirtschaft*.

Admittance to university programmes is neither regulated nor restricted in Germany, as the educational system is financed by the state through tax income. Private universities are a comparatively recent innovation in Germany and there are still relatively few.

Universities (*Universitäten*, *Wissenschaftliche Hochschulen*, and *Technische Hochschulen*) should transfer basic scientific and methodical knowledge to students.[3] The aim is to establish a connection between an excellent qualification for the future career and a working method on a scientific and methodological basis.

Fachhochschulen (universities of applied sciences) can best be characterised by their practical specialisation to a specific profession and the close ties of their curricula to a certain industry.[4]

Berufsakademien (universities of co-operative education) are characterised by the dual structure of the education. During the three-year period of studies, the student spends three months of each semester at the *Berufsakademie* followed by practical experience at his company for the rest of the period. The *Berufsakademien* have the same legal rights as the universities of applied sciences (*Fachhochschulen*).

At German universities there is a traditional separation between the *Grundstudium* (foundation studies) which ends with the "pre"-diploma and the main studies, leading to graduation.

Courses at *Fachhochschulen* (universities of applied sciences) generally last for three years. At universities, the study time is a minimum of four years, but normally students study for five years before they graduate.

Real estate related knowledge is particularly included in the study courses for:

- Architecture;
- Business administration;
- Engineering;
- Law;
- Political economics; and
- Urban/Regional planning.

Here, however, only partial aspects are usually covered, which do not facilitate any overlapping studies. The following sections concentrate on study courses with an economic focus. A distinction is made between educational programmes mainly aimed at school leavers (student education) and further training for professionals (executive education).

Until recently, special property-related academic courses were virtually non-existent in Germany. The lack of high-quality programmes became evident from the beginning of the 1990^s, when the property market began a sharp downward movement at the same time as a structural change caused by a higher degree of internationalisation. International investors were lured into the German property market by the promise of the high demand for property and consequently high yields in the former East Germany. The appearance of foreign companies, with their highly qualified and experienced professionals, in the German property market drew attention to the lack of academic education.

Education providers responded quickly. In 1990, the ebs Immobilienakademie at the European Business School was the first. Ten years later, a wider range of programmes is on offer by universities, universities of applied science, and universities of co-operative education and associated academies. This article concentrates on these academic study courses.

9.2.2   Student Education

9.2.2.1   Study Courses at Universities

9.2.2.1.1   Overview

State-run universities in Germany are slowly responding to the property sector's growing need for staff with an academic background. Only a few universities offer a real estate related specialisation, within their study courses in business administration / political economics.

At present, Chairs in business administration relating to real estate exist only at the (private) European Business School (endowed Chair of Real Estate) and at the (state-run) University of Leipzig (Institute of Real Estate Management) graduates of which can also go on to the higher degree of Dr. rer. pol. (similar to Ph.D.).

For both student and executive education, the interdisciplinary approach to real estate education is typical.

An overview of the different real estate related programmes at universities in Germany is shown in Table 2.

Table 2: Real Estate Programmes at Universities*

Name and address of provider	Programme and Degree	Length and Cost
European Business School (ebs) Stiftungslehrstuhl Immobilienökonomie Schloß Reichartshausen D-65375 Oestrich-Winkel	- Business Administration with major in Real Estate; founded 1994 RICS accredited - Dipl.-Kaufmann (after 8 semesters)	- 8 semesters including 4 semesters of Real Estate Education - 4,750 Euro per semester + registration fee
University of Karlsruhe (TH) Institut für Entscheidungs- theorie und Unternehmens- forschung – Ökonomie und Ökologie des Wohnungsbaus Postfach 6880 D-76128 Karlsruhe	- Economic Engineering with major in ecology and eco- nomics of residential con- struction; founded in Feb. 1998 - Dipl.-Wirtschaftsingenieur	- 9 semesters of engineer- ing + 1 semester diploma thesis - no tuition fees
University of Cologne Institut für Wohnungsrecht und Wohnungswirtschaft at the University of Cologne Klosterstr. 79b D-50931 Köln	- Residential Business Affairs; founded 1994 - Housing Economics - Dipl-Kaufmann; Dipl.- Volkswirt; Dipl.- Handelslehrer + Certificate in housing economics	- 9 semesters business administration including 3 semesters for housing economics - no tuition fees

Name and address of provider	Programme and Degree	Length and Cost
University of Leipzig Stiftungslehrstuhl für Grund- stücks- und Wohnungswirt- schaft Marschnerstr. 31 D-04109 Leipzig	- Business administration with elective in Residential Property and Real Estate affairs; founded 1994 - Dipl.-Kaufmann	- 9 semesters business administration with major - no tuition fees
University of Mannheim Lehrstuhl für Volkswirt- schaftslehre und Geographie Gebäude A 5-6 D-68131 Mannheim	- Residential Property Science - Dipl.-Volkswirt	- 9 semesters of econom- ics with major - no tuition fees
University of Münster Schloßplatz 2 D-48149 Münster	- Economics in Regional Planning - Dipl.-Volkswirt; Dipl.- Kaufmann; Dipl.-Geograph	- 9 semesters with major - no tuition fees

all tables only use the male form of the academic degrees

9.2.2.1.2 European Business School

The European Business School (ebs) in Oestrich-Winkel is not only the oldest privately-run university for business administration in Germany, but was also the first university to implement a business administration pro- gramme with a major in *Immobilienökonomie* (real estate economics). The Chair of business administration and real estate was founded in 1994 and is now financed by 20 leading companies, mainly from the property and bank- ing industries.

The ebs offers a full-time business administration programme, lasting eight semesters. It comprises four semesters of undergraduate courses, two semesters of studies abroad and two semesters of graduate courses. Students choose two majors out of eight for the final part of the programme. Real estate economics is one of the majors. The majors are part of the diploma examination and are also subjects that students can choose for their diploma theses. Students majoring in real estate economics have the chance to achieve a double qualification. Instead of their normally scheduled semesters at two universities in different foreign countries, they can opt to study for a full year at the Georgia State University (GSU) in Atlanta, to acquire a Mas- ter's degree in Real Estate. This is either a Master of Science in Real Estate or a Master of Business Administration with concentration in real estate. They can also opt to spend one year at the University of Hong Kong to earn their Master's designation (Master of Science in Real Estate).

After eight semesters, the students are awarded the degree of *Diplom- Kaufmann*, which is equivalent to an MBA degree. As this degree (with ma- jor in real estate) is accredited by the RICS, graduates can also proceed to the Chartered Surveyor designation, subject to satisfying the normal requirements for professional experience and the APC.

9.2.2.1.3   University of Leipzig

Leipzig University has a very long history. Before World War II it was one of the highest-regarded German universities. All this was wiped out in the post-war era when Leipzig was part of communist East Germany. After German reunification the former East German universities struggled with a large number of challenges, including the adaptation of the curricula of their Business Administration Faculties to Western market economy standards.

On the other hand, this start from zero offered the chance to design programmes to cater for the demands of the economy. One outcome is the newly established Institute of Real Estate Management. Private companies finance this institute, an unusual arrangement at a state-financed university in Germany.

The Institute of Real Estate Management was established in 1994. The subject is a major within the Business Administration programme at the University of Leipzig. Officially, the programme takes 9 semesters, but due to the fact that Leipzig is a public University without tuition fees, the actual time spent by students may well be longer. A stay at a University abroad is not compulsory but depends on the initiative of each student.

Efforts have been commenced to gain RICS accreditation for the programme at the University of Leipzig. This is expected to be granted in the near future.

9.2.2.2   Study Courses at Universities of Applied Sciences and at Universities of Co-operative Education

In recent years, real estate business specialisation subjects have been created at many *Fachhochschulen* (FH) and *Berufsakademien* (BA). These courses in real estate economics, which are described in detail in table 3 and 4, usually lead to the degree *Diplom-Betriebswirt (FH)* or *Diplom-Betriebswirt (BA)*.

In addition, there are study courses concentrating on facility management in some engineering faculties. Table 5 gives information on these courses, which award a range of different degrees.

Table 3: Real Estate Programmes at Universities of Applied Sciences

Name and address of provider	Programme and Degree	Length and Cost
Fachhochschule Anhalt Strenzfelder Allee 28 D-06406 Bernburg	- Immobilienwirtschaft; subject of specialisation in the business administration programme; founded 1995 - Dipl.-Betriebswirt (FH)	- 8 semesters including 1 semester practical working experience - no tuition fees
	- Immobilienwirtschaft / Real Estate Management; founded 1996 - Dipl.-Betriebswirt (FH) der Immobilienwirtschaft	- 8 semesters including 1 semester practical working experience - no tuition fees
FHTW Berlin Fachhochschule für Technik und Wirtschaft FB-3 – Wirtschaftswissenschaften Treskowallee 8 D-10313 Berlin	- Business Administration with major in Real Estate Management; founded 1996 - RICS accredited - Dipl.-Kaufmann (FH)	- 8 semesters including 1 semester practical working experience - no tuition fees
Fachhochschule Biberach (linked to ist Bauakademie) Karlstr. 11 D-88400 Biberach	- Business Administration (Construction); founded 1983 - Dipl.-Ingenieur (FH)	- 8 semesters including 2 semesters practical working experience - no tuition fees
	- Project Management (Construction) ; founded 1991 - Dipl.-Ingenieur (FH)	- 8 semesters including 2 semesters practical working experience - no tuition fees
	- Business Administration for Construction Engineers and Architects; founded 1988 - Dipl.-Wirtschaftsingenieur (FH)	- 3 intensive courses each January and February; followed by diploma thesis - 2,685 Euro per course unit; no fees for tests and diploma thesis
Fachhochschule Hildesheim-Holzminden Fachbereich B Haarmannplatz 3 D-37603 Holzminden	- Real Estate Management - Dipl.-Wirtschaftsingenieur (FH)	- 4 years full time programme - no tuition fees
Fachhochschule Lippe Fachbereich Bauingenieurwesen Emilienstr. 45 D-32756 Detmold	- Postgraduate course in Real Estate Management only for graduates of the business administration programme; founded 1985 - Certificate in addition to the university diploma	- 3 semesters - no tuition fees

Name and address of provider	Programme and Degree	Length and Cost
Fachhochschule Nürtingen Hochschule für Wirtschaft, Landwirtschaft und Landespflege Neckarsteige 6-10 D-72622 Nürtingen	- Real Estate Management; founded 1998 - Dipl.-Betriebswirt (FH)	- 8 semesters including 2 semesters of practical working experience - no tuition fees
	- Elective "Real Estate Management" within the business administration programme; founded 1984 - Dipl.-Betriebswirt (FH)	- 2 semesters; 6 hours per week - no tuition fees
	- City planning; founded 1998 - Dipl.-Ingenieur (FH)	- 8 semesters including 2 semesters of practical working experience - no tuition fees
IBS International Business School Lippstadt Im Eichholz D-59556 Lippstadt	- International Manager for Real Estate and Financial Services; founded July 1997 - IBS-Diplom "Betriebswirt für Immobilien und Finanzdienstleistungen"	- 3 years full time programme with practice during term holidays - Registration 1,000 Euro; 3,550 Euro per semester
Hochschule Zittau/Görlitz (FH) Fachbereich Bauwesen Theodor-Körner-Allee 16 D-02763 Zittau	- Residential and Real Estate Economics; founded 1994 - Dipl.-Wirtschaftsingenieur (FH)	- 8 semesters including 1 semester of practical working experience - no tuiton fees

Table 4: Real Estate Programmes at Universities of Co-operative Education

Name and address of provider	Programme and Degree	Length and Cost
Berufsakademie Berlin Staatliche Studienakademie Berlin Neue Bahnhofsstraße 13-15 10245 Berlin	- Real Estate Economics; founded in 1993 - Dipl.-Betriebswirt (BA)	- 3 years with change between theoretical education and practical training - no tuition fees - Companies, which offer training places, pay students during their stay
Berufsakademie Mannheim Staatliche Studienakademie Immobilienwirtschaft Coblitzweg 7 D-68163 Mannheim	- Real Estate Management; founded October 1996 - Dipl.-Betriebswirt (BA)	- 6 semesters; ca. 2,500 hrs.; per semester 12 weeks theory and 12 weeks practice - companies: negotiable - rate for students: 43.50 Euro fee per semester

Name and address of provider	Programme and Degree	Length and Cost
Berufsakademie Sachsen Staatliche Studienakademie Leipzig Schönauer Str. 113a D-04207 Leipzig	- Real Estate Management; founded 1993 RICS accredited - Dipl.-Betriebswirt (BA)	- 6 semesters; ca. 400 hrs. practical and theoretical education per semester; - no tuition fees
Berufsakademie Stuttgart Immobilienwirtschaft Postfach 100563 D-70004 Stuttgart	- Real Estate Management with specialisation; founded October 1997 RICS accredited - Dipl.-Betriebswirt (BA)	- 3 years with change between 3 months theoretical education and 3 months practical training - no tuiton fees - Companies, which offer training places, pay the students during the 3 months stay

Table 5: Facilities Management Programmes at Universities of Applied Sciences

Name and address of provider	Programme and Degree	Length and Cost
Fachhochschule Albstadt-Sigmaringen Anton-Günther-Straße 51 D-72488 Sigmaringen	- Facility Management - Dipl.-Ingenieur (FH), bzw. Dipl.-Facility Manager (GEFMA)	- 8 semesters plus diploma thesis period (generally 1 semester) - no tuition fees
FHTW Berlin Fachhochschule für Technik und Wirtschaft Ingenieurwissenschaften I Treskowallee 8 D-10318 Berlin	- Studiengang Technisches Gebäudemanagement (FM) - Dipl.-Ingenieur (FH)	- 8 semesters - no tuition fees
Fachhochschule Gelsenkirchen Neidenburger Str. 10 D-45877 Gelsenkirchen	- Facility Management - Dipl.-Wirtschaftsingenieur (FH)	- 8 semesters - no tuition fees
Fachhochschule Gießen-Friedberg Wilhelm-Leuschner-Str. 13 D-61169 Friedberg	- Facility Management - Dipl.-Wirtschaftsingenieur (FH) - founded in 1999	- 8 semesters - no tuition fees
Fachhochschule Münster Josefstr. 2 D-48151 Münster	- Wahlfach Facility Management - Dipl.-Oecotrophologe (FH)	- 1 semester - no tuition fees

Name and address of provider	Programme and Degree	Length and Cost
Technische Fachhochschule Wildau Bahnhofstraße D-15745 Wildau	- Facility Management at the Faculty of Engineering - Wirtschaftsingenieur (FH)	- 8 semesters - no tuition fees
Hochschule Zittau/Görlitz (FH) Fachbereich Bauwesen Theodor-Körner-Allee 16 D-02763 Zittau	- Facility and Infrastructural Management; founded in 2000 - Bachelor of Facility Management; Dipl.-Ingenieur (FH); Master of Engineering	- 6 (Bachelor), 8 (Dipl.) or 10 (Master) semesters - no tuition fees

9.2.3   Executive Education

The academic situation, which has been unsatisfactory for many years, and the great attractiveness of the property sector, have had a combined effect on recruitment. A large percentage of the employees who have been recruited are either college graduates lacking any real estate-related education, or persons without a college degree, e.g. commercial or technical staff from the property and housing business. For these staff, a wide range of training possibilities has been developed, ranging from one day seminars to qualification studies lasting one to two years.

9.2.3.1   Study Courses at Universities

9.2.3.1.1   Overview
With the foundation of the Real Estate Academy at the European Business School (ebs Immobilienakademie) in 1990, comprehensive property-related further training to university standard was first introduced to Germany. A further education study course in Real Estate Management was accredited in 1992 (and retrospectively to 1990) as the first study course in continental Europe accredited by the Royal Institution of Chartered Surveyors.

Other than the ebs Immobilienakademie, there are only three university-like establishments in the market:
- The *Führungsakademie der Wohnungs- und Immobilienwirtschaft (FWI)* at the University of Bochum, with the qualification *Diplomierter Wohnungs- und Immobilienwirt (FWI);*
- The *European Institute for postgraduate education* at the Technical University of Dresden (eipos) with an integration study course in real estate economics; and

- The *Deutsche Immobilienakademie* at the University of Freiburg, with diverse programmes.

9.2.3.1.2   European Business School (ebs) Immobilienakademie

In 2000, the ebs Immobilienakademie celebrated its 10th anniversary and is therefore the oldest institution in the German market offering postgraduate programmes in Real Estate. The ebs Immobilienakademie was awarded RICS accreditation of its programme in 1992, for all courses and years retrospectively, thus allowing all its graduates exemption from the RICS membership examinations. As the academic director of the ebs Immobilienakademie is also the Professor of Real Estate at the European Business School, the academic approach is interdisciplinary as well.

The programme is designed as a part-time course of 1-year duration, with tuition split into two terms. A block of 2 weeks tuition is followed by 10 weeks of weekend tuition on Fridays and Saturdays. A maximum of 45 students per course is admitted.

Over the years, the ebs Immobilienakademie has gained a high reputation in the market, resulting in a correspondingly high demand for its courses. The consequence was the opening of branches in Berlin and in Munich. Courses start in Oestrich–Winkel in January and July, each January in Berlin and in Munich each July.

Annually, around 90 participants graduate at the headquarters in Oestrich-Winkel, with around 45 graduates each in the Berlin and Munich branches.

The courses end with the award of the title *Immobilienökonom* (ebs). The ebs Immobilienakademie has received the accreditation as an "Accredited Centre" from the Royal Institution of Chartered Surveyors. It is the first and only institution in continental Europe to achieve this status.

Due to the growing demand in the area of Corporate Real Estate Management and Facilities Management the ebs Immobilienakademie started a new course in 1998. This programme, Corporate Real Estate Management / Facilities Management, offers, in a 1 year programme (32 days of tuition and 2 months of private studies) a twin education in this field. After joint basic tuition the courses split into CREM and into FM groups with separately designed, intensive courses for each of the programmes. The programmes start once a year in May.

The graduates are awarded the title of Corporate Real Estate Manager (ebs) or Facilities Manager (ebs).

The ebs Immobilienakademie has received accreditation from the Royal Institution of Chartered Surveyors for both programmes in 1999.

The programmes have been designed in close co-operation with IFMA (the International Facility Management Association) and also meet the standards of the International Development Research Council (IDRC) thus providing a wide range of international acceptance.

With the intensive study course in Retail Properties, run in co-operation with the German Council of Shopping Centres (GCSC), the ebs Immobilienakademie offers a further postgraduate study course with the qualification "Certified Shopping Center Manager (ebs/GCSC)".

9.2.3.1.3   Führungsakademie der Wohnungs- und Immobilienwirtschaft (FWI)

The FWI is also a young institution in the market. It is backed by the Ruhr-Universität Bochum and companies from the housing industry. The programme reflects its name by stressing the topic of residential and housing affairs. The *Fachstudium Wohnungs- und Immobilienwirtschaft* is scheduled for an overall duration of 2 years, which divides into 5 units of 12 days each year. This is extended by home studies based on a catalogue of compulsory literature.

The programme, accredited by the RICS, starts every autumn and grants the title of *Diplomierter Wohnungs- und Immobilienfachwirt* (FWI).

Graduates are exempted from the RICS membership examinations and can therefore become members of the Royal Institution of Chartered Surveyors subject to fulfilling the usual requirements.

9.2.3.2   Study Courses at Universities of Applied Sciences and at Universities of Cooperative Education

There are a large number of further training study courses that are offered by technical colleges and professional academies. Especially worth mentioning are:

- The *Akademie der Immobilienwirtschaft (ADI)* at the Professional Academy of Stuttgart, whose further education study course in Real Property Economics is recognised by the Royal Institution of Chartered Surveyors;
- The *Fachhochschule Anhalt* with its study course in Property Valuation;
- The *Bauakademie* at the *Fachhochschule Biberach*;
- The *Institut für immobilienwirtschaftliche Studien (iSt)* with its programme in Real Estate Management;
- The *Fachhochschule Nürnberg* with a further training study course in Facility Management;
- The *Fachhochschule Nordostniedersachsen* with a further training study course in Project Management.

In addition, there are academies that are run by associations and companies, local government and business academies, and a large number of private business providers. In this market segment three institutions in particular have achieved positions of importance:

- The *HypZert* further training course, leading to the qualification of Property Surveyor for Mortgage Valuations;
- The Institute for Corporate Real Estate Management;
- The Institute for Facility Management, in co-operation with the Hanzehogeschool in Groningen.

The only programme that has received RICS accreditation (in 1999) is offered by the *Akademie der Immobilienwirtschaft (ADI)*. It is partly private and partly state-financed as it works in close co-operation with the *Berufsakademie* Stuttgart, which is a public institution. The programme offered is scheduled for five trimesters, comprising 15 months in total and is called *Aufbaustudium Immobilienökonomie*.

So far enrolment will be once a year. The title awarded is *Immobilienökonom* (ADI). A branch was opened in Leipzig in 2000.

9.3   Real Estate Research

9.3.1   Research Approaches

9.3.1.1   Overview

Real Estate related research in Germany is as new as the academic discipline. The approach to research differs from those taken in the United States or in Great Britain. In the American literature, the multidisciplinary and the financial management approach can be distinguished, whereby the financial management approach prevails. In Great Britain a more valuation-related perspective is more common.[5]

Although the field of real estate research is seen as a special sector of managerial economics, the disciplines interrelated with the different aspects of real estate research make it more than simply a branch of managerial science. There are close ties to e.g. engineering, law, and city and regional planning, which force anybody active in this field to maintain an interdisciplinary footing.

The interdisciplinary approach is dominant in Germany.[6]

9.3.1.2   The "House of Real Estate Economics" as an illustration

To help visualise the scientific concept, the "House of Real Estate Economics" diagram was developed in around 1993. As in real life, the imaginary building has been changed several times. Figure 1 shows the present situation. This helps to differentiate between management, institutional, typological and interdisciplinary aspects, all of which will be examined in more detail in the following paragraphs.

The focus lies on the interdisciplinary aspects, because here the main differences between Great Britain, the US and Germany can be found.

9.3.1.3   Elements of the scientific discipline Real Estate Economics

9.3.1.3.1   Interdisciplinary aspects

The foundation of real estate economics is business administration, but not until the disciplines of economics, law, spatial planning, architecture and engineering are integrated does the "House of Real Estate" acquire the necessary stability. Finally interdisciplinary references serve to provide space for the multi-dimensionality of real estate already mentioned, within the framework of a scientific investigation.

The application of *business administration* addresses above all the management of economic subjects concerned with real estate.

The specific leadership aspects of the management of real estate companies include – as with other companies – planning, organisation, control and accounting. Planning concerns itself primarily with company and real estate related objectives and also the basic strategies of real estate companies. Organisation is concerned in the first instance with the design of the structure and process elements. Control has as its task to contribute to the meeting of the company's objectives regarding processes as well as results. The balance sheet and profit and loss statement are the most important instruments of commercial accounting.

The specific configuration of the individual aspects differs more or less strongly according to the type of real estate company.

Economics may generate important knowledge for the management of the company. Decisions about real estate are influenced to a considerable degree by macroeconomic factors such as the inflation rate, interest rate levels, rates of tax, and exchange rates. Many questions at the interface between economics and real estate economics have been only inadequately researched in Germany, such as the connection between overall commercial and real estate cycles or the effects of certain economic policy instruments on the real estate business.

Figure 1: "House of Real Estate Economics"
Framework for Real Estate Economics as a Scientific Discipline

Real Estate Economics

Management Aspects

Portfolio-management	CREM	PREM	Real Estate Analysis	Real Estate Appraisal	Real Estate Investment	Real Estate Finance	Real Estate Marketing	Project Development	Construction Project Management	Facilities Management
Strategy-related Aspects			Function-specific Aspects					Phase-oriented Aspects		

Institutional Aspects
- Real Estate Developers
- Real Estate Investors
- Construction Companies
- Real Estate Financial Institutions
- Real Estate Service Providers
- Real Estate Users
- Others

Typological Aspects
- Commercial Real Estate
- Residential Real Estate
- Industrial Real Estate
- Special Real Estate

Interdisciplinary Aspects

Economics	Law	Spatial Planning	Architecture	Engineering
Business Administration				

The interfaces between real estate economics and *law* are wide-ranging and diverse. Most activities concerned with real estate involve contracts. Particularly the legal aspects of land register law, private property law, law of tenancy, public planning and building law, private building law, residential property law, the property management law, estate agent law and the tax law must all be considered. Laws and ordinances have an effect on the business administrative decisions of real estate management and affect the specific functional and phase-oriented aspects as well as the strategy-related aspects.

Spatial planning has the task of putting in order and developing certain areas (regions), on the one hand according to the people's needs, such as dwellings, work, education, supply, recreation, traffic and social communication, and on the other hand according to natural, economic and social resources. Spatial planning is mostly understood as an umbrella term for urban planning, regional planning and national state planning. The "Bird's Eye View" of the spatial planner and the individual perspective of the project developer lead in practice quite often to problems in the realisation of real estate projects. Between spatial planning and real estate economics there also exists a need for interdisciplinary research. Current issues of great relevance are, for instance, the mediation process, urban entertainment centres, and the public-private partnership.

The discipline of *architecture* concerns itself primarily with the design of building structures. Real estate economics criteria such as economic feasibility and the requirements of users have, until now, played only a small part in this specialist area. This conflict of interest can be attributed to the artistic self-conception of architects on the one hand and the economic interests of project developers, investors and occupiers of space on the other hand. For interdisciplinary research this opens up an interesting field of research, such as for example the investigation of the relationship between high-grade architecture and real estate value appreciation.

Engineering is a wide-ranging discipline, which not only includes the classical fields of civil and land surveying engineering (geodesy), but increasingly also the field of technical building services, which is of importance for facilities management. Themes such as ecological building, cost-effective building and the optimisation of costs in use lie at the interface to real estate economics.

9.3.1.3.2 Institutional Aspects

There is a wide spectrum of companies in the building, real estate and financial sectors, the management of which is marked through particular features. For example planning, organisation and control and also accounting differ more or less considerably according to the company, depending on whether for example a project developer, an investor, a real estate manager or real estate agent is being considered.

9.3.1.3.3 Typological Aspects

The real estate typological aspects include the analysis, structuring and solution of problems, which arise from involvement with individual types of real estate. A strongly simplified system distinguishes between commercial, residential, industrial and special real estate. Each type of real estate and its occupants have special real estate management requirements.

9.3.1.3.4 Management Aspects

Within this category a distinction can be made between phase-oriented, function-specific and strategy-related aspects. Whereas phase-oriented aspects stand for the temporal determinant in the life cycle of real estate, the functional approach has regard to the real estate-related particularities of business administrative functions. Strategy-related aspects, on the other hand, are concerned with the portfolio management of investors and corporate and public real estate management.

9.3.1.4 Conclusion

The interdisciplinary approach, developed by the ebs Real Estate Academy and by the endowed Chair of real estate at the European Business School, in the tradition of James A. Graaskamp[7], constitutes an invitation to the other disciplines to follow the same route. In addition, the subjects of economics, law, spatial planning, engineering and architecture have to open themselves up to questions of real estate economics. This will not only bring the science further but also enhance technical communication among professionals in the construction, real estate and finance sectors as well as related industries and will thus in the end increase effectiveness and efficiency.

9.3.2 Real Estate Research Societies

Gesellschaft für Immobilienwirtschaftliche Forschung (gif)
(Society of Property Researchers, Germany)
Wilhelmstraße 12
D-65185 Wiesbaden
Tel.: 0611-33 44 970 / Fax: 0611-33 44 975

This Society has about 450 members, from academia and industry. Although established fairly recently, it has already contributed to the field of research. The members of the society are organised in various teams or circles of specialists in the most important fields of property related issues, such as property investment or yield and performance measuring. The teams deal with subjects that need e.g. more standardisation, or a higher quality of product. The society and its teams have published various guidelines to enhance the market performance and appearance of products such as closed-end property funds. Publications so far are:

- *Richtlinie zur Berechnung der Mietfläche für Büroraum*
  (Guidelines for the calculation of the lettable area of office properties)
- *Richtlinie zur Berechnung der Mietfläche für Handelsraum*
  (Guidelines for the calculation of the lettable area of retail properties)
- *Empfehlung zur Prospektierung geschlossener Immobilienfonds*
  (Recommendations for the content of brochures for closed-end property funds)
- *Empfehlung zur Berechnung von Prognoserenditen für geschlossene Immobilienfonds* (Recommendations on the calculation of forecast yields for closed-end property funds)
- *Empfehlung zur Ermittlung des Verkehrswertes von werdendem Bauland*
  (Recommendation for the valuation of future development land)

9.4   Real Estate Journals

There are no academic real estate journals in Germany. All articles appear in "practice" journals in the German language, normally with no English summary. The most popular journals are:

- Immobilien Praxis+Recht (Real Estate Practice and Law)
- Immobilienmanager (Real Estate Manager)
- Immobilienzeitung (Real Estate Newspaper)
- Der langfristige Kredit (The Long-term Credit)
- Der Sachverständige (The Real Estate Expert)

The journal *GuG* (Grundstuecksmarkt und Grundstueckswert) comes closest to the style of an academic journal in the Anglo-American sense.

The research society *gif* is understood to be making efforts to found an academic journal.

9.5   Conclusion

Study courses have been and are being continuously created and have been just as frequently discontinued, so that the above listing cannot claim to be exhaustive. Developments in recent years, which have resulted in the establishment of educational opportunities for the property industry, particularly at technical côlleges and professional academies, must be welcomed unreservedly. However, this increasing supply has not changed the fact that the European Business School (ebs), and the ebs Immobilienakademie play a leading part in education and further training for property professions with regard to their range of programmes, the quality of lecturers and participants, and the number of graduates.

Two main quality criteria underline this statement:

- The majority of members of the *Deutscher Verband Chartered Surveyors* has been educated at ebs.
- When asked to name well-known postgraduate facilities, personnel managers from German Real Estate Companies named the ebs in first place by a large margin.[8]

NOTES

[1] For easier understanding, an adhoc translation of the meaning of the organisation names is given in brackets.

[2] „e.V." meaning „eingetragener Verein" = registered company.

[3] Source: Hochschulrektorenkonferenz, Konzept zur Entwicklung der Hochschulen in Deutschland, Dokumente zur Hochschulreform 75/1992, 2. Aufl., Bonn 1992, p. 16.

[4] Compare to: Wissenschaftsrat, Empfehlungen zu den Perspektiven der Hochschulen in den 90er Jahren, Köln 1988, p. 105.

[5] Karl-Werner Schulte / Gisela Schulte-Daxboek: Immobilienökonomie – ein Vergleich des ebs Aus- und Weiterbildungskonzeptes mit den „Real Estate Studies" in Großbritannien und den USA, in: 10 Jahre ebs Immobilienakademie, Festschrift, 2000, p. 58-63.

[6] Karl-Werner Schulte, Immobilienökonomie – ein innovatives Lehr- und Forschungskonzept, in: 10 Jahre ebs Immobilienakademie, Festschrift, p. 36-47; Schulte, Karl-Werner (Hrsg.); Immobilienökonomie, Band I, Betriebswirtschaftliche Grundlagen, 2. Aufl., München 2000, p. 97-115.

[7] James R. DeLisle / Elaine Worzala, Essays in Honor of James A. Graaskamp: Ten Years After, 2000.

[8] Real Estate 5/2000.

ACKNOWLEDGEMENTS

The author would like to acknowledge the support of Nico Rottke MSRE, research assistant at the European Business School Real Estate Academy, and Ian Coombs MRICS, Director of Healey & Baker.

Chapter 10

Great Britain

Nick French
The University of Reading, Reading, Great Britain

Scarlett Palmer
The University of Reading, Reading, Great Britain

10.1 Introduction

This chapter on real estate and property education in Great Britain traces the development of professional training in land and property from its earliest manifestation to the present day.[1]

The generic, and often confusing, term that applies to all professionals involved in the field of property[2] and land is Surveyor. Surveying developed as a profession in a similar way to other core professions such as law and accountancy. Historically, the traditional model for training surveyors, as with the other professions, was through the young professional being trained on the job by a recognised master in that trade. This process was known as "articles" and, although this term no longer applies in the UK to surveyors, the process of work experience remains a mainstay of the training process today.

10.2 History of Surveying

Initially, the bulk of the surveying profession was based in rural communities where they were the managers of the large rural estates and where they would be responsible for the management of the farm; maintaining and renewing the estate properties; collecting rents from estate workers etc. Their role was varied and divers but most surveyors would be involved in all these forms of work.

However, with the industrial revolution and the resulting increased urbanisation, surveying skills were needed outside the traditional rural areas and many surveyors moved to towns and cities to take advantage of the increased workload. It was at this time that the profession started to specialise and many professionals became involved in only a single element of the surveying process. Some would specialise in the costing and management of new construction; some would concentrate on maintaining existing buildings; some on the management and collection of rents from let properties and some would develop skills in the pricing and sale of properties as that part of the market developed.

This specialisation led to the development of a number of special interest groups and societies that helped to regulate and control their specific area of the profession. Eventually, in 1868, the plethora of surveying clubs and societies joined together to form one society; The Institution of Surveyors. The initial membership of this body was under 200 but by 1881 that membership had doubled and the Crown granted the society a Royal Charter to create the Royal Institution of Chartered Surveyor [RICS] (see 10.4 below). The RICS was not the only surveying body in existence, but it was the largest and over time the smaller societies that remained autonomous have generally amalgamated with the RICS[3]. This chapter will therefore describe and annotate the property training process in the UK principally from the standpoint of the RICS.

This unified and Royal Institution developed the regulation of its membership beyond the application of professional ethics and standards, a central tenet of any professional body, to establish and oversee the education of surveyors within its ambit. Initially the RICS laid down minimum standards for acceptable knowledge and skills, but this led to a wish to oversee and examine these requirements. Thus in the early 20th century, the Institution introduced the requirement that all trainee surveyors (apprentices), under their auspices, should take professional examinations to prove their proficiency. This was the bedrock of the training and education provisions that exist today and are discussed below.

10.3 The Breadth of Surveying in the UK.

It is interesting to note that in the UK, due to the organic evolution of surveying as one united profession, the various fields of expertise involved in the land, property and construction industries can all involve surveyors. This is not necessarily the case in other countries, where different professions have subsumed the various activities. Construction advice, for example, which falls within the brief of a surveyor in the UK, may be dealt with by an architect, lawyer or civil engineer in parts of Europe or the USA. The work is principally the same, however the profession undertaking the work may vary.

Figure 1: The Property Life Cycle

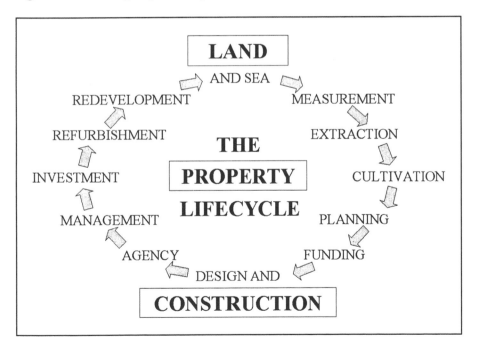

This is discussed in more depth in the other chapters. It should also be noted that although this chapter specifically refers to the UK surveying profession, the reach of the UK surveyor is now international and many commonwealth countries follow the same pattern of training and regulation either through their own indigenous professional bodies or via the RICS in the UK.

Surveyors in the UK are therefore involved in all aspects of land, property, construction and the associated environmental issues. Figure 1 illustrates the life cycle of a property. The surveyor can be involved in all the areas described.

10.4 Royal Institution of Chartered Surveyors

The Royal Institution of Chartered Surveyors is the largest property, land and construction professional body in the UK although it has recently realigned itself as a global organisation. Under the terms of its Royal Charter the members of the RICS are required at all times to act in the public interest. The Institution is committed to upholding standards of competency and integrity among its 83,000 full members, 3000 technical surveyors[4] and 21,000 student members[5]. One of the principal means for the RICS to maintain standards is through its educational programme.

The RICS sets, monitors and enforces standards in two principal areas; education and training and professional conduct. Compliance with these standards entitles the member to use the term chartered surveyor or technical surveyor depending upon their level of membership. The three levels are Fellow of the RICS (FRICS), Professional Member (MRICS)[6] or Technical Member (TechSurv).

To further illustrate the diversity of the profession, the RICS which previously had been divided into separate "divisions" related to the central themes of the profession[7], has chosen to unite all the disparate elements of the profession and disband the divisions. Members of the RICS are now represented by separate special groups of "faculties". These are listed in table 1.

Table 1: Separate special groups of "faculties"

Antiques and Fine Arts	Management Consultancy
Building Surveying	Minerals and Waste Management
Commercial Property	Planning and Development
Construction	Plant and Machinery
Dispute resolution	Project Management
Environment	Residential Property
Facilities management	Rural
Geomatics	Valuation

As discussed earlier, the RICS used to set and regulate its own examinations which were generally undertaken on a part-time basis through correspondence or evening courses or full-time at a dedicated educational establishment. However, in 1995 the RICS set its own examinations for the last time and chose instead to accredit, initially the courses and latterly the educational establishment, providing full time and part time degree or diploma programmes.

10.5 Educational Programmes accredited by the Royal Institution of Chartered Surveyors

There are currently more than 180 RICS accredited courses worldwide at undergraduate or postgraduate levels (RICS, 1998) and a student must successfully complete one of these courses in one of the approved subjects (which still tend to relate to the old divisions of the RICS) to be allowed to register for the Institution's postgraduate professional training programme or APC (see 10.7 below). The RICS is currently reviewing its system of accreditation of degree and other educational courses that permit graduates to gain entry to the APC. The proposed model (as at December 2000) is for the RICS to enter partnerships with Higher Education Institutions who operate relevant courses to the various specialisms within surveying. These institutions must demonstrate evidence of good quality teaching, high entry requirements, scholarly activity amongst the staff and subsequent student entry into the profession.

A number of minimum thresholds have been established; based on measurable inputs and outputs such as the Teaching Quality Audit and Research Assessment Exercise[8] scores, minimum 'A' level (and equivalent) scores and percentage of graduates obtaining relevant occupation (with a relatively wide definition of 'relevant').

Higher Education Institutions which fall below these thresholds will either not be offered a partnership agreement or will have any existing partnership removed; subsequent student entrants to the course will not be entitled to enter the APC of the RICS, although students already on courses will be allowed to enter after graduation.

Higher Education Institutions who are in partnership will be subject to an annual partnership monitoring visit which will review the operation of courses within the partnership and debate future directions and needs for both parties to the partnership. In addition to the annual monitoring of the institution, the RICS will also be involved in the external examiner system for each relevant course.

The external examiner system favoured by the RICS mimics and dovetails into the normal procedures of all UK universities. All degree courses in all subjects in the UK (and many commonwealth countries) must appoint external examiners (persons, academic or otherwise, who are recognised as experts in their field) to oversee and monitor the examination process of the parent university. Although this is a university or (other Higher Education institution) mechanism, the RICS can monitor any appointments made by an institution within the partnership agreement and question their validity. Normally, for vocational courses a mix academic and practitioner externals would be expected as well as a mix of external examining experience. As a result, courses in partnership tend to have RICS members as externals but this is not necessarily the case. The objective of the system is to ensure that standards are upheld but also to marry academic with vocational course philosophy and content. There are various modes of study at the various institutions in partnership, which are listed in Table 2.

Table 2: various modes of study at various institutions in partnership

Full-time Route	Part-time Route
The most common academic surveying education is a full-time 3 year RICS accredited degree or diploma, followed by a minimum of 2 years structured training in the form of the APC.	Some colleges and universities offer degree or diploma courses on a part-time basis. These are normally 5 years in duration and the final year may count toward the required 2 year APC.
Distance Learning Route	**Sandwich Route**
There are some RICS accredited degree or diploma courses that can be taken by correspondence whilst in employment. These are normally 4 years in duration. The fourth year may count toward the required 2 year APC.	Some colleges and universities offer degree or diploma courses that include a 1 year industrial placement. These are normally 4 years in duration and the sandwich year may count toward the required 2 year APC.
Full-time Postgraduate Route	**Part-time Postgraduate Route**
Students who have completed a first degree in a non-property related (non-cognate) degree can take a 1 year postgraduate degree or diploma course followed by a minimum of 2 years structured training in the form of the APC.	Students who have completed a first degree in a non-property related (non-cognate) degree can take a 2 year part-time postgraduate degree or diploma course followed by a minimum of 2 years structured training in the form of the APC.

This breadth of degree subject and mode of study is designed to encourage as many good students into the profession as possible. A full list of accredited course available in the UK is attached at Appendix 1.

10.6 Non-degree Educational Programmes in Great Britain

Although the vast majority of surveyors will qualify via degree or diploma courses as noted above, there are currently national government initiatives that may allow alternative, non degree/diploma, routes for qualification.

One such initiative is the introduction of property related National Vocational Qualifications (NVQs) in England and Wales and Scottish Vocational Qualifications (SVQs) in Scotland. These are vocational based qualifications that are assessed on the basis of performance rather than academic achievement. They are therefore likely to be most applicable, although not exclusively as some schools are now teaching NVQ/SVQs, to students who are in full time employment and wish a route to qualification whilst working.

In some respects the NVQ/SVQ route is analogous with the old articles system but with the benefit of a vocational and transferable qualification, plus a clearer career progression. At the time of writing these qualifications for property are in their infancy but they are likely to become a viable alternative to the academic routes of entry into the profession. The providers of NVQ/SVQs are the local education authorities via the secondary or tertiary college/school system.

10.7 The Assessment of Professional Competence

The experience component of the training is undertaken in an office of qualified surveyors, either in private practice or a public sector organisation. All prospective chartered surveyors must have at least two years of on the job training that must be approved in advance by the RICS. At least one year of the experience must be completed after the accredited degree or diploma.

Candidates must keep a formal record of practical training experience. This is monitored and regularly approved by a sponsor who is usually a chartered surveyor in a senior position in the organisation where the candidate is working. The RICS inspects the candidate's record halfway through their experience and either approves it or suggests specific areas where further experience will be helpful. At the end of the two year practical training, the record is inspected again and either passed or referred for more experience.

Having completed all of the above, the last stage of qualification is a Final Professional or Technical Assessment interview, which is administered by the RICS. In most cases, the candidate presents examples of past work or deals with a specific task set by the RICS. The approach adopted depends upon the candidate's area of work. The assessment ensures that the candidate is fully aware of the responsibilities of a chartered or technical surveyor and that they have the necessary skills and knowledge to solve typical professional problems.

On passing the Final Professional or Technical Assessment interview, the candidate is admitted as a full professional associate or technical surveyor of the Royal Institution of Chartered Surveyors and has the right to use the letters ARICS or TechRICS after their name.

The RICS (1998) defines competencies for the APC across a wide range of property and other surveying activities. The competencies set out the required standards that must be met in order to qualify for a particular division of the RICS or surveying specialism. All candidates must master certain *common core competencies* for general practice surveying, namely: personal and interpersonal skills, business skills, data, information and information technology, professional practice, law, measurement and mapping. In relation to general practice requirements *compulsory core competencies* include: a minimum of Level 3 valuation, Level 1 property inspection and Level 1 drawings. The common and compulsory core competencies are mandatory for all APC candidates and are assessed at the final assessment interview.

In addition candidates are required to select *optional core competencies* from a range of activities defined as general practice. For example in the case of valuation the three levels are as follows:

– Level 1: recognise the purpose and mandatory requirements of any valuation, assimilate pre-valuation documentation and identify, measure and record all relevant factors;
– Level 2: identify, select, assemble and analyse relevant comparable evidence. Apply the various valuation techniques and methodology and understand the consequence of using these methods;
– Level 3: apply data analyses to relevant valuation methods for the required purpose and assist in the preparation of advice and reports.

Under the RICS byelaws, all members of the RICS are required both to undertake Continuous Professional Development (CPD) and to provide the Institution, when required, with evidence of doing so. Regulations made under the byelaw require every member to complete a minimum of 60 hours CPD in each period of three consecutive years, normally a minimum of 20 hours in every year. The RICS carries out a programme of random checks on members' compliance with the byelaw and regulations. According to the RICS website[9] these checks have produced overwhelming evidence that the great majority of members have no difficulty in complying with the regulations and are often exceeding the required minimum CPD.

10.8 The Institute of Revenues Rating and Valuation

One specialised society that still exists outside the auspices of the RICS is the Institute of Revenues Rating and Valuation (IRRV). This is a specialised professional body of property professionals involved in the levying, collection and administration of local taxes. The IRRV works closely with the RICS to produce joint guidance notes in a number of specific areas of practice. There is a large overlap of membership with the RICS and most IRRV members are also RICS qualified.

The IRRV does however administer its own examinations system in addition to the granting of exemptions in lieu of other professional qualifications. Tuition is available direct from the IRRV via its own designed and administered distance learning courses or via day release courses offered by a number of universities and colleges.

10.9 National Association of Estate Agents

The National Association of Estate Agents (NAEA) was established in 1962 and membership is open to practising estate agents. As with the IRRV, there are overlaps with the work of chartered surveyors, but in recent years many estate agents have opted for membership of the NAEA in preference to the RICS. The reasons for this may lie in the simpler and less stringent requirements for qualification; to become an associate member of the NAEA candidates need only pass one admissions test and have a number of years experience. Alternatively, if the candidate already has another professional qualification or NVQ, they are exempt from the admission test.

A benefit of membership is that NAEA members are able to gain professional certificates in their core areas of work, namely the Certificate of Practice in Estate Agency (CPEA) and a Certificate in Residential Lettings and Management (CRLM). These are examination based via distance learning programmes purchased from NAEA.

10.10 European Society of Chartered Surveyors

Based in Brussels, the European Society of Chartered Surveyors (ESCS) is a Europe-wide federation of national associations of chartered surveyors. Members come from most European Union states, as well as an increasing number of eastern European countries. The ESCS acts as a single voice for all chartered surveyors working in Europe and serves as a forum for like-minded professionals who are able to consult their counterparts across borders. The ESCS and their members are regulated the RICS in London.

The ESCS is made up of national associations assisted by an elected Board of chartered surveyors. The Board initiates the strategies and policies of the ESCS and proposes these to the representatives of the national associations of chartered surveyors. The national associations supervise and implement decisions taken by Board members and representatives of national associations at General Meetings. The ESCS Secretariat facilitates the co-ordination and implementation of decisions.

On the educational side, the ESCS identifies and develops university level surveying courses across Europe. Nationals from Belgium, France, Germany, Hungary, Ireland, the Netherlands and Poland and the United Kingdom can follow university courses in their own countries to obtain their academic qualifications prior to becoming chartered surveyors. Further courses are under consideration in Austria, Denmark, Greece, Italy, Portugal and Spain.

10.11 Conclusion

From its early origins in rural communities the surveying profession has now developed into an eclectic, yet unified, body in the UK. The Royal Institution of Chartered Surveyors commands a pre-eminent position in the property industry both at home and abroad. The education process is an integral element of ensuring the continuation and maintenance of standards within the profession. More than any other country in the world there is a strong and direct partnership between the education providers (principally the universities) and the profession.

REFERENCES

RICS (1998) *APC Requirements & Competencies,* 2nd ed, Royal Institution of Chartered
    Surveyors, Coventry.
RICS (2000) *The RICS Prospectus to Surveying Education*, Fourth Edition, GTI Specialist
    Publishers Ltd, Wallingford, Oxon.

NOTES

[1] The United Kingdom comprises England, Scotland, Wales (together known as Great Britain) and Northern Ireland. This chapter deals only with the sovereign states of Great Britain; Northern Ireland is covered in the chapter of Ireland.

[2] The UK term relating to the physical construction and management of buildings is "property". This is often referred to internationally as "real estate" and although this international term is beginning to find acceptance in the UK, the term property is still dominant and will be used throughout this chapter.

[3] The most recent and prominent amalgamation was in 2000, when the Incorporated Society of Valuers and Auctioneers (ISVA) voted in favour of a merger. Prior to that amalgamation, ISVA was the second largest property related professional body in the UK with its own code of professional ethics and educational requirements. The educational route with the ISVA was principally via its own professional examinations. Apart from some transi-

tional procedures put in place to allow existing ISVA students to continue their qualification route, all future students will qualify via the normal RICS partnered degree/diploma route (see on).

[4] A technical surveyor is a subset of the profession involved in the more technical and less eclectic work. The members of this group were previously members of the Society of Surveying Technicians until it amalgamated with the RICS in 1998.

[5] Student Members include those students in education who have chosen to join in advance of the completion of their studies (membership is non mandatory) and Probational members (membership is mandatory) who are in employment undertaking pragmatic training.

[6] MRICS was previously known, until 2001, as ARICS or Associate of RICS

[7] The RICS was, until 2000, divided into a number of separate divisions; General Practice Division (which is related to work in commercial and residential property); Building Surveying (which is related to advice on the design, maintenance and construction of buildings); Rural Practice Division (which is related to farms, country estates and forestry); Planning and Development Division (which is related to the planning, financing and development of new buildings); Quantity Surveying (which is related to project management and costing of new buildings); Mineral and Environmental Management (which is related to the management and extraction of natural resources); and Geomatics (previously Land and Hydrographic which relates to the measurement and mapping of the land and the built environment)

[8] Higher Education Institutions in the UK are subject to periodic review of both teaching and research by the Higher Education Funding Council on behalf of central government. Teaching quality and research are assessed by peer review and departments or unit of assessment are awarded a score for each of these areas. These scores are now being used by the RICS as a measure of quality when considering partnerships.

[9] The RICS Website can be found at www.RICS.org

USEFUL ADDRESSES

The Royal Institution of Chartered Surveyors
12 Great George Street,
Parliament Square,
London, SW1P 3AD
Tel: +44 (0)207 222 7000, Email: info@rics.org.uk , Website: www.RICS.org

European Society of Chartered Surveyors
Avenue de Cortenbergh, 52
1000 Brussels
Belgium
Tel: +32 2 733 10 19, Website: www.ESCS.org

APPENDIX

based on Tables included in *The RICS Prospectus to Surveying Education*, Forth Edition, GTI Specialist. Used with permission.

Institution	Level	Course Title	Mode
University of Aberdeen	BLE	Land Economy	FT
	BSc/BSc (Hons)	Marine Resource Management	FT
	DipLE/MLE	Land Economy	FT
University of Abertay Dundee	BSc (Hons)	Quantity Surveying	FT/S
Anglia Polytechnic University	BSc (Hons)	Building Surveying	FT/S/PT
	BSc (Hons)	Planning and Development Surveying	FT/S/PT
	BSc (Hons)	Property Management	FT/S/PT
	BSc (Hons)	Quantity Surveying	FT/S/PT
Bolton Institute	BSc (Hons)	Quantity Surveying	FT/S/PT
University of Brighton	BSc (Hons)	Building Surveying	FT/S/PT
University of the West of England Bristol	BSc (Hons)	Building Surveying	FT/S/PT
	BA (Hons)	Housing Policy and Management	FT/S/PT
	BSc (Hons)	Quantity Surveying	FT/S/PT
	BA (Hons)	Planning and Development	FT/PT
	BSc (Hons)	Valuation and Estate Management	FT/S
	BSc/BSc (Hons)	Real Estate (Valuation and Management)	FT
	Dip/MA	Housing studies	FT/S/PT
Cambourne School of Mines, Exete	BEng (Hons)	Minerals Surveying and Resource Management	FT
	BEng (Hons)	Minerals Surveying and Resource Management With European Study	FT
Cambridge University	BA (Hons)	Land Economy	FT
University of Central Lancashire	BSc (Hons)	Quantity Surveying	FT/S/PT
	BSc (Hons)	Building Surveying	FT/S/PT
University of Central England in Birmingham	BSc (Hons)	Estate Management	FT/PT
	BSc (Hons)	Quantity Surveying	FT/PT
	BSc (Hons)	Building Surveying	FT/S/PT
City University	BSc (Hons)	Real Estate Finance and Investment	FT
	Dip/MA	Property Valuation and Law	FT/PT
	BEng	Civil Engineering with Surveying	FT/S
	MEng	Civil Engineering with Surveying	FT/S
	MSc	Property Valuation and Law	FT/PT
The College of Estate Management	Diploma	Suveying	D
	BSc	Estate Management	D
Coventry University	BSc (Hons)	Building Surveying	FT/S/PT
De Montfort University	BSc (Hons)	Land Management	FT/PT
	BSc (Hons)	Business Property Management	FT/PT
	BSc (Hons)	Rural Land Management	FT

Institution	Level	Course Title	Mode
	BSc (Hons)	Planning and Development	FT
	BSc (Hons)	Building Surveying	FT/PT
University of East London	BSc (Hons)	Surveying and Mapping Science	FT/PT
	BSc (Hons)	Geographial and Land Information Management	FT/PT
University of Glamorgan	BSc (Hons)˙	Quantity Surveying	FT/S/PT
	BSc (Hons)	Building Surveying	FT/S
	BSc (Hons)	Estate Management	FT/S
	BSc/BSc (Hons)	Minerals Surveying and Resource Development	FT/S
	BSc	Surveying for Resource Development	FT/S
	BSc/BSc (Hons)	Estate Management Surveying	FT
University of Glasgow	BSc/BSc (Hons)	Topographic Science	FT
Glasgow Caledonian University	BSc (Hons)	Quantity Surveying	S/PT
	BSc (Hons)	Building Surveying	S
	BSc (Hons)	Property Management and Development	FT/S/PT
	BSc/BSc (Hons)	Building Services Quantity Surveying	FT
The University of Greenwich	BSc (Hons)	Building Surveying	FT/S/PT
	BSc (Hons)	Estate Management	FT/S/PT
	BSc (Hons)	Quantity Surveying	FT/S/PT
Harper Adams University College	BSc (Hons)	Rural Enterprise and Land Management	FT/S
	MSc	Rural Environmental Amenity and Land Management	FT/PT
Heriot Watt University	BSc/BSc (Hons)	Building Surveying	FT
	BSc/BSc (Hons)	Building Economics and Quantity Surveying	FT
	BSc/BSc (Hons)	Estate Management	FT
	BSc/BSc (Hons)	Building Services Quantity Surveying	FT
	MSc	Marine Resource Management	FT/PT
Kingston University	BSc (Hons)	Building Surveying	FT/S/PT
	BSc (Hons)	Envionmental Real Estate	FT/S
	BSc (Hons)	Property Planning and Development	FT/S
	BSc (Hons)	Quantity Surveying Consultancy	FT/S/PT
	BSc (Hons)	Real Estate Management	FT/S/PT
	MSc	Immobilia (European Real Estate Studies)	FT/PT
Leeds Metropolitan University	BSc (Hons)	Quantity Surveying	FT/S/PT
	BSc (Hons)	Building Surveying	FT/S/PT
Liverpool John Moores University	BSc/BSc (Hons)	Urban Estate Management	FT/PT
	BSc/BSc (Hons)	Quantity Surveying	FT/S/PT
	MSc	Commercial Property Management	FT

Institution	Level	Course Title	Mode
University College London	Dip/MSc	Photogrammetry with Remote Sensing	FT
	Dip/MSc	Surveying	FT
	Dip/MSc	Geographic Information Science	FT
Loughborough University	BSc (Hons)	Commercial Management and Quantity Surveying	S
University of Luton	BSc (Hons)	Building Surveying	FT/S/PT
Manchester College of Arts and Technology	Diploma	Valuation	D
UMIST	BSc (Hons)	Commercial Management and Quantity Surveying	S
Napier University	Seeking Acc	Building Surveying	
	Seeking Acc	Estate Management	
	Seeking Acc	Quantity Surveying	
	Seeking Acc	Planning and Development	
University of Newcastle Upon Tyne	BSc (joint Hons)	Surveying and Mapping Science with another science subject	FT
	BSc (Hons)	Surveying and Mapping Science	FT
North East Wales Institute	BSc (Hons)	Estate Management	FT
University of Northumbria at Newcastle	BA (Hons)	Housing	FT/S/PT
	BSc (Hons)	Quantity Surveying	S/PT
	BSc (Hons)	Building Surveying	S/PT
	BSc (Hons)	Estate Management	FT/S/PT
	BSc (Hons)	Planning and Development Surveying	FT/S/PT
The University of Nottingham	BEng	Civil Engineering	FT
	BEng/MEng	Mining Engineering	FT
	Dip/MSc	Engineering Suveying and Geodosy	FT/PT
	MSc	Geographial Information Systems	FT/PT
Nottingham Trent University	BSc (Hons)	Building Surveying	FT/S/PT
	BSc (Hons)	Real Estate Management	FT/S/PT
	BSc (Hons)	Planning and Development	FT/S/PT
	BEng (Hons)	Surveying for Engineering	FT/S/PT
	BSc (Hons)	Surveying for Engineering	FT/S/PT
	BSc (Hons)	Cost Management of Building Engineering Services	PT
	BSc (Hons)	Estate Surveying	FT/S/PT
	BEng (Hons)	Civil Engineering Surveying	FT/S
	BSc (Hons)	Civil Engineering Surveying	FT/S
	MSc	Real Estate (in conjunction The Technical University of Budapest)	PT
	Diploma	Quantity Surveying	PT
Oaklands University	BSc (Hons)	Quantity Surveying	PT
Oxford Brookes University	BSc (Hons)	Real Estate Management	FT
	BSc (Hons)	Real Estate Management (by open learning in Singapore)	O

Institution	Level	Course Title	Mode
University of Paisley	BSc/BSc (Hons)	Real Estate Management	FT/S/PT
	Dip/MSc	Urban Property Appraisal	FT/PT
University of Plymouth	BSc (Hons)	Building Surveying and the Environment	FT/S/PT
	Dip/MSc	Hydrology	FT/PT
University of Portsmouth	BSc (Hons)	Real Estate Management (at Seale-Hayne)	FT/PT
	BSc (Hons)	Quantity Surveying	FT/PT
	BSc (Hons)	Property Development	FT
	BSc (Hons)	Land Management	FT
	MSc	Coastal and Marine Resource Management	FT/PT
The University of Reading	BSc (Hons)	Building Surveying	FT
	BSc (Hons)	Quantity Surveying	FT
	BSc (Hons)	Construction Management Engineering and Surveying	FT
	BSc (Hons)	Land Management	FT
	BSc (Hons)	Investment and Finance in Property	FT
	BSc (Hons) with Dip/MSc	Land Management with Dip/MSc Urban Planning and Development	FT
	MSc	Land Management	FT
The Robert Gordon University	BSc (Hons)	Building Surveying	FT/S/PT
	BSc (Hons)	Quantity Surveying	FT/S/PT
	BSc/BSc (Hons)	Marine Resource Management	FT/S/PT
The Royal Agricultural College	BSc (Hons)	Rural Land Management	FT
	MSc	Rural Estate Manananagement	FT
The Royal Naval Hydrographic School		Long Hydrographic Course	FT
The Royal School of Military Survey	MSc	Defence Geographic Information	FT
University of Salford	BSc (Hons)	Building Surveying	FT/S
	BSc (Hons)	Quantity Surveying	FT/S
	BSc (Hons)	Property Management and Investment	FT
	BSc (Hons)	Surveying (3 pathways)	PT
Sheffield Hallam University	BSc (Hons)	Building Surveying	FT/S/PT
	BSc (Hons)	Quantity Surveying	FT/S/PT
	BSc (Hons)	Business Property Management	FT/S/PT
	BSc (Hons	Environmental Land Management	FT/S/PT
	BSc (Hons)	Facilities Management	FT/S/PT
	BSc (Hons)	Property Management	FT/S/PT
	BSc (Hons)	Urban Land Economics	FT/S
	BSc (Hons)	Property Appraisal	FT/S
	BSc (Hons)	Property Development	FT/S
	BA (Hons)	Housing Studies	FT/S/PT
	Dip/MSc	Housing Policy and Practice	FT/PT

Institution	Level	Course Title	Mode
	Dip/MSc	Property Valuation and Management	FT/PT
Southampton Institute	BA (Hons)	Fine Arts Valuation	FT/PT
South Bank University	BSc (Hons)	Building Surveying	FT/S/PT
	BSc (Hons)	Estate Management	FT/S/PT
	BSc (Hons)	Quantity Surveying	FT/S/PT
	Dip/MSc	Estate Management	FT/PT
	Dip/MSc	Property Development and Planning	FT/PT
	MSc	Building Surveying	PT
	MSc	Quantity Surveying	PT
Staffordshire University	BSc (Hons)	Building Surveying	FT
	BSc (Hons)	Quantity Surveying	FT
	BSc (Hons)	Valuation Surveying	FT
	BSc (Hons)	Property with Business Studies	FT
University of Ulster	BSc (Hons)	Surveying	FT/S/PT
University of Wales College Cardiff	BSc (Hons)	Marine Geography	FT/S
University of Westminster	BSc (Hons)	Urban Estate Management	FT
	BSc (Hons)	Quantity Surveying	FT/PT
	BSc (Hons)	Building Surveying	FT
	BSc (Hons)	Housing Management and Development	FT
University of Wolverhampton	BSc (Hons)	Building Surveying	FT/S/PT
	BSc (Hons)	Quantity Surveying	FT/S/PT

Chapter 11

Greece

Sotiris Tsolacos
Jones Lang LaSalle, London, Great Britain

11.1 Introduction

It is now acknowledged that real estate is a multidisciplinary subject area that reflects the complexities and the dynamic character of the real estate markets. Despite the distinctive characteristics of this market, real estate studies as a field were slow to emerge in the majority of the European countries, as the articles in this book illustrate. Even in the UK and Ireland, two countries where a longer tradition of real estate education existed, and to an extent in the Netherlands and Sweden, interaction for example with the frontiers of urban economics, financial investment, institutional economics, geography and land behaviour was not strong. In other countries an engineering tradition to real estate education, with the focus on construction and to some extent investment aspect of the property market, had existed (Hedvall and Leiwo, 2000). Real estate education in Greece has broadly mirrored this trend and it can be argued that the notion of real estate education was largely synonymous with civil engineering and land surveying. The real estate professionals were seen to be those who were initiating and managing developments, usually civil engineers, and real estate agents who were involved in brokerage work only. Real estate education as it is currently perceived began to be appreciated in Greece after the mid-1990s.

This paper aims to explain the evolution of real estate education in Greece especially in the period 1980 to mid-1995. The paper explores the factors that prevented academic establishments and other organisations to offer real estate education in the past and restricted progress towards developing courses in the same way that other European countries, which had been characterised by a similar lack of education, were making steps forward during the 1980s and the 1990s. Subsequently, the discussion identifies the influences which have given rise to the recently acknowledged need for explicit real estate education, as it is perceived today, in the Greek environment. This is a strongly market driven need that is now challenging for education providers. Finally, the potential and future trends in real estate education in Greece are critically examined.

The rest of the paper is organised onto four sections. Section two outlines the obstacles that restricted the provision of real estate education either from the academic sector or professional organisations. Section three discusses the sources of the market need for real estate education that became apparent in the second half of the 1990s. Section four focuses on the current and future providers of real estate education in Greece. The last section summarises the arguments and assesses the future of real estate education in Greece.

11.2 Main reasons for the lack of real estate education

11.2.1 Political and economic factors

In general, a persistently unstable political environment and low rates of economic development affect the evolution of the education system as a whole in the longer term. Certain fields such as finance, investment and real estate can be belatedly developed since more advanced and stable investment and finance environments are required. Political instability, that was the result of a civil war that ended in 1950, turbulent relations with neighbouring Turkey, a continuous confrontation between right and left parties, a coup d'etat in 1967 and a junta that lasted for seven years and the Cyprus trouble in 1974, characterised Greece's political arena from the second world war period until the mid-1970s. During this period the main focus of the Universities courses was on traditional fields (f.i. medicine, engineering, education) and land studies would not feature in the programmes. The political situation turned towards being more stable in the second half of the 1970s.

Following the accession of Greece to the European Union in 1981 a more settled political environment began to emerge that could facilitate innovation in Greek education at the University level. However, when the socialists took office in 1981 and although a more stable political environment was emerging, the prevailing philosophy up to the mid-1990s was that real estate was associated with or it was in the heart of capitalism especially from an investment point of view. Real estate education would have been difficult to be born in the Greek political and ideological environment of the 1980s as universities would not have the backing of the education authorities if initiatives had been taken. These attitudes began to change in the mid-1990s as both firms and the public were becoming increasingly aware of the investment characteristics of land and buildings.

In the aftermath of the second world war the Greek economy went through a period of reconstruction as the rest of Europe did. The political instability that characterised the country had a significant effect on the economic performance. The reconstruction period was prolonged and despite the high growth rates (about 8% annual average in the 1960s), the agricultural sector was the most significant until the beginning of 1970s. The 1980s have been for most European countries a period of fiscal consolidation and steady economic expansion. The macroeconomic policies followed by the Socialist government in the 1980s were imprudent and maintained high inflation, interest rates and public debts. Regional policies were also not so successful. For example, Kourliouros (1997) argued that the attempts of the Socialist government to plan industrial location in the metropolis of Greater Athens was not achieved in practice. This author analysed the importance of both economic and political/ideological dimensions that were promoting an anti-industrialist mentality. The macroeconomic situation and the regional problems underpinned the growth of fields such as urban and regional studies a trend that had began in several European countries much earlier. However, as in the European urban and regional environment, real estate markets were not seen as playing a significant role in the regional economy or urban growth and did not receive academic attention.

In the early 1990s, Greece did not escape the Pan-European recession. Since 1993 economic policies were put in place to meet the Maastricht convergence criteria. This brought in the necessary macroeconomic policy discipline and political will to modernise all spheres of the economy. The public began to appreciate the necessary economic restructuring for joining the

European monetary system. The traditional philosophies of the socialist government were gradually abandoned in favour of a more market economy approach especially in the second half of the 1990s. This could facilitate the creation of a new environment for universities to revisit their course portfolio and move towards offering new courses for which there was a market demand such as real estate courses.

Political instability, incompatible ideologies and economic growth cannot be seen as the sole dimensions behind the lack of real estate education especially when there is no market need for such education. In the case of Greece, subject areas which constitute important ingredients in real estate studies, such as investment, planning and spatial economics, had not prospered in Greek academia.

11.2.2 The investment market

Until recently Greece was characterised by an under-developed capital and investment market. The trend of liberalisation and modernisation that Europe experienced after the turbulent 1970s was not seen in the Greek capital market. A large number of inefficient state banks, which were representing the bulk of financial intermediaries in the 1980s, absence of institutional investors and an underdeveloped market for stocks, bonds and other financial products could summarise the financial investment environment until the beginning of the 1990s. A strongly unionised labour was fiercely opposed to policies of privatisation to modernise the industry and increase its efficiency as the case was elsewhere in Europe. In such an environment of course the field of property investment remains in darkness. However, despite the absence of any explicit property investment market, state banks and other organisations held, and still hold, substantial portfolios of land and buildings. Until recently, however, no systematic attempt had been made to utilise these portfolios that would require advice from analysts with real estate investment education background.

In the absence of financial investment products to attract the savings of the public, bank deposits represented the main investment channel. This type of investment was particularly attractive in the periods of high interest rates that prevailed in Greece until the mid-1990s (short term rates in 1980s were nearly 20% and government bond income returns over 15%). On the other hand, it can be argued that the strong tendency of Greeks to use their savings to build their own house has affected the popularity of new financial products over time. Traditionally, the general public would consider investment in land and houses as a secure investment. This could extend to illegally built houses in areas where no town plans existed. The relaxed Greek planning system had made investment in land by individuals a fairly safe operation through legalising illegally built properties. Also, in a high-inflationary environment the view was that investment in land was the safest investment. Of course, this view had also been prevailed not only among the general public but also among professionals, in more sophisticated property markets, such as in the UK. Therefore, this attitude of the general public reduced the demand for financial investment products.

Similar views about the advantages of investment in land in periods of high inflation were prevailing among businesses. Ownership of land and buildings also strengthened the balance sheets. Moreover, the lending policies of banks, that required the building or land as a collateral for borrowing, did not increase flexibility in the market. There was not therefore an apparent need to consider the benefits of sale and lease back arrangements (for which the legislation was only put in 1998). In such an investment environment real estate education, in this case property investment, was bound to lag behind.

Finally, taxation was not favourable for either property owners or property investors. In an economic situation where the governments run significant budget deficits and government revenues suffer from tax evasion, property cannot escape the imposition of levies. There is a large number of taxes (over 40 types) and the owner is responsible for paying them. These taxes range from taxes on property income, use, sale, municipal taxes and other. Market participants, mainly owners and the construction industry had lobbied for changes to property tax legislation. However, in the 1980s and in the beginning of the 1990s, government tax legislation to favour property owners would have had a significant political cost to the Socialist party. Overall, the tax position of the country towards property still cannot be considered favourable to property investment.

11.2.3 The planning environment

In addition to the situation of an undeveloped investment field, another ingredient of real estate studies, planning education was late to emerge. Labrianidis and Deffner (1999) argued that both planning and geography teaching in Greek Universities has until recently been extremely limited, as there were no planning and geography departments which contrasted with the substantial research in these fields since the 1960s. These authors also point that planning was never seen as a profession. Members of the powerful Chamber of Commerce, most of them with engineering background, could call themselves planners and experts in the property market. Despite the excessive research in other European countries on the effects of planning policies on the function of the local property market and economic development, academic research and education toward evaluating the effects of the

Greek planning system was very limited. Thus, the belated start of planning education and geography in Greek universities can be seen as another reason for the delayed appreciation of the real estate market as a distinct field of education.

11.2.4 Real estate related units in University programmes

An examination of the curricula of a number of Universities reveals that units related to real estate and space are offered in several of their programmes. Units such as building construction, quantity surveying, real estate valuation, land management and land policy are included in the course syllabuses of civil engineering, architecture and land surveying (topography) departments have included in the syllabuses of their courses units relevant to real estate. Urban and regional studied departments have also offered units which relate to real estate studies. Urban and economic geography, applications of GIS, models of urban planning, environmental planning are delivered. Property led urban regeneration policies which were launched in the early 1980s in the UK did not foster a more explicit study of the real estate market in these departments. Across these departments, however, real estate related units have been mostly offered on an optional basis and just complement the main subjects in the course. Moreover, they are orientated towards supporting the general direction of the individual departments and cannot be seen as a part of real estate education.

The courses offered in economic and business departments in the country have also ignored the real estate user, development or investment market. The behaviour of fixed capital investment is a main study area in economics degrees but building structures have not been considered as constituting a market of their own and as a part of fixed capital investment which is determined in a different way from equipment investment. Moreover, the neo-classical approach taught in economic departments was limiting the development of spatial economics units. The neo-classical theory does not have an explicit treatment to space (land and building structures). Based on the strong assumptions about flexibility in the prices of products and inputs and free mobility of the factors of production it was expected that any market, including the land market, would be able to reach equilibrium. The recognition of the distinct place of real estate economics in the sphere of mainstream economics is only a recent phenomenon not only in Greece but also elsewhere in Europe. Finally, business and finance departments have not explicitly treated property finance and property investment issues in their course portfolios.

11.2.5 Lack of engagement of professional bodies in real estate education

The presence of organisations which relate to the real estate field can play a significant part to promote education and research. In Greece three bodies have represented for a considerable time the interest of different groups within the real estate profession. The Greek Real Estate Federation, which is affiliated to FIABCI, is the main body representing the interests of estate agents throughout the country. The Body of Sworn-in-Valuers, which is a member of European Group of Valuers' Associations (TEGoVA) and the International Valuation Standard Committee (IVSC), was established in 1979 with the aim to endorse appraisal standards in the Greek property market. The Hellenic Property Federation is the body of real estate property owners in Greece. This organisation is one of the country members, which make up the International Union of Property Owners (UIPI).

One of the objectives of these organisations is to promote knowledge on property issues among their members and pursue continuous professional development. Mainly they have acted as lobbying organisations and providers of guidelines and advice to their members. They have also been involved in organising seminars and panel discussions. However, they have not been involved in a formal education programme of real estate education in Greece either by associating with a University or by setting out the themes that students should study in order to become real estate professionals. But such involvement would be difficult as it is doubtful to what extent, even at the present time, these organisations appreciate the interdisciplinary nature of the market and therefore any involvement would not have resulted in a complete real estate programme.

An attempt to close this gap was made by the Greek Association of Chartered Surveyors (GACS) which is the local organisation of chartered surveyors practising in Greece and the Greek branch of the European Society of Chartered Surveyors. The latter has undertaken a course development initiative in many European countries. GACS recently attempted to apply this initiative to Greece with the co-operation of an Athens based university the Panteion University of Social and Political Sciences. Even in this case, a brand new degree was not developed. Students who successfully finish four semesters in the post-graduate degree in Economic and Regional Development can attend in a fifth semester in which four subjects are taught: principles of construction, real estate investment, real estate valuation and real estate development. The purpose is for students to achieve chartered surveyor qualifications through APCs. This is a very new course and its potential is discussed in the next section.

Overall, the existing organisations have been inadequate to advance real estate education in Greece. The fact that they all produce commentaries to explain the state of the market and evaluate the effects of government policies on real estate and support seminars is a positive aspect but involvement in real estate education requires further commitment. Recently, another organisation was launched, the Hellenic Institute of Valuation. Its aim is to promote the 'science of valuation' in Greece. In the press release announcing its launch, the first aim is the organisation of special education programmes, seminars, lectures and other activities for the valuation of real estate and other fixed assets. It remains to be seen how effectively these aims will be pursued.

11.3 The need for real estate education

New trends in all spheres of economic life have recently generated a need for real estate education. This section concentrates on four key trends.

11.3.1 The changing investment environment

If it was land, houses and bank deposits that the average Greek investor would consider as investments in the past, the stock exchange market and a wide range of financial projects offer now new opportunities. A network of financial advisors cover even the smaller towns where younger generations in particular can receive advice and monitor their investments. As the investment market becomes more sophisticated and the public becomes increasingly aware of the opportunities that a variety of financial products offer, property investment is bound to benefit. As an example, throughout the 1990s several private and state owned banks set up mutual funds. These funds were successful stories and their size in terms of value increased dramatically towards the late 1990s. Utilising this experience, banks are now launching property mutual funds, such as REITs in the US and open ended funds in Germany.

This trend towards property funds is aided by several factors. Investors have acknowledged the potential offered by the property market. Issues associated with direct property investment, such as liquidity, marketability and large initial capital outlays, that gave rise to securitized vehicles in other countries underpin this trend in Greece. The need for the consolidation of balance sheets of large state organisations, such as state owned banks, has led these organisations to realise the market potential of their vast property holdings. The birth of these funds will require expertise that will favour those with solid investment and real estate education background. It is clear that appropriate advice cannot be offered by the 'traditional real estate professionals' in Greece from backgrounds such as engineering as property funds with their tendency to trade at a discount to net asset value and their inconsistent relationship with the underlying direct property market represent distinctive investment media. The need for real estate investment expertise has resulted in several organisations employing foreign firms as advisors or employing Greek nationals who have received relevant education abroad mainly in the UK and in the US.

11.3.2 The major infrastructure projects and Olympics 2004

Greece is undergoing now a substantial programme of infrastructure projects. Some of these projects affect whole regions, such as transport projects, and other are more confined to the city level. The region of Athens is transformed as the city is also preparing for the Olympics of 2004. Landowners see the potential investment value of their sites soaring partly as a result of these infrastructure projects. Their behaviour could become irrational in the sense that hope values could damage development activity. At the same time developers may be driven by excess optimism and over-react. Planning and development authorities realise that future plans will have to ensure that pressures in property markets are balanced so that local and regional development plans are put in practice in order to avoid the chaotic urban sprawl of the past. In this environment the provision of real estate services by firms can only be worthy if the individuals involved understand property market dynamics.

11.3.3 Sophistication of the clients

D'Arcy and Tsolacos (2000) highlight trends in Europe that are expected to affect real estate education and research. These authors argued that as clients become more sophisticated, the providers of real estate services need to respond to this trend by offering good quality service and advice. This will force the providers of services to adopt more scientific means of market analysis. Both domestic and international investors who consider investing in Greek real estate, especially in the run up to the Olympics games, will put pressure for more sophisticated real estate market advice. In addition indigenous firms and local branches of international providers of real estate services will attempt to strengthen their competitive position by employing analysts who have received real estate education and are equipped with those strengths that can face up to the new challenges.

11.3.4 European influences

In the last decade academic institutions throughout Europe moved towards developing real estate degrees. The launch of such degrees is expected to provide an incentive for the development of similar degrees in Greece. With a pool of real estate courses around Europe, that are developed in diverse institutional environments, it will be easier for Greek academics to structure a programme and adapt it to the realities of the country. Real estate firms realise the need to employ professionals with specialised knowledge that can be offered by real estate degrees. Moreover, real estate research meetings, such as the conference of the European Real Estate Society, and other European forums, which demonstrate the need for interaction between participants in the real estate field, receive greater publicity and illustrates that a real estate education culture has emerged in Europe. Overall, the implication of these developments is that both universities and firms realise that a new breed of real estate professionals, who have to some extent a common education basis, is generated.

11.4 The potential of future providers of real estate education

11.4.1 Universities

Given the needs of the market for real estate specialists, universities are expected to be the main providers of real estate education in Greece. Given the fact that urban and regional studies departments along with rural and land surveying departments have offered units relating to real estate, one would expect that universities could utilise their experience in different units and develop real estate degrees. This can be facilitated by exchanging experiences between universities or linked to other academic establishments across Europe through the various staff exchange programmes. To date this expectation has not been fulfilled. This can be attributable to several factors including bureaucratic procedures within the universities, no full realisation of the need for real estate education, lack of qualified staff and so forth.

The success of the recent initiative by the Panteion University of Social and Political Sciences and the Greek Association of Chartered Surveyors (GACS) to offer specialised education to the postgraduates of the Regional and Economic Development degree remains to be seen. This stream was introduced last year and despite the employment offers to students it still has not been fully incorporated into the University's programme as a distinct degree. In addition, GACS have not issued clear guidelines about how APC training will take place for students to receive chartered surveyor status. Other attempts to introduce explicitly real estate in university degrees has not been made (at least at the time of writing this article) and it is unlikely to be made in the immediate future. Proposals for academic real estate education in Greece will emerge slowly for the reasons outlined in the previous paragraph. Moreover, the Greek academic sector has not given any signals of synchronisation with the initiatives undertaken in other European universities for the launch of real estate courses.

11.4.2 Real estate organisations

It was argued earlier that organisations representing professional interests in the real estate market have not assisted in promoting academic real estate education in Greece. The exception is the recent attempt of the Greek Association of Chartered Surveyors to set up a degree but yet there are several issues that should be addressed. The future involvement of the other organisations is very unlikely judging from their past track record. The future involvement of all organisations in real estate education will be restricted for three main reasons. First of all, their linkages with the Universities are limited. As a result a forum which can provide the basis for exchange of ideas is not in place. Second, the *raison d'etre* of these organisations is to safeguard the interests of the professionals they represent (property owners, estate agents, chartered surveyors and so forth) and raise their profile. Third, lack of real estate education and understanding of the interdisciplinary nature of the real estate markets. Real estate bodies in Greece have not fully realised the spectrum of inputs from outside their own field for a more complete analysis of the real estate market.

11.4.3 Companies

The third group of real estate education provision is private firms. Companies have been quick to recognise the need for analysts who have real estate education background. Areas where companies seek expertise include property investment, economic analysis of real property markets, appraisal and property financing. Companies have attempted to close this gap through appointments of staff (both senior and other) with real estate qualifications from foreign universities. Their presence would help companies to offer 'in-house' training in real estate that universities or professional organisations cannot provide. Future real estate analysts are more likely to receive training in companies than universities and real estate professional organisations.

11.5 Conclusions and the future

This paper discusses the lack of real estate education in Greece until the mid-1990s. However, until the beginning of the last decade this has been a general phenomenon in the majority of the continental European countries. The paper attempted to identify the key factors that restricted real estate education in the past. These factors ranged from economic-political, to an undeveloped investment environment and lack of academic attention. It was never considered a new function in the academic field. But also education in related subject areas, such as planning and finance, had not been developed either. Due to the dominance of civil engineers in the development market the development industry, banks and authorities never appreciated the interdisciplinary character of real estate market analysis and the necessity for distinct real estate education.

The discussion also highlighted the need for real estate education that has arisen from another of trends in the Greek environment. A notable development is the increasing sophistication of the investment market that has resulted from the liberalisation of the financial system and the presence of international operators. Greece is now undergoing a period of insanity about real estate. Property now receives significant attention by investors and also the government. Recently the government decided to introduce legislation for property unit trusts. Several banks who have been unit trust providers in the 1990s are getting involved. Private and public corporation now see the need to utilise their property assets and also see the need for expert advice. It is this appreciation that resulted in a large interest by the both private companies and real estate organisations in the 6th ERES meeting in Athens.

Against this background one expects that universities, and in particular departments of regional studies and planning or departments of land surveying to respond to this requirement. The discussion in this paper reviewed the potential of future real estate education providers in Greece. The conclusions are not considered encouraging. The universities appear sluggish to yet acknowledge real estate as a distinct discipline and even if they do so it is doubtful whether real estate degrees can be introduced as new courses or developed within the existing course structures. Due to the structure of the Greek academic system, this process will be lengthier in public Universities. Moreover, with the exception of the Greek Association of Chartered Surveyors it is not clear whether the other societies are willing to engage in the provision of real estate education through an academic establishment or otherwise.

It is interesting however to note that despite the publicity of real estate conferences and meetings in Europe and the fact that the number of real estate courses appearing in continental European countries increases constantly, the Greek Universities are lagging behind. In the recent ERES conference in Bordeaux not a single Greek University was present this of course the lack of research in this area. This leaves us to conclude that graduates of foreign institutions will meet the need for such expertise. For example, the number of Greek students in the main UK universities who offer real estate courses can confirm this. However, the demand in the market will not be met. In house training of newly employed will also cover for the absence of such courses. This in the medium term may deter the development of real estate education as it will appear that the needs are met. In the longer term however it will provide the basis to acknowledge the field as distinct from civil engineering, land surveying, planning, environmental, regional economics courses.

REFERENCES

D'Arcy, E. and Tsolacos, S. (2000) Property research in Europe: moving forward through engagement, Journal of Property Investment and Finance 18(3), 284-90.

Hedvall, K. and Leiwo, K. (2000) Vocational and higher-level real estate education in Finland, paper presented at the 7th European Real Estate Society conference, Bordeaux, 13-15 June, 2000.

Kourliouros, E. (1997) Planning industrial location in Greater Athens: the interaction between deindustrialisation and anti-industrialism during the 1980s, *European Planning Studies* 5(4), 435-60.

Labrianidis, L. and Deffner, A. (1999) The development of planning education and its relation to the belated start of Geography teaching in Greek universities, *European Planning Studies* 7(2), 243-53.

Chapter 12

Ireland

Alastair Adair
University of Ulster, Newtownabbey, Ireland

Brendan Williams
Dublin Institute of Technology, Dublin, Ireland

Elizabeth Brown
formerly University of Ulster, Newtownabbey, Ireland

12.1 Introduction

The chapter on real estate education in Ireland encompasses both political jurisdictions within the island of Ireland namely the Republic of Ireland, which is a sovereign state, and Northern Ireland, which is part of the United Kingdom. In terms of historical development the education and training of property professionals in Ireland has undergone major changes over the past two decades. Traditionally the model for educating and training property professionals comprised two elements namely, on the job learning supplemented by part-time, evening study, either classroom based or by correspondence. Under this model assessment of the learning process was by external examinations organised by the professional bodies. Over time, the increasing volume and complexity of knowledge in every professional sector together with the provision of full-time college based education and training led to the development of externally moderated courses recognised by professional organisations. In addition the professional bodies developed a system of validation of professional competence of graduates through approved work-based experience. The lifelong educational experience is supplemented by programmes of certified continuous professional development in order to keep members informed of the changing work environment. Today, externally set and moderated professional examinations for property professionals have virtually all been replaced by full or part-time accredited college-based courses (Davis, 1999).

The development of educational provision for property professionals further reflects wider changes within the global environment which is increasingly characterised by rapid, continuous and pervasive technological and socio-economic changes. High quality and continually improving standards of education and training, underpinned by research and development, are increasingly recognised as being the bedrock of a successful knowledge-based economy. As part of these global processes, education for the professions, of which property is only one, is undergoing major adjustment in response to the changing needs of society (Davis, 1999).

Real estate education in Ireland focuses on the needs of several professional bodies which, depending on their constitution, either operate within or across the political jurisdictions. For example, the Society of Chartered Surveyors operates solely within the Republic of Ireland whereas its sister organisation the Royal Institution of Chartered Surveyors is the equivalent body in Northern Ireland. In contrast the Irish Auctioneers and Valuers Institute, the Incorporated Society of Valuers and Auctioneers and the Inland Revenue Rating Valuers all operate across both jurisdictions. These organisations represent the principal professional bodies in Ireland in terms of standard of education, governmental and legislative requirements for land and property professional membership and perceived status within the profession. In addition two other professional organisations are considered in the chapter namely the Institute of Professional Auctioneers and Valuers and the National Association of Estate Agents. The route to membership, categories of membership and other regulatory controls are outlined in Exhibit 1. The discussion in sections 12.2 to 12.8 addresses the requirements of the professional bodies in terms of their educational provision. Full-time and part-time courses are offered at a number of institutions which are located in the key population centres, namely the Dublin Institute of Technology, Limerick and Galway Mayo Institute of Technology and the University of Ulster. The discussion in sections 12.9 to 12.12 outlines the real estate educational provision in each of these institutions. The final section (12.13) of the chapter comprises a discussion of issues influencing the education of property professionals in Ireland.

12.2 Society of Chartered Surveyors

The Society of Chartered Surveyors (SCS) is the representative professional body for chartered surveyors practising in the Republic of Ireland. The organisation has reciprocal arrangements with the Royal Institution of Chartered Surveyors (RICS) based in the UK which represents chartered surveyors at an international level. The origins of the Society are traced back to 1895, when a group of Irish surveyors amalgamated with the Royal Institution of Chartered Surveyors, in the UK, as a branch. This remained the case until 1993, when it became an independent body.

There are seven categories of chartered surveyor in terms of areas of practice namely, building surveying, minerals surveying, quantity surveying, rural and land agency, general practice and planning and development surveying. The general practice surveyor or chartered valuation surveyor is principally involved in real estate matters. This category undertakes a variety of activities but is mainly involved in estate agency, valuation, development and management of property in both the public and private sectors. Over 1000 surveyors, in total, work in all areas of property and construction in Ireland (Exhibit 1).

Members qualify to two levels of qualifications namely, associate or fellow and such members are entitled to reciprocal membership of the RICS in the UK. The Society has its headquarters in Dublin and a Munster group operates in Cork with a Western group based in Limerick. To qualify as a general practice or chartered valuation surveyor, a candidate must either pass or obtain exemption from the examinations of the SCS. The Society recognises degree level courses at Dublin Institute of Technology (DIT) and Limerick Institute of Technology (LIT) as providing exemption from such examinations. Additionally, candidates must complete an Assessment of Professional Competence (APC) which is a two year period of training and work experience relating to the specialised area in which the candidate wishes to practice.

The objective of the APC, which includes structured training and experience, is to satisfy the Society that the candidate has reached an acceptable level of proficiency. Amongst other criteria, this process is intended to establish that candidates: can apply theoretical knowledge; have developed communications and report writing skills; understand and intend to act in accordance with the Society's Rules of Conduct; and have developed the confidence to work in an unsupervised role (Society of Chartered Surveyors, 1999). The APC consists of: a twenty-four month training period involving the keeping of a diary and record of progress; an interim submission after twelve months; professional development/structured learning; a final submission and attendance at an assessment centre for presentation and interview. In particular, the Summary of Experience and Critical Analysis Project Submission are a significant aspect of the final assessment and interviews. Failure to satisfy the assessors results in a referral process and is subject to a written appeals procedure.

12.3 Royal Institution of Chartered Surveyors

The Royal Institution of Chartered Surveyors (RICS) is the largest property, land and construction professional body in Northern Ireland with circa 984 members operating across seven divisions. The general practice division with 104 fellows and 278 associate members is the largest of the RICS divisions in the province. At the time of writing the RICS is undertaking a major strategic review under the title *Agenda for Change* and sweeping changes are proposed including the replacement of divisions with faculties. There are two main entry routes to full RICS membership, the accredited degree route for candidates with little or no previous professional experience and a route by professional experience (Exhibit 1).

Alternatively educational courses can be used as the educational component of qualification as a technical surveyor (TechRICS). A technical surveyor can later apply to undertake the Assessment of Professional Competence (APC) to become a chartered surveyor. Currently there are over 180 accredited courses world-wide at undergraduate or postgraduate levels (RICS, 1998a) however the University of Ulster is the sole accredited university centre in Northern Ireland. Possession of an accredited degree or diploma will enable a candidate to register for the Institution's postgraduate professional training programme or APC. The RICS offers full reciprocity with the Society of Chartered Surveyors in the Republic of Ireland (section 12.2).

The RICS operates a system of accreditation which distinguishes between accredited centres and other centres offering accredited courses. The two categories are defined as follows:

– an **accredited centre** is a designated faculty, school or department of an academic institution, which offers one or more accredited courses provid-

ing admission to the Institution's APC for seven or more years during which at least one successful course re-accreditation will have taken place.
–   other centres will be academic institutions which have offered accredited courses providing admission to the Institution's APC, for less than seven years.

Accredited centres have greater flexibility for introducing new under-graduate and postgraduate surveying programmes without a visit actually taking place. This is designed to encourage innovation and evolution in course development. New programmes offered by an accredited centre, which are designed to provide admission to the APC, are subject to a simpli-fied form of accreditation by the RICS. Accredited courses at undergraduate and postgraduate level and accredited centres are monitored annually and, subject to satisfactory reports, remain in continuous approval. Accredited centres are required to submit at the end of each year annual course review reports; the number of students entering accredited courses including direct entrants, entry profile details, cohort progression and graduate output statis-tics; external examiners' reports; details of any staff or other resource changes within the last twelve months; and revised course documentation and revalidation reports where applicable.

Normally one review will take place in any seven year period. Visits will be conducted on a centre basis to review all surveying courses with extant approval. The purpose of a review visit will be to assess the custodianship of surveying education by an accredited centre. The visit will focus on issues arising from the process of annual monitoring. The role of the external examiner approved by the RICS Surveying Courses Board is seen as one of the most effective ways of monitoring standards and maintaining the profes-sional relevance of the courses satisfying the RICS academic requirements for professional qualification and admission to the APC.

The experience component of the qualification is undertaken in an office of qualified surveyors, either in private practice or a public sector organisa-tion. All prospective chartered surveyors must have at least two years of on the job training which must be approved in advance by the RICS. At least one year of the experience must be completed after the accredited degree or diploma.

Full time students typically do two years of practical training after they graduate. Sandwich students can count the sandwich year (if it is spent work-ing in a surveying office) as one year's experience and then do a second year after graduation. Part time students can similarly count their final year (if working in a surveying office) towards their practical experience, leaving one year to complete after graduation. Professionally relevant research undertaken as part of an accredited surveying course can also count towards the practical experience.

Candidates keep a formal record of practical training experience. On completion of the experience element the last stage of qualification is a final professional or technical assessment, which is administered by the RICS. In most cases, examples will be presented by the candidate of past work or the candidate will be set a specific task. Normally all candidates are asked to discuss their work in a professional interview.

The RICS (1998b) defines competencies for the APC across a wide range of property and other surveying activities. The competencies set out the required standards in order to qualify for a particular division of the RICS or surveying specialism. All candidates must master certain *common core competencies* for general practice surveying, namely: personal and interpersonal skills, business skills, data, information and information technology, professional practice, law, measurement and mapping. In relation to general practice requirements *compulsory core competencies* include: a minimum of Level 3 valuation, Level 1 property inspection and Level 1 drawings. The common and compulsory core competencies are mandatory for all APC candidates and are assessed at the final assessment interview.

In addition candidates are required to select *optional core competencies* from a range of activities defined as general practice. For example in the case of valuation the three levels are as follows:

- Level 1: recognise the purpose and mandatory requirements of any valuation, assimilate pre-valuation documentation and identify, measure and record all relevant factors
- Level 2: identify, select, assemble and analyse relevant comparable evidence. Apply the various valuation techniques and methodology and understand the consequence of using these methods
- Level 3: apply data analyses to relevant valuation methods for the required purpose and assist in the preparation of advice and reports

Under the RICS bye-laws, all members of the RICS are required both to undertake Continuous Professional Development (CPD) and to provide the Institution, when required, with evidence of doing so. Regulations made under the bye-law require every member to complete a minimum of 60 hours CPD in every period of three consecutive years, normally a minimum of 20 hours in every year. The RICS carries out a programme of random checks on members' compliance with the bye-law and regulations. According to the RICS these checks have produced overwhelming evidence that the great majority of members have no difficulty in complying with the regulations and are often exceeding the required minimum CPD.

12.4 Irish Auctioneers and Valuers Institute

The Irish Auctioneers and Valuers Institute (IAVI) is the largest professional representative property organisation in Ireland. Operating in both
Northern Ireland and the Republic of Ireland, it has approximately 1,450
members and 500 member firms (Exhibit 1). The Institute aims to provide
representation for the property profession, serve its members and the public
as well as furthering educational standards (IAVI, 1999). The organisation
operates under a regional structure, which deals with local matters, with a
national council and headquarters with eight permanent staff located in Dublin. The Institute's Compensation fund, run via mandatory subscriptions
from member firms, exists to provide the public with protection for deposits
lodged with IAVI member firms. Self-regulation includes members being
bound by a code of professional conduct with a public complaints procedure.

Full membership of the IAVI involves satisfying one of the following
conditions: successful completion of a recognised diploma/degree and one
year's approved practice experience; passing all parts of the IAVI Direct
Final Examination; or hold a professional qualification recognised by the
IAVI and have appropriate practical experience. Associate membership is
available to qualified employees in IAVI member companies practising only
in the residential and agricultural land sectors. Qualification for this membership is also dependent on passing the IAVI Residential and Land Agency
Course.

IAVI approved college degree courses are offered by the Dublin Institute
of Technology (DIT), Limerick Institute of Technology, University of Ulster
and the DIT/IAVI Partners Degree Programme. IAVI approved college diploma programmes are offered by the Dublin Institute of Technology and
Galway Mayo Institute of Technology.

The IAVI offers its own B.Sc. Property Studies course which is a four-
year honours degree programme for practitioners in the property area in
partnership with the Dublin Institute of Technology. The first intake of this
programme commenced in 1999 with the resources of the IAVI and DIT
available to all students. An important innovative element of this programme
is the incorporation of monitored experiential learning as an essential component of the programme. In addition an IAVI Residential and Land Agency
is open to applicants who work on a full-tine basis in the property profession. Applicants must have passed the National Leaving Certificate or its
equivalent. The course is for one year and subjects are Residential and Land
Valuation, Agency Practice, Rural Resources, Law and Residential Construction. Successful candidates who become associate members are prohibited from opening for business on their own account.

12.5 Incorporated Society of Valuers and Auctioneers

The Incorporated Society of Valuers and Auctioneers (ISVA) is a Great Britain based organisation with a membership of the order of 58 in Northern Ireland and 35 in the Republic. Membership is open to valuers and other property professionals operating in both the public and private sectors. The ISVA qualification is recognised by the Civil Service Commission, the Inland Revenue, the principal clearing banks, the building societies, the Council of Mortgage Lenders, the Local Government Training Board, the Stock Exchange, by private and public practices and within the First Directive (89/48 EEC) for the mutual recognition of qualifications within the EU.

At the time of writing a merger of the RICS and the ISVA is about to be effected. Both RICS and ISVA members have voted in favour of the merger which came into effect on 1 January 2000.

12.6 The Institute of Revenues Rating and Valuation

Arguably the most specialised of the various real estate professional bodies in Ireland is the Institute of Revenues Rating and Valuation (IRRV), which is the professional body of those involved in the levying, collection and administration of local revenues (e.g. property rates and council taxes). Its focus is on the promotion of professionalism throughout the entire local revenues procedures. It is the leading awarding body in the UK for valuation for rating purposes. Its membership encompasses both the professional administrators as well as the property valuers involved in the operation of local revenues, so it is not exclusively a real estate profession.

The categories of membership are: corporate, technician, student, affiliate, retired and honorary. The IRRV has a very small membership in the island of Ireland (35 in Northern Ireland and 7 in the Republic of Ireland), the vast majority of whom are valuers and also members of the RICS (Exhibit 1). There is representation from Northern Ireland on the Institute Council.

The routes to membership are by internally administered examinations or by exemption due to other professional qualifications. The IRRV examinations include specialised papers for rating valuation and appeals. Tuition is available through a distance-learning scheme administered by the University of Wales College, Newport. In addition there are a number of college-based courses in Scotland, England and Wales.

In addition to examination based qualification the Institute is also a founder member of the Awarding Body for the Built Environment, which administers valuation NVQs. It is developing competence-based qualifications for the Valuation Office Agency. The routes to membership are by examinations set by an independent Examining Board chaired by the former Local Government Ombudsman, Sir David Yardley.

The valuation of property for rating purposes is one of the most closely regulated areas of professional real estate practice, the bases of valuation being set down in the relevant rating statutes. Professional rating valuers are employed both in the public sector, preparing rating valuations, and in the private sector negotiating appeals against rating valuation assessments. The Institute has a Valuers Group to promote the interests of rating valuers. The IRRV membership regulations include a voluntary CPD scheme.

12.7 National Association of Estate Agents

The National Association of Estate Agents (NAEA) was established in 1962 and has a membership in Northern Ireland of 75 Fellows, 45 Associates, 20 Affiliates and 2 Special Associates (Exhibit 1). Membership of the Association is open to practising estate agents and to become an Associate member candidates must pass an admissions test and have a number of years experience. Those holding a professional qualification or NVQ Level 3 are exempt from the admission test. Those who are too young or do not have required experience join as affiliate members. NAEA offers a Certificate of Practice in Estate Agency (CPEA) and a Certificate in Residential Lettings and Management (CRLM). Both qualifications are examination based and both are achieved via distance learning programmes purchased from NAEA.

The Certificate of Practice in Estate Agency (CPEA) comprises Estate Agency Practice and Marketing, Legal Aspects of Estate Agency, Valuation and Building Construction and Management for Estate Agents. The Certificate in Residential Lettings and Management (CRLM) comprises Legal Aspects of Lettings and Management, Lettings and Management Practice and Marketing, and Business Management for Lettings Agency.

CPEA and CRLM are required for upgrading to Fellow. Alternatively candidates can undertake NVQ Level 3 in Residential Estate Agency or Lettings and Property Management Agency, and then take one examination to either gain CPEA or CRLM. The College of Estate Management in Reading also offers a course similar to CPEA which is not linked to NAEA although possession of their qualification will give upgrading to Fellow. Manchester College of Arts and Technology has recently started a pilot part-time course leading to CPEA and hope to do the same with CRLM. No previous qualifications are required to study or take examinations for CPEA or CRLM.

From the beginning of 1997 all corporate grade principles, partners and directors became bound by the Association's Code of Practice. CPD is mandatory for all members of the Association at Affiliate, Associate and Fellow grade who joined after the 1 January 1998. Members are required to fulfil 12 hours of CPD (8 hours by attendance at any relevant educational event, and up to 4 hours from relevant private study) in each year. Attainment of the required number of CPD hours is a requirement for upgrading to Associate or Fellow.

12.8 The Institute of Professional Auctioneers and Valuers

The Institute of Professional Auctioneers and Valuers (IPAV) was established in 1971 as a representative body for qualified licensed auctioneers, valuers and estate agents in Ireland. There are seven categories of IPAV membership namely, Honorary, Associate, Fellow, Affiliate, Overseas, Northern Ireland and Licentiate (Exhibit 1).

Services offered by IPAV members include sales, valuations and other services associated with all types of property including agricultural land. The IPAV designs its own courses which are audited by a panel of external examiners. These courses include: a Certificate in Auctioneering and Estate Agency Practice; Higher Diploma of Education in Estate Management Surveying; Diploma of Higher Education in Property Management and Valuation; Certificate of Proficiency in Auctioneering and Estate Agency Practice (Adults); and Certificate/Diploma in Fine & Decorative Arts.

On completion of the Certificate in Auctioneering and Estate Agency Practice, successful students may progress to the Diploma of Higher Education in Property Management and Valuation. Holders of this Diploma may then proceed to the University of Glamorgan, UK to complete a B.Sc. (Hons) in Property Management and Valuation (Auctioneering).

IPAV is a self-regulatory body, which seeks to promote professional standards among its members who subscribe to a Deposit Protection Fund.

12.9 Dublin Institute of Technology

The Dublin Institute of Technology (DIT) is an autonomous university-level institution formed under the DIT Act, 1992. It is constituted from a range of existing colleges of technology and other colleges and now provides third level education to some 22,000 students, making it the largest such establishment in the Republic of Ireland (Goldsmith, 1999). The Institute is currently being restructured on a Faculty basis. DIT has played a leading role in technological and business education in Ireland and is closely involved with the industrial, professional, economic and cultural developments. In particular, real estate education is associated with the Faculty of the Built Environment, which incorporates the School of Surveying.

The Faculty of the Built Environment has developed as a centre of excellence for the disciplines of the built environment in Ireland, which involves the effective planning, development, management and provision of professional services. This involves a broad range of academic programmes across the disciplines of architecture, real estate, construction, environmental planning and management integrated with the relevant skills involved in the construction process. This is supported by applied research and a continuing development programme with a broad range of national and international links.

Full time education for the real estate area includes two full time courses, a four year degree programme in Property Economics and a three year certificate/diploma programme entitled Auctioneering, Valuation and Estate Agency (DIT, 1999). A part time course is also offered in Property Studies over four years in partnership with the Irish Auctioneers and Valuers Institute. The Institute has also developed a two year part-time M.Sc. in Planning and Development to provide for the educational requirements for practice as a planning and development surveyor. Professional accreditation for this course is pending validation in Spring 2000.

12.9.1 BSc Hons Property Economics

This is a four-year full time honours degree course, which traditionally has been undertaken by students aiming for careers in property appraisal, development, investment and town planning. The course provides students with an education in the financial, legal, planning and construction aspects of property in the context of this investment market and the general economy.

Final year subjects include Planning, Urban Economics, Valuations, Investment Analysis. Other subjects studied include Construction, Law, Economics and Quantitative Analysis. On completion of the course, students are awarded an honours B.Sc. (Surveying). On successful completion of a test of professional competence, holders of the award are eligible for corporate membership of the Society of Chartered Surveyors and the Royal Institution of Chartered Surveyors in the UK. They are also exempted from membership examinations of the Irish Auctioneers and Valuers Institute and the Intermediate Examination of the Royal Town Planning Institute.

The minimum educational entry requirement for this course is the National Leaving Certificate with passes in six courses with at least two subjects at Grade C3 or higher on Higher Level papers. Subjects passed must include English and Mathematics. This is the normal entry standard for university level courses in Ireland. Mature applicants may be considered for admission by interview and are not required to meet normal entry requirements.

12.9.2 Diploma in Auctioneering, Valuation and Estate Agency:

This course involves a two-year certificate with candidates who achieve the required standard proceeding to the Diploma stage. Subjects studied include Valuations, Construction, Economics, Property Management, Law and Marketing. The course is aimed at students who wish to make a career in auctioneering and estate agency. The Diploma is recognised as exempting holders from the membership examinations of the Irish Auctioneers and Valuers Institute and the Institute of Professional Auctioneers and Valuers. Students from this course may apply for advanced entry to the Property Economics Degree Course at DIT or related degree courses in the UK.

The minimum educational requirement for this course is the National Leaving Certificate with passes in five subjects including Mathematics and English or Irish or an equivalent qualification.

12.9.3 BSc Hons Property Studies

This is a part-time course run by the Irish Auctioneers and Valuers Institute with DIT. Entry is open to property practitioners holding a recognised academic qualification. The course is a four-year part-time honours degree programme run on a part-time basis at the Faculty of the Built Environment, DIT. Students are placed in study groups on the basis of geographical location with experienced academic back-up support provided. A dedicated Internet website is provided for further support along with access to DIT learning facilities. Work experience forms a vital part of this degree programme and is monitored on a structured basis. The examination system for the course combines continuous assessment, written examinations, feasibility study and dissertation.

Candidates for entry must either hold recognised national educational awards such as university degrees/national diplomas, have passed relevant professional examinations or be eligible by virtue of having a minimum of five years experience in the property profession and be at least 25 years of age. Entry is possible depending on the above criteria from Year 1 to Year 3 level.(IAVI, 1999).

12.9.4 MSc in Planning and Development

This is a two-year part-time course aimed at broadening the knowledge and skills base of professionals working in the built environment area. The course specifically provides the educational requirements for practice as a planning and development surveyor. Subjects include Valuations, Law, Urban Land Economics, Planning and Development Policies, site visits and a dissertation.

The entry requirement is possession of a recognised professional qualification in planning, architecture, surveying, engineering, law, accountancy or an appropriate honours degree and a minimum of 3 years suitable work experience in the built environment field.

12.10 Galway Mayo Institute of Technology

Formerly, the Regional Technical College for the Western Region of Ireland, the Galway and Mayo Institute of Technology (GMIT) delivers programmes across five schools. The property course is delivered in the School of Engineering located within the main Galway College Campus. A distinctive feature of professional courses at GMIT is the inclusion in all such courses of a requirement to study a modern European language.

National Diploma in Business Studies (Property Valuation and Estate Agency)

The aim of this course is to provide education and training to enable candidates to practise as auctioneers, estate agents, valuers and other roles within the property sector. The minimum entry requirements for the course are the National Leaving Certificate with Grade D3 of higher in five subjects. The course is of three years duration and subjects include Valuations, Economics, Law, Building Studies, Modern Languages, Planning and Property Marketing and Development. The course graduates are qualified to apply for full membership of the Irish Auctioneers and Valuers Institute and recognition is currently being sought for membership of the Society of Chartered Surveyors. A number of the graduates of the existing programme opt to continue their studies to degree level at UK universities.

12.11 Limerick Institute of Technology

Formerly the Regional Technical College, Limerick, Limerick Institute of Technology (LIT) now operates under a governing body established under the Regional Technical Colleges Act 1992. Historical roots for the Institute date back to an 1852 School of Arts & Crafts and responsibility passed to the City of Limerick Vocational Educational Authority in 1930. The Institute has developed to modern times as a significant contributor to the industrial, commercial and cultural development of the mid-west region. At the School of the Built Environment, the property/real estate course is entitled a professional degree/diploma in chartered surveying (Property Valuation and Management).

– BSc Property Valuation and Management

This course was introduced with the significant expansion, which occurred in LIT in the 1990s, with the development of a number of degree programmes including property in the built environment area. The Property Valuation and Management Course (PVM) is designed to develop a thorough understanding of the dynamic economic, management and investment principles which shape the property market. The course also is expected to assist students gain a thorough knowledge of construction and maintenance of buildings and planning and regulatory processes, which govern their use.

The course is a four-year sandwich, consisting of two years full time study followed by one year of practical experience and a fourth year in full time study. The minimum entry requirement is the Leaving Certificate Examination with Grade D3 of higher in five subjects, including Mathematics and English, two of the subjects must be at a minimum of Grade C3 on higher papers.

Course subjects include: Property Valuation
                           Economics
                           Construction Technology
                           Law
                           Economics
                           Urban Development Management &
                               Planning

Successful graduates of the PVM Course gain full exemption from the professional examinations of the Society of Chartered surveyors in Ireland, the Irish Auctioneers and Valuers Institute and the Royal Institution of Chartered Surveyors. The Institute has validation arrangements in place by which the degree award for this course is by Heriot-Watt University, Edinburgh, Scotland.

12.12 The University of Ulster

The University of Ulster is the sole provider of degree level real estate courses in Northern Ireland. Course delivery takes place at the University's Jordanstown campus, in Newtownabbey on the northern outskirts of Belfast. The School of the Built Environment within the Faculty of Engineering offers real estate courses at honours and masters degree levels.

12.12.1   BSc (Hons) Surveying (with Specialisms)

The BSc (Hons) Surveying (with Specialisms) programme is offered in both full-time and part-time modes of study. For students intending to enter one of the real estate professions, the Estate Management Specialism would be the preferred route. This course is fully accredited by the RICS, IAVI and ISVA.

By full-time study the degree takes four years, the third year being a placement or sandwich year spent in supervised work experience in an approved professional office. By part-time study the programme takes up to six years, with those employed in relevant work being exempted from the placement period. In either mode, students offering prior relevant qualifications or substantial relevant prior experience may be eligible for partial exemptions from the taught modules.

All subjects in the course are taught from first principles, with no required pre-entry subjects other than GCSE Maths and English at grade "C" or better. Approximately half the entrants come from an A-level background (entry requirements minimum 18 points, average circa 21 points), but increasing numbers come from the more vocational BTEC and GNVQ routes. The asking grades from these qualifications are set at levels deemed to equate to the A-level points levels. Overseas applicants must prove ability in the English language. For mature applicants (over 21 years of age at admission) the required academic entrance standards can be viewed more flexibly, with work experience compensating for lack of academic qualifications. This course is a popular route for the more successful students from BTEC courses at local institutes of further and higher education to upgrade their BTEC qualifications in order to achieve membership of the RICS and/or other professional institutes.

Whilst admission to the course is not based on quotas for each specialism, typically circa 30 full-time students per year elect for the Estate Management specialism, of whom 2-3 may be mature entrants. The majority of students are from Northern Ireland, but usually there will be 2 or 3 from the Republic of Ireland and perhaps also 2 or 3 from SE Asia. In addition there is an annual intake of part-time entrants, usually circa 5 students, who normally will have been working for at least two years in a real estate or closely related organisation.

The core areas of study within the course are economics, building construction, land law, property market and development economics, planning law and property valuation, with some choice of modules in final year. In final year every student undertakes a dissertation involving a major piece of independent research in a real estate related area.

The course is based on a first year, which introduces the basic principles of economics, law, building construction, property development and surveying practice. The second year develops in more detail the specialised areas of planning, property valuation, land law and urban economics. The third (placement) year is a vital element of the course which exposes the student to real-life practice, demonstrating the application of the theory and the integration of the various elements of study within the context of real estate practice. It is an important personal development exercise for the less experienced students and a valuable opportunity to establish personal network contacts within the professions for all students. Many students who impress employers during their placement year are offered permanent employment by them on graduation. The final year provides a deeper examination of specialist knowledge and current issues in professional practice in relation to the development, valuation and appraisal, and management of property. The choice of dissertation topic allows the student to specialise within his or her chosen field.

12.12.2 MSc Real Estate and Facilities Management

A post-graduate taught MSc in Real Estate and Facilities Management is also offered, currently only available by part-time study. A recently introduced programme, it replaces the MSc in Property Development, (first intake 1999/2000), and has not yet been submitted to any professional bodies for accreditation.

The course covers business management and finance, corporate real estate strategy, project and facilities management, and real estate appraisal, finance and markets. It is designed to appeal to graduates from other disciplines who find their career paths leading to managerial positions with responsibility for property asset development and management within both the public and private sectors. The taught programme extends over two academic years, with students subsequently undertaking a research thesis to complete the masters qualification.

The core staff responsible for delivery of the courses at the University of Ulster are mainly RICS and IAVI qualified, with a mixture of public and private sector professional experience. On the MSc programme staff from other construction-related professional organisations share the teaching. In addition both courses make extensive use of guest lecturers from the property industry to give specialised lectures and case studies from recent professional practice.

12.13 Issues Influencing the Education of Property Professionals

The property curriculum taught in the colleges reflects many influences relating to political, legal, social, economic and environmental differences within Ireland as well as specific property market variations attributable to the local area. However at a broad level a consideration of the real estate curriculum normally focuses on two major issues. The first concerns the curriculum paradigm in particular the knowledge and skill base required for current and perceived future professional needs. The typical property curriculum comprises modules or subjects with discrete content which are grouped into a course or programme that is usually subject to professional body accreditation. The structure of the course or programme in terms of integration and coherence and the sequencing and content of the modules will reflect the requirements of the accrediting professional organisation as well as the specialisms and strengths of the faculty. The aim of the curriculum is to provide effective real property decision makers, professionals armed with the concepts, techniques and skills required to solve current and future problems (Black et al, 1996).

The second issue concerns the learning paradigm or how the curriculum is taught. The most common approach is the textbook model which seeks to utilise the most up-to-date literature so that students understand and can apply current techniques in the discipline (Epley, 1996). In this model the typical learning environment is passive in nature, built upon the lecture-seminar/discussion model which may or may not involve students in the learning process depending upon the interest and skill of the tutor. Butler, Guntermann and Wolverton (1998) have identified the principal shortfall of the textbook model as whether or not it produces students who can function successfully in the real estate business due to its limited ability to confront reality. In order to integrate theory and practice many property courses utilise a period of placement or work experience varying from one year to shorter periods so that students are exposed to real life situations. In other situations students are exposed to real life problems through integrated project work whereby they have to proffer solutions comparable to those expected in practice. Such learning environments are essential in property courses as employers expect graduates to possess skills enabling them to work in an active environment of changing concepts, new technology and collaborative relationships. Thus, the learning paradigm requires a change from the traditional passive educational delivery system into a more proactive environment of active learning and real world experience.

These learning environments highlight that real estate as an applied discipline is both multi-disciplinary and inter-disciplinary. In contrast to the

United States, where most real estate schools are located in university business or finance departments, in Ireland, like the UK, the discipline is predominantly related to built environment disciplines such as quantity surveying, construction, civil engineering and architecture. Within Ireland the primary focus of most property courses is the valuation of land and buildings with other modules and subjects supporting this central area of specialism. However as Graaskamp argued real estate is a multi-disciplinary synthesis and should be taught as a process of dynamic interactions (Graaskamp 1976). Real estate is multi-disciplinary in nature as competent understanding requires knowledge of a combination of disciplines for example, commercial site selection involves understanding of geography, geology, civil engineering, landscape architecture, architecture, economics, finance, accounting, marketing, law and psychology. In addition real estate is inter-disciplinary because it blends concepts and theories of several traditional disciplines to create a new synthesis. For example, discounted cash flow analysis is the result of an inter-disciplinary blending of accounting, finance and economics (Black et al, 1996).

Currently much attention is being focused on the skills of real estate graduates and their ability to operate within an increasingly sophisticated business environment. Criticisms have been made that the profession needs to utilise the same financial language as investors. In particular property terms such as ERVs, years purchase and equivalent yield mean little to investors and their advisers who are used to dealing with net present value, internal rate of return and volatility concepts. The argument for greater integration of business skills into the real estate curriculum is increasingly occupying the education debate. The practice of property investment has made significant advances in the past decade nevertheless investment performance from property in recent years has generally disappointed investors. Consequently through a desire of multi-asset managers to understand and impose discipline upon property or through property professionals seeking to do a better job, considerable effort has been expended in the last decade in bringing property into line with other assets.

The manifestation of the influence of investment markets on property is demonstrated in the techniques deployed to evaluate assets, construct portfolios and assess future incomes and returns. Discounted cash flow methodology, the basic tool of modern portfolio theory, and an ever more sophisticated level of rent and total return forecasting at finer and finer spatial scales have all been increasingly deployed. There is a further manifestation of this change, namely in the language used within the property industry. The multifarious yields used in traditional property valuation are being replaced or at least being accompanied by internal rates of return and to a lesser extent net present values. In addition the importance of research informing property investment theory and practice has become increasingly recognised. Nevertheless it is considered that due to data constraints and a marked reluctance by property professionals to utilise sophisticated investment techniques understanding within the field of property has remained experiential rather than research based. Intellectually, property has been, until recently left far behind other investment fields such as equities and bonds.

The growth of a research culture within real estate is being promoted by annual conferences sponsored by the RICS (Cutting Edge), the European Real Estate Society (ERES), the American Real Estate Society (ARES) and the American Real Estate and Urban Economics Association (AREUEA). A primary function of these conferences is the enhancement of research and publication opportunities for academics, and to a lesser degree, professionals in the property field. The topics of papers presented at annual meetings reflect the diversity of the property field for example, investment, valuation, agency, corporate finance, international, law, market analysis, corporate real estate and taxation. The breadth of activity clearly demonstrates a richly construed field (Black et al, 1996). Cogent questions about the role of property as an investment vehicle have led to essential research being undertaken not only in the spirit of academic enquiry but more importantly because such research is essential to the profession, investors and occupiers. It is in the interest of the profession that colleges undertake research both to support academic standards and to ensure that they produce the best possible graduates who posses up-to-date and relevant knowledge.

The real estate curriculum must evolve in order to meet the needs of the profession in terms of producing graduates at the highest managerial and technical levels. The way forward in developing the curriculum lies in the application of rigorous thought to all types of professional problems with full support from the profession. Among key issues are the funding of education and research, the provision of information and data to form the basis for research projects and finally the more ready acceptance of new ideas and the willingness to challenge old ones. The profession must evolve to meet these challenges as it has evolved in the past, or it will wither away. Developments in real estate education and research will, in the long run, determine the future of real estate as a profession.

APPENDIX

Exhibit 1: Real Estate Education in Ireland

	SCS	RICS	IAVI
Route to Membership **Accredited degree route**	-accredited diploma/degree -minimum 24 months monitored experience -interim submission -critical analysis -final assessment to include presentation on critical analysis and interview	-accredited UG or PG degree -minimum 24 months of monitored experience -interim submission -critical analysis -final assessment interview	-successful completion of recognised course plus at least one year's approved professional experience -Institute now moving towards degree-level minimum standard
Professional experience route / Institute Examinations	-A Direct Entry -candidates over 30 years of age -10 years relevant experience -sit full diet of final examinations set by SCS -12 months monitored experience -final assessment including critical analysis and interview -B Professional Entry -candidates hold cognate degree or equivalent professional qualification -10 years relevant experience -sit three examinations in direct final examinations -12 months monitored experience -final assessment including critical analysis and interview	-non-accredited university degree or professional qualification -minimum 10 years relevant experience -minimum 3 core modules normally from final year of an accredited course or equivalent -minimum 12 months of monitored experience -critical analysis -final assessment interview	-direct final examinations of IAVI with appropriate practical experience. From October 1999 entrants required to follow 4-year part-time degree -holders of other professional qualifications recognised by the Institute and appropriate professional experience -Successful completion of Institute's one-year residential and land agency course for Associate Membership
Accredited institutions	-SCS accredits courses - not institutions.· -courses at Dublin Institute of Technology, Limerick Institute of Technology	-RICS recognises over 180 approved courses worldwide -NI - University of Ulster BSc Hons	-Property Management & Valuation - LIT - Property Economics - Dublin Institute of Technology

	SCS	RICS	IAVI
		Surveying with Specialisms (Estate Management)	-BSc (Hons) Surveying [Est. Mgt.] - University of Ulster
			-Other appropriate overseas degree courses
			-Auctioneering, Valuation & Estate Agency - DIT
			-National Diploma in Business Studies - GMIT
			-Other appropriate overseas diploma courses
Categories of Membership	-Members -Probationers	-Fellow -Member -Probationer -Student	-Fellow -Member -Associate

	SCS		RICS		IAVI
Number of members	GP	P&D	GP	P&D	Membership c. 1,450, of which c. 200 are fellows
	Members 400	30	Members		
	Probationers 220	N.A.	(984) Fellow 104	4	
			Member 278	2	
			Probationers		
			(214) 64	1	
			Students		
			(212) 78	5	
National Regulations of Professional Practice	Auctioneers and Estate Agents Acts		Property Misdescriptions Act and Estate Agents Act		Auctioneers & House Agents Acts 1947 and 1967 (as amended by 1993 Finance Act) require Estate Agents/Auctioneers in R.O.I. to be licensed to carry Insurance Board and to have business accounts certified. N.I. as per RICS etc.
Professional Membership Regulations	-SCS bye laws and regulations - covers standard issues e.g. Professional Conduct, Insurances, CPD Regulations		-RICS publishes Rules of Conduct and Disciplinary Procedures -Conduct of professional activities or insurers, advertising		-Code of Conduct covers: -professional Ethics - including conflict of interest, confidentiality, duty of care and profes-

	SCS	RICS	IAVI
		-Conflicts of interest	sional standards
		-Practice details particularly adherence to AVS Committee & A V Manual	-compliance with statutory licensing and accounting requirements
		-Properties outside UK, IVSC guidelines to be followed	-compliance with CPD requirements
		-Compulsory PII Regulations	-disciplinary procedures - Disciplinary Committee has powers of reprimand, fines, suspensions and expulsion
		-Members Accounts Regulations	
		-CPD Regulations	

Role of professional body

	SCS	RICS	IAVI
Design of accredited courses	-regulation of accredited courses -guidance for courses seeking accreditation -development and delivery of Society direct final examinations	-regulations for accredited centres (institution offered course(s) for 7 years) and accredited courses. Guidelines for design of courses seeking accreditation.	-design of Institute's own courses -Education Committee involved with colleges in design of new courses
Monitoring of accredited courses	-revalidation process for existing courses every five years -regular monitoring of specific details dealt with by Education Committee	-annual monitoring of specified details	-review visits to institutions offering accredited courses (5-yearly intervals)
Delivery of teaching	-specified in course structure and documentation	-teaching methods must be specified as part of wider course structure and contact	-majority of teachers are full time third level college lecturers -members also involved with teaching of own courses and input as visiting lecturers on recognised courses
Placement supervised work experience	-contributes to APC	-contributes to APC	-under review
Post-graduation supervised work experience	-monitored by SCS	-monitored by RICS	-monitored by IAVI
Commis-sioning	-Research committee makes awards on annual	-RICS Education Trust - twice yearly round	

	SCS	RICS	IAVI
Real Estate research	basis -CPD and seminar programmes	of awards	
Undertaking Real Estate research	-occasional sponsored research -publication of property and construction review quarterly magazine -practice handbook updated regularly	-RE research published as part of RICS Research Findings Series and published research reports	

	IRRV	NAEA	IPAV
Routes to Membership			
Accredited Course Route	-Tuition offered by distance learning or day release courses at a range of Great Britain colleges. No course delivery in Ireland.	-Certificate of Practice in Real Estate Agency (CPEA) and Certificate in Residential Lettings and Management (CRLM). Distance learning, exam based offered by NAEA.	-Successful completion of recognised course plus two years professional experience.
Professional Experience Route / Institute Examinations	-Internally administered examinations, including specialised examinations for Rating Valuation and Appeals. -Holders of other professional qualifications eligible for full or partial exemption from the Institute's examinations.	-Associate member must pass admissions test and have number of years experience. Holders of a professional qualification or NVQ Level 3 are exempt from admissions test. -Affiliate member - too young: lack experience.	-Seven years experience in the auctioneering business. -Successful completion of IPAV evening course and two years professional experience.
Accredited Institutions	IRRV distance education	-Manchester CAT offers pilot p-t course -College of Estate Management offers similar course to CPEA.	-Senior College, Dun Laoghaire, Dublin, Ireland. -Cork College of Commerce, Ireland. -University of Glamorgan, U.K.
Categories of Membership	Corporate Technician Student Affiliate	Fellow Associate Affiliate Special Associate	Honorary Licentiate/Student Affiliate Associate

	IRRV	NAEA	IPAV
Routes to Membership			
	Retired Honorary		Fellow Overseas Northern Ireland
Number of Members	ROI 7, NI 35 of these 36 are also members of the RICS. 35 are full corporate members, 1 affiliated member and 6 are retired.	NI Fellow 75 Associate 45 Affiliate 20 Special Associate 2	Honorary 6 Licentiate/Student 185 Affiliate 14 Associate 478 Fellow 18 Overseas 2 Northern Ireland 10 713
National Regulations of Professional Practice		Property Misdescriptions Act and Estate Agents Act.	Auctioneers and House Agents Acts 1947 and 1967 (as amended by 1993 Finance Act) require auctioneers/ estate agents in the Republic of Ireland to be licensed to carry insurance bond and to have business accounts certified. Northern Ireland: Property Misdescriptions Act and Estate Agents Act.
Professional Membership Regulations	Promotion of professional voluntary CPD scheme. NB: Institute includes non-valuer practitioners involved in levying, collections and administration of local revenues.	Code of Practice for Residential Agents Rules of Conduct: duty to maintain separate client's accounts; duty of care and maintaining professional standards.	Code of Conduct covers: -Duties to clients and professional ethics; -Disciplinary procedures; -Duties in terms of agency terms.
Role of Professional Body			
Design of accredited courses	-Design of Institute's own courses.		-Design of Institute's own courses; -Academic Council involved with educational institutions in development of new courses.
Monitoring of accredited courses	-Regular monitoring of delivery at local centres.		-Ongoing by Academic Council.
Delivery of teaching			

	IRRV	NAEA	IPAV
Routes to Membership			
Placement supervised work experience			-Not part of IPAV courses.
Commissioning Real Estate research			-Under review.
Undertaking Real Estate research			-Publication of performance index for Irish housing market.

REFERENCES

Black, R T, Carn, N G, Diaz III, J and Rabianski, J (1996). The Role of the American Real Estate Society in Defining and Pumolgating the Study of Real Property *Journal of Real Estate Research,* 12(2), 183-194.

Butler, J Q, Guntermann, K L and Wolverton, M (1998). Integrating the Real Estate Curriculum, *Journal of Real Estate Practice and Education*, Vol 1(1), 51-66.

Davis, J P (1999) Educating Property Professionals for a Changing World, *Property Valuer,* Vol 18(3), 14-16.

DIT (1999), *Faculty of the Built Environment Entry 2000 Prospectus.* Dublin Institute of Technology, Dublin.

Epley, D R (1996). The current body of knowledge used in real estate education and issues in need of further research, *Journal of Real Estate Research*, 12(2), 229-236.

Goldsmith, B (1999), *DIT Official website*, Dublin Institute of Technology, Dublin.

Graaskamp, J A (1976). Redefining the Role of University Education in Real Estate and Urban Land Economics, *Real Estate Appraiser,* 42(2), 23-28.

IAVI (1999). *BSc (Hons) in Property Studies. Part-time course document.* Irish Auctioneers and Valuers Institute, Dublin.

IPAV (1999) *Corporate Booklet,* Institute of Professional Auctioneers and Valuers, Dublin.

RICS (1998a) *The Official Guide to Surveying Education*, Second, Edition, GTI Specialist Publishers Ltd, Wallingford, Oxon.

RICS (1998b) *APC Requirements & Competencies,* 2nd ed, Royal Institution of Charteered Surveyors, Coventry.

Society of Chartered Surveyors.(1999) *Guide to APC for Candidates and Employers*, Society of Chartered Surveyors, Dublin.

Wolverton, M, Butler, J and Guntermann, K (1997). Denying Traditional Senses: Lessons about Program Change, *Teaching in Higher Education*, 2(3), 295-312.

Chapter 13

Israel

Daniel Gat
Technion, Israel Institute of Technology, Haifa, Israel

13.1 Introduction

Real Estate Education in Israel is only at an embryonic stage. There are few serious real estate programmes, and of these, only one is a bona-fide university level curriculum aiming at an academic degree. I shall describe the few programmes that exist according to the following categories: the academic-degree programme (chapter 13.3.1); non-degree programmes at universities and colleges (13.3.2); general unfocused programmes including short-term workshops (13.3.3). Before turning to the programmes, I shall start with a brief description of the Israeli real estate scene.

13.2 The Israeli Real Estate Scene

13.2.1 The Demand Side

Israel is a small country with a population of 6 million. However, building activity is usually very brisk since it is a society that encourages immigration and which also has a fairly high natural rate of increase, especially when compared to other societies of similar socio-economic status. Diagram1 summarises Israel's construction history over the last 40 years. It shows not only the level of construction but also the degree to which it ebbs and flows. As might be expected, housing construction dominates all other types.

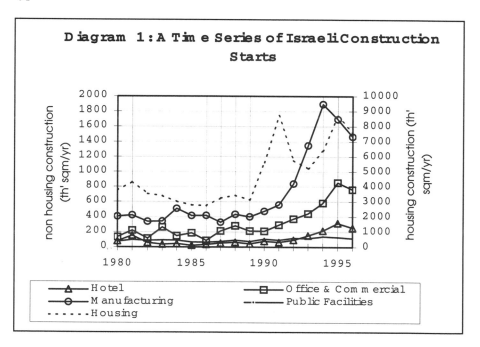

Diagram 1: A Time Series of Israeli Construction Starts

13.2.2 The Supply Side – Private & Public

In the past, the supply side has been dominated by government and quasi-government entrepreneurial organisations, especially during years of high immigration. With the growing trend towards privatisation and a market dominated economy, three parallel changes are occurring: (1) Most of the recent construction is being initiated by the private market. (2) The private market's structure, formerly comprised of numerous small builders, each putting up one or two condominium buildings per year, has been transformed. Much of the construction is now dominated by a few score of very large builders, many of whom are traded on the Tel Aviv Stock Exchange. (3) The real estate services sector has become more specialised, differentiated and computerised. This includes, *inter alia*, the provision of instant mortgages – over the phone or via the Internet; working drawings being wired between designer, consulting engineer or builder; construction tenders being submitted over the net; and property rental and sales advertising over the net.

All of these changes would appear to require a major upgrading of the professional real estate workforce, but strangely enough, little of that is taking place. Following a few words on the special situation of the government's (state) monopoly of the land-market, the rest of this paper will report in brief on the Real Estate studies scene in Israel.

13.2.3 Israel's Land Administration

Central government is a major player in the Israeli land market, even more so than in countries which are well known for their social housing tradition (e.g. Holland and Switzerland). Although the direct supply of new housing by central government has receded, over 90 percent of the remaining developable land is owned - and tightly controlled - by the Israel Land Administration (ILA). As a rule, the ILA does not sell land and, when it does relinquish control, it is via a leasing arrangement that severely constrains the lessee. For example, changing or upgrading the land-use status needs ILA approval, and also entails the payment of an approval fee. Such fees may often reduce the potential profit, even to the point of making the proposed changes no longer commercially viable.

For such reasons, a major part of the education and subsequent practice of real estate appraisers is devoted to learning about the ILA's rules and the interpretation of their financial implications.

The small number of lawyers and financial consultants who are familiar with the ILA rules, in addition to their knowledge of tax laws, are in great demand. One would therefore expect that real-estate law and finance-oriented academic programmes would flourish. This is hardly the case however.

I will begin my description of the Israeli real estate educational field with the one possible exception.

13.3 Real Estate Education in Israel

13.3.1 The Academic-Degree Programme at HDC

The only academic, degree-oriented real-estate programme was set up five years ago at the Herzelia Inter Disciplinary Center (HIDC) which is an accredited, private college. HIDC specialises in Law and other business related professions. For help in setting up the real estate programme, HIDC established an early connection with Prof. Peter Linneman of the Wharton School of Business in the USA, and it maintains close ties with that school. The purpose and scope of the programme is best described by its formal Statement of Vision:

> "The Real Estate Program at HID offers students the opportunity to combine a B.A. in business administration with a major in real estate studies. This unique program provides students with both a solid theoretical background and an intensive practical experience in the areas of international and Israeli real estate markets. The program promotes understanding of, the capability to analyse complex and sophisticated issues of the business world with a specific reference to the real estate dimension. The numerous courses are based on a variety of academic disciplines that are essential for real estate decision-making: Economics, Law, Engineering, Marketing, Finance, Appraisal, and others. A particular emphasis placed upon real estate entrepreneurship within the business environment."

Enrolment and target audience. According to Dr. Danny Ben-Shahar, the programme chair:

> "The real estate programme is offered to both business students and students in the joint law and business programme. These are only undergraduate programmes for now, although we are planning to open our first Master's programme next year...
>
> ...The programme is far more appealing to students in the law and business programme than to students studying merely business. While this is very common in other business schools worldwide (where the real estate department is generally small compared to finance or marketing for example), I believe that this is also a consequence of the local economic situation. Having said the above, I would assess that the real estate pro-

gramme is probably about 20% of the law-business programme and about 10% of the business programme."

Past annual enrolments for the programme have been as high as 60, but have dropped to approximately 40 during the past two years. Ben-Shahar says that this is probably a consequence of the recent severe real-estate slump.

Curriculum. The real estate curriculum is characterised by a shift in weight from general business courses during the early semesters, adding more and more real estate courses, many of which are electives, towards the second half of the programme. A typical Bachelor-of-Business-in-RE curriculum is shown in the appendix.

Industry placement of programme graduates. Law and business graduates are mostly placed in law offices specialising in real estate. Business students are employed mostly within the real estate and finance areas.

Faculty. There are very few permanent members of staff at HIDC. The school relies on a core of under a dozen permanent lecturers, many of whom are recent Ph.D.s, and a large number of external academic lecturers.

13.3.2 Certificate (non-degree) programmes at universities and colleges

13.3.2.1 Overview

Non-degree real estate certificate programmes are offered at three institutions: the Technion's extension programme; the Tel Aviv University Social Sciences department; and the Israel Management College, which has active branches in all the major cities. The three institutions offer programmes in real estate assessment and in brokerage.

The importance of the appraisal programmes stems from their main purpose, which is to prepare students for the government's Department of Justice (JD) examinations, and for those required by the Israeli Land Assessors Association, which maintains a quasi-monopoly in valuation. The JD's exams are a necessary pre-requisite for professionals wishing to have their work recognised by the courts. Similarly, brokers now formally qualify by taking the Bureau of Brokerage examination required by law. This has created a market for brokerage courses.

The following three academic institutions offer certificate (non-degree) programmes in real estate assessment and in brokerage:

- The Technion Continuing Studies Department (in Haifa)
- Tel Aviv University Social Sciences Department
- The Israel Management College (with branches in Haifa & Tel Aviv)

The programmes offered by these institutions are similar, since they are aimed at similar audiences and have a common goal: to familiarise participants with the fundamentals of real estate and to prepare them for formal state-approved examinations. Therefore, only the first set, the two Technion programmes, will be described.

13.3.2.2 Real Estate Assessment and Real Estate Asset Management.

This programme has a dual purpose: to endow the participant with a knowledge base useful for coping with real estate assessment problems; and to prepare the student for the Real Estate Assessors' formal examination. Admittance to the programme is usually limited to persons with a college education, but others with proven practical experience are also considered. The programme lasts for two academic years and is based on 460 credit hours. Study subjects include: assessment tables – their construction and application; asset measurement; planning and construction fundamentals and planning and construction law; city planning; construction engineering and construction costs; economics and the Israeli economy; law, including the land registration and taxation laws; asset management; rights in land; land use; and land transactions. Students are required to succeed in all of the examinations before being awarded their certificate.

13.3.2.3 Real Estate Development, Management and Brokerage.

This programme also has a dual purpose: to endow the student with practical and theoretical knowledge which is helpful to those who are or would like to be involved in real estate management, including: brokers, architects, builders, lawyers, and construction firm managers. Admittance is open to anyone holding a high-school certificate. The programme lasts one year and is based on 180 credit hours. The material studied covers that which is required by the official brokerage exam. The list of study subjects, which is rather long, includes: the Israeli real estate market; fundamentals of real estate brokerage; real estate taxation; brokerage laws and regulations; marketing, sales promotion and public relations; real estate transactions; investment feasibility; real estate financing; business plan preparation for a real estate project; contracts; corporate structure; civil engineering basics.

13.3.3 General Studies Real Estate Programmes

The Haifa University Extension Studies programme offers the most ambitious real estate programme of the third type. According to the stated purpose of the Haifa-University programme *"the real estate studies programme offers two tracks that enable participants to specialise and acquire all the knowledge necessary to succeed in the real estate brokerage exams required by law.*" However, course descriptions, in their effort to recruit students, are often guilty of unwarranted self-praise.

The first track, called *Basic Real Estate Studies*, lasts a year and requires 80 credit hours. Its stated purpose is: "to widen professional horizons, by endowing participants with the basic necessary tools... The programme is aimed at persons interested in future real estate work, e.g. brokers, consultants, etc."

The second track is entitled *Entrepreneurial Real Estate Management*. It also lasts a year, but requires 150 credit hours. It is aimed at "professionals working in real estate or those wishing to initiate a real estate project, including developers, investors, brokers, employees of construction firms, and anyone who wishes to enhance his/her real estate knowledge."

The Haifa University programme does not offer any more details regarding its course material and accordingly seems to lack focus.

As well as the Haifa University programme, this category includes short and medium term workshops, lasting from a couple of days to a few months. These workshops are often advertised in the news media. Sometimes real estate service companies, whose business is brokerage, valuation or real estate management and consulting, offer them. The purpose of these workshops is presumably more promotional than educational.

13.3.4 Other real estate and related studies

It is rather surprising that while there are many economics and business-management degree-programmes in Israeli colleges and universities, real estate studies have not taken off. As already stated, apart from the HIDC programme, no academic institutions offer RE programmes. Only one of them offers RE for-credit courses. The Technion runs two elective RE courses, one at entry level and an advanced RE economics seminar, both of which are offered to graduate city- and regional planning students. These two courses have generated a brisk and steady enrolment over their ten-year lifetime. In addition, related courses in urban economics and in location theory are taught as part of several graduate degree programmes in Urban Studies at the universities of Tel Aviv, Bar Ilan, Jerusalem-Hebrew and Ben Gurion in the Negev.

13.4 Post Script

Even as I write this paper, I have been invited to join a Technion committee whose purpose is to prepare a detailed proposal for a Master's in Real Estate program. This task was initiated by the Dean of Extension Studies, and it is part of a deliberate Technion policy to transform the Extension Studies into a set of fully accredited academic graduate programs. It also reflects a realization that the need for an MRE exists and is rising. As further evidence of this need, it is interesting to report the following: During the first week of May 2001 I had participated in the real estate session of the Israeli Economic Society's annual meeting. The session, chaired by Dr. Danny Ben-Shahar, (mentioned elsewhere in this paper) was heavily attended by real estate practitioners, public as well as private, by bankers and by researchers, including members of the Central Bank research unit. This was in sharp contrast to the negligible attendance of the same session two years ago.

REFERENCES

Herzelia Inter-disciplinary Center (HIDC), Ted Arison Business School
Technion – Israel Institue of Technology, Continuing Studies
Haifa University, Continuing Studies
Tel Aviv University, Social Sciences Department
The Israel Management College

ACKNOWLEDGEMENTS

I wish to thank Dr. Danny Ben Shahar for responding quickly and in detail to a sequence of questions regarding his real estate programme at HIDC. Much of the rest of the material in the paper is based on the following Internet home pages:

APPENDIX 1

The Herzelia Interdisciplinary Center RE Curriculum

Semester 1	Semester 2
Public Law Computer and Communications	Business Communication in English
Fundamentals Fundamentals of Accounting	Mathematics II
Social Psychology of Management	Statistics I
Law of Contract	Introduction to the Business Firm
Introduction to Micro-Economics	Israel's Middle Eastern Neighbours
Business Communication in English	Information Systems in Management
Mathematics I	Corporation Law
	Introduction to Macro Economics

Semester 3	Semester 4
Foundations of Finance	Research Methods and Marketing Research
Organizational Behavior I	Managerial Accounting
Principles of Marketing Management	Principles to Operations Management
Statistics II	The Firm in the Middle East
Taxation Law	Introduction to Econometrics
Introduction to Operations Research	Theory of Investments
The Consumer and the Firm in the Economy	Critical Thinking
Macro Economics	Organizational Behavior II
Environment Real-Estate Courses:	Real-Estate Courses:
Town Planning and Building Law	Urban Economics
Information Technologies Courses:	Land Use Policy
Introduction to Computer Science with	Law of Property
Visual Basic	Information Technologies Courses:
Systems Analysis and Software	Communications and Networks
Engineering I	Systems Analysis and Software
	Engineering II
	Database Management
	Tourism & Hotels Management Courses:
	Introduction to Tourism and Hotels management (Elective)

Semester 5	Semester 6
Seminar in Business Administration I	Seminar in Business Administration II
Economics of Israel	The Capital Market in Israel
Financial Statement Analysis	Economics of Israel
Finance Courses :	The Firm in the Global Market
Securities Regulation	Business Administration in the Internet Age
Real Estate Finance	(Elective)
Risk Management and Trading	Finance Courses :
Simulation games and Negotiation Processes	Introduction to Banking
Investment Banking	Credit Evaluation and Management
Pricing Policy (Elective)	Law of Banking and Bank Securities
Real-Estate Courses :	Trading Systems on Stock Exchanges
Real Estate Finance	Financial Securities Evaluation and Trading
Land Enterpreneurship	Antitrust (Elective)
Transaction related to the Isreali Land Administration	Applied & Empirical Research in Finance and Economics (Elective)
Issues in Town Planning	
Pricing Policy (Elective)	

Information Technologies Courses :
    Software Development with Visual
    Basic
    Introduction to Multimedia Program-
    ming
    Final Project
Marketing Courses :
    Introduction to Business Multimedia
    Consumer and Marketing Legislation
    Distribution Policies Consumer Beha-
    vior
    Project Course I
    Intellectual Property Law (Elective)
Managerial Decision-Making (Elective)

Real Estate Courses :
    Simulation games and Negotiation Proc-
    esses
    International Real Estate
    Research Methods and Marketing Re-
    search
    Financial Securities Evaluation and Trad-
    ing
    Law of Banking and Bank Securities
    (Elective)
    Antitrust (Elective)
    Topics in Applied Real Estate Finance
    (Elective)
    Seminar in Finance and Applied Econom-
    ics (Elective)
Information Technologies Courses :
    Simulation games and Negotiation Proc-
    esses
    Selected topics in Networking, Internet
    and Information
    Final Project II
    High-Tech Entrepreneurship (Elective)
    Computer Law (Elective)
Marketing Courses :
    Global Marketing
    Interactive Marketing
    Pricing Policy
    Product Policy
    Simulation games and Negotiation Proc-
    esses
    Integrated Marketing Communication
    Project Course II
    Public Relations - Reputation and Vision
    Antitrust (Elective)
Direct and Database Marketing (Elective)

Chapter 14

Italy

Maurizio d'Amato
1st School of Engineering, Polytechnic of Bari, Bari, Italy

14.1 Introduction[1]

There are two main recurring models of real estate education. The first is the model followed in the U.S. business schools[2], in which real estate is essentially viewed as a particular aspect of financial resource allocation. In this context, real estate education is taught with a financial perspective, as a subset of accounting, finance and urban economy. The second approach could be referred to as the British RICS model. This institution has accredited courses where real property is studied from several perspectives, including Economics, Law, Construction, Planning, Finance and Management. In Italy there is not one only one recognised institution which accredits coordinates and promotes courses on real estate. Real estate problems are essentially analysed from legal, planning and technical perspectives. The U.S. type of approach has not been developed.

14.2 Emerging Aspects in the Italian Real Estate Market

It is possible to observe some emerging aspects of the Italian real estate market.

In the past, the Italian real estate market was characterised by a preponderance of "conventional values". According to the "Equo Canone Law" (392/78), residential rents were based on a mathematical formula, and were generally lower than open-market rents. This law has been partially changed by a recent reform (L.431/98) which allows the opportunity for free negotiation of leases. The organisation and procedures of the Land Registry are starting to be changed in order to bring fiscal and market valuations closer to each other.

Unfortunately, the high tax burden on property transactions means that the real price paid in a transaction is still difficult to ascertain as part of the real price may not be officially declared . This is the reason why real estate market data are generally kept confidential and the provision of accurate real estate analysis and forecasting is quite difficult.

As a consequence, importance is being placed on the contribution stimulated and offered by Prof. Simonotti[3] who, for the first time, has defined standards for collection of real estate data.

The latest emerging aspect is the increasing integration between the real estate and capital markets with the introduction and growth of the Italian REIT known as *Fondi Chiusi Immobiliari*, which is in the form of a "blind pool" closed real estate fund. Others funds include *DB Fondi Chiusi Immobiliari*, *Credito Italiano Fondi Chiusi Immobiliari*, *Polis* and *BNL Fondi Chiusi Immobiliari*. These new players have defined a new, increasingly strategic role for real estate finance and call for qualified professionals to carry out real estate appraisal. There is also growth in the number of real estate investors. In fact, a lot of great companies as Pirelli, Fiat, Mediaset and Telecom create specific companies devoted to their own real estate portfolio management.

14.3 Italian Education and Training in Real Estate Appraisal

Historically, there was a link between the Italian and French bodies of technical knowledge. For instance, the first Italian laws of public works (2248/1865; 350/1895) and expropriation (2539/1865) were based on French

patterns. Similar to the French experience,[4] in Italy the main aspects studied in real estate education are:
- Architecture and Urbanistics
- Technical
- Legal

There is no single institution offering a specific course in real estate appraisal[5]. Real estate market problems are studied in several fragmented courses and institutions at different levels.

In the secondary schools, real estate education and cost appreciation is offered in *Istituti Tecnici per Geometri* and *Istituti Tecnici Periti Agrari*. The former school provides an education for construction managers and the latter school is devoted to the education of agricultural consultant.

14.3.1 Graduate Education

At undergraduate level, real estate is taught in the schools of Engineering, Agronomy and Architecture. Traditionally, real estate education was initially developed in the schools of Agronomy. All these schools offer a variety of programmes. In the schools of Architecture, the problems of cost appreciation, environmental goods evaluation, planning evaluation, public works and real estate appraisal are the most important subjects studied. In the faculties of Engineering, real estate courses are essentially devoted to economics, real estate appraisal methods, cost appreciation, planning evaluation and construction management. In the faculties of Agronomy, real estate problems linked to real estate valuation through legal problems and an increasing interest in environmental and urbanistic aspects are studied.

The main valuation approaches taught are the market value, cost and income approaches. In few faculties, discounted cash flow analysis and the market comparison approach are included.

During the last few years, environmental economics, economic evaluation of public goods and evaluation problems in planning have assumed an increasing role[6] in the above-mentioned schools

In many schools, research is mainly focused on the evaluation of problems of sustainable development.

It is rare for schools of economics to have a professor devoted to real estate appraisal.

14.3.2 Post-graduate Education

At post-graduate level, courses tend to be more involved in economic and financial aspects. There are no courses devoted to the real estate market and appraisal ("U.S. approach") in Italy, except for the MBA postgraduate course at the Economic University of Bocconi. This school organises several brief courses, the main aim of which is to develop knowledge of real estate marketing, modern real estate portfolio theory, and real estate valuation and finance, among both professionals and academics. The school has plans to develop a specific Master's Course on these problems. Another private school, called **FREI**, directly organised by Reddy's Group, has developed courses in co-operation with the Finance, Insurance and Real Estate Department of the University of Florida in Gainesville.

Domus Academy in Milan has recently been founded in order to develop courses focused on the technical, economic and legal problem of real estate. Last year, one of the most important private real estate market research institute called "*Scenari Immobiliari*" started organizing several courses for professionals in Rome and in Milan.

In a way comparable with the French situation, the Italian education system emphasises the legal, planning and technical aspects of the real estate market.

Real estate education from ***legal and planning perspectives*** is studied in several courses offered by *Fondazione Giovanni Astengo* (the Giovanni Astengo Foundation) whose principal interest is in the Land Register, Project Financing, and Urban and Territorial Planning. Several universities have developed postgraduate courses, especially in planning and environmental problems[7]

LUISS Management School has recently developed a general course on the technical and legal problems of real estate management.

From a ***technical*** point of view the Di.Tec-Department of the Polytechnic in Milan runs other courses focused essentially on real estate and facility management.[8]

DAU, a Department of 1st School of Engineering of Polytechnic in Bari, together with seven other European Universities[9], offers a Master's in Construction Engineering,

One of the most important private schools in the south of Italy is CSEI in Bari. This school organises, *inter alia*, a specific course on "Construction Management" each year.

Both ***legal*** and ***economic*** points of view are developed in the Master's in *Real Estate Market and Territorial Planning* organised by COREP, a fairly well-known post-graduate school of the Polytechnic in Turin. All over Italy, several faculties of Architecture, Engineering, and Agronomy have initiated Ph.D. courses devoted to real estate markets, especially from technical, building and urbanistic perspectives.

14.3.3 Academic Association and Real Estate Journals

One of the most important academic real estate forums is CeSET. This is an organisation involved in environmental, planning and real estate market problems. It holds an annual forum whose participants come from the academic and professional worlds in several parts of Italy.

CeSET publishes an important review, *AESTIMUM*, which is open to contributions by foreign academic researchers. Another important and historic review is *Estimo e Territorio*. As may be seen, urbanistic problems are becoming more and more important. Another traditional journal is *Rivista del Dipartimento del Territorio* (Land Register Review) previously called *Rivista dei Servizi Tecnici ed Erariali* which is focused more on real estate appraisal problems and the land register. These journals usually publish the most important Italian academic contributions. There is also the recently-founded *Quaderni di Economia del Territorio* (Land Economics Review) a twice-yearly review published by the Polytechnic of Milan and managed by Prof. Sergio Mattia. The Polytechnic of Milan is also managing an attempt to develop a specific Italian institution, in order to harmonise Italian and foreign valuation principles. The name of this new institution is *Istituto Italiano di Valutazione* (Italian Institute of Valuation) IsiVi. This important institution is a member of TeGOVA and is hardly working on harmonization between Italian and European real estate valuation procedures.

There is an increasing interest in harmonization of real estate procedures between Italy and Europe. On behalf of Tecnoborsa (a research Institute of national Council of Real Estate Exchange) and the most important professional associations and real estate companies, professionals and academics developed a specific "Blue Book" on real estate appraisal in Italy has been developed.[10]

Reddy's group publishes a journal called *Economia Immobiliare* which is concerned with the real estate market and analysis problems. An important and professional journal published by "Il Sole 24 ore", an editorial group, is *Il Consulente Immobiliare* (the Real Estate Consultant). This is the most important practice-oriented journal for real estate advisers in Italy.

14.3.4 Professionals and Research Centres

Property appraisals are usually carried out by engineers, architects, agronomists, quantity surveyors or accountants. Members of these professions also act as expert witnesses in the courts.

According to law n.39/89, real estate brokers must have taken a course and passed an examination before being authorised to practice. Graduates in

Economy, Law Architecture, Engineering, however, can commence immediately after receiving an authorisation from the local Chamber of Commerce.

This public agency organises two-month courses for the admission of new real estate brokers, covering some elements of the legal and technical problems of property.

The memberships of professional organisations such as FIAIP (Italian Federation of Professional Real Estate Brokers) and FIMAA (Italian Federation of General Brokers) are mainly made up of real estate brokers. FIAIP, in co-operation with the Polytechnic of Milan, organises professional courses for real estate brokers.

Recently, this cooperation has been developed with the Polytechnic of Bari, too. In fact, the first course of DEI (Real Estate Economics and Law) is going to start in May, 2001.

Another important association is the Italian Association of Real Estate Counsellors (AICI). It organises several forums on real estate market problems, in co-operation with important Italian financial journals.

The large real estate consultants, such as the Reddy's group and the Real Estate Advisory Group, who both promote internal courses, play another important role in real estate education.

In addition, the major franchisers in real estate brokerage, e.g. Gabetti and Tecnocasa amongst others, have arranged internal courses covering real estate valuation practice from a technical and a legal point of view.

Specific courses for condominiums and property management are organised by ANACI (Italian Association of Condominium and Property Manager) although there is no specific law to set a requirement for authorisation or a curriculum for people working in this field.

Several important annual real estate forums are organised by major real estate research centres such as Nomisma, Scenari Immobiliari and CRESME, CENSIS. Due to a lack of official data, both scientific research and private centres have some difficulty in providing accurate real estate market analysis and forecasting.

14.4 Conclusion

It is possible to conclude that:

– The Italian real estate education system, analogous to the French one, emphasises urbanistic, architecture and the technical aspects of real properties.
– In all the faculties where real estate appraisal is taught, the scientific interest of researchers in environmental matters and planning problems is growing.

- Due to the introduction of REIT and the creation of new, larger companies in real estate management, courses in the fields of real estate marketing and finance are being initiated.
- There is a problem of market research and analysis, in the absence of data.
- There is an increasing necessity to provide specific courses for real estate professionals.
- There is a lack of connections with international groups and institutions such as TEGOVA and the RICS.
- In the field of education and training for real estate appraisal, there is a complete absence in our educational system both of economics-oriented and MBA programs, except for those at LUISS and Bocconi.

REFERENCES

[1] I would like to thank Dott.Paola Lunghini for the useful suggestions. The responsibility for assertions rests with the author.

[2] This interesting brief distinction is made in R.Goodchild (2000), Real Estate Education: Denman's Forgotten Dimension, CD Rom of Paper n.043 of 7th European Real Estate Society Meeting in Bordeaux.

[3] See Marco Simonotti and Maurizio d'Amato (2000),Qualità dell'Informazione e Valutazione Immobiliare, Quaderni di Economia e del Territorio n.1, Ed. Società Aperta Milan.

[4] See Ingrid Nappi-Choulet (1999) The Recent Emergence of Real Estate Education in French Business Schools: The Paradox of the French Experience, Paper of 6th meeting of ERES in Athens, Greece.

[5] See A.M.Lunghini (1992), Valutare è Prevedere, in AICI Progetto Multiseminar, edited by Centro Studi AICI and Milan Popular Bank, p.111.

[6] See the works of Prof. Fusco Girard. Among the others see L.F.Girard (1994) Risorse Architettoniche e Culturali: Valutazioni e Strategie di Conservazione, una analisi introduttiva, Franco Angeli, Milano ; L.F.Girard (1993) (edited by) Estimo ed Economia Ambientale: le Nuove Frontiere della Valutazione, Franco Angeli, Milano L.F.Girard (edited by) (1997),Le Valutazioni per lo Sviluppo Sostenibile della Città e del Territorio , Franco Angeli, Milano.

[7] See for example the postgraduate course managed by the Faculty of Architecture of University of Rome, or by 1st School of Engineering of Polytechnic of Bari and Faculty of Engineering of University of Calabria.

[8] There are several courses generally co-ordinated by Prof. O. Tronconi.

[9] The following universities take part to this European Master's: Coventry University (UK), Santander and Valencia University (ESP) Esbijerg University (DAN) University of Potenza (ITA) University of Porto (PORTUGAL) , Polytechnic of Bari (ITA).

[10] Tecnoborsa, (2000) Codice delle Valutazioni Immobiliari, Italian Property Valuation Standard.

Chapter 15

The Netherlands

Paul Kohnstamm
*Stichting voor Beleggings- en Vastgoedkunde,Centre for Investment and Real Estate,
Amsterdam, Netherlands*

15.1 Introduction

This paper describes a number of the most important real estate programmes at universities and higher vocational institutes (polytechnics) in the
Netherlands.[1] Real estate education takes place at different levels. We will
differentiate between undergraduate, graduate and post-graduate courses.
Although Dutch students are used to foreign languages, as they use a number
of English and American textbooks, there are at this moment no programmes
available in foreign languages. Therefore it is not very meaningful to go into
detail of the different programmes. We expect the first post-graduate courses
in English in the year 2003.

Chapter 15.2 describes the organisation of the Dutch real estate profession. Chapter 15.3 concentrates on the real estate courses that are offered by universities and polytechnics.

Chapter 15.4 describes post-graduate courses, and Chapter 15.5 focuses on real estate research and real estate journals.

15.2 The real estate profession

Real estate brokers and appraisers in the Netherlands are required to have a licence, which they receive after obtaining the SVM (Institution for Education of Brokers) diploma. There are no minimum entrance qualifications for admission to this diploma. However, the level of the SVM examination is clearly below normal university undergraduate level. After having obtained the SVM diploma, which is recognised and approved by the state authorities, and after a training period in a brokerage firm, candidates can apply for the official title of *makelaar* (real estate broker). Until now the Chamber of Commerce keeps a register of surveyors. Annually approximately 800 people successfully complete the SVM examination and around 3100 *makelaars* are currently registered. From march 1st 2001 the system has been changed. There is no role for the Chamber of Commerce and the name "makelaar" is not anymore protected.

Since 1995, a special diploma has been available for real estate appraisers who work for municipalities. The real estate appraisal tax law demands special valuation capabilities.

There are a number of institutions that offer real estate courses leading to the SVM-diploma. The largest is the *Stichting Opleiding Makelaars* (SOM), which is the training institute of the *Nederlandse Vereniging van Makelaars* NVM, the Dutch Association of Realtors.[2] In addition to the NVM there are two smaller professional bodies, the *Landelijke Makelaars Vereniging (LMV)* and the *Vereniging Bemiddeling Onroerend Goed* (VBO).[3]

Until now there is no official CPD programme in the Netherlands for licensed *makelaars*, but members of the NVM are obliged to comply with an internal CPD system. From now on there will be a CPD system in place.

15.3 Real estate education in universities and polytechnics

15.3.1 Polytechnics

The polytechnics (HEAO) in Groningen and Eindhoven offer a specialisation in real estate. Their courses are accredited by the SVM and the RICS in London. The course at the HEAO takes 4 years. Every year about 50 students are awarded the diploma. The course level is comparable to RICS-accredited undergraduate courses in the UK. Both polytechnics collaborate with the NVM.

There are other polytechnics that offer real estate courses (The Hague, Haarlem, Deventer, Larenstijn and Utrecht), but they specialise in real estate management, or agricultural real estate. Some of them offer degrees that are recognised by SVM.

15.3.2 Real estate education at Universities

There is no official academic 'real estate' degree offered by universities in the Netherlands. In this respect the Netherlands differs from the UK. However, there are a number of universities that offer real estate courses, and universities where real estate can be chosen as a Major.

15.3.2.1 Technical University Delft

The school of architecture at the Technical University of Delft offers two specialisations: 'construction management' and 'real estate management'. The department was founded in 1990 and is the most important real estate department at technical universities in the Netherlands. Corporate real estate and construction management are important subjects. Every year, approximately 130 students are awarded a degree (ir) as engineer. The alumni find their way into all kinds of real estate jobs. Professor Hans de Jonge is chairman of the department. Associate professors are Soeters and Van der Toorn Vrijthof. For more information: bmvb@bk.tudelft.nl.

15.3.2.2 Technical University Eindhoven

Eindhoven also offers a two-year course in 'Real Estate Management' at its school of architecture and construction. In this course the emphasis is placed more on building management. The total programme of two years leads to the title Master of Real Estate. Professor Wim Keeris is head of the department. For more information: infovgm@euforce.tue.nl.

15.3.2.3 University of Amsterdam

In the faculty of Economics and Econometrics, students can specialise in real estate within the finance department. Three courses are available: Land Economics; Real Estate Finance and Investment; and Real Estate Markets. During their studies, which normally take 4-5 years, students may spend one year on real estate subjects. Each year about 50 students attend these courses. Professor Piet Eichholtz and Professor Paul Kohnstamm lead the real estate department. Gerjan Vos is associate professor.

This department has a close relationship with the SBV School of Real Estate (SBV). For more information: gjavos@fee.uva.nl.

15.3.2.4 University of Maastricht

The Faculty of Economics and Business Administration offers a course 'Institutional Investment'. Each year around 30 undergraduate and graduate students attend this course which takes one semester. Professor Piet Eichholtz leads this department. This course has two parts. The first part focuses on real estate investments for institutional investors. In the second part, the institutional investments are addressed in a wider setting. For more information: www.unimaas.nl.

15.3.2.5 University of Groningen

In the Faculty of Economic Geography, Professor Ed Nozeman teaches 'Real Estate Development and Retail Property'. The main subjects taught on this course are the underlying aspects of the location pattern of companies, office users and retailers. The course takes one semester and is for graduate students. For more information: www.eco.rug.nl.

15.4 Post-graduate courses in the Netherlands

15.4.1 'Master of Real Estate' (MRE) at the SBV School of Real Estate (SBV)

The SBV started this programme in 1989 in co-operation with the Faculty of Economics and Econometrics at the University of Amsterdam. The Dutch Association of Property Developers (Neprom) and the Dutch Association of Realtors (NVM) were the founding fathers. The Master's course takes two years on a part-time basis. It covers the full extent of the profession and is meant for so-called "high potentials" in the field, who are already contributing to the strategic management of their organisations. The target annual enrolment is 39. The minimum entrance qualifications for admission to the postgraduate course are a university degree or Higher Vocational Education degree (in law, economics, social geography, architecture or civil engineering) and at least five years' relevant professional experience.

The MRE programme is accredited by RICS and is accepted as the top course in real estate studies in the Netherlands. During the last 11 years 350 students have been awarded the degree.

Alumni are found in senior positions in all real estate sectors.

The curriculum is comparable to postgraduate courses in the UK and the USA. Students have to write a thesis at the end of the two-year term.

The curriculum consists of the following subjects:

- Finance in general
- Real Estate valuation
- Real estate finance
- Planning and environmental law
- Investment analysis
- Corporate real estate
- Portfolio management
- Urban Economics
- Civil and fiscal law, zoning and environment Real estate Marketing
- Landlord and tenant legislation
- Real estate products and markets
    - Housing
    - Offices
    - Retail
    - Industrial

The assessment procedure for Real Estate Studies consists of 14 examinations; participation in excursions and workshops; and the dissertation. Students pass *the exams* in Real Estate Studies if they successfully complete all these parts within three years of starting the course.

More than 60 lecturers, both academics and real estate practitioners, are involved in the programme.

Leo Uittenbogaard is managing director of SBV, Professor Paul Kohnstamm is chairman of the board. Members of the scientific staff are: Tom Berkhout MRE, Rob Crassee MRE FRICS, Pieter van Hulten, Arthur Marquard and Gerjan Vos. For more information: pieter@sbv.uva.nl or www.sbv.vastgoed.nl.

The SBV maintains a documentation centre, which specialises in commercial real estate. The centre is open to the public. Visitors can use the specially developed system of real estate keywords to undertake specific searches. The documentation centre is the largest real estate library in The Netherlands.

15.4.2 Post academic courses at the SBV

In these courses the emphasis lies on a specific part of real estate studies. They are intended for highly-qualified real estate employees, who are looking for specialised knowledge about particular real estate subjects. They are academic courses with no element of vocational training.

'Market Analysis' focuses on market research and marketability analysis.

'Investment Analysis' aims at feasibility analysis and risk analysis of different types of property. Both courses combine scientific knowledge with practical problem-solving education, in a highly intensive twelve-week schedule. Every year, a limited number of about twenty students is admitted to each of the courses. For more information: arthur@sbv.uva.nl or www.sbv.vastgoed.nl.

15.4.3 Neprom-course

The Dutch Association of Property Developers (Neprom) started a real estate development course in 1984. The course consists of 12 lecture days. The curriculum is based upon real estate development in the widest sense of the word. Each year around 100 participants attend the course, for which there is no specific entry level. Some people subsequently continue their studies by joining the SBV Master's programme. All lecturers are specialists, working in the real estate field.

At the end of the course the students receive a certificate of attendance. There are no examinations.

15.4.4 Novam

The Novam course concentrates on real estate management. It is a two-year part-time programme for university graduates with at least two years' working experience. Although the workload is lighter than the SBV course, with 35 lecture days it is still a heavy programme. A maximum of 25 students is allowed per course. There are now more than 350 alumni.

The curriculum has 7 subjects:

Real estate markets; Negotiation; Real estate finance; Public, private and tax law; Land economics; Portfolio and facility management; Project and account management.

The organiser of the Novam-course is Nederlands Studie Centrum in cooperation with the Fontys Hogeschool Eindhoven. For more information: www.nsc.nl.

15.5 Real Estate Research

15.5.1 Overview

All universities with real estate courses and many real estate consulting firms carry out research as part of their activities. During the last 10 years, more than 15 real estate researchers have been awarded Ph.D.s at Dutch universities. Real estate companies participate in research programmes, either financially or by providing specialist knowledge and data. At the Technical University of Delft, two large multi-client projects have taken place. In 1994 a large research project about the future of the office market in the Netherlands was undertaken, and in 1998 a project about the future of the retail market.

Many researchers attend and contribute to the well-known world research conferences like ARES, ERES, AREUA and the RICS Cutting Edge conferences.

15.5.2 Real estate research societies

De *Vereniging van Vastgoed Onderzoekers in Nederland* (VOGON) is the Dutch Association of Property Researchers, which was established in 1991. There are now 120 members, from universities, private companies, pension funds and investment funds. All members of VOGON are, collectively, members of ERES (European Real Estate Society). From the year 2000 they will receive *ongoing* all the ARES publications free of charge. For more information: pieter@sbv.uva.nl

15.5.3 Real estate journals

VastGoedMarkt is the leading general real estate journal in the Netherlands. In co-operation with VOGON, a scientific supplement is published four times a year. More than 13,000 copies of these supplements are distributed to the subscribers of *VastGoedMarkt*. Both national and international research is covered.

NOTES

[1] In 1998 The Center for Investment and Real Estate (SBV) has made an inventory of real estate education in the Netherlands, which gives a general overview of the different levels.

[2] Website: www.nvm.nl

[3] Website: www.lmv.nl and www.vbo.nl

Chapter 16

Poland

Stanisław Belniak
Akademia Ekonomiczna w Krakowie, Cracow, Poland

16.1 Introduction

As for any system of production or services, the real estate market also needs an intellectual backup. What is required in this area is the analysis of market mechanisms; investigation of legal prerequisites and growth trends; creating new forms and methods of activity on the market; comparing the experience of other countries, etc. It is also necessary to train specialists employed by the institutions serving the real estate market; to publish the results of market analysis; and to prepare codes of practice and manuals for use both by intermediaries and clients operating in market.

People active in the market also require knowledge of other disciplines such as tax laws, insurance, finance and loans, marketing, technical details of transactions, amortisation and valuation of buildings.

Specialists in those disciplines should also be aware of the existence and growth of real estate market and be able to provide necessary solutions and proposals for legal regulations.

Specialists in both the core and peripheral fields of real estate market are organised in appropriate teams or institutions and they jointly provide research and training support.

Neither the Polish estate market nor the specialists working within it have reached a stage of maturity: they are still undergoing the process of organisation and growth. A preliminary attempt to identify organisations active in education and training in the real estate market distinguished three basic categories providing intellectual support:

– chairs at higher schools of economics, agriculture and universities
– R&D departments of economic institutions
– various consulting and service institutions and societies

16.2 Higher schools

Higher schools in Poland follow a traditional model of education. Teaching is conducted on full time, evening and extra-mural (part-time) courses. Education comprises lectures, classes and a short internship (usually one month) that form part of the curriculum.

Full time studies take from four and a half to five years. Graduates are granted an M.A. degree in a particular specialisation, e.g. economics of real estate, real estate management, real estate valuation, etc.

Evening and part-time studies are conducted in two cycles. The first cycle takes three years, and upon the completion a graduate is awarded a B.A. degree in a particular specialisation. Following this, graduates may pursue another course, a year and a half to two years. Having passed the final examinations and defended his or her thesis, the candidate is granted an M.A. degree in a given specialisation. The specialisation is noted on the M.A. diploma.

Four state-run schools and two private schools in Poland provide most of the comprehensive higher level education in real estate. (Table 1). Those schools have included the term "real estate" in the names of their professional chairs, and include the following establishments:

State-run schools
- Main School of Commerce in Warsaw: Chair of Investment and Real Estate
- University of Łódź: Chair of Investment and Real Estate Economics
- Cracow University of Economics: Chair of Real Estate and Investment Process Economics
- Warmińsko-Mazurski University

Private schools
- Higher School of Real Estate Management in Warsaw
- Małopolska Higher School of Economics in Tarnów: Chair of Real Estate and Insurance

The chairs have elaborated detailed curricula for teaching, based on western experience, have collected basic stock of American and European writing on the subject, and have been running seminars since 1992.

The faculties of architecture and town planning at many Polish technical universities include some elements of real estate in their research programmes and their courses. The chairs of geodesy and cartography of technical universities and higher schools of agriculture primarily provide a significant contribution to the process. The faculty staff of those schools take an active part in the education training new groups of specialists.

The curricula of full-time and evening courses taught in Poland provide 3,000 contact hours. Half of this time is assigned to general subjects such as economics, accounting, the theory of organisation, management, marketing, law, tax laws, and 1200 to 1400 hours are devoted to specialised subjects. These include knowledge on real estate markets, the investment process, real estate economics, valuation methods, assessment of investment risk , financing of real estate, credit procedures (including mortgage loans).

In Poland, every year approximately 300 students complete specialised training courses on those subjects. Those achieving success are awarded diploma in Real Estate Management.

About 100 scholars are professionally engaged in research and teaching at 10 universities.

Polish universities also provide post-graduate studies in real estate valuation, trading real estate, and real estate management. Post-graduate studies last a minimum of one year and comprise at least 240 hours of lectures and classes. A dissertation, which must be defended in front of the commission, concludes the studies. The faculties teaching those courses include both scholars from higher schools as well as eminent real estate practitioners.

Three types of real estate professionals in Poland, viz. real estate expert, real estate agent, and real estate manager require licences. Before the President of the Office of Housing and Urban Growth will grant a licence, the applicant has to qualify in front of a State Qualification Commission.

The qualification process comprises three stages:

Stage One - A qualifying commission determines whether the applicant possesses the required background and whether the documents submitted prove that the requirements set by the Regulation on Real Estate of 1997 have been satisfied.

The commission requires candidates to satisfy different conditions for the below listed qualifications:

A. Real Estate Expert
– master's degree of any university
– post-graduate studies in real estate valuation
– internship

B. Real Estate Manager
– GCSE (General certificate of Secondary Education)
– specialised course
– internship
  or
– higher education in real estate
– internship

C. Real Estate Intermediary
– GCSE
– specialised course
– internship
  or
– higher education in real estate
– internship

Post-graduate studies and specialised courses must be accredited by the Office of Housing and Urban Growth. Documents required for accreditation include:

– an internship log book and a report on the course of internship in real estate trade, real estate valuation, real estate management, or a certificate proving completion at least six months' professional training within the above mentioned areas prior to January 1, 1998;
– a curriculum vitae.

Applicants wishing to receive a real estate expert certificate have to submit 15 real estate valuations to the qualifying commission. The Regulations of the State Qualification Commission specify in detail how many valuations, calculated by prescribed methods, have to be submitted.

During Stage Two the Commission administers a written test including 100 questions for a real estate agent and real estate manager qualification and 90 questions and one task to be solved by applicants aspiring to become a real estate experts. The questions are selected from topics prescribed by the President of the Office of Housing and Urban Growth as a minimum curriculum for specialised courses and post-graduate studies of the relevant disciplines. An applicant must score at least 70% points to be successful.

In Stage Three, a qualifying commission assesses practical skills of an applicant with reference to his or her internship log book, or real estate valuations in the case of aspiring real estate experts.

All examinations required for real estate agents, real estate managers, and real estate valuators are taken in front of a commission accredited by the President of the Office of Housing and Urban Growth. The members of the commissions are scholars and practitioners (for case studies). In this way a continual raising of standards of real estate education can be ensured.

Higher schools in Poland are engaged in research as well as offering courses within the above areas.

16.3 Research and development departments at economic establishments

The above group comprises a small number of institutions engaged in physical planning, i.e. the Institute of Housing in Warsaw and its Cracow subsidiary.

For many years the institute has been engaged in studies on the volume and structure of housing stock in Poland, the organisation of its management, and the economics of real estate exploitation. Statutory activities of the Institute provide for studies of real estate market; legal status of buildings; valuation of buildings, apartments and land in the cities; organisation of real estate tenders, and trading real estate.

Additionally, the IH contributes significantly to the education of new real estate teachers specialising in trading real estate and real estate management.

Once the courses have complied with the minimum curricula requirement they are accredited by the OHUG.

The Institute of Physical and Municipal Planning has made a significant contribution to study of housing resources and mechanisms of allocation of land for investment purposes. Its Warsaw seat and Cracow subsidiary both actively participated in the elaboration of legal and economic aspects of a new category of property ownership i.e. municipal property. By organising training courses, conferences and symposia the IPMP contributes to raising the standard of education of many managers and administrators of real estate in Poland.

The Institute of Building Technology in Warsaw has always supported real estate market in the assessment of technical worthiness of buildings.

16.4 Consulting and service institutions and societies

The third entity giving intellectual support to real estate market is Cracow Real Estate Institute. The foundation publishes "The World of Real Estate" quarterly, promotes the establishment of real estate market, and encourages investment activity, education and ethics in real estate transactions nationwide. Apart from research activity, CREI runs workshops for the candidates aspiring to become managers and agents. CREI co-operates with the schools of higher education in this area, and it has signed long-term agreements with most of them.

16.4.1 The Polish Federation of Real Estate Market

The next institution, the Polish Federation of Real Estate Market, includes within its ranks 17 regional societies of real estate agents. The societies run internships and workshops as well as specialised courses for real estate agents, in close co-operation with the schools of higher education. This co-operation, carried out according to agreed terms, guarantees appropriate educational standards for the courses. All the courses conclude with an internal examination, and participants receive a certificate entitling them to sit for a state examination. Curricula of those courses are validated by the OHUG and each of them is given a certification number. This proves that a course has met the minimum curriculum requirement, and that it includes at least 240 hours of lectures and classes. When applying for a certification number the authority organising a course must present the credentials of lecturers.

Currently there are approximately 2500 licensed real estate agents in Poland.

16.4.2 The Polish Federation of Real Estate Managers' and Administrators' Societies and the Polish Union of Real Estate Owners

The Polish Federation of Real Estate Managers' and Administrators' Societies and the Polish Union of Real Estate Owners are mainly involved in organising and running professional internships for real estate managers. The curricula of such internships are also validated by the OHUG. Internships last minimum 6 months and are run by certified real estate managers.

Currently there are about 5000 licensed real estate managers in Poland.

16.4.3 The Polish Federation of Real Property Experts' Societies

Real estate valuation is most closely regulated part of real estate internship. Local societies of real estate experts run internships, workshops, and specialised courses. All candidates aspiring to become a real estate expert must have:

1. A defined basic knowledge of economics, business, collection of data, economic and financial analysis, law, accounting, geodesy, building technology, etc.
2. Specialised knowledge encompassing approaches, methods and techniques of valuation, mathematics, statistics, technical drawing, map reading, etc. Both are prerequisite to sitting for a state examination.

Regional societies of real estate experts run specialised courses and actively participate in the examination of the State Qualifying Commission. Their training input is based on close contacts with the schools of higher education.

There are currently approximately 3500 real estate experts in Poland.

16.4.4 State Real Estate Council

The State Real Estate Council was established in 1999. It acts as an advisory body to the President of OHUG. The council comprises 50 specialists, from different economic departments and universities. The Council deals with four different problems, i.e. real estate market, real estate turnover, physical planning, and real estate databases.

The primary objective of the Council is to give opinion on drafts of amendments or updates to the relevant legislation.

Recently the Council validated minimum curricula taught at postgraduate studies and supplementary courses on real estate valuation and the courses for real estate agents and managers.

16.5 Conclusion

It is ten years since the introduction of free market economy into Poland, and the emergence of three new professions, i.e. real estate expert, real estate agent, and real estate manager. It appears that the best quality education in the real estate area is provided by schools of higher learning and internships.

Graduates of real estate economics taught at several Polish universities (Table 2) learn the basics of investment process, building resources, and real estate market. They also know the rudiments of the technical assessment of buildings, organisation of real estate transactions, and real estate management. Those graduates are also prepared to assume the capacities of independent developers on the real estate market and to become highly qualified managers of municipal property within local government bodies.

APPENDIX

Table 1: Real Estate Education in Poland

Routes to Membership	Society of Real Estate Experts	Society of Real Estate Agents	Society of Real Estate Managers
Accredited degree route	– accredited by a University diploma – minimum six months' supervised internship – 15 valuations – state exam	– accredited by a B.A. or M.A. University diploma – minimum six months' supervised internship – state exam	– accredited by a B.A. or M.A. university diploma – minimum six months' supervised internship – state exam
Professional career path	– higher studies (not accredited) – post-graduate studies-accredited (min. 1 year) – six months' supervised intern-ship and 15 valuation reports or, – 5 years' service and 10 valuation reports – state exam	– secondary or higher education (not accredited) – post-graduate studies, accredited, min. 1 year – accredited course min. 240 hrs – internal exam – minimum 6 months' supervised internship or, – 5 years' certified service – state exam	– secondary or higher education (not accredited) – post-graduate studies, accredited, min. 1 year – accredited course, min. 240 hrs – internal exam – minimum six months supervised internship, or – 5 years' certified service – state exam
Accredited Institutions	– Warmińsko-Mazurski University in Olsztyn – full-time evening part-time – post-grad. studies run by 8 state or pri-	– Cracow University of Economics – Main School of Commerce in Warsaw – Higher School of Real Estate Man-	– UE in Cracow – MSC in Warsaw – HSREM in Warsaw – UE in Poznań – MHSE in Tarnów full time evening

Routes to Membership	Society of Real Estate Experts	Society of Real Estate Agents	Society of Real Estate Managers
	vate universities	agement in Warsaw	part-time
		— Małopolska Higher School of Economics in Tarnów	— post-grad. studies
			— accredited specialised courses
		— University of Łódź full-time evening part-time	Approx. 40 courses run each year by various state and private institutions
		— accredited specialised courses Approx. 60 various courses run each year by state and private institutions	
Internships	— Society of Real Estate Experts	— Society of Real Estate Agents	— Society of Real Estate Managers
	— run by certified real estate experts, supervised by OHUG	— run by certified agents, supervised by OHUG	— certified managers, supervised by OHUG
	— workshops run by the society or universities	— workshops run by the society or universities	— workshops run by the society or universities
Commissioned studies	— State and private higher schools, Research and Development Institutes, private consulting firms, foundations (e.g. Cracow Real Estate Institute)		
Research work	— State and private higher schools, R&D Institutes, Main Census Office, Cracow Real Estate Institute		

Table 2 Syllabus of Real estate Management Studies

- Major: Economics Specialisation: Economics of Real Estate

Obligatory subjects	Number of hours
1. Economics of contracting enterprises	45
2. Building technology 101	30
3. Management in investment process	30
4. Pricing of contracting work	30
5. Economic-financial analysis of enterprises	30
6. Real estate market	30
7. Investment and contracting market	30
8. Real estate management	45
9. Restructuring of enterprises	30

Elective subjects	Number of hours
10. Geodesy and geology 101	30
11. Legal basis of real estate management	30
12. Strategy of financing of investment projects and real estate	30

Elective subjects	Number of hours
13. Physical planning 101	30
14. Functioning of territorial self-government	30
Students select 90 hours of suggested subjects in semester VI	
15. Housing policy	30
16. Management of municipal property	30
17. Marketing in building and real estate management	15
18. Management of housing resources	30
19. Building tenders and contracts	30
Students select 60 hours of suggested subjects in semester VII	
20.Taxes in investment and real estate	30
21. Economics of architectural and building planning	30
22. Valuation of real estate and enterprises	30
23. Banking services for investment and real estate	30
24. Computer lab	15
25. Creativity and innovation	15
Students select 90 hours of suggested subjects in semester VIII	
26. Issue and turnover of securities	15
27. Economics of historical objects renovation	30
28. Property insurance	15
29. Investment process in shaping the environment	15
30. Management of organisation growth	30
31. Transactions and negotiations in real estate turnover	30
32. Sociology of cities	15
33. Human resources management	15
Students select 120 hours of suggested subjects in semester IX	

REFERENCES

Belniak S., Kałkowski L., Naukowcy o nieruchomościach, Home and Market 1994.
Vademecum Studenta, University of Economics 1999.
Polski Rynek Nieruchomości, Unikat Promocja Media 1999.
Regulation on real estate turnover, Journal of Law, Issue 115/1997.
Law on Higher Education, Journal of Law, Issue 63/1991.

Chapter 17

Slovenia

Maruška Šubic Kovač
University of Ljubljana, Faculty of Civil and Geodetic Engineering, Municipal Economics Institute, Ljubljana, Slovenia

17.1 Introduction

The sweeping social and political changes in Eastern Europe at the end of the 1980s were mirrored in Slovenia. The right to own private property was guaranteed by the new Constitution and a free real estate market was developed. The need for market valuation of real estate became more and more pronounced.

Many real estate agencies were founded in the early 1990s. The field of real estate brokerage was not legally regulated. Owing to the lack of data on the real estate market in Slovenia, the real estate valuers are still using the so-called administrative valuation from the past socialist period, whilst on the other hand, clients are increasingly demanding market valuations.

The transition to a settled market and to market valuation of real estate is closely connected with the availability of appropriate education and training for property professionals. The development of education in this field in Slovenia is only just beginning. Slovenian universities offer only a few subjects in the field of real estate, although the professional bodies are occupied with the provision of special courses and annual congresses.

This paper focuses on the provision of real estate education from various points of view:

- professional higher and university study:
  - a) Faculty of Civil and Geodetic Engineering at the University of Ljubljana,
  - b) Faculty of Civil Engineering of Maribor at the University of Maribor.

- training of property professionals within the:
  - a) Association of Sworn-in Valuers and Experts in Civil Engineering,
  - b) Slovenian Institute of Auditors,
  - c) Exchange of Real Estate, and
  - d) Economic Association of Interests of Real Estate Agencies.

The only current legal requirements are those prescribing the extent of education and special examinations for sworn-in valuers and experts in civil engineering, and valuers within the Slovenian Institute of Auditors.

The majority of sworn-in valuers and experts in civil engineering in Slovenia have had a technical education. Most of them have a fundamental education in civil engineering. For this reason, this paper will only analyse the courses, at higher and university education level, at the Faculty of Civil and Geodetic Engineering of Ljubljana and the Faculty of Civil Engineering of Maribor.

The Higher Education Act (*Zakon o visokem šolstvu,* Official Gazette of RS No 67/93), passed in 1993, evolved at the time when the process of rapprochement to Europe dictated the integration and standardisation of higher education. For this reason, the Act provided for numerous changes in university education. Courses are now organised as either:

- a 3-year professional higher education course, or
- a 4-year university course.

The Faculty of Civil and Geodetic Engineering at the University of Ljubljana has also prepared new courses in civil construction as well as in geodesy.

17.2 Faculty of Civil and Geodetic Engineering at the University of Ljubljana

Despite a long history of academic education in Slovenia, the University of Ljubljana was formally established as late as 1919. The number of faculties and colleges has increased considerably over the years. At the present the University comprises 23 faculties, academies and colleges. It has more than 43,000 students and offers a variety of postgraduate studies (M.Sc. and Ph.D. degrees) within its current 248 courses.

The Professional Higher Education Course in Civil Engineering and the University Course in Civil Engineering include five main subject areas:

– Hydraulic Engineering,
– Municipal Engineering,
– Structural Engineering,
– Project Management,
– Traffic Technical Engineering.

The study of Civil Engineering in general is both directly and indirectly linked with real estate. The subjects under the Municipal Engineering unit are focusing on the planning and the acquisition, development and management of building land, and real estate valuation. In the University course, the contents of subjects as Municipal Economics, Urban Planning, Urbanistics, Regional Planning and The Basics of Spatial Regulation have been updated. In the higher expert course a new subject, "Building Land Development and Valuation" has been added to the existing "Municipal Economics and Legislation concerning Civil Engineering".

In the *Department of Geodetic Engineering*, changes to the content of the teaching programme were defined within the TEMPUS S-JEP Phare 11001-96 Project, which includes the Department of Geodetic Engineering and the national professional institutions as well as numerous European universities. The essential objective of the structural TEMPUS Project, called "The Improvement of Education concerning the Environment and Infrastructure", is to reform some of the existing courses at the Faculty as regards urban and regional planning and integral real estate management.

An analysis at the Faculty of Civil and Geodetic Engineering at Ljubljana showed that the existing academic educational structure of the Department of Geodetic Engineering did not satisfy the prevailing requirements in the geodesic field, nor those of the general public. It was discovered that up to 70% of Geodesy graduates were active in real estate management, real estate cadasters, public administration, real estate valuation, or spatial planning. The existing course programmes do not cover these fields to any satisfactory extent.

Following the analysis of the situation, of problems within the relevant field and of the needs of the users and possible solutions, new educational programmes were prepared. The professional Higher Education Study of Geodetic Engineering and the University Study of Geodetic Engineering now offer two study orientations:

– Geodetic Engineering
– Spatial Engineering.

The amended Geodesy course now includes subjects in the field of real estate and valuation. In particular the course in Spatial Engineering includes:

– The Fundamentals of Law,
– Business Economics,
– Introduction to Public Law,
– Real Estate Law, and
– Real Estate Valuation.

17.3 Faculty of Civil Engineering at the University of Maribor

The University of Maribor was founded in 1959, to fulfil the need for a university centre in north-eastern Slovenia. The University evolved from the Association of School Institutions of Higher Education in 1975. At that time Maribor and the northern parts of Slovenia had a constant shortage of university-educated professionals, in particular economists, engineers, and both primary and secondary schoolteachers. The University of Maribor includes six faculties, which offer 80 undergraduate and 40 postgraduate programs. There are approximately 14,000 students at the University.

The studies at the Faculty of Civil Engineering at the University of Maribor include the education activity and scientific research, divided between three different courses:

1. "Civil Engineering",
2. "Traffic/Transportation Engineering" and
3. "Industrial Engineering".

Postgraduate studies include specialisation courses, Master's and Doctorates.

The subject "Real Estate Valuation" is part of the aforementioned three courses. One of the courses, "Industrial Engineering", provides knowledge in solving professional, development and management tasks in the sphere of industry. For this reason, this course provides a much deeper coverage of economics than the other two. The subject "Urban planning" is included only in the professional higher education study program of "Civil Engineering".

Graduates from the Faculty of Civil and Geodetic Engineering at the University of Ljubljana and the Faculty of Civil Engineering at the University of Maribor acquire only limited theoretical and practical knowledge in the field of real estate valuation during their studies. Additional training, after completing the course, can lead to appointment either as sworn-in valuers and experts in civil construction in the Ministry of Justice of the Republic of Slovenia, or as certified real estate valuers in the Slovenian Institute of Auditors.

17.4 Association of Sworn-In Valuers and Experts in Civil Engineering of Slovenia

In Slovenia, sworn-in valuers and experts in civil engineering were formerly organised within sections of the individual primary courts of justice. There were 9 sections.

Under the new Courts Act (*Zakon o sodiščih*, Official Gazette of RS No.19/ 94) of 1994, the power of nomination was transferred from the primary courts to the Ministry of Justice. On the initiative of the same Ministry, the Association of Sworn-in Valuers and Experts in Civil Engineering of Slovenia was established in 1997.

The Minister responsible for the judicature appoints sworn-in valuers. Under the Courts Act (Article 87), a sworn-in valuer may be anyone who:

- is a citizen of the Republic of Slovenia and a fluent speaker of Slovenian,
- has attained his/her majority,
- has not been found guilty of a criminal offence, owing to which he/she would be morally unsuitable for the performance of his/her work,
- has the appropriate expert knowledge and abilities for the work of a particular type of valuer.

The Act, therefore, does not impose any educational requirements on candidates. As there were also no such restrictions in the past, sworn-in valuers included many people who had only secondary school education. The exact number of sworn-in valuers in the field of civil engineering is not known, as the records of valuers have not been updated.

The law states that the Minister of Justice may order applicants for the status of sworn-in valuer to sit a special proficiency examination, before a commission of experts in the applicant's future field of activity.

During the past four years, the Association of Sworn-in Valuers and Experts in the field of Civil Engineering, has organised preparatory courses for applicant valuers. Applicants may attend the courses after they have studied the prescribed literature. The courses are currently of informative nature only, as they last for only three days, including two days of lectures and the presentation of a model valuation report, plus a day of consultations.

The examination includes:

– a written section – a valuation report, prepared at home by the applicant,
– written answers to shorter questions, under examination conditions, and
– an oral examination in relation to both the above parts.

In order to pass the examination, the applicant must present an appropriate valuation report and obtain at least 75% of the possible marks in the answers to shorter questions. All applicants must also attend the oral examination. The candidate must pass both the written and oral parts of the examination.

Despite the opposition of some applicants, the Ministry of Justice wishes to restrict the award to appropriately trained experts and insists on this mode of selection for the appointment of sworn-in valuers.

In 2000, an Act amending the Courts Act (Official Gazette of Republic of Slovenia, No. 28/2000) was passed. Persons applying for the position of sworn-in valuer must have at least six years' professional experience, in addition to a university education, and must pass a proficiency examination every five years. Sworn-in valuers are obliged to co-operate in professional consultations, convened for this purpose by the competent national authorities.

17.5 Slovenian Institute of Auditors

Even today, sworn-in valuers mainly use administrative methods of real estate valuation from the past socialist period, although several valuers holding the certificate have been trained in market-related valuation methods.

The latter are divided between:

- valuers holding the Certificate of the Agency of the Republic of Slovenia for Promotion of Economic and Company Reconstruction, and
- valuers holding the Licence of the Agency of the Republic of Slovenia for Promotion of Economic and Company Reconstruction, which was re-named the "Certificate of a Designated Real Estate Valuer of the Slove-nian Institute of Auditors" in 1998.

The start of major changes that introduced market-related methods to real estate valuation took place in 1992. At that time, experts of the American Society of Appraisers (ASA) in conjunction with the Agency of the Republic of Slovenia for Promotion of Economic and Company Reconstruction, or-ganised a training seminar in real estate valuation as part of the company privatisation process. The seminar mainly dealt with real estate valuation methods used by the ASA experts. Success in the subsequent examination, including three intermediate and one final test, sufficed for the award of the above-mentioned Certificate of the Agency of the Republic of Slovenia for Promotion of Economic and Company Reconstruction. Subject to presenting an appropriately prepared valuation report, and passing an oral examination, applicants could also be awarded the Licence of the Agency of the Republic of Slovenia for Promotion of Economic and Company Reconstruction.

The Slovenian Institute of Auditors was established in 1994 as the repre-sentative body of qualified licensed auctioneers and valuers in Slovenia. It issues licences to real estate valuers, and prescribes special training pro-grammes for new applicants.

An applicant wishing to sit the examination for registered certified real estate valuers must:

- have a university education,
- have appropriate working experience in each individual field defined in the Rules,
- speak fluent Slovenian,
- not have been (may not be) found guilty of a criminal offence which would make them unworthy of their profession,
- meet the requirements of the code of professional ethics.

In order to acquire the qualification of attested real estate valuer, there are envisaged:

- 132 hours of lectures in valuation,
- 15 hours of lectures in accounting and taxation,
- 15 hours of lectures in business finance,
  i.e. 162 hours of lectures in total.

The expert examination is in two parts. In the first part, the applicant is examined in individual subjects. In the second part he/she presents and substantiates the work done and replies orally to the questions asked. Upon passing the examination, the certificate awarded is valid for a limited time only. A real estate valuer may prolong its validity by collecting a certain number of points from supplementary training within a five-year period. The exact requirements are governed by special rules on the recognition of supplementary training for the prolongation of validity of the licence or entry in the register.

The Slovenian Institute of Auditors has applied a systematic approach to the internal certification of real estate valuers. As the system has only been in force for a little over a year, it has yet to produce its first successful candidates.

17.6 The Exchange of Real Estate and Economic Association of Interests of Real Estate Agencies

As mentioned in the introduction, real estate brokerage has not yet been regulated by law in Slovenia. There are at present no regulations for the award of licences for this activity. Nevertheless, there is a need for supplementary training in this field.

Slovenia currently has two major associations, in the field of real estate agency, which are involved in the training of agents:

– The Exchange of Real Estate, and
– The Economic Association of Interests of Real Estate Agencies.

The two associations are implementing a programme to grant internal licences to real estate agents. A voluntarily acquired licence functions as a quality certificate and as proof of the real estate agent's relevant expertise, required for the provision of good-quality professional services. There are however no statutory conditions for the award of a licence or a certificate.

The Exchange of Real Estate organises training under the auspices of the Ministry of Labour, Family and Social Affairs. The training programme for the award of a licence in real estate agency in trade includes 40 hours of training, that includes, as follows:

– General part,
– Bases of material law,
– Agency agreements and real estate brokerage,
– Fiscal and administrative law,
– Related topics.

The licence may be granted to applicants who pass the written and oral examination.

Additionally, the Information Exchange of Real Estate regularly organises training in the fields of civil construction, spatial planning and real estate valuation. The training course comprises 48 hours of lectures. The main objective of the course is to familiarise real estate agents, whose basic education was not in civil construction, with some relevant expertise. The Information Exchange of Real Estate aims to contribute to an improvement in the professional standards of real estate agents.

The course programme includes the following subjects:

- Market valuation of real estate,
- Valuation reports,
- Spatial planning,
- Basics of architecture,
- Renovation of buildings, and
- Energy efficiency in buildings.

Participants who pass the examination are awarded a certificate in civil construction expertise, spatial planning and real estate valuation.

The Exchange of Real Estate started its training programme approximately a year ago. Experience has shown that there is great interest in such lectures, not only from real estate agents, but also from civil servants and municipal officials.

Each year the Association of Sworn-in Valuers and Experts in Civil Engineering of Slovenia, the Slovenian Institute of Auditors, the Exchange of Real Estate and the Economic Association of Interests of the Real Estate Agencies organise an annual conference for property professionals. Attendance at the conference qualifies as "supplementary education" for the purposes of renewal of licences.

17.7 Conclusion

The need for supplementary training in the field of real estate in Slovenia arises from the everyday practice. A transition from administrative to market valuation of real estate requires a different approach, which can only be attained through appropriate education and training.

To begin with, real estate education and training in Slovenia was included in higher and university education, as well as supplementary training. In the 1990s the Faculty of Civil and Geodetic Engineering at the University of Ljubljana revised its teaching programmes and course content for subjects of both direct and indirect relevance to real estate. Valuation practitioners have been developing their own training programmes, which will need to be included in, or carried out in accordance with, the proposed certification system which is under preparation. The first steps in organising the field of real estate education in Slovenia have, therefore, already been taken.

REFERENCES

Courts Act, Official Gazette of Republic of Slovenia, No.19/1994.
Faculty of Civil and Geodetic Engineering, 1998, University of Ljubljana.
Rules on Valuers, Official Gazette of Republic of Slovenia, No.20/1995.
Science in Slovenia, 1993, Ministry of Science and Technology of the Republic of Slovenia, Ljubljana.
Act amending the Courts Act, Official Gazette of Republic of Slovenia, No. 28/2000.
Šubic Kovač, M., 1998, Inertia of the Administrative Valuation Methods and Introduction of Marketing Real Estate Valuation - Case study of Slovenia, International Real Estate Conference, Maastricht [ERES /AREUEA].
Šubic Kovač, M., 1999, Development of Education and Profession in the Field of Real Estate Valuation in Slovenia International Real Estate Conference, Athens [ERES].
kamen.uni-mb.si
fgg.uni-lj.si
www.si-revizija.si
www.uni-mb.si

Chapter 18

Spain and Portugal

Paloma Taltavull de La Paz
Universidad de Alicante, Dpto. Analisis Economico Aplicado, Alicante, Spain

18.1 Introduction

To describe real estate education in Spain and Portugal is not an easy task. Although there are strong similarities, in terms of institutions and functions, in the structure of the real estate systems in both countries, there are also major differences in the organisation of their real estate professions and educational systems.

Spain and Portugal share, with Italy and France, a system of institutions to control and defend property rights. There is a group of official institutions, from different Ministries, which belong to a system that registers each property when it is constructed, when it is sold and when it is mortgaged or rented, as well as recording its value. There are some close similarities between the Spanish and Portuguese institutions.

Another similarity is that neither country has any official real estate courses in its universities. However, some research groups belonging to specific departments in the universities have part of their staff working in this field.

The real estate markets in both countries have grown very quickly during the last fifteen years, resulting in demand for more, and higher quality, real estate services. This means that both markets need specialised, qualified real estate professionals although there is no leading institution to direct their education.

The aim of this article is to attempt to clarify the present situation in each country and to explain the structure of such real estate education as exists, at various levels, in Spain.

The article is organised as follows: Part I is dedicated to Spain and part II to Portugal. In each section, the professions currently active in the real estate market and property construction are explained. The different levels of degree available in the universities and the institutions that promote education and research are then described. Finally, some conclusions are presented for each country.

18.2 Real Estate Education in Spain

18.2.1 Introductory notes about the Real Estate Market and Organisations

Spain has an expanding economy, with major possibilities of further growth, as is demonstrated by its GDP, which has increased at a faster rate than those of other European countries during the last few years. Part of this expansion is driven by the very active construction sector, in both building and civil engineering, throughout the country. This process demonstrates that the real estate market is of major, and increasing, importance to the whole economy. This applies to the expansion of urban areas by the building process, as well as present and future demands on real estate services through development and real estate investment.

Property and the real estate markets are highly regulated in Spain. This can include taking control of existing properties until their ownership is registered. Each step of the property process has different rules to cover ownership rights and taxes. Property control is carried out by two institutions in Spain: the first is the *Registro de la Propiedad* (Property Registry), where changes of ownership and any other circumstances affecting properties, such as charges (e.g. mortgages, judgement debts) can be registered. All property transactions or any other changes in the circumstances of real estate must be made in writing in a notarised public document and will subsequently be entered in the relevant register.

The second institution is the *Catastro de la Propiedad Rústica y Urbana,* (rural and urban property cadaster). This institution is part of the Ministry of Economy. It identifies and registers all real property in Spain. Its objective is to maintain a database of properties, to catalogue them and their locations, and also their base values for property taxation purposes. The aim is to exercise better control over properties and their owners. The cadastral value indicates the total amount of real estate wealth possessed, by families and in general, in the Spanish economy. It is considered as an indication of long-term value, because it is usually lower than actual market values at any particular time. In order to control existing properties the system has to be dynamic, registering building projects and new properties as they are built. The base for cadastral values is usually revised every 10 to 15 years.

Real estate laws cover all aspects, from building control to the taxation of purchases and values, and the provision of services in the market, with regulations for real estate managers and agents. With some recent exceptions (see below) the law restricts the right to provide real estate services to professionals belonging to bodies called *Colegios Oficiales* (Official bodies, in the same way as for other professions) in order to guarantee a minimum level of education and to strengthen consumer rights.

The modernisation of the Spanish economy and increased requirements for infrastructure for residential and non-residential construction have coincided at a time when the business cycle is accelerating, increasing construction activity rates, in the well-known process called building boom. This applies not only to housing but also to commercial, industrial and office development. It is particularly evident in the geographic areas where higher levels of economic growth and expansion are occurring. These include the two major urban centres, Madrid and Barcelona; the whole Mediterranean coast (the so-called Mediterranean Axis) especially from Valencia southwards; Aragon; the Basque and Navarrese countries; and the islands. In these areas, growth in construction activity has generated new demands for real estate management and brokerage services, adapted to modern market requirements. The demand for new real estate services, as well as laws and regulations and the expansion of new technologies, have all contributed to the need for new, specialised education for real estate professionals.

The necessity for new techniques is driving a large-scale entrance to the market of new agents, many of them without becoming members of the *Colegio Oficial* (official professional body). According to Spanish Law, this institution has exclusive powers to unify, organise and ensure the quality of real estate services. At the same time, however, movement towards an open market for services in Spain has meant that people without qualifications are allowed to offer services in the market. This process is leading to an increased number of firms that are operating outside the standard rules, particularly those concerning ethics, and an apparent market disruption that has resulted in reduced consumer protection.

During the 1990s Spain saw important changes: the attempt to modernise the market following strong growth in construction and the specialisation of services; and the development of real estate education in the universities, driven by demand from professionals in this sector. At present, there is an unstable situation, with the changes in progress, which could open the way towards a greater specialisation in the real estate market.

18.2.2 Real estate professions

Existing Spanish laws related to the real estate professions govern all services supplied in the market. They restrict the right to practise to members of the *Colegios Oficiales* (official professional bodies), resulting in a contradiction between the regulations and market practice. The *Colegios* cover a range from technical professions, e.g. architects, quantity surveyors and engineers, to those more concerned with the real estate market, e.g. estate agents and real estate managers. Valuers and appraisers are subject to different, more recent regulations.

Development promoters in Spain are a group that plays a very important part in the construction process. Their role is at the interface between investment and project management, so they could be regarded as being in the services sector. They have a very important entrepreneurial character and they do not have regulations to limit their performance. They may be members of developers' associations, which have co-ordinated their activity in each area for many years, although they are not forced to belong to them. Some of these are very old and well-respected associations.

The various professions recognised in the real estate market in Spain are shown in Table 1.

Table 1: Real Estate Professions in Spain

Activity	Colegio Oficiale/ Professional Body	Type of Profession
Design and residential projects	yes	Arquitectos y Arquitectos Técnicos
Planning	yes	Arquitectos superiores e Ingenieros
Design and civil engineering projects	yes	Ingenieros

Activity	Colegio Oficiale/ Professional Body	Type of Profession
Real estate brokers and estate agents	yes	Agentes de la Propiedad Inmobiliaria (API's)
Property management	yes	Administradores de Fincas - Spanish law says that they are trustees and responsible for the maintenance, conservation and correct management of the property - They can manage both urban and rural properties
Appraisers	no	It is not a specific profession. Technical architects, estate agents and all professionals registered in the Bank of Spain's list of Appraisers may value properties.
Promoters	no	Not a recognised profession: their role is closer than investors and project management.
Real Estate Analysis	no	Not a recognised profession

The more restricted development of real estate specialities in Spain necessitates a comparison with a typical classification of real estate activities in the rest of Europe, in order to assess how they are affected by public regulation. Table 2 shows this comparative analysis:

Table 2: Professions and activities inside the Real Estate Markets in Spain and Europe

Activity	Spanish equivalent	Colegio Oficiale / (belong to a prof. body)	regulated	Professional body
Design and construction projects	Proyectos y dirección de obras	yes	yes	Colegio Profesional de Arquitectos y de Arquitectos Técnicos
Planning	Planeamiento	yes	yes	Colegio Profesional de Arquitectos y de Arquitectos Técnicos
Development- promotion	Promoción	no	no	Promotores-inversores
Valuation-appraisal	Tasadores-valoradores	no	yes	Bank of Spain Registry of Appraisers
Property Investment Analysis	Análisis de inversión inmobiliaria	no	no	Bank institutions. Investment Funds
Property Management (urban and rural)	Administración de Fincas	yes	yes	Colegio de Administradores de Fincas
Real Estate Management	Gestión de activos inmobiliarios	no	no	Asesores, administradores, sociedades de in-

Activity	Spanish equivalent	Colegio Oficiale / (belong to a prof. body)	regulated	Professional body
				versión
Construction management	Promotores	no	no	Developers firms
Estate Agents	Intermediación de bienes inmobiliarios	yes	no	Colegio de Agentes de la Propiedad Inmobiliaria
Real estate finance, investment	Analistas financiación inmobiliaria	no	no	Finance Banks

18.2.2.1 Regulated and unregulated Professions

Most types of professional activity are regulated in Spain. The real estate professions are no exception, being protected by standard rules 'against intruders', which restrict the market to practitioners belonging to a professional body, as already noted. These bodies exist to co-ordinate and control professional activities having an implicit civil liability. They regulate the limits of practice in order to safeguard consumer's interests. To comply with official regulations, professionals active in a field that is the responsibility of a specific *Colegio* (professional body) are required to belong to it and to adopt its rules and standards in their practice.

Membership of the *Colegios* is usually applied for after the award of an official academic title. This is the case for *inter alia* engineers, architects, technical architects, quantity surveyors, and lawyers. However, for other real estate professionals such as property managers or brokers, entry to the profession is regulated in different ways, which, up to the present, do not include a requirement for specific studies. Each *Colegio* has responsibility for education: it should teach and examine candidates for membership, provide specialised courses and set examinations, in conjunction with the relevant Ministry. The *Ministerio de Fomento* (Ministry of Development) awards successful candidates a professional skill title, as real estate manager or broker. The Ministry has the authority to award the title to people passing the exams, as well as those that have an academic degree in a similar speciality. Only those holding an official title and belonging to a professional body (membership is automatic after obtaining the title) may offer their services in the Spanish real estate market. Real estate brokerage is, however, an exception (see below).

Up to June 2000, two professional bodies in the field were required to offer educational facilities: *Colegio de Administradores de Fincas* and *Agentes de la Propiedad Inmobiliaria (API's)*. The former has resolved the situation by transferring its responsibilities for education to Spanish universities (there were 12 offering courses in this field in the 1999-2000 academic year). The universities organise the curriculum, its content, and teach and examine each speciality. A similar change took place in Architecture and Engineering a long time ago when these degrees were created.

From June 2000, the Government decided to liberalise some service activities, including that of real estate broker. This means that they have eliminated the market restriction and the obligation to belong to a *Colegio* for real estate agents.

18.2.2.2 Professional bodies and their regulation

Colegios (professional bodies) linked with the real estate market include those covering professions such as engineering, architecture, estate agency and property administration. Table 3 shows those currently in existence, the legislation under which they were created, and their fields of responsibility. The first two *Colegios* are responsible for real estate services only. However, the *Colegios* for engineering, architecture and technical architecture are responsible for the processes of construction and design, as well as planning and urbanism.

On the other hand, there are two other groups – *Tasadores* (appraisers) and *Promotores* (promoters) – who are not subject to membership of a *Colegio*, although they are recognised and regulated in some respects.

The *Tasadores* (Appraisers) are a body recently created by the Administration in order to have a professional group to carry out real estate valuation for financial purposes. It is obligatory to instruct an Appraiser when authorisation is required to give a mortgage loan for the purchase or refinancing of a property. Only people with a university degree in architecture (medium or high level university degree) or a comparable specialisation can carry out this work. They must also be registered in the Registry of Appraisal of the Bank of Spain. There is no *Colegio* with responsibility for Appraisers: both firms and individual professionals can practise in the market.

The main reason for the regulation of this activity by central authority is the mortgage rules. This law allows financial institutions to issue real estate shares (*cédulas hipotecarias*) only where mortgages do not exceed 80% of the property value. This value is used by financial institutions to apply risk and credit restriction ratios.

This rule made it necessary to create an official register of Appraisers, who are responsible for certifying property values as a guarantee for the financial institutions, thereby reducing risk and, indirectly, improving the flow of finance to the construction industry.

Promoters act as agents, managing projects and the funds to finance construction. They have a mixed role between investment and project management. They are usually entrepreneurial and professional, and very integrated in construction activity in their towns or cities. They decide on the type of construction and its design, according to planning requirements, acquire land and negotiate finance, and manage the execution of design and construction.

Table 3: Professional Bodies and their Responsibilities

Colegio / Professional body	Created by	Responsibilities
AGENTES DE LA PRO-PIEDAD INMOBILIARIA (API's) (real estate agents)	Decreto del 17.12.1948, num 1949/65 Decreto 4.12.69, num 3248/69, that publishes its own rules (estatutos). Decreto 2.6.00, that liberal-ises estate agent activity	- Marketing and property advertising - Property brokerage - Valuation
ADMINISTRADORES DE FINCAS (real estate managers)	Ley de Propiedad Horizontal, 21.7.1960, art. 12 y 18 R.Decreto 639 de 1 de abril de 1968, that create the offi-cial Professional Body (de creación del Colegio de Ad-ministradores de Fincas) Decreto del 28.1.69, which publishes its own rules (es-tatutos).	- Property management (urban and rural) - Building maintenance and repair (housing and other building) - Facility management
ARQUITECTOS (architects)	Real Decreto del Ministerio de Obras Públicas y Urba-nismo del 13.5.77 y del 16.2.83, , that created the official Professional Body	- Project design - Urban planning - Cartography - Urban development
ARQUITECTOS TÉCNICOS (technical architects or build-ing engineers)	Regulación original de la profesión de 1935 Real Decreto del Ministerio de Obras Públicas y Urba-nismo del 13.5.77 y del 16.2.83, , that created the official Professional Body Ley 7/1997, that updated its own rules (que actualiza los estatutos del Colegio Profe-sional)	- Building Pathology - Construction management - Valuation and appraisal
INGENIEROS (engineers)	Real Decreto del Ministerio de Obras Públicas y Urba-nismo del 13.5.77 y del 16.2.83, that created the	- Civil engineering, infra-structures - Urban development - Geodesics and geophysics

Colegio / Professional body	Created by	Responsibilities
	oficial Professional Body	- Ground engineering - Mineral exploitation - Oceanography
REAL ESTATE PROFESSIONALS AND ACTIVITIES NOT SUBJECT TO PROFESSIONAL BODIES		
TASADORES (appraisers)	Decreto del Banco de España that created the official Appraisal Registry (sobre la creación del Registro General de Tasadores)	- Appraisal and property valuations for financial purposes
PROMOTORES (promoters, developers)	Ley Sindical de 1977, that created the official entrepreneurship Organisation (por la que se crean las organizaciones empresariales y sindicales)	- Construction management - Finance and investment - Project management

Source. RICS, APC requirements and competencies and cited legislation. See http://www.arquitectura-tecnica.org, http://www.PROVIA.es

18.2.3 University degrees in real estate in Spain

18.2.3.1 Overview

From the beginning of the 1990s, Universities in Spain began to enter the process of training real estate agents, leaving the responsibility for providing education with the *Colegios Oficiales* but taking over the design and practice of courses. The *Ministerio de Fomento* (Ministry of Construction) remains in control because there are no specific official[1] courses in the real estate market: the most exhaustive training is focused on technical careers such as architecture and engineering (e.g. for assessors).

The multidisciplinary character of real estate education means that groups of studies which are concerned with a particular aspect of this profession are often covered in other specialisations, such as law or building construction

On the other hand, the lack of maturity of the Spanish real estate market and related financial markets has resulted in an underprovision of specialisations such as management, marketing and investment techniques. This has acted as a brake on the modernisation of real estate training and education at university level and its relationship with professional institutions.

When talking about university studies in Spain, official real estate education is focused in the areas of technical careers, such as architecture and engineering, in the first and second cycle. There were no specific studies for this sector in the public university system, especially in areas such as management, marketing, brokerage and finances. General questions in these areas will be integrated in the titles of Economics, Geography and Finances, until the real estate undergraduate courses appear.

One of the main difficulties of introducing real estate studies in Spanish universities is the distribution of the curriculum over subject areas that are the responsibility of different faculties.

As many universities do not offer the whole range of studies necessary for real estate courses, not all are able to introduce them. In the 1990s, however, some Spanish universities started offering specialised courses for real estate agents, focussing on law and economics[2].

In 1997, three universities offered such courses: the University of Alcala (Madrid); the University of Barcelona; and the University of Alicante. In 1999 there were 8 universities offering courses, all of them including the basic curriculum required by the Ministry of Development for the award of a professional title to their graduates. During 2000 this trend continued, making it probable that a course in official Spanish real estate studies could begin in two years. The importance of official studies is primarily because other ("non-official") courses are not recognised by the government and do not have any public support. The qualifications they confer cannot be validated in terms of the possibility of joining the official Estate Ministry as a civil servant.

The basic curriculum in Real Estate Studies is shown in Chart 5. It is designed to cover specific training in the services of brokerage, management and real estate promotion.

Apart from these university courses, there are other specific courses intended to educate professionals with intensive groups in some subjects, either as a Master's course or as specialisations inside other university studies. Master's courses in valuation are promoted by different branches of the Treasury Department (mainly the Land Registry) in order to produce a body of specialists in the different systems of controlling value: land registry, special statutory valuations (ruins, development, expropriation, etc.) mortgages and insurance.

Higher degree studies are the way in which real estate studies are introduced for specialisation at research level. There is not a great variety of them in the Spanish universities at present. They tend to specialise in e.g. the analysis of real estate market finance, or development, depending on the department and the specialisation the programme offers.

18.2.3.2 Real Estate Curricula at the Universities

Courses in real estate studies have an identical formal structure to those of other subjects in Spanish universities.

As mentioned above, there are 8 universities in Spain teaching this speciality. All of them offer a three year degree, which is a technical course with a maximum range of contact time from 180 to 240 credits (1 credit = 10 hours of theoretical and practical lectures). Individual subjects have from 4.5 to 6 credits: they are organised in semesters.

Table 4 shows the universities concerned, together with the name of the faculty offering real estate studies. They have all agreed a common core-studies curriculum.

Table 4: Undergraduate Courses in Real Estate in Spanish Universities

University	Core subjects	Number of Specialities	Faculty	Number of students
U. de Alcalá (Madrid)	yes	1	Derecho (Law)	120
U. Autónoma de Barcelona	yes	3	Derecho (Law)	160
U. de Alicante	yes	3	Económicas (Economics)	80
U. de Valencia	yes	1	Politécnica (Polytechnic)	100
U. Castilla-La Mancha	yes	1	Derecho (Law)	40
U. Católica de Murcia	yes	1	Privada (no facultades) Private – no faculties	30
U. País Vasco (Bilbao)	yes	1	Económicas (Economics)	40
U. Málaga	yes	1	Económicas (Economics)	40

Source: own research

Most of the universities offer only one specialisation in real estate administration, the result of the agreement with the real estate Professional Bodies mentioned above. Two of them, Barcelona and Alicante, offer three specialisations: construction management for development companies; real estate and property administration; and real estate brokerage. The course at Alicante has a larger technological component and also offers an analysis of the real estate market from an economic point of view.

The core curriculum integrates the main knowledge needed by real estate professionals, reflecting the large legal component necessary because of the high level of regulation of real estate in Spain, both concerning the market and in the construction process (Table 5).

Universities have the freedom to offer specialised studies around this agreed core, according to the aims of their courses. Both Alicante and Barcelona Universities have a similar design of the subjects because the stronger specialisations they offer. Alicante University additionally offers an important body of new technology studies, integrated into the course for real estate agents.

Table 5: Core Subjects in Real Estate Undergraduate Courses in Spain

Knowledge Area	Credit
I.- Law	
A.- Introduction to Law, Public and Private Law	4.5
B.- Civil Law. Contracts, property rights, Urban Housing Rent Law	21
C.- Administrative, Planning and Urban Law	6.0
D.- Tax Law	9.0
E.-Ethics in Real Estate	4.5
Total law knowledge	45.0
II.- Economics and Management	
F.- General and Real Estate Economics	12
G.- Accounting and Finance	14
H.- General and Real Estate Management	6
Total economics knowledge	32
III.- Instruments and skills	
I.- Mathematics and statistics	9
J.- Information systems, nets and virtual tools	9
Total instruments and skills	18
IV.- Building technology	
K.- Technology of buildings	4.5
L.- Building and facilities maintenance, security regulation of buildings	4.5
M.- Appraisal and real estate valuation	6
Total building technology	15
TOTAL	111

Source: own research

18.2.3.3 Real Estate studies and new technologies

Real Estate professionals need to use new technologies to improve the quality of their services. One of the characteristics of their activities is the quantity of information they must handle. In this regard, the University of Alicante offers the only real estate course in Spain to include new technologies as a subject in its programme. The course includes a knowledge of the basic software required for everyday work, the use of Geographic Information Systems in property and portfolio management, uses of the Internet, remote information sources and the design of virtual offices. The subject is taught in different stages to maximise learning efficiency: one topic is covered in each semester of the three-year course.

Taking into account the lower specialisation in Spain in this area, the course also offers economics and finance in relation to the real estate market. This includes an introduction to market analysis, studies of profitability and portfolio composition, and real estate finance. These topics, which are commonly found in university courses in other European countries, are completely new in Spain.

The basic elements include, firstly, knowledge about the real estate sector, its legal framework and its relationships with the Spanish and international economic structures, which is taught through the subjects of law and economics. Secondly, students acquire a complete knowledge of administration and business management techniques, particularly in accounting, marketing and finance systems. Finally, statistics and mathematics are specially applied to the techniques of economic analysis, based on a wide knowledge of the most advanced computer techniques. The structure of the subjects is shown in table 6.

Table 6: Structure of Subjects in the first, second and third Year

First year

Number of subjects	Subject	Total Credits
2	Building Technology: Design and construction principles	9.5
2	Real Estate Law: Principles and Property Rights	12
2	Economics: Principles of macro- and microeconomics. Financial Systems.	9.5
2	Information Technology: Basic Software and Data Bases	9
1	Management. Principles	6
1	Statistics	6
1	Financial Mathematics	4.5
1	Accounting Principles	4.5
1	Ethics in Real Estate	4.5

Second year

Number of subjects	Subject	Total Credits
1	Property Management	6
2	Building Technology: Construction and services	9
1	Real Estate Law: Urban Housing Rent Law	9
1	Real Estate Market Economy, general and Spanish real estate market	6

Number of subjects	Subject	Total Credits
1	Real Estate Taxes System	6
1	Work Market Spanish Law	4.5
1	Human Resources Management	4.5
2	Information Technology: GIS and Information networks	12
1	Real Estate Marketing. Principles	6
1	Advertising Techniques. Principles	4.5
Options		
1	Economic Analysis tools	4.5
1	Real Estate Marketing: Case Studies	4.5
1	GIS- Case Studies	4.5

Third year

Number of subjects	Subject	Total Credits
1	Building Technology: Facilities	4.5
1	Real Estate Law: Urban Law and Planning. Principles	6
1	Investment and Finance Real Estate	6
1	Information Technology: Networks of information II	6
1	Information Technology: Virtual tools	6
1	Principles of Valuation	6
2	Applied Foreign Language: English, French, German	9
Options:		
2	Property Management: residential and non-residential buildings	12
1	Building Technology: Maintenance of services	6
3	Real Estate Law: Administrative and Processes Law	14
1	Real Estate Law: Urban Law and Planning II	4.5
1	Real Estate Agent Image. Applied Advertising Techniques	4.5
1	Real Estate Cycles Analysis and Forecast	4.5
1	International Real Estate Markets	4.5
1	Housing Policy	4.5
1	Security on Building Process Law	4.5
1	Taxes Law. Case Studies	4.5
2	Property Management. Case Studies	9

18.2.3.4 Methods of teaching.

The teaching methods of the courses are based on the system of credits usual in Spanish universities. Under the system, each subject has a predetermined number of hours of contact time (lectures and practicals) which is equal to 10 hours per credit assigned. For example, a subject with 6 credits would have 60 hours of lectures and practicals. At the end of the course, students must have obtained a minimum of 225 credits in order to be awarded the Diploma. These credits are confirmed when the examinations for each subject are passed. The lectures are exclusive to real estate students. Attendance is compulsory for at least 80% of the total course time. The method is to attend classes, to write essays and to sit examinations.

Students are examined on the content of each subject and the recommended bibliography. Evaluation of students is by the final examinations, although each professor has power to decide to evaluate through essays in subjects with high practical content. The maximum number of opportunities students have in order to pass the exam is six in each subject.

Students at the University of Alicante can use a wide variety of virtual educational tools in "Campus Virtual" (http://www.ua.es). This is an innovative tool that allows the professor to run tutorial sessions, keep control over students, contact them, and send students up-to-date materials and information to improve their learning. Students also use other sources at the University, such as books in the central library, virtual library, computer rooms, and study rooms. Other services for students include:

- The Student Council: the most important organ for the students, it is also an information centre and has created several working committees (culture, services, environment, and sports).
- Office of Initiative for Employment (GIPE): promotes practical experience with firms, helps to complete the students' training and to find employment.
- University Defender: its function is keeping a watch on activities, guaranteeing the rights and interests of the members of the students. There are also services of mediation and conciliation, if required.

The International Relation Centre has developed a complete structure to support students' mobility and to make access for overseas students to the University of Alicante easier. It helps in matters such as lodging and Spanish courses.

18.2.4 Research

The immaturity of real estate studies in Spain and the lack of specialised researchers means that there is no tradition of real estate research in the Spanish universities. Research into construction technology, based in technical faculties such as architecture or engineering, is very advanced. However, economic, financial and taxation analysis is not well developed. The majority of researchers can be classified into two areas:

- Macroeconomics, related to construction activity and housing in all their aspects. Institutions promoting this research include the Banco de España (macroeconomic aspects) the Argentaria Foundation (housing and affordability) and the Ministry of Development, in matters related to Housing Facilities policy and the creation of databases.
- Financial institutions and Public Bodies from Regional Communities are important sources of research by funding.

The Economic Analysis of Housing has an important focus related to problems of affordability, market analysis, demographic determinants, selection of housing, taxes and planning.

There are no official real estate societies in Spain other than the Promoters' associations and the *Colegios Oficiales* (professional bodies) mentioned above. There is no association of owners, for instance.

There are also few magazines exclusively covering real estate, apart from some with just local influence. Some of the most important magazines, such as *Revista Española de Financiación de la Vivienda* of the Banco Hipotecario de España are unfortunately no longer published. At present the most important ones are connected with groups of promoters such as *Revista de la Construcción Tanitpress RCT*, which has important technical content, or *Euroconstruct*, a magazine covering innovation in European construction matters.

18.2.5 Conclusion

Real estate studies in Spain are starting to develop as a result of co-operation between Promoters, the *Colegios Oficiales*, and the universities. The advantages of this arrangement is that courses can have a high practical content, which will facilitate collaboration and support in the processes of research.

The current importance of, *inter alia*, development, the growth of urban areas and the demand for real estate services, mean that this specialisation will be very important in the near future. The number of courses available at university level will increase. In the same way, it is possible that the universities will dedicate part of their research facilities to this sector, expanding their already specialised departments. This process can be carried out at the same time as the standardisation of all aspects of real estate training in Europe.

18.3 Some Notes about Real Estate Market in Portugal

The Portuguese real estate market has remarkable similarities with Spain, in terms of structure, institutions and functions. There are, however, sufficient differences to require that it be viewed as a separate market. These include its property law, the institutionalisation of its professions, and education.

Following a brief description, the particularities of its organisations are explained in the following sections, in accordance with the information available.

18.3.1 Structure of the regulation of property and real estate activities

The system of regulation in Portugal follows similar principles to that of Spain, in that there is a structure of institutions, which exercises control of properties and their uses.

The property registry, *Registro Predial* records details of properties as well as changes in their ownership and charges to which they are subject. The institution is independent, although it is a public body. In addition to its main function as a registry, it is also a source of real estate information, as the registers are public. As in Spain, the managers of the registry, *Registradores de la Propiedad*, belong to a specific profession, to which entry is regulated.

The urban real estate cadaster, *Cadastro Imobiliário Urbano*, belongs to the fiscal directorate (*Direcçao General de Contribuçoes e Impostos*) of the Ministry of Economics. Its principal role is similar to the Spanish Cadaster, i.e. the control of real estate properties and ownership and also assessment of property values for taxation purposes. It is also responsible for the control and management of urban areas.

A third type of institution in Portugal is the Chamber of Property (*Cámaras de la Propiedad*) of each municipality. These organisations manage specific aspects of urban property and act as a link between owners and tenants. In Spain, the equivalent institutions were abolished in the 1980s, although since the 1990s some cities have reintroduced them.

There are other institutions, mainly branches of different government departments, which hold details and values of property in Portugal. For example the Ministry of Cultural Heritage classifies historic buildings and the National Education Ministry publishes *Inventario e Valorizaçao do Património Imobiliário Artístico e Histórico da Naçao* (Inventory and Valuation of the Artistic and Historic Real Estate Heritage of Portugal).

On purchase, property ownership should be verified by a notary, in a process that is more formal than a simple private contract of sale. As in

Spain, property rights are transferred when the notary has completed the documents. The change of ownership must then be entered in the Property Registry.

18.3.2 Real Estate activities and professionals in Portugal.

There is a wide range of regulation of real estate activities, from technical rules controlling construction to tax and valuation. Unlike Spain, Portugal does not have restrictions on the right to provide real estate services and there are no *Colegios oficiales* with exclusive power over certain areas. This means that real estate professionals have different forms of association. For example, quantity surveyors are normally members of *Sindicato dos Agentes Technicos de Arquitectura e Engenharia* (the association of architectural and engineering technicians) while appraisers belong to an association named *Associaçao Portuguesa de Avaliaçoes de Engenharia* (Portuguese Association of Engineering Appraisers)

In Portugal, real estate appraisers, managers, promoters and brokers, are all considered to be real estate professionals, although only brokers are regulated by law. The regulations require that brokers should have had at least 60 hours of relevant education provided by an officially licensed institution. As in Spain, promoters have an important role in the development and construction process. Portugal also has long-standing associations to co-ordinate these activities

On the other hand, real estate and property managers are not regarded as real estate professionals. Their activities are specifically governed, as in Spain, by the *Ley do Propiedade Horizontal* (Horizontal[3] Property Law) as a 'leader or procurator that acts for and in, the interests of the condominium owner'[4]. Their role is, therefore, regulated in terms of rights and obligations, although not regarded as the province of a qualified professional. Any person representing the owner of a property may carry it out, whether or not they have had specific or recognised education or training.

Table 7 shows the range of real estate professions in Portugal. It includes a non- exhaustive list of the different types of associations.

Membership of the professional bodies is usually applied for directly after being awarded an official academic qualification (in the case of architects, technical architects, engineers and appraisers), obtaining degree in a Higher Education Institution with an official licence (*mediators imobiliarios* - agents) or on appointment, in the case of property managers.

Table 7: Real Estate Professionals in Portugal

Profession	Regulation	Activity	Association
REAL ESTATE BROKERS (mediadores imobiliários)	Regulated- 60 hours at least of real estate education	-Marketing and property advertising -Property brokers	Associaçao do Mediadoras Imobiliárias do Norte
PROPERTY MANAGERS (administradores de propiedad o mandatarios)	Ley do Propiedade Horizontal	-Property management (urban and rural) -Building maintenance and repair (housing and other building) - Facility management	
ARCHITECTS	Graduated Education and Licensed	-Project design -Urban planning -Cartography -Urban development	
ARQUITECTOS TÉCNICOS	Graduated Education and Licensed	-Building Pathology -Construction management	Sindicato dos Agentes Technicos de Arquitectura e Engenharia,
ENGINEERING (Engenharia)	Graduated Education and Licensed	-Civil engineering, infrastructures -Urban development -Geodesy y geophysics -Ground engineering -Mineral exploitation -Oceanography	
APPRAISERS (Avaliadores imobiliários)	real estate education at university level	-Appraisal and property valuations for financial purposes	Associaçao Portuguesa de Avaliaçoes de Engenharia
PROMOTERS (Promotores)	None	-Construction management -Finance and investment -Project management	Fomento Imobiliário, Cooperativa de Habitaçao e Construçao. Sociedade Nacional de Fomento Imobiliario.

Source: own research

18.3.3 University real estate education and research in Portugal

In Portugal, there are no specific real estate courses in the universities, although there are some departments that specialise in the analysis of real estate sectors and offer specific education on selected topics. Real estate education is provided by institutions licensed by the Education Ministry to teach and to grant professional qualifications. One example is the *Escola Superior do Actividades Imobiliárias* - ESAI (High School of Real Estate Activities) in Lisbon.

Universities and other institutions specialising in real estate studies (i.e. carrying out research or with some degree of education in real topics) may be classified as follows:

a) **Official Studies**
 − Instituto Superior de Economia e Gestao. Universidade Técnica de Lisboa (Lisbon University)
 − Facultad de Economía (Economics Faculty), Univ. Nova de Lisboa
 − Instituto superior de Ciencias del Trabajo y de la Empresa. Univ. Lisboa (Lisbon University)
 − Dpto. de Geografía Humana e Planeamiento Regional e Local, Univ. Lisboa (Lisbon University)
 − Facultad de Engenharia, Univ. Do Porto

b) **Private**
 − Escola Superior de Actividades Imobiliárias (ESAI), (licensed by the Education Ministry.

c) **Other**
 − Centro de Estudos Territoriais ISCTE
 − Sociedade Nacional de Fomento Imobiliário, Cooperativa de Habitaçao e Construçao.
 − Empresa de Consultadoria de Investimento Imobiliário

According to the publications available, real estate research is mainly carried out in various specialised departments of Portuguese universities, in doctoral programs developing very concrete aspects of real estate, technical as well as economic and financial. Other institutions that are trying to improve real estate research are public bodies related to the government, such as the Culture Ministry, Education Ministry, and financial institutions, e.g. the National Society of Real Estate Credit (*Sociedade Nacional de Crédito Imobiliário*).

There are a number of specialised magazines and journals, e.g. Mercado Imobiliario, Confidencial Imobiliario, Investimento Imobiliário o Imobiliario (revista especializada em negócios).

NOTES

[1] Undergraduate courses in Universities are 'non-official' that means designed and run by each University.

[2] These titles are the result of different agreement between the training schools, (mainly the school of Real Estate Administrators and also the Real Estate Agents in Barcelona), and the universities of every area to develop the training of this group.

[3] The word "horizontal" is used to refer to the type of property. A 'horizontal' property means a share of the total building, e.g. an apartment inside a block, which itself is 'common' property for all owners as distinct from the private property in each apartment. The specific law that create rules on this type of properties is, in Spain and in Portugal, the Horizontal Property Law – Ley de Propiedad Horizontal.

[4] Ley do Propiedade Horizontal, secçao III, cap.3 'Administraçao do condominio'.

REFERENCES

Alonso Sánchez, B.1995, El Administrador de Fincas en el régimen de la Propiedad Horizontal, Aranzadi Civil, num. 20, pags. 11-33.

Antunes, A. and Severino, N, 1991, Guia Jurídico do Arrendamento e Condominio, edit. Heptágono, Lisboa.

Butler, J.Q., Guntermann, K.L. and Wolverton, M, 1998, Integrating the Real Estate Curriculum, Journal of Real Estate Practice and Education, vol 1(1), pags. 51-66.

Consejo General de Colegios de Administradores de Fincas, 1999, Texto de la Ley de Propiedad Horizontal, Madrid.

Correia, M. 1994, Mediadoras imobiliarias, Asociaçao das Mediadoras Imobiliárias do Norte.O Porto.

Cossa, Mario S.(1994), Imobiliario: investimentos, organizaçao e gestao, Licenciatura em Gestao de Empresas, Instituto Superior de Economía e Gestao, Universidade Técnica de Lisboa.

De La Fuente Junto, Angel, 1974, El Registro de la Propiedad en los sistemas Latinos, Centro de Estudios Hipotecarios, Madrid, tomo I.

Decreto del 17.12.1949, num 1949,65 sobre la creación del Colegio de Agentes de la Propiedad Inmobiliaria.

Decreto del 28.1.69, que publica los estatutos.

Decreto num 3248/69 del 4.12.69, que publica los estatutos del Colegio de Agentes de la Propiedad Inmobiliaria.

Expreso Guia Imobiliário de Portugal, varios números.

Harris, Robert, G,1984, The Values of Economic Theory in Management Education, Economic theory and management Education, 74(2), pags. 122-126.

Ley 10/1992 del 30 de abril sobre la Propiedad Horizontal.

Ley 2/1988 del 23 de febrero sobre la Propiedad Horizontal.

Ley 3/1990 del 21 de junio sobre la Propiedad Horizontal.

Ley 49/1960 del 21.7.1960, sobre la Propiedad Horizontal.

Ley 7/1997, que actualiza los estatutos del Colegio Profesional de Arquitectura Técnica.

Ley de Reforma de la Propiedad Horizontal, del 18.3.1999.

Ley num. 49/1960, del 21 de julio sobre Propiedad Horizontal.

Ley Sindical de 1977, por la que se crean las organizaciones empresariales y sindicales.

Mendes, Isabel P.,1992, O registro predial e a segurança jurídica nos negócios imobiliários: estudos apresentados no IX Congresso Internacional de Direito Registral, Coimbra.

Moitinho de Almeida, 1996, Propiedade Horizontal, Almedina, Coimbra.

R.Decreto de 1 de abril de 1968, de creación del Colegio de Administradores de Fincas.

Rabianski, J.S. and Black, R.t, 1998, Real Property Brokerage Education and License Law, Journal of Real Estate Practice and Education, vol 1(1), pags. 21-38.

Real Decreto del Ministerio de Obras Públicas y Urbanismo del 13.5.77 y del 16.2.83, sobre creación del Colegio Profesional de Arquitectura Técnica.

Roulac, Stephen E., 1996, Innovative Thought Leadership and the Community of Real Estate Scholars, The Journal of Real Estate Research, vol. 12(3), pags 315-322.

Royal Institution of Chartered Surveyors (RICS), APC Requirements & Competencies. Assessment of Professional Competence, London.

Chapter 19

Sweden

Stellan Lundström
Department of Real Estate & Construction Management, The Royal Institute of Technology, Stockholm, Sweden

19.1 Introduction

The origin of the Swedish real estate education on an academic level was in the professions of surveying, forestry and agronomy. Until the 1960s, research and education in the field of real estate economics was primarily concerned with rural issues. The main subjects were valuation, and compensation related to land consolidation and expropriation.

In 1965, a professorship in Real Estate Economics was established at the School of Surveying, which is located at the Royal Institute of Technology (*Kungliga Tekniska Hoegskolan*, KTH) in Stockholm. This professorship has been the foundation of a strong property profession in Sweden. The real estate curriculum at KTH has been a benchmark for academics in Sweden for the last ten years. There are no similar professorships, either elsewhere in Sweden, or in any of the other Nordic countries (Denmark, Iceland, Norway and Finland).

The real estate curriculum at KTH has gradually turned towards Urban Economics. By 1980, almost all elements of agricultural economics had been phased out. Since then, some 800 students have been awarded Master's degrees in surveying (4½ years of study) with a specialisation in real estate economics. The majority of them are meanwhile employed within four types of enterprise:

- Private and public real estate companies,
- Institutional investors,
- Real estate consulting firms,
- Banks and other types of financial institutions.

In the last few years, almost all traditional valuation firms have been taken over by real estate consulting firms. All of them have international partners or other connections. A new trend is also for traditional accounting firms to open real estate divisions. This rapid restructuring of the market for real estate consultancy will continue, influenced by the integration of the real estate market into the capital market.

The major strength of academically qualified property professionals was originally in the field of valuation and investment analysis. During the last 20 years, research and a special designed curriculum has resulted in fast growth in jobs dealing with asset and property management. At the start of the new millennium there is a clear tendency for transaction-based assignments to increase. Corporate finance and brokerage are areas that are developing.

19.2 Swedish real property in brief

In 1999, the total Swedish real property stock was valued at some 4,600 billion SEK

(1 USD = 8 SEK). Total assets in Sweden could be valued at roughly 7,200 billion SEK (equivalent to four times the GDP of around 1,800 billion SEK). Real property therefore accounts for more than 50 % of total assets. Table 1 shows that, notably, the listed companies[1] hold real property with an estimated market value of 180 billion SEK, which is about 4% of the total real property value.

The commercial transaction market, which comprises the five first categories in Table 1, has an annual volume of some 100 billion SEK. The real estate crisis in Sweden had ended by 1995 and has been followed by un-precedented restructuring activities. Proactive management of real estate portfolios will continue to expand and will increase the need for academic skills in areas like asset management and corporate finance.

Operation, maintenance and investment costs for property occupiers within the rental sector (including owner-occupiers and the public sector) can be estimated at some 200 billion SEK a year. By tradition, almost all property management activities in Sweden have been carried out in-house. This scenario is undergoing change, with big Swedish corporations like Ericsson being the forerunners with extensive programs for outsourcing and facility management.

Table 1: The Swedish real property sector, year 1999, by company/real property type and estimated market value (1 USD = 8 SEK).[2]

Type of Company / Real Property	Market Value (Billion SEK)
Public real property companies	180
Institutional investors	170
Private owners of residential and commercial property	320
Municipal housing companies	320
Owner-Occupiers (Industrial)	320
Public sector real property	350
Tenant-owned real property (co-operatives)	250
Detached houses and holiday houses	1,800
Agricultural and forest property	600
Other real property: Power plants etc	200
Total	4,600

19.3 Private institutions

The Association of Real Estate Economics (SFF) now has about 600 members. SFF started in the 1960's as an organisation primarily for valuers. The scope is now broader and almost all types of property professionals can be members. The main SFF activities are short courses and seminars, which are open to the public.

In 1994, SFF established a private authorisation scheme for valuers, with three types of authorisation. Some 150 valuers now hold a general authorisa-tion for valuation of all types of property, 20 valuers hold authorisations for agricultural property only, and there are 40 authorised residential property valuers. It is a requirement that general valuers should have had at least 3½ years (140 credits) of university studies in areas such as mathematics, statis-tics, computer science, accounting, macro- and microeconomics, general business economics, real estate economics, real estate law, building and development technique.[3]

A couple of hundred full and part time valuers, mainly of residential properties, are not authorised as authorisation is not compulsory. By time has the professional buyers of valuation services recognized the importance of having a kind of quality guarantee for the information provided within the valuation report. This recognition of the authorization is not obvious in the same way for individuals buying valuation service two or three times during there life time. Authorisation is then not primarily working as a consumer protection.

A Swedish property index (SFI) was established for commercial property in 1997. The total index portfolio in the year 2000 was close to 200 billion SEK. A special valuation guideline for the index states that all valuations should be undertaken by authorised valuers or people with corresponding competence. More than 80% of all index valuations are conducted by discounted cash flow analysis, with feedback of all parameter assumptions, together with information about the actual outcome from property management.

In Sweden there are about 4,700 real estate brokers. The special law controlling brokers states that a broker should be publicly registered and under public control. From 1998, all newly-registered brokers must have at least two years (80 credits) of academic education in the areas of real estate brokerage, civil and real estate law, tax law, building and valuation technique and general business economics.

The status of the property and asset management sectors has gradually improved as young people with academic education in both business and real estate economics enter the field. So far there are no licensing or authorisation schemes for people working in property and asset management.

19.4 Research in Real Estate Economics

Research with a prime focus on real estate economics is undertaken at three universities:

1. the Department of Real Estate & Construction Management at KTH in Stockholm;
2. the Institute of Housing Research at Uppsala University (located in the city of Gaevle);
3. the Department of Finance at the Stockholm School of Economics.

The KTH department has seven professors, associate professors or senior lecturers with a doctoral degree in general economics or real estate economics[4]. There are about ten ongoing research projects in the areas of valuation, investment analysis, property management, property cycles, housing, and urban economics. Currently there are eight doctoral students active in the area of Real Estate Economics. The research approaches are on a wide scale, from quantitative financial economics to normative institutional and behavioural approaches.

The Institute of Housing Research in Gaevle has two professors who deal with housing economics[5]. The Institute hosts the European Network for Housing Research, ENHR. As an interdisciplinary centre, with some 40 people employed, it is one of the biggest research centres in Europe. The research group has no formal link to any educational programme in real estate economics.

Stockholm School of Economics has one professor[6] who covers research topics related to real estate economics. The school offers an elective Master's course (5 credits) in real estate finance. The school has no educational programmes devoted to real estate economics.

Research results are normally presented in internal, departmental series of research reports. An increasing proportion of research reports are written in English. As there is no Swedish or Scandinavian academic journal for Real Estate Economics, most of the research results are presented at international conferences and in journals in the UK and USA.

19.5 The KTH and Lund Curricula

In the year 2000 there were two universities in Sweden with Master's programmes in real estate economics - KTH in Stockholm and the University of Lund. The Swedish University of Agricultural Science in Uppsala also offers courses in real estate economics. Undergraduate (Bachelor's degree) programmes, where a considerable amount of the courses cover real estate economics, can be found at the polytechnics of Gaevle/Sandviken, Trollhaettan, Karlstad and Malmoe. Another 20 universities and polytechnics have courses in economics where real estate economics is a part.

Real estate economics at KTH in Stockholm is part of the study programme in Surveying. The formal title of the degree is Master of Science in Surveying with specialisation in Building & Real Estate Economics. The nominal study time is 4½ years. All students enter the school to fulfil the Master's programme. Unlike many other universities around the world, there is no possibility for the award of a Bachelor's degree after three years.

Every year approximately 110 students are admitted to the school of surveying. After two years of common studies, the students can choose between three main programmes: 1) Surveying & Mapping; 2) Land Development & Management; 3) Building & Real Estate Economics. About half the group of

110 normally chooses Building & Real Estate Economics. In this group, for many years, there has been a 50/50 mix of male and female students.

The first two years of studies have courses that are common for the whole of KTH, but also courses that should give a perspective of the broader surveying science. This inevitably means that some of the courses are far from tailor-made for real estate economists. The first two years of studies (80 credits) cover the following topics: Mathematics and statistics (22); GIS and mapping (17); Land engineering and construction (10); General business economics (9); Data and programming (8); Civil law (5); Land management (5); Ecology (4).

During the third and fourth years students have the possibility to formulate an individual study plan. Courses can, subject to approval, be taken at KTH or at any other university in Sweden or abroad. The third and fourth years of courses at KTH are all in modules of 5 credits, which means that a total of 16 courses must be chosen. The following 21 courses are provided by KTH. Students having a special interest in real state economics take courses 4-8 and add courses like 13-17 to obtain different applications, which may be useful for their first employment:

1. Operations, Maintenance and Modernisation Techniques
2. Buildings and Building Services Engineering
3. Management
4. Real Estate Economics
5. Business Cycles in Construction and Real Estate Markets*
6. Investment Analysis*
7. Financial Analysis*
8. Real Estate Finance and Economics*
9. Environmental Economics
10. Urban Land Economics
11. Law of Real Estate
12. Law of Leaseholds
13. Market Analysis and Marketing*
14. Real Estate Brokerage
15. Management Control
16. Real Estate Management
17. Real Estate Valuation*
18. Information Technology in Construction
19. Construction Management
20. Facilities Management*
21. Construction Economics

(*These courses are given in English)

The applied courses are based upon case studies and a problem-based learning approach is used. All courses with the standard 5 credits are based on 30 hours of lectures and 30 hours of classroom work. The assessment of each course is always based on a mixture of exercises and a written examination. All courses include oral and written presentations. Textbooks in English are used in almost all courses, even if the course is given in Swedish.

The Master of Science studies are completed by a thesis (20 credits). As part of the thesis work the students have to study theory of science and research methodology. Suggested topics for theses are provided by the school and the industry in co-operation. In some cases private firms also give limited financial support to students for work of special interest.

A school of surveying was established at the University of Lund in the beginning of the 1990's. The intake is 30 students each year and the programme is largely similar to the KTH programme. So far there are no staff with higher academic degrees in real estate economics.

19.6 International Master's programmes

In 1998, an international Master's program (40 course credits plus 20 credits for thesis work) in Real Estate & Construction Management was established at KTH. In the first year, 15 students from Europe, Africa and Asia entered the program. For the academic year 2000/2001 the name of the programme has been changed to Real Estate Management. The body of the programme consists of those courses in the main KTH MSc programme which are given in English (marked with an asterisk in the above list).

In 1996, KTH launched a specially designed Master's program in Land Management for students from the former Soviet Union. Every year 30 students from Russia, The Baltic States, Ukraine and Belarus take courses (40 credits) in areas such as Land Information Systems, Real Estate Law, Business Economics, Real Estate Economics and Valuation. Thesis work (20 credits) is carried out in the home country. The Swedish government finances the whole programme. The objective is for students to return to their home universities in order to create an academic body in real estate.

19.7 Executive education

Every year, the Department for Real Estate & Construction Management at KTH gives a couple of courses, of 5 credits each, which are specially designed for real estate executives. 30 to 50 students attend each course. During the last 15 years about 1,200 executives have taken courses such as Real Estate Valuation, Mortgage Underwriting, Management Control of the Real Estate Firm, Real Estate Management in the Public Sector, and Facilities

Management. Executive courses are regarded as a valuable link between KTH and the industry.

19.8 Conclusion

The presence of a relatively large academic department, devoted to real estate economics, has had a profound effect on the property profession in Sweden. The location, within an institute of technology and the school of surveying, provides both opportunities and restrictions. There is the possibility for an interdisciplinary approach, with a strong mathematical base, having a mixture of law, planning, environmental issues and economics. However, economics is never the "core business" at an institute of technology and the possibilities for expansion of the economics part of the curriculum are limited. One could say that real estate economists will never be economists!

NOTES

[1] 27 real estate companies are listed at the Stockholm stock exchange. Four public construction companies are also holders of considerable real estate portfolios. A higher number of public real estate companies in Europe is only found in the UK.

[2] The numbers are basically from the Swedish General Assessment, updated by The Swedish Property Index, SFI.

[3] The high number of valuers with a general authorisation is explained by the fact that the academic education of valuers is only found within the broad Master's programs at KTH and the University of Lund.

[4] Roland Andersson, Mats Boman, Hakan Bejrum, Hans Lind, Stellan Lundstroem, Erik Persson and Kurt Psilander.

[5] Bengt Turner and Rune Wigren.

[6] Professor Peter Englund

Chapter 20

Switzerland

Philippe Favarger
Swiss Federal Institute of Technology, Lausanne, Switzerland

Martin Hoesli
University of Geneva; HEC, Geneva, Switzerland and University of Aberdeen, Department of Accountancy & Finance, Aberdeen, Scotland

20.1 Introduction

In Switzerland, there are few restrictions on entry to the real estate professions: no specific training course, nor success in any specific examination, is required. This means that anybody can decide to be an appraiser, a property manager or a broker. As is the case for several other industries in Switzerland, real estate professionals usually complete an apprenticeship in the field, or earn a more general university degree in a field such as economics, business or law. Several training opportunities, however, are offered in

Switzerland, either in universities or related to professional bodies. A feature of Swiss real estate education is that professional and university training programmes are not linked, so that no exemptions are available.

This chapter is organised as follows. We first discuss real estate education in universities. We then present Swiss real estate professional bodies. Training and certificates offered by these bodies are discussed next. Finally, real estate publications in Switzerland are presented.

20.2 Real Estate Education in Universities

Real estate education in Swiss universities is limited, compared with the situation in other countries. There are some undergraduate courses, however, and the Swiss Institute of Technology in Lausanne has recently launched a Master's degree in real estate appraisal. Although some lectures of the FAME (international centre for Financial Asset Management and Engineering) doctoral programme in finance are devoted to real estate, no doctoral course in real estate exists in Switzerland.

As mentioned, the Swiss Federal Institute of Technology in Lausanne offers a Master's degree in real estate appraisal, jointly with the Universities of Fribourg and Geneva and the Collège suisse des experts architectes (CSEA). This degree covers three fields: the legal framework of the judicial assessment of real estate, the defects in buildings, and real estate valuation. Each field is covered by a module that can be attended independently of the others. The main courses include:

- Legal framework: judicial organisation, procedures in civil courts, the assessment process, appraisal for private purposes, the responsibility of the expert, and arbitration.
- Defects in buildings: the mechanical, thermal and hydric equilibria, the deficiencies of structures, materials and components, and the diagnosis of defects in structures, services, installations and comfort.
- Real estate valuation: real estate economics and finance, statistics, and valuation methods (the sales comparison method, the income approach and the depreciated cost approach).

The duration of the full course is almost two years (600 hours of teaching and exercises plus 600 hours for the Master's thesis). Participants may work part-time (80%) during the course. To register for the Master's degree, a candidate should have a university degree. The course is mainly designed for architects and engineers – the former usually acting as valuers in Switzerland, but graduates in economics or social sciences may also attend.

At the University of Geneva, it is possible to earn a "minor" in urban and real estate studies at the undergraduate level (*licence*). (A minor is a second field of specialisation, which a student chooses in addition to his/her main field of study or "major".) A student who chooses this minor will have to take a number of courses in urban and real estate studies (approximately 500 hours). These courses include planning, finance, real estate investments, economics, urban geography and history. The University of Geneva also offers both an undergraduate and a postgraduate course in real estate investments as part of its business curriculum, and an undergraduate course in real estate economics at its Institute of Architecture.

The University of St.Gallen also offers an undergraduate course in real estate economics and finance, as part of its economics curriculum.

20.3 Real Estate Professional Bodies

The main professional associations encompass property managers, brokers, condominium managers and in some cases developers. These bodies are organised at *canton* level (*cantons* are the unit of regional government in Switzerland). Some cantons (such as Geneva, for instance) have several professional societies, whereas most other cantons have only one. The associations are grouped by language spoken in the respective cantons (German, French or Italian), rather than nationally. For German- and Italian-speaking cantons, the grouping is the *Schweizerischer Verband der Immobilien-Treuhänder* (SVIT – Swiss association of real estate managers), whereas the *Union suisse des professionnels de l'immobilier* (USPI – Swiss union of property professionals) covers the French-speaking cantons.

There are also professional bodies for real estate appraisers. In French-speaking Switzerland, the *Chambre d'experts en estimations immobilières* (CEI – chamber of real estate valuers) is part of the SVIT. In German-speaking Switzerland, the two appraisers' associations (*Schweizerische Vereinigung kantonaler Grundstückbewertungexperten*, SVKG – Swiss association of canton land valuers; and the *Schweizerischer Immobilien-schätzer-Verband*, SIV – Swiss property valuers' association) are independent entities. There is also a national body, which encompasses both real estate appraisers and technical assessors (the *Collège suisse des experts architectes*, CSEA).

20.4 Training and Certificates offered by Professional Bodies

The Swiss Society of Financial Analysts and Portfolio Managers (SSFP) offers two diplomas in finance. The first programme is aimed mainly at financial analysts and portfolio managers and leads to the Certified International Investment Analyst (CIIA™) diploma. Whereas this diploma places only marginal focus on real estate, the other diploma (Federal Diploma for Experts in Finance and Investments) encompasses all classes of assets, with 40 hours being devoted to real estate (real estate economics, valuation, indices, portfolio management and financing). This diploma is intended for experts in finance and investments. The duration of each diploma programme is one year.

The professional bodies organise courses which lead to three certificates: the *Brevet fédéral de gérant d'immeubles* (certificate for property managers), the *Diplôme fédéral de régisseur et courtier en immeubles* (diploma for property managers and brokers) and the *Brevet fédéral d'expert en estimations immobilières* (certificate for property valuers). The certificate for property managers is a foundation training course, whereas the diploma is at a higher level and is intended for professionals who want to start their own business. All three programmes lead to nationally recognised designations and courses are offered both in German (in Zurich) and in French (in Lausanne). It is possible to enrol for the examinations without having attended the courses.

As is the case throughout the Swiss real estate industry, it is not compulsory to hold a certificate or diploma in order to be a property manager, broker or appraiser. An exception to this is in some German-speaking cantons, where a recognised qualification is required for real estate brokers. In some cantons, it is compulsory to hold the certificate for property managers in order to join a professional body. Before being allowed to train apprentices, those who do not hold either the certificate or the diploma for property managers must attend a special course.

To register for the examinations of the certificate for property managers (*Brevet fédéral de gérant d'immeubles*), the successful completion of an apprenticeship (three years) and a minimum of four years of practical experience in real estate are required. The duration of the part-time course is one year (142 hours of teaching). The main subjects encompass law, real estate brokerage, real estate management and accounting.

To register for the diploma for property managers and brokers (*Diplôme fédéral de régisseur et courtier en immeubles*), a candidate must either:

a) have finished his/her apprenticeship (three years) and have a minimum of six years of practical experience in real estate, or

b) hold the *Brevet fédéral de gérant d'immeubles* with an additional two years of practical experience.

The duration of the part-time course is two years (342 hours of teaching). In addition to the subjects covered at certificate level, the diploma course includes the subjects of taxation, planning, brokerage, appraisal, management, political economy, marketing and construction.

To register for the examinations of the certificate for property valuers (*Brevet fédéral d'expert en estimations immobilières*), the successful completion of an apprenticeship, a high school or technical school qualification, or the certificate for property managers, or the diploma for property managers and brokers, plus a total of six years' practical experience in real estate are required. The duration of the part-time course is two to three semesters (174 hours of teaching). The main subjects are law, real estate valuation, political economy, planning and technology.

In Geneva, the *Institut d'Etudes Immobilières* (Institute for Real Estate Studies) offers a diploma in real estate. In order to apply for admission to this diploma, students must hold a degree in either business, law, or architecture. The students of the Institute take courses both at the University of Geneva (in business and law) and within the Institute. The main courses include: law, accountancy, finance, real estate valuation, real estate investments, subsidised housing, taxation, real estate development, and institutional investment. Approximately 140 hours of tuition at the Institute and 200 hours at the University are required for holders of an undergraduate degree in either business or law (400 hours for the holders of an undergraduate degree in architecture). The duration of the programme is one year.

20.5 Real Estate Publications

Consistent with the paucity of real estate education in the country, there are no academic real estate journals in Switzerland. Real estate papers typically appear in either the economics journal (*Swiss Journal of Economics and Statistics*), the finance journal (*Financial Markets and Portfolio Management*) or the accounting journal (*Der Schweizer Treuhänder*). Several professional real estate periodicals are published, however (e.g. *Immobilien Business, Immobilier romand, der Immobilien Treuhänder, Propriété, der Schweizerische Hauseigentümer* and *Immobilia*).

REFERENCES

Fierz, K. (1998) *Wert und Zins bei Immobilien*, Schriftenreihe der Treuhandkammer Band 56, Zurich.

Hoesli, M., Bender, A. R. and Favarger, P. (1996) "Switzerland", *in European Valuation Practice – Theory and Techniques*, Adair, A., Downie, M. L., McGreal, S. and Vos, G. (Eds), London: E & FN Spon, pp. 249-264.

Hoesli, M., Giaccotto, C. and Favarger, P. (1997) "Three new real estate price indices for Geneva, Switzerland", *The Journal of Real Estate Finance and Economics*, 15(1), pp. 93-109.

Hoesli, M. and Hamelink, F. (1997) "An examination of the role of Geneva and Zurich housing in Swiss institutional portfolios", *Journal of Property Valuation and Investment*, 15(4), pp. 354-371.

Hoesli, M. and MacGregor, B. D. (2000*) Property Investment – Principles and Practice of Portfolio Management*, Harlow: Longman.

Naegeli, W. and Wenger, H. (1997) *Der Liegenschaftenschätzer*, Zurich: Schultess Polygraphischer Verlag.

Sohre, P., Ships, B. and Jaeger, F. (1993) *Hypothekarkreditmarkt*, Chur: Verlag Rüegger.

Wüest und Partner (2000) *Immo-Monitoring 2000*, Zurich: Verlag W&P.

Chapter 21

Turkey

Zeynep Önder
Bilkent University, Faculty of Business Administration, Bilkent, Ankara, Turkey

21.1 Introduction

Real estate was always considered to be a traditional investment choice in Turkey because of the unavailability of other investment alternatives, such as stocks and bonds, before the establishment of the Istanbul Stock Exchange (ISE) in 1986. According to the results of the 1994 Household Income Distribution Survey, the home ownership rate in Turkey was very high by international comparison, at 70.88 percent. In addition, most of household incomes are used for housing-related expenditures. However, despite the importance of real estate to Turkey, research and education in this field have been very limited. Education has developed as the need has arisen, while research has been carried out as the necessary data have become available. In this paper, first, the background to the Turkish real estate market will be described. Then, the real estate professions, education and research in Turkey will be discussed.

21.2 Background

Since the 1950s, the migration of households from rural areas to the cities has increased the demand for housing in urban areas (Şenyapılı and Türel, 1996). The mortgage market has not been well developed in Turkey: buying a house therefore requires a large amount of capital. Lenders' requirements for a permanent income and high levels of equity led to development of slum houses on the outskirts of the cities. The limited amount of land available in the cities has also substantially increased in value. The supply of land has been increased by the development of new urban areas on the outskirts of the cities and by the legalisation of development on the previously unauthorised land where slum houses were located. Allowing the development of higher buildings in the inner cities has also increased densities.

The Housing Development Authority (HDA), established in 1984, has helped to increase housing production. It provides housing finance to co-operatives and other builders of multi-family housing units; sells housing units built on the Authority's land; and provides finance for housing units built on municipal land. 85 percent of the total amount of loans provided by the HDA have been taken by co-operatives. Through co-operatives, the HDA provides loans to individuals who purchase housing units that the co-operatives have built. There is a limit to the amount that can be borrowed, based on the size of the housing unit. These loans are medium to long term, 5- year or 10-year loans with relatively low interest rates.

Real estate investment trusts are new to Turkish investors. They were established only recently, after the preparation of the necessary regulations in 1995. The first real estate investment trust was offered in 1998. These trusts and their organising companies will increase the need for research into commercial real estate.

21.3 Property Professions

The property professions in Turkey can be divided into five categories: developers, appraisers, investors, brokers and property managers. Although some professional associations exist, their regulation and licensing are not well established except for development planners and real estate investment companies. There are special regulations regarding to the qualifications of the development planners and the real estate investment companies are regulated by the Capital Market Board of Turkey.[1]

In Turkey, most developers are involved in housing projects. For example, according to the State Institute of Statistics (1997), in 1997 92.95 percent of fully and partially completed buildings (out of a total number of 58,028 buildings) were residential while only 6.15 percent were commercial or industrial. Housing therefore constitutes by far the major part of the new construction. Moreover, 105 of the 109 members of the Turkish Contractors' Association are involved in the development of residential and commercial properties. Türel (1996) examined some characteristics of the developers that are involved in residential development projects.[2] His sample consisted of small-scale builders, those that built residential properties as contractors for co-operatives receiving loans from the HDA, and large-scale developers constructing the satellite-city type of residential and commercial developments. He found that the majority of these builders were civil engineers or architects. 77 percent of the builders in his sample were involved in building properties for sale, while the rest were contractors for co-operatives or the state. Although one third of the builders purchased land by payment before construction, most of them acquired it by offering some of the units of the property to be constructed to the previous owner of the land.

According to Turkish law, development planners are required to have some qualifications. For example, in order to plan a development on land of up to 200 hectares, with a projected population of less than 10,000, planners must satisfy three conditions. They must have:

1. at least an M.Sc. degree in city and regional planning or urban design and a B.Sc. degree in city planning or architecture,
2. experience as a planner in public or private planning organisations, and
3. achieved success in urban planning competitions.

There are increased educational, experience and achievements requirements for planners of larger areas of land and more heavily populated areas.

Real estate brokers in Turkey are not required to have any special education or licence to undertake their profession: most of them consider real estate brokerage to be their secondary occupation. They have developed haphazardly, since the late 1970s, as small-scale entrepreneurs. In addition to arranging buying, selling or renting of property on behalf of a principal, in return for a fee or a commission, some also act as real estate investment consultants or experts in real estate appraisal.

The first formal organisation for the real estate brokerage profession in Turkey was the Ankara Realtors' Organisation, which was established in 1991. However, not all brokerage firms in Ankara are members of the organisation, neither are they required to be members in order to become a real estate broker. Ankara brokers secured a chamber in Ankara Chamber of

Commerce in 1999. This implies that real estate brokerage has begun to be recognised as a profession in Ankara. However, this factor does not apply to the whole country.[3]

There are two types of real estate agencies in Turkey: individual real estate brokers and brokerage chains. Some individual real estate brokers are members of realtors' organisations. Since there is no statutory regulation of the real estate brokerage market, the realtor organisations try to regulate the market themselves. For example, members of the Ankara Realtors' Organisation are required to have taken some courses before they may act as a real estate broker. The courses include deed registration, land survey, real estate marketing, real estate law and city planning. Members are not allowed to undertake any other profession except that of real estate agent or real estate consultant. They are required to use standard types of contract. The level of fees to be charged is also determined by the organisation.

Hafızoğulları (1997) surveyed a randomly-selected sample of individual real estate brokers in Ankara. She found that only 11.3 percent of them had more than 10 years' experience while almost two-thirds of her sample had less than 6 years' experience. 86.8 percent of the brokers had another occupation apart from real estate brokerage. 12.2 percent of them worked alone, without any supporting personnel. These results indicate that real estate brokerage tends to be regarded as a second job rather than as a professional service in Turkey.

The "chain" real estate brokers are not the members of the Realtors Organisation. However, in order to become a member of a chain real estate company, they must take some courses offered by their parent company and pay a franchising fee. They provide a kind of multiple listing service. Each member gives all the information available to the central real estate database, which is regularly updated.

Two types of appraisal companies, government-supported and private, are engaged in real estate valuation and consulting. There are two government-supported appraisal companies. Both of these originally operated as special appraisal departments within the two public banks. They subsequently separated from their banks and became independent appraisal firms. These two companies are allowed to carry out real estate appraisal by the Capital Market Board of Turkey for the real estate investment companies traded in the ISE. There are no specific regulations controlling the formation of a private appraisal company. Some real estate brokers also act as property appraisers. They are not required to obtain a license or to hold any qualification in order to become an appraiser. There are a few companies that specialise in real estate appraisal and consulting. Private appraisers are usually architecture graduates and usually have an MBA degree.

As at December 1999, the stocks of eight real estate investment companies were traded on the ISE. The companies are allowed to invest in residential and commercial real estate and real estate development projects. Real estate investment companies formed the Association of the Real Estate Investment Companies, which now has twelve members, in 1999. They include the companies whose shares are traded on the ISE and those that are expected to be traded there in the future. The aims of the Association include giving direction to the real estate business; motivating the development of shopping centres, commercial properties and satellite cities; setting standards in terms of quality control, appraisal, finance and marketing in real estate (by co-ordinating with the government and the local management); and increasing inner-city rehabilitation and redevelopment plans.

The real estate investment companies are exempt from income taxes. Although all of them also invest in equities, they differ in terms of the composition of their real estate portfolios. Three of the currently listed companies concentrate on land development projects; one of them invests in shopping malls and commercial properties; another two companies invest in housing. The others do not invest in development projects but have buildings and land in their portfolios. Construction companies own two of the investment companies; a public bank owns one, and private banks own the others.

In general, properties are managed by their resident owners. Very few companies have been established to provide property management services. Construction firms have however established such companies after they have developed residential areas with multi-family housing units or commercial buildings. The firms usually act as a department of the construction company that built the residential or commercial properties, with the aim of satisfying current occupiers in order to increase the marketability of unsold apartments, houses, offices or shops. Their services include maintenance, security, landscaping and cleaning. However, there is no legal framework for the continued provision of these services.

21.4 Real Estate Programs at Universities

There are no special real estate departments or real estate specialities in the Turkish universities. Unfortunately, neither real estate finance nor property appraisal courses have been offered in any departments. However, several departments offer some courses related to real estate at undergraduate level. For example, a few economics departments offer urban economics courses as electives. The curricula of the city and regional planning departments, of which there are seven in Turkey, include many courses related to real estate. During the 1997-1998 academic year, 292 students graduated from the city and regional planning and urban design departments.

In general, the emphasis in the city and regional planning departments is on housing. Students are required to take an urban economics course. The principles of housing, housing research, and housing problems are examples of other courses that are offered in these departments. Land use and urban land policy are offered in addition to housing courses. In all of the city and regional planning departments, geographic information systems and neo-classical location theory courses are also taught.

Even though there are no real estate departments at either undergraduate or postgraduate levels, students of the Masters and Ph.D. programmes may specialise in real estate when writing their thesis. There were 283 theses on real estate subjects in the period between 1985 and 1997.[4] Table 1 shows the classification of these theses according to degree and discipline. Theses were written in several disciplines, including city and regional planning, economics, public administration, management, architecture and law. Since there are no real estate departments in the universities, the faculty members supervising the theses are also listed in this table, with their discipline and title, in order to give an idea of the faculties involved.

Table 1: Classification of Real Estate Theses by Discipline

Discipline	Type of Thesis			Faculty Members				
	Master	*Ph.D.*	*Total*	*Full Prof.*	*Assoc. Prof.*	*Assist. Prof.*	*Instruc-tor*	*Total*
City and Regional Planning	57	12	69	19	9	7	2	38
Architecture	52	15	67	30	14	2	2	49
Management	35	7	42	13	7	5	1	26
Economics	30	7	37	15	6	6	0	27
Law	16	3	19	9	5	1	0	15
Civil Engineering	10	2	12	3	3	0	1	7
Public Administration	8	1	9	2	1	2	0	5
Geography	8	0	8	1	0	1	0	2
Landscape Architecture	5	2	7	3	4	0	0	7
Other*	12	1	13	4	4	3	1	12
Total	233	50	283	100	53	28	7	188

The theses in other category are from several disciplines: three in environmental engineering, three in agricultural engineering, two in industrial engineering, three in sociology, one in psychology and one in statistics.

Table 2 shows the grouping of these theses into major real estate subjects using the *Journal of Real Estate Literature* classification system. As Table 2 indicates, the number of real estate theses has increased over the years. Almost a quarter of the theses concerned "Real Estate Business/Industry".

"Government policy/planning" is another major subject area, probably because the majority of the theses were written in city planning and architecture departments. "Institutions" appears to be another popular subject. There were only two studies in the subject area of "Type of Contract/Transaction." The lack of popularity of this subject may be due to the absence of a mortgage market, mortgage-backed securities or options in Turkey.

Table 2: Classification of Theses about Real Estate, 1985 – 1997
based on the Classification System of *Journal of Real Estate Literature*

Subject \ Years	85	86	87	88	89	90	91	92	93	94	95	96	97*	total
Theory/Methods	0	0	0	1	0	3	2	1	0	0	2	3	2	14
Type of Real Estate	0	2	0	2	3	3	5	2	9	7	9	7	2	51
Type of Contract/Transaction	0	0	0	0	0	0	0	0	1	0	0	1	0	2
Real Estate Business/Industry	1	1	0	2	1	3	7	6	6	9	12	11	8	67
Type of Decisions	0	1	0	0	4	0	1	5	2	4	2	3	1	23
Government Policy/Planning	0	2	2	2	4	1	4	4	5	7	8	5	6	50
Institutions	0	3	3	3	2	2	4	3	2	6	2	2	5	37
Macro Trends/Market Analysis	1	2	3	1	0	3	0	1	2	5	2	2	0	22
Real Estate Law	0	1	0	1	3	1	0	3	1	1	3	3	0	17
Total	2	12	8	12	17	16	23	25	28	39	40	37	24	283

*Because of the unavailability of the list of all of the theses defended during 1997, these numbers do not include all of the theses during 1997.

Table 3 presents a more detailed classification of the topics of Master and Ph.D. theses for the period 1985 to 1997, using the detailed classification system of *Journal of Real Estate Literature*. The hedonic and spatial analyses are applications of theory, classified in "Theory Methods". The majority of theses are about housing and housing policy (120 and 330 respectively). In addition to residential housing, there is research about the development of vacation houses in coastal areas. A great deal of research about homebuilding during the 1990s investigated the impact of the HDA. Land use controls in several parts of Turkey, the problem of slum houses, government policies about slum houses, and the affordability of housing by low-income households have all been extensively examined. Municipal authorities, co-operatives and the HDA are included in the "Institutions' category in order to take into consideration the special characteristics of the Turkish housing system. Housing co-operatives have become very important in increasing the supply of housing, especially since the HDA was established. Research on housing co-operatives ranges from their cost accounting and their organisa-tional structures to their impact on housing supply. Most of the studies listed on Table 3 are very descriptive. Because of the unavailability of data, survey methods were used and the data were often collected by using question-naires.

Table 3: Detailed Classification of Theses about Real Estate
based on the Classification System of *Journal of Real Estate Literature*.

Subjects	Years			
	85-89	90-93	94-97	total
000 Theory/Methods				
010 Hedonic Theory	0	0	1	1
020 Spatial/Location Theory	1	6	6	13
100 Type of Real Estate				
120 Housing	5	9	11	25
120 Summer houses (vacation)	1	2	4	7
130 Apartments	0	0	2	2
140 Office Buildings	0	1	2	3
150 Shopping Centers/Retail Space	1	5	2	8
160 Hotels/Motels	0	1	2	3
170 Industrial	0	0	1	1
190 Other (elderly)	0	1	1	2
200 Type of Contract/Transaction				
220 Mortgages	0	0	1	1
270 Mortgage Backed Securities	0	1	0	1
300 Real Estate Business/Industry				
310 Appraisal/Valuation/Consulting	1	4	3	8
320 Brokerage	0	1	4	5
330 Development/Homebuilding	3	12	26	41
350 Corporate	1	0	0	1
360 Property Management	0	1	1	2
370 Syndications/REIT/Partnerships	0	2	2	4
390 Architecture/Title Insurance	0	2	4	6
400 Type of Decisions				
410 Investment/Valuation	1	0	1	2
423 Housing Finance	2	6	7	15
440 Sale-Leaseback	1	1	0	2
470 Location	1	1	2	4
500 Government Policy/Planning				
510 Land Use Controls/Zoning	4	9	15	28
520 Eminent Domain	0	2	0	2
530 Property Taxes	0	0	2	2
560 Other (housing policy)	6	3	9	17
600 Institutions				
600 Municipalities	1	2	2	5
600 Co-operatives	10	7	8	25
600 Housing Development Authority	0	2	1	3
630 Banks	0	1	3	4

Subjects	Years			
	85-89	**90-93**	**94-97**	**total**
700 Macro Trends/Market Analysis				
710 Demographics/Population	4	2	6	12
720 Cycles	0	1	0	1
730 Economic Base/Input-Output	3	3	3	9
800 Real Estate Law	5	5	7	17
Total	51	93	139	283

21.5 Real Estate Research Centres

There is only one real estate research centre in Turkey: The Centre for Housing Research at the Middle East Technical University, Faculty of Architecture. It was established in 1986 in order to co-ordinate housing-related research activities at the university. It aims to develop research projects on various aspects of housing, such as housing supply, housing finance, and housing acquisition. Creating a database for housing research is also among the Centre's objectives. Its current research projects include: economic effects of housing investment; unauthorised home building; the impact of multi-family housing production on urban development; and the role of family characteristics, gender issues and social groups on desired housing characteristics.

21.6 Journals

No scientific journal focuses specifically on Turkish real estate markets. However, the journal *M.E.T.U. Journal of the Faculty of Architecture*, published by the Faculty of Architecture at the Middle East Technical University, does so.[5] It is a biannual, refereed publication, first published in 1981. It publishes papers contributing to the development of knowledge in human-environment relations, design and planning. It accepts both theoretical and applied papers, with the emphasis mainly on urban planning and urban development rather than real estate finance and investment. The submission of papers to this journal is open to anyone, not just members of the Faculty of Architecture at Middle East Technical University.

21.7 Conclusion

Most of the real estate research in Turkey is concentrated on housing and housing policy. Compared to U.S. real estate research, real estate research in Turkey has been focused mostly on planning, land development and housing policy and less on real estate finance and investment. Research in the field of commercial real estate and REITs is very limited. However, the development of research in these areas is expected, following the recent establishment of real estate investment companies in Turkey.

Currently, there are no real estate departments in the Turkish universities. However, some universities are planning to establish departments in this field. No real estate finance courses are offered in any university at present but there are plans to offer them as elective courses in some management departments.

The education and licensing of the real estate professions have also been developing.

The availability of data is the major problem for real estate researchers in Turkey. For example, there is no house value index. Only rents, prices of utilities and maintenance costs are reflected as housing expenses in the Turkish Consumer Price Index calculations. However, improvements in the availability of data are expected in the future. One step in this improvement process, at the end of 1998, was the initiation of efforts by the State Institutes of Statistics to construct a hedonic house value index.

The chronic high inflation experienced over the last three decades is another obstacle to the development of a mortgage market in Turkey. The absence of a properly functioning mortgage market has reduced the importance of real estate finance. The emphasis has therefore been on urban and land planning and development. However, recent research has shown that a high level of inflation not only restricts the creation of a properly functioning mortgage market but also influences the behaviour of returns from real estate in Turkey (Önder, 2000).

NOTES

[1] The Capital Market Board of Turkey is like the U.S. Securities and Exchange Commission.

[2] His sample consisted of 246 house builders in twelve cities that responded to the questionnaire that was sent by mail.

[3] Ankara Realtors Organization has been the head office of the Union of Realtors Association in Turkey. There are fourteen members of this union. All of the members are the realtors associations formed in fourteen cities in Turkey, Adana, Adapazari, Ankara, Antalya, Bursa, Denizli, Icel, Istanbul, Izmir, Konya, Samsun, Usak, Tekirdag and Yalova. There is no specific requirement to form a realtors' organization. The founding members of the organization have to apply to the city governor in order to form this association.

[4] The figures on Year 1997 do not include all of the theses defended during 1997.

[5] The Faculty of Engineering and Architecture in three universities (Cukurova, Gazi and Selcuk Universities) have their journal. However, the emphasis in these journals is on architecture rather than urban planning or regional science.

REFERENCES

Hafızoğulları, B. Gül. 1997. *The Roles and nature of Mediating Agencies in the Real Estate Market after the 1980s: Brokerage Sector in Ankara*. Unpublished M.S. Thesis. Middle East Technical University, Department of Urban Policy Planning and Local Governments.

Önder, Zeynep. 2000. "High Inflation and Returns on Residential Real Estate: Evidence from Turkey," *Applied Economics*. vol. 37(7): 917-931.

Şenyapılı, Tansu and Ali Türel. 1996. *Ankara'da Gecekondu Oluşum Süreci ve Ruhsatlı Konut Sorunu*. Ankara: Batıbirlik Yayınları.

State Institute of Statistics Prime Ministry Republic of Turkey. 1997. *Building Construction Statistics*. Ankara: State Institute of Statistics, Printing Division.

Türel, Ali. 1996. *Konut Üreticileri*. T.C. Başbakanlık Toplu Konut Idaresi Başkanlığı, Konut Araştırmaları Dizisi, No. 14, Ankara: ODTÜ Basım Işliği.

III

REAL ESTATE EDUCATION IN
NORTHERN AMERICA

Chapter 22

Canada

Stanley Hamilton
Faculty of Commerce & Business Administration, University of British Columbia, Vancouver, Canada

Graham McIntosh
Faculty of Commerce & Business Administration, University of British Columbia, Vancouver, Canada

22.1 Introduction

In order to appreciate the structure of real estate education in Canada, it is necessary to have some understanding of two important institutional arrangements. It should first be noted that Canada is a (physically) large country, but with a small population: a country somewhat larger than the USA, but with a population of approximately 33 million. Moreover, approximately two-thirds of the population live in three metropolitan centres (Montreal,

Toronto and Vancouver). As a consequence, the cost of developing and offering education packages in real estate must be amortized over a small dispersed population.

Second, it is important to note that the Canadian Constitution divides the powers to make laws between the federal and provincial governments. The provinces have sole responsibility to make laws concerning property and civil rights, education, municipal organization, professions and licensing, and all matters of a purely local nature. Consequently all statutory laws relating to the regulation of real estate professional bodies, licensing and education fall under the domain of the 10 provinces and territories (hereafter referred to as "the provinces"). While there are a number of important voluntary national organizations in real estate, the mandatory or statutory organizations are provincial, with each province having somewhat different requirements[1]. As one might suspect, many of the provincial organizations will share common features, but the differences can be significant.

Hence real estate education in Canada is provided to a small population scattered over a large geographic area and governed by the provincial and territorial governments, each specifying some local requirements. This has the potential to generate costly fragmented education programs. Fortunately the provincial governments have exhibited an increasing willingness to cooperate and recognize one another's programs. Real estate is not the only service sector to suffer from this political fragmentation: the same issues apply to the accounting profession, the medical profession and the legal profession. But in the case of the real estate profession, the challenges are increasingly more acute as the individual firms tend to operate in more than one jurisdiction. The provincial variations continue to present greater challenges to the mobility of the real estate professionals in Canada.

While the combination of the large geographic area and small population has significant cost implications, the suppliers of the education programs have sought ways to reduce costs. One obvious alternative is to rely more upon distributed or distance education. Indeed large portions of the professional real estate education are delivered by distance methods with examination centres established at remote sites.

In the next section of the paper we establish the scope of the real estate profession. This is important since each sub-sector has a different set of educational requirements. We then examine the education demands for each sub-sector in the profession. Since the demand for real estate education is primarily a derived demand, derived from the specific requirements of each sub-sector, it is important to understand the nature of the regulatory requirements. Next we examine the independent suppliers of the education for the various real estate sub-sectors. The paper concludes with some speculation as to the future of real estate education in Canada.

22.2 Scope of the Real Estate Industry

From an economic perspective, the "real estate industry" in Canada is considered to be part of the service sector and is comprised of three main areas: brokerage, valuation and property management[2]. Brokerage mainly involves the buying, selling and leasing of real property, but also includes the intermediation of mortgage lending by non-financial institutions. Valuation (or appraisal) is composed of services that determine the value of properties for a variety of purposes including but not limited to, buying, selling, lending, estate planning, investment, taxation (personal, corporate and property), insurance, leasing, development feasibility, and expropriation. Property management is the final area and involves the day-to-day management of the individual real estate assets. Real estate development and institutional mortgage lending are excluded from this analysis since they differ in a fundamental manner from the other service activities in that they involve the principals and as such, are not subject to regulatory educational requirements. For example, one must be licensed in Canada to sell real estate, but not to sell your own properties or those of your employer.

The brokerage, valuation and management functions are typically further categorized by the type of property usage: residential (individual owner-occupied) or investment (ICI: Industrial, Commercial (office/retail) and Investment (usually residential)) and these categories convey somewhat different educational requirements. In terms of dollar volume of activity and people employed, residential sales is by far the largest brokerage sub-sector in Canada. The appraisal services are more often categorized either by reference to valuation activities for a wide range of private purposes or appraisal (or assessment) for real property tax purposes. In the former, the appraiser is generally acting on behalf of a range of clients while in the case of assessment the appraiser is generally an employee of a single public agency valuing according to some provincial statutory specifications. Given that real estate brokerage accounts for the largest number of individuals employed in the real estate sector, we begin with this group. Property management is considered next as many of the educational requirements overlap with the brokerage sector. The appraisal sector will be addressed last. But before analyzing the requirements of the various sub-sectors, it is helpful to discuss briefly the nature, role and implications of public and private regulation and the implications for education.

22.3 Public and Private Regulation in Real Estate in Canada

To the extent that the demand for real estate education is derived from the educational requirements of the regulatory bodies, it is to helpful distinguish between public and private regulations. The public regulation of both the professions and their education implies that the provincial governments have the constitutional authority to set licensing and certification standards and to set the educational (and other) standards for entry and for continuing education and for professional conduct. At the present time, all provinces have mandated minimum licensing requirements for real estate brokerage[3], seven provinces have specific licensing requirements for property management and, most provinces require licensing or certification for mortgage brokerage. On the other hand, only two provinces (New Brunswick and Nova Scotia) have instituted licensing requirements specifically for appraisers) while the province of Quebec requires that appraisers be members of a provincial regulatory body. In other provinces where a licensee can do other work, the coverage of the license need not be so broad. In all other provinces it is possible to undertake appraisal assignments without being licensed (although the practice of appraisal is often permitted under the real estate brokerage licensing provisions one need not hold a brokerage licensee to do appraisal work except in these three provinces.) In each case these mandated licensing requirements include educational requirements.

The particular structuring of the licensing systems generally reflects the nature of the restrictions applied to licensees. For example, in British Columbia a licensed salesperson may not hold another job. As a consequence, the work permitted under the brokerage license is broad and includes appraisal. At the same time, if a person just wanted to do appraisal work in British Columbia they would not need to be licensed.

In those cases cited above it is necessary to acquire and hold a license or certification to practice. In these cases the corresponding educational requirements are mandatory. In contrast there are a number of important private regulatory (professional) bodies in Canada that have educational admission standards, but where membership is "voluntary". However, in some cases membership in these private professional bodies, while not mandatory, is necessary for professional success. Hence the nature of the educational requirements of these private regulatory bodies will also contribute to the demand for real estate education. Indeed in many cases these private professional bodies have higher educational standards than many of the public regulatory agencies. And indeed there is some logic to such differences. Since the public regulations have the potential to prohibit one from practicing, the standard is generally set as the "minimum standard to protect the public." In contrast, most private professional bodies seek to product differentiate and their educational and experience requirements are an important part of this product differentiation.

22.4 Real Estate Brokerage

22.4.1 Public Regulation

The most common model of organization for the professions, including real estate, is to have provincial bodies operating under provincial regulations and a national body comprised of the provincial organizations. The provincial bodies ensure the provincial standards are respected while the national body focuses on issues of common interest at the national (and often international level.) In some instances there will be two parallel systems: one for the public regulation and one for the private (professional) bodies. The organizational structure for real estate brokerage follows this model. At the core is the individual licensee. In all provinces the individual must meet the educational (and other) requirements for a license[4]. In most provinces this license will permit the individual to do brokerage (either residential or non-residential), property management or appraisals. In three provinces property management requires a separate license while in two provinces appraisal requires a separate license[5].

The majority of the licensees (approximately 66,000 in Canada in 1999) will belong to one of the 112 local or multiple listing service (MLS) real estate boards. These real estate boards first started in Canada in 1888 with the Vancouver real estate board, one of the first in North America. Membership in these local boards is not mandatory for the licensees, but these MLS boards process approximately 85% of all residential listings, hence membership is an economic, if not legal, requirement[6]. These boards account for a much lower percentage of all non-residential listings and sales, and virtually no leasing activity, hence there is less incentive for licensees specializing in non-residential brokerage and leasing to join the local boards. Membership in the local real estate boards is typically restricted to licensed individuals, with provision for other associate members. In general the local real estate boards do not have additional educational requirements for membership beyond that of the licensee, but they do have as part of their mandate to promote and develop continuing professional education[7].

In all provinces there exists a provincial real estate association (for example the British Columbia Real Estate Association or BCREA) that represent their provincial real estate boards. Such provincial organizations have been in operation in Canada since Ontario formed the first in 1922. With only rare exceptions, all boards elect to join their provincial associations. In general the provincial associations have no specific educational requirements since their "members" are essentially derived through the local real estate boards. However, these provincial associations do promote voluntary education for licensees.

These provincial associations in turn belong to the national real estate brokerage association, the Canadian Real Estate Association or CREA, formed in 1943. Hence the national real estate brokerage organization is, in reality, an association of provincial organizations, and the provincial associations are in turn an association of local real estate boards. The primary mission of CREA is to represent its members at the national level of government and to act as a watchdog on national legislation pertaining to the real estate industry. CREA has a Code of Ethics and Standards of Professional Conduct that are universally adopted by the provincial boards. It does not however prescribe the minimum standards of permissive performance, but rather the performance "the public may reasonably expect" and makes that norm the standard for members. CREA also serves as the international link for real estate brokerage in Canada as the member to FIABC[8].

It follows that the only mandatory public educational standards are those set by the provincial licensing authorities. However, the local real estate boards, provincial real estate associations and CREA do promote education for their members, but this level of education is voluntary and not a condition for membership in the boards.

In all provinces the government has established a quasi-independent licensing agency, such as a Real Estate Council, and charged this agency with the responsibility to prescribe, design and deliver the licensing education. In all provinces save British Columbia the licensing agency has assigned the responsibility for education to the provincial trade associations. Educational institutions, to the extent they are involved, do so as part of the programs managed by the provincial trade association. The one exception is British Columbia where, for over 40 years, the Real Estate Council has used the University of British Columbia as the primary provider of the licensing education.

The precise nature of the educational requirements varies from province to province, but in all cases the total mandatory entry level licensing education is less than one year full-time equivalent study. It is difficult to be precise since many of the provinces have a self-paced study program. The longest program of study appears to be in Quebec where students are required to complete 240 hours of college level credit in five different subjects. At the other extreme, several provinces require something in the order of five days of lectures and self-study. A similar range of educational requirements also applies for the second level of license, the agent or broker license. Quebec has the longest requirement at 255 hours or five college level courses and several provinces require as little as 20 hours.

While the provinces have significant differences in the length of the entry-level educational programs, there is more agreement as to the subject matters to be covered. The focus is clearly on the more professional side and the topics include law of contracts, property law, finance, ethics, valuation, construction, leasing and property management. These topics are clearly designed to build a foundation of knowledge relating to the interests in real estate and the contractual arrangements relating to use and ownership. The topics relating to promotion, marketing and sales skills, office management and human resource management are not common in the entry-level programs. Indeed even at the second or senior level of licensing these personal development topics are not common: agents or nominees appear to mainly study the same topics, but in more depth, perhaps adding a bit of non-residential to the program.

22.4.2 Private Regulation

The local real estate boards, provincial associations and CREA constitute the organized "trade" associations for real estate brokerage. There is generally a parallel set of institutions representing the "professional" bodies. These operate along much the same lines with provincial institutes and a national body. In the case of real estate brokerage, the principal professional organization is the Real Estate Institute of Canada (REIC), formed in 1955 as the Canadian Institute of Realtors, and later renamed REIC[9]. The mission of REIC is" Establishing, maintaining, promoting and advancing high standards of practice through education, certification and accreditation in occupations concerning real estate". Membership in REIC is voluntary. REIC offers a number of professional designations (see Exhibit 1) covering almost all aspects of real estate including brokerage, real estate finance, appraisal, leasing and property management. A rigorous education program is a standard of admission. The current educational standard for membership in REIC (and REIBC, the Real Estate Institute of British Columbia) falls short of the requirements for a typical university degree, but are well beyond that required for licensing purposes. Depending upon the specialization selected, the education requirements typically involve the equivalent of 6-8 university courses. Typically the topics covered may be similar to those covered in a licensing program, but they are covered in greater depth, and at the level of university courses. The program of study may be characterized as a highly focussed professional program requiring approximately the equivalent of one full-time academic year (approximately 30 university credits). While both REIC and REIBC have well-developed programs of study, the delivery is generally done by the academic community[10]. At the present time neither professional body requires a university degree as a condition of membership.

22.5 Appraisal

22.5.1 Public Regulation

The discipline of appraisal has not attracted the same level of public regulation as the brokerage industry. While one can speculate on why this is so, the fact remains that only a minority of provinces have elected to demand separate licensing for appraisers. There is no need to repeat the nature of the public regulatory regime since it follows a pattern almost identical to that for real estate brokerage, except that the numbers are significantly smaller. The program of study dictated by the public regulators, where applicable, would be similar in length to that for the brokerage sector. However, unlike brokerage where professional membership is uncommon, appraisers are expected to have achieved a much higher level of professional education: it would be difficult for an appraiser who has simply met the mandatory educational requirements set out by the provinces to be successful. Clients demand more, and in general they demand the equivalent of the standards set by the Appraisal Institute of Canada.

22.5.2 Private Regulation

While many of the major appraisal professional bodies from other developed countries are represented (and recognized) in Canada, the dominant national professional body is the Appraisal Institute of Canada. The Appraisal Institute of Canada was formed in 1938 and is Canada's most widely recognized professional appraisal organization. The Institute is dedicated to serving the public interest through continually advancing high standards for the appraisal profession by granting use of the CRA (Canadian Residential Appraiser) and AACI (Accredited Appraiser Canadian Institute) designations.

The Institute currently has more than 4,500 members across Canada. Designated members are widely respected by the courts, real estate corporations, chartered banks, trust companies, mortgage lending institutions, all levels of government and private individuals. Indeed, many users of appraisal services will only accept appraisal reports completed by individuals who hold the designations AACI or CRA.

The Appraisal Institute of Canada's mission is to represent, support and advance their members as the professionals of choice in the counselling, analysis and appraisal of real property, and protect the public interest by developing and maintaining high standards of professional practice. To this end, the Appraisal Institute has a strong educational requirement for membership.

With currently 4,500 members, the Appraisal Institute's membership is approximately 8% of the number of brokerage licenses. Hence the need to offer the educational programs in a cost effective distance education mode.

For many years the Institute offered its own educational programs, both direct to members and through other academic institutions, primarily colleges[11]. The Institute set the standards and delivered many of the courses. Currently a candidate must complete the specified nine courses to earn their CRA designation and complete 16 specified courses for the AACI designation. The specified courses are heavily focussed on the core appraisal topics. Candidates are not offered a breadth of electives. Recently the Institute entered into an agreement with the University of British Columbia whereby the University delivered all educational programs on behalf of the Institute. The agreement is not exclusive so other academic institutions also offer some of the required courses. The Institute requires that candidates must hold an undergraduate degree before qualifying for the designation AACI. There is no specific undergraduate concentration required.

While the Appraisal Institute of Canada is the leading national appraisal organization in Canada, other appraisal professions are recognized, but none compares in importance or market penetration. For example, the Real Estate Institute of Canada has an appraisal specialization, but the Real Estate Institute of Canada is much more a representative of the brokerage sectors, not the appraisal sector. As a consequence, the Appraisal Institute is generally regarded as the "national voice" for appraisers and their educational standards generally set the benchmark.

A group of separate, but related, organizations are the assessment organizations across Canada. Two organizations provide leadership in the area of assessment: the Institute of Municipal Assessors and the International Association of Assessing Officers (IAAO) from the USA. The former promotes education and offers a certification program (Associate IMA and Member IMA) while the latter recognizes one or more of the Canadian programs for their Residential Evaluation Specialist (RVS) and Certified Assessment Evaluator (CAE). The required program of study is offered through a number of suppliers in Canada. While membership is voluntary, some provincial authorities recognize the certifications and provide financial incentives to their employees who complete the programs. In general these education programs would be equivalent to a one-year full-time college program.

22.6 Property Management

22.6.1 Public Regulation

There is little to add concerning the public regulation of property management. In those provinces that regulate property management under a separate program, the structure and delivery system remain very similar to that used for real estate brokerage. The principle differences in the education material include a greater focus on leasing (as opposed to selling) real estate and a greater emphasis on construction and accounting. But even in these cases the differences are measured in "chapters", not courses.

The length of the education programs and much of the content remain similar. In those provinces where property management is included under the broader-based real estate license, the educational requirements are as described earlier.

22.6.2 Private Regulation

The one major property management certification, the CPM, is offered through the Institute of Real Estate Management (IREM), a Division of the Real Estate Institute of Canada. The program requires approximately four years of part-time study, the equivalent of a full year of university credit. The Institute offers courses throughout Canada on a reasonably regular basis, but the Institute also recognizes the core offerings from a number of other suppliers.

Other organizations from the USA are also represented in the Canadian property management field, but they do not offer a certification program customized for the Canadian market.

22.7 Summary: Demand for Real Estate Education

In summary, demand for real estate education in Canada starts with the largest sub-sector, the real estate brokerage sector. The demand for education in real estate brokerage is primarily created by the provincial public regulatory regimes and the mandatory programs are generally less than the equivalent to one part-time year of university study. This constitutes the significant majority of all professionals in the real estate sector, and of all new entrants to the industry. The voluntary educational programs for admission to the professional institutes for brokerage are, at a maximum, equivalent to one year full-time university study, but the membership in the professional bodies is only a fraction of the number of licensees[12]. As a consequence, the trade associations with a much higher participation rate (some-times reaching 100% of licensees) have significantly more political power. As one can see, the volume of education demanded (students x course hours) generated from this sector of real estate is actually quite limited – and this is the largest sub-sector of real estate.

The field of appraisal has fewer mandatory certification requirements, but they do have stronger private regulatory power. Membership in the Appraisal Institute of Canada is for all practical purposes a requirement for anyone wanting to do non-residential appraisals or to work for the federal government and crown corporations. Members of the Real Estate Institute of Canada holding their appraisal certification are recognized, but the Real Estate Institute has its primary strength in brokerage and property management. Given that the Appraisal Institute of Canada now requires a university degree for full membership, this sets the highest standards of all bodies in Canada. In the case of property management, the highest requirement is equivalent to one year of full-time study.

The derived demand for real estate education in all sub-sectors remains at a reasonably low level. Aside from the Appraisal Institute of Canada, individual corporate requirements and individual preferences, there is little call for degree programs in Canada.

22.8 Suppliers of Real Estate Education in Canada

22.8.1 Overview

The primary suppliers of real estate education in Canada include both the various professional and trade organizations and the academic community. In general, the professional and trade organizations play a major role in designing and delivering the licensing and certification programs. In most cases the provincial authorities will recognize a role for the colleges and universities for program delivery, but the program design is typically under the domain of the professions and trades. As might be expected, the professions are under some pressure to recognize the potential roles for their own provincial academic institutions. As a consequence, many colleges offer some or all parts of the various licensing and certificate programs applicable to their own province, typically as part of their continuing education programs offered on a part time basis or through distance education methods.

The educational programs for the professional institutes, at a higher level than the typical licensing programs, are also offered by a number of colleges and universities and these are more likely offered as university credit courses. Examples include the basic economics courses, mathematics and statistics and English (generally business writing skills). However, few colleges or universities offer credit courses covering the more industry specific real estate courses. The simple fact is that the demand for such courses is too limited to justify having the universities and colleges offer anything but the broadest based courses.

22.8.2 University of British Columbia

If one limits the analysis to academic institutions having a current capacity to deliver comprehensive programs specializing in real estate, then only two universities meet the definition. And of these, one specializes in real estate development that falls outside the scope of this paper. The oldest, strongest and most comprehensive real estate programs are offered by the Faculty of Commerce & Business Administration at the University of British Columbia. UBC, with support from the real estate industry in British Columbia, started their real estate programs in 1958. The package of programs included all real estate licensing programs required by the province, a four year distance diploma program, certificate programs, executive education seminars, Bachelor, Masters and PhD programs, a distance Bachelor program and a comprehensive research program. UBC currently has five full time tenured faculty specializing in urban land economics (real estate), and a staff of 15 creating, managing and delivering distance education.

The licensing programs are designed to meet all qualifications for licensing in British Columbia, including brokerage, property management and mortgage lending[13]. The university acts as the academic advisor to the Real Estate Council, the quasi-public body charged with responsibility for licensing in the province. All programs are offered by distance education, with tutorials and lectures provided in limited cases. The university sets and grades the examinations, reporting grades to the Council who issues the license.

UBC also provides a four-year Urban Land Economics (ULE) Diploma program with specializations in real estate assessment, property management, real estate finance and appraisal. A new option in real estate marketing is scheduled to begin in 2002. The program curriculum is set by UBC, with input from an industry advisory committee. The diploma program is equivalent to one full year of university courses (33 credits). The certificate program in Assessment is 15 credits. These programs are offered by distance education. The certificate program in Assessment is recognized across Canada and meets the requirements for the professional assessment organizations. The ULE Diploma also serves as the education program for the various designations offered by the Real Estate Institute of Canada (and the Real Estate Institute of B.C.)

UBC offers the entire AIC educational programs on behalf of the Appraisal Institute of Canada[14]. This program overlaps to a significant degree with the ULE Diploma program and is also provided by distance delivery. Unlike the ULE Diploma program, the Appraisal Institute of Canada has retained control over the overall curriculum, but UBC serves as an academic advisor. This program is offered on behalf of the Appraisal Institute of Canada and the ULE Diploma program combine to satisfy the education standards for the major professional bodies in Canada.

The two undergraduate programs include a full time four year Bachelors program[15] with a specialization in real estate (Bachelor of Commerce and Business Administration) that has been offered since 1959 and a new distance education Bachelors program (Bachelor of Business in Real Estate) in real estate offered since 1998 in co-operation with the Open University in British Columbia[16,17]. These programs generally satisfy the academic requirements of the major professional real estate bodies in Canada, with some exceptions that require further study of the unique provincial legal materials. The full time MBA program offers a number of graduate level courses, in urban land economics and real estate, but the primary graduate level program is a full time MSc program specializing in Urban Land Economics. The PhD program in Urban Land Economics is a full time program of study.

One of the principle reasons why UBC has such commitment to real estate is the leadership exhibited by the real estate industry in the province. The industry has provided strong leadership and financial support for the development and delivery of real estate programs over a 43 year period. Initially this support came from annual grants and scholarships. However, the real estate profession established The Real Estate Foundation in 1985, the first such Foundation in Canada, and this Foundation now provides financial support to all educational institutions, professional and trade organizations in the province that seek to offer real estate programs or undertake research in the discipline[18].

22.8.3 York University

York University, through the Schulich School of Business at York University in Ontario[19], offers a MBA program with a specialization in real estate development. The Schulich School also offers a 21 credit diploma program in real estate development. While real estate development falls outside the scope of this paper, the York program is cited since their graduates do not limit their careers to development. Many find careers in brokerage, real estate finance and real estate asset management.

22.8.4 Other Universities

A number of other universities offer some courses in real estate, either as electives in another specialization in a degree program or as part of a continuing education program. Almost without exception, these universities would have no more that one academic involved in the discipline.

22.8.5 Colleges

A number of colleges in Canada offer programs specializing in real estate, appraisal or property management. In all cases the programs are designed to meet the academic standards for one of the professional bodies. Perhaps the four most comprehensive programs are the real estate development program offered at Kwantlen University College[20] (B.C.), the real estate programs offered by Seneca College[21], the largest college system in Ontario, the program at Lakeland College in Alberta and the two year diploma program offered by the British Columbia Institute of Technology (BCIT). In the case of Kwantlen, the program is a two-year program specializing in real estate with an emphasis on appraisal. Seneca College offers two real estate programs: a two-year diploma program in real property assessment and a two-year diploma program in Assessment and Appraisal. Lakeland College[22] offers a two-year program in Appraisal and Assessment. The two-year program at BCIT is a full time program. This program is conducted in support of the Appraisal Institute of Canada's education requirements.

There are a number of other colleges offering portions of a program or individual courses as electives in other programs. In many cases the program offerings are part of their continuing education programs rather than part of their regular college credit program.

22.9 Summary

It was noted at the outset that Canada is a large country with a small population. As a consequence the local demand for real estate education is seldom sufficient to justify a comprehensive full-time program of study. Distance education plays a major role. These facts, coupled with the ultimate authority of the provinces to control both education and the professions have resulted in some degree of fragmentation in program offerings. In addition, the fact that real estate brokerage, the largest sub-sector in the real estate industry, primarily attracts mid-career individual dictates reliance on distant education. Moreover this entry-level education is under the direction of a Council and, in all provinces except British Columbia, is delivered under the direction of the trade associations in real estate.

Only one major university has a full range of offerings in real estate, supported by full-time research faculty, and this has been the case for over 40 years. Once again this reflects the small market in Canada. The fact the university is in British Columbia reflects the leadership shown by the real estate profession some 40 years ago when the industry initiated their strong commitment to education. The fact this industry support continues today has helped promote real estate education within the province.

Exhibit 1

Major Real Estate Designations Applicable in Canada

1. Real Estate Institute of Canada

FRI	Fellow of the Real Estate Institute of Canada
CPM	Certified Property Manager, Institute of Real Estate Management
CRF	Certified in Real Estate Finance, Real Estate Institute of Canada
CLP	Certified in Land Planning and Development, Real Estate Institute of Canada
CMN	Certified in the Marketing of Real Estate, Real Estate Institute of Canada
ALO	Accredited Leasing Officer, Real Estate Institute of Canada
ARM	Accredited Real Estate Manager, Real Estate Institute of Canada
RI(BC)	Real Estate Institute of British Columbia .

2. Appraisal Institute of Canada

AACI	Accredited Appraiser Canadian Institute, Appraisal Institute of Canada
CRA	Certified Residential Appraiser, Appraisal Institute of Canada

3. International Association of Assessing Officers

RES	Residential Evaluation Specialist, International Association of Assessing Officers
CAE	Certified Assessment Evaluator, International Association of Assessing Officers

4. Others

CPRPM	Certified Professional Residential Property Manager, Professional Association of Managing Agents
RPA	Real Property Administrator, Building Owners and Managers Institute
MVA(R)	Market Value Appraiser, Canadian Real Estate Association

*The list is limited to designations that have a unique Canadian element and that apply to more than one province. Many of the designations from other countries are also used in Canada, but without any significant Canadian content, for example, the RICS designation is used and recognized in Canada.

NOTES

[1] There are a number of important national statutes that impact the real estate industry, such as the federal *Competition Act.* Beginning in 1976 the services, such as real estate brokerage, came under the purview of the *Combines Investigation Act*, predecessor of the *Competition Act.* However, these have no specific educational requirements.

[2] This definition closely relates to the Standard Industrial Classification (SIC) employed by Statistics Canada.

[3] In most cases the regulations create two licenses: an entry-level license often called an agent or broker or salespersons license, and a more advanced license for the broker or agent. The agent's license is generally designed for the individual responsible for the operation of the office or firm, hence more management focussed. The concept of a single license to serve all purposes is gaining popularity.

[4] British Columbia enacted one of the earliest real estate acts in North America in 1919.

[5] But in the other provinces an individual may do appraisal work without any license.

[6] Access to the MLS data and marketing processes is limited to members. The MLS sales currently account for over 335,000 sales and $53 billion in volume (1999 totals). For up to date information, contact <realtors.mls.ca/crea>.

[7] The local boards also adopt and maintain a Code of Ethics and Standard of Business Practice.

[8] Federation Internationale des Administrateurs de Biens et de Conseil Immobiliers.

[9] REIC is a national body, but operates primarily through provincial and local chapters. The one exception is British Columbia where both the local chapters of REIC operate along with a separate provincial body, the Real Estate Institute of British Columbia. This arrangement reflects the strong provincial bias that was present in the 1950's when the Real Estate Institute of British Columbia (REIBC) formed its own professional body. Today there are two organizations attempting to represent the professional arm of real estate brokerage in British Columbia, but they do exhibit a major degree of cooperation. The existence of a national body with local or provincial chapters is not inconsistent with the constitutional arrangements since membership is voluntary in this institute.

[10] For example, the University of British Columbia offers the distance education courses necessary for membership in each professional body

[11] The role of the Institute and admission requirements for membership are very similar to that of the American Appraisal Institute.

[12] For every 100 licensees active in real estate, approximately 10 will be members of the professional body.

[13] See <info@realestate.commerce.ubc.ca>.

[14] UBC is not the exclusive provider of education for the Appraisal Institute of Canada, but it is the primary provider and is responsible for assisting the AIC with the development of program materials. Other colleges across Canada deliver portions of the program for the AIC.

[15] See <commerce.ubc.ca>

[16] The Open University is a separate university established in British Columbia to deliver distance education.

[17] See <www.commerce.ubc.ca>

[18] See <www.landcentre.ca/foundation> The Real Estate Foundation is a philanthropic organization created in 1985. The Foundation is a non-profit corporation. The Foundation strives to provide benefits that accrue to the communities of British Columbia. The Foundation's mission is: "to use its resources for the benefit of British Columbians by support-

ing efforts that improve all aspects of land use and real estate practices." The Foundation provides both project funding and endowment grants to non-profit organizations, including educational institutions. Endowment grants are available only to organizations with charitable status. The Foundation enjoys wide latitude to interpret and execute its mission.

[19] See <dr.ssb.yorku.ca>

[20] See <Kwantlen.bc.ca>

[21] See <www.senecac.on.ca>

[22] See<lakelandc.ab.ca>

Chapter 23

United States

James R. Webb
Department of Finance, James J. Nance College of Business, Cleveland State University, Cleveland, USA

Halbert C. Smith
University of Florida, Florida, USA

23.1 Introduction

Real estate education and research has a long history in the U.S.A. The largest professional organization in real estate is for real estate sales people (National Association of REALTORS®). It has had as many as one million members in years past. However, the U.S.A. now has about twenty-five different professional organizations dedicated to virtually every area of the profession and all property types. The following list is undoubtedly incomplete, but will convey the flavor and the current level of activity within the real estate profession. See Table 1.

Table 1: A Partial List of U.S. Professional Real Estate Organizations

- Appraisal Institute (valuation)
- Association of Foreign Investors in U.S. Real Estate
- BOMA International (property/asset management)
- Counselors of Real Estate
- International Association of Corporate Real Estate Executives
- International Council of Shopping Centers
- International Development Research Council
- Mortgage Bankers' Association
- National Association of Industrial and Office Properties
- National Association of Real Estate Investment Managers
- National Association of Real Estate Investment Trusts
- National Association of REALTORS
- National Council of Real Estate Investment Fiduciaries
- National Investment Center for the Seniors Housing & Care Industries
- National Multi Housing Council
- Pension Real Estate Association
- Research Institute for Housing America
- Society of Industrial and Office REALTORS
- Urban Land Institute

Licensing/certification is required for people in brokerage (agency) and valuation by virtually all 50 states in the U.S. All areas of real estate have designations available through their professional organization, but the others usually do not require licensing. Investment advisors have to register. The designations are earned by a combination of experience and classes/exams. These can be quite substantial and involve several years of effort in some cases. The U.S. is quite large (281,000,000 people, approximately) and therefore, most areas in real estate often have more than one professional organization that caters to people.

23.2 Real Estate Education at Universities

The U.S. has several hundred public and several hundred private universities. Approximately 200 of these offer real estate classes, usually as an area of specialization in the finance department of a College of Business. Occasionally, real estate is found in planning or urban economics. In the U.S., the core real estate curriculum consists of real estate finance, real estate invest-ment and valuation. Additional classes are usually offered in Departments of Economics (urban) or Urban Planning.

In addition to the real estate class offerings at universities, junior colleges (two year colleges aimed at vocational training, sometimes called polytech-nics in other parts of the world) throughout the U.S. almost all offer real estate. However these classes are aimed at training/licensing so a person can quickly go into real estate - generally brokerage (agency).

Several, perhaps thirty or more, universities offer either real estate mas-ter's degrees or M.B.A. degrees with specialization in real estate. As many as fifteen universities offer doctorates in real estate, but probably only five to seven put out graduates on a regular basis.

Faculty at universities in the U.S. must have a doctorate. At junior (two year) colleges, bachelor and master's degrees are acceptable. Faculty for classes offered by professional groups do not have absolute requirements, except those of the offering professional organization.

23.3 Real Estate Research in the U.S.

23.3.1 Overview

Virtually all real estate research is done at universities. Some profes-sional organizations claim to do some research, but it is mostly just data gathering and no statistical tests are performed or hypotheses tested. A very few professional organizations fund academic research in their area.

There are two academic real estate organizations in the United States. They are the American Real Estate and Urban Economics Association (AREUEA- founded in 1965) and the American Real Estate Society (ARES-founded in 1985). AREUEA has one journal and ARES currently has four journals and one more in the planning stage. See Table 2 for a listing of these and other U.S.A. based real estate journals.

Each of these academic real estate organizations has an annual confer-ence where academic papers are presented and discussed, in addition to pan-els on current events. This is done to promote communication about aca-demic research amongst real estate faculty and practicing professionals that are interested in real estate research. The AREUEA meetings tend to empha-size housing issues, while the ARES meetings tend to emphasize real estate investment and finance issues. However, both contain a broad array of top-ics.

Since the first two academic real estate organizations in the world were started in the U.S., a brief history of these organizations should be insightful.

Most of the peer reviewed academic research in the U.S. is affected by these two organizations.

Table 2: U.S.A. Based Real Estate Journals

I. Academic Organizations
    1. American Real Estate Society (ARES)
        a. Journal of Real Estate Research (6/year)
        b. Journal of Real Estate Portfolio Management (4/year)
        c. Journal of Real Estate Literature (2/year)
        d. Journal of Real Estate Practice and Education (1/year)
        e. Journal of Real Estate Strategy (in planning)
    2. American Real Estate and Urban Economics Association (AREUEA)
        a. Real Estate Economics (4/year)

II. Professional Organizations
    1. Appraisal Institute (AI)
        a. The Appraisal Journal (4/year)
    2. Counselors of Real Estate (CRE)
        a. Real Estate Issues (4/year)

III. Other
    1. Fannie Mae Foundation
        a. Journal of Housing Research (4/year)
        b. Housing Policy Debate (4/year)
    2. Journal of Real Estate Finance and Economics (4/ year)
    3. Housing Economics (4/year)

23.3.2 Academic Real Estate Prior to 1964

Academic real estate existed to a very limited extent during the 1930's and early 1940's. Courses and programs were offered at several universities, such as New York University, University of Wisconsin, Ohio State University, University of Florida, University of Michigan, and Indiana University. Real Estate scholars such as Richard M. Hurd, Richard T. Ely, Richard U. Ratcliff, Henry E. Hoagland, and Homer Hoyt occupied positions in these universities and government agencies. Richard M. Hurd, in 1910, published the first important book in the modern age of real estate, *Principals of Land Values.* Homer Hoyt's study, entitled *One Hundred Years of Land Values in Chicago,* and his later work with the Federal Housing Administration leading to the sector theory, helped solidify the field. The land economics textbook of Richard T. Ely, and the real estate texts of Earnest M. Fisher, Henry E. Hoagland and Arthur M. Weimer, and Homer Hoyt were regarded as important contributions and were studied by many students. Richard U. Ratcliff's emergence at the end of this period led to his major role as a transitional scholar between the older, more institutionally oriented scholars and those of the modern age.

Soon after the end of World War II, university business programs experienced a rapid increase in the number of students. Some of these students wanted to study real estate, and many courses were added, often with an institutional and/or brokerage (agency) orientation, since brokerage was by far the largest component of the real estate business. Real estate law also became a popular offering at the time to accompany brokerage courses. Then, in the early 1950's, the Carnegie Foundation and the Ford Foundation commissioned studies of undergraduate business schools and their programs under the direction of Gordon and Howell and Pierson. Their conclusions were that undergraduate programs were insufficiently analytical and too institutional and vocationally oriented. They recommended that business schools offer only a course or two in the core fields of marketing, finance, and management. They also recommended that the number of courses in "minor" fields, such as real estate and insurance, be reduced and that the remaining courses be made much more analytical, and that real estate should not be included in the "core curriculum".

Real estate programs and courses were hit hard by these recommendations. Business school deans cut back drastically, or eliminated real estate offerings entirely in some schools. Those real estate courses that remained were restructured and most real estate departments and faculty were moved to finance departments. Real estate faculty and programs were in decline for several years afterwards. Then, in the late 1950's and early 1960's real estate, began to recover, since there was considerable demand by students for real estate instruction as the economy expanded. The emphasis, however, switched to appraisal and finance, with some real estate law and away from brokerage (agency). In the early 1960's investment analysis began to be recognized as an important topic, providing an integrational framework for the other courses and representing an analytical basis for real estate decision making.

Although the 1950's are often regarded as a low period for academic real estate, some important progress occurred. With the blossoming of M.B.A programs, many programs included a course or two in real estate, and some programs included real estate as an area of concentration. The University of Wisconsin was notable for its more specialized M.S. program in real estate appraisal and investment. Also, a few universities recognized real estate as a major or minor in Ph.D. programs, and Indiana University included real estate as a field for D.B.A. candidates who had to show proficiency in five fields that were considered equal, (i.e., fields not designated as major or minor, as in traditional Ph.D. programs).

Beginning in the 1950's Indiana University, under the leadership of Arthur M. Weimer, became the largest producer of real estate doctorates and real estate faculty. Weimer had co-authored, with Homer Hoyt, the most widely used real estate textbook of the period and he forcefully promoted the development of real estate as a legitimate academic field. Fred Case, George Pinell, Maury Seldin, Robert O. Harvey, James Gillies, and Stephen Messner are some of the more notable real estate doctorates given during this period.

Other major universities having doctoral programs in real estate in the 1950's and 1960's were the University of Illinois, under the academic leadership of Robert O. Harvey; UCLA under the academic leadership of Fred Case, James Gillies, and Leo Grebler; University of Wisconsin, under the academic leadership of Richard Ratcliff, Richard Andrews, and later James Graaskamp; Pennsylvania State University, University of Pennsylvania, under the academic leadership of David T. Rowlands; and University of Texas. Several other universities would be added to this list in the 1970's and 1980's including University of Georgia, Georgia State University, University of Florida, University of North Carolina, and University of California at Berkeley.

Prior to 1964 there was no academic organization serving the needs of real estate faculty members. Likewise, there were no academic real estate journals. Real estate faculty members tended to attend two meetings; the Allied Social Science Association (ASSA) meetings that included meetings of the American Economic Association (AEA), American Finance Association (AFA), American Marketing Association, and some other, more specialized economic associations. The American Marketing Association broke away from ASSA in approximately 1968. The AFA occasionally had papers on some aspect of real estate finance, and the AEA had some papers on housing and related real estate concerns. But it certainly is not an understatement to say that none of these organizations served the needs of university real estate faculty.

Some real estate faculty also attended conventions of the National Association of Real Estate Boards (NAREB), later to be called the National Association of REALTORS (NAR). NAREB was an organization for brokerage (agency) and had an Education Committee that held a meeting at the NAREB conventions, usually on the campus of a local university. Although real estate faculty participated in these meeting, they did not present papers or discuss academic topics. Rather, the meetings were concerned with REALTOR education and training, and the means and extent to which real estate faculty might participate in such educational and training programs.

These meetings certainly did not provide a suitable forum for real estate academics.

23.3.3 Founding of the American Real Estate and Urban Economics Association

The NAREB convention in 1964 was held in Los Angeles, and the "Education Committee" meeting was held on campus of USC. During the lunch break and a brief walk on campus, George Bloom is reported to have said top Hal Smith, "This meeting is unsatisfactory for real estate academics, and we've got to start a new organization to meet the needs of real estate academics." Hal is reported to have agreed totally with him and offered to do anything he could to help him.

Although time was short, they contacted as many real estate academics as they could and invited all of them who would be attending the ASSA meetings in Chicago at the end of December that same year to meet and discuss formation of the new organization. The group met on December 29, 1964, and informally appointed George Bloom as President, Raymond Emery as Vice-President, and Halbert C. Smith as Secretary-Treasurer for the coming year. After considerable discussion of the pros and cons of the name, American Real Estate Association was finally chosen as most directly representing the essence of the new organization. The name was also consistent with other academic organizations to whose stature they aspired, such as the American Finance Association, American Economic Association, *et al.* It was argued that such affiliation would provide more prestige than being separated from the other academic organizations and that such joint meetings would permit more interaction among organizations.

During 1965, the organization was incorporated in Ohio as the American Real Estate Association (AREA), and efforts were made to sign up members and to encourage them to meet in New York at the ASSA meetings the following year. Approximately 100 members were obtained during that first year, with perhaps 50 or 60 attending the New York meetings. At that first "official" meeting, George Bloom was elected President, David T. Rowlands Vice-President, and Halbert C. Smith Secretary-Treasurer. AREA had some time slots on the ASSA program, and for the first time academic papers were presented.

The major item of business that occurred that year was a report from the President that NAREB objected to the name American Real Estate Association because it believed that the public would think it was another trade association in competition with NAREB. While we tried to reassure NAREB this was not the case, their attorneys were insistent and suggested that we change the name to American Association of Real Estate Educators. Not wishing to be identified solely as teachers, or to be viewed as out-of-step with the older, more prestigious academic organizations, the membership defeated that proposal.

Urban economics was then viewed as a more academically respected field than real estate, so it was proposed that urban economics be included in the name. It was pointed out that the real estate center at the University of California at Berkeley was named the "Center for Real Estate and Urban Economics", and a new center had been formed at the University of Connecticut with the name "Center for Real Estate and Urban Economic Studies". Therefore, the membership finally settled on the current name, American Real Estate and Urban Economics Association (AREUEA).

23.3.4 Early Years of AREUEA

The early years of AREUEA could be characterized as inclusive. They desperately tried to obtain (attract) as many members as possible, and all members were encourages to submit papers for participation at the annual meetings. In the beginning *Proceedings* of the annual meetings were edited by Carl J. Tschappat and published by the Association.

Since we were striving for academic acceptance, and the Association had only a limited number of slots on the ASSA program schedule, the Program Committee and Chairman exercised strong control over which papers were accepted for presentation. Each paper submitted was reviewed by members of the Program Committee, and a significant percent (25-30%) were rejected. This was perhaps the beginning of the feeling by some members that the association was "exclusive" and biased against (1) purely real estate research and (2) papers and faculty members from smaller universities and programs.

Hal Smith appointed a committee during his presidency (19XX) to study the feasibility of a journal, and these efforts paid off with the founding of the *AREUEA Journal* in 1973 during Norb Stefaniak's tenure as President (now retitled *Real Estate Economics*).

Herman Berkman had, from the beginning of his involvement in AREUEA, pushed for the inclusion of urban economists, planners, and members of related disciplines in AREUEA. Therefore, during his presidency, a major push was started to attract these people to the organization.

But by the early to mid-1980's there was a growing feeling among many real estate faculty that AREUEA was not meeting their needs. Places on the program of the annual meetings were relatively few, resulting in the rejection of a high percentage of proposed papers for presentation. The *Journal* was serving as an outlet for topics on planning, urban economics, general economics, and others, often to the exclusion of micro-real estate topics, and the organization's small structure prevented many real estate academics from participating in the organization's deliberations and activities.

Furthermore, the Association's officers were not chosen strictly on the basis of prior work and contribution to the organization, but also on the basis of perceived academic reputation. Thus, those who worked on behalf of the organization sometimes saw themselves passed over for officer positions in favor of others who had not labored long and diligently in the organizational trenches. In order to meet these feelings in a limited way, the organization sanctioned some regional meetings. It was at the Southern Regional Meetings of AREUEA in 1985 that the idea of forming another academic organization took root.

At the 1985 AREUEA annual meetings a panel discussion was presented, with remarks by four past AREUEA presidents. Bill Kinnard, Herman Berkman, Hugh Nourse, and John Weicher. At this meeting Hugh Nourse stated that the organization had suffered from three principal criticisms: (1) The organization is closed; it is hard to participate in the organization's functions and operation, (2) The *Journal* publishes articles that are too planning and macro oriented, and (3) the organization has not responded to professional issues of interest to real estate faculty.

At that panel discussion, Nourse largely defended the organization, but noted that a new academic organization had been initiated. He predicted that only one organization would survive, and it would be whichever organization best met the needs of core real estate faculty. A number of years later Nourse admitted that his forecast about only one of the two organizations surviving had been wrong, but noted that his other implied prediction had been correct: "The organization that would meet the needs of the core membership, academic real estate faculty, would thrive. That organization is the American Real Estate Society" (Nourse, 1996).

23.3.5 The American Real Estate Society (1985-Present)

The American Real Estate Society (ARES) was founded in April of 1985 in Nashville Tennessee, by approximately 44 people, at what was the third meeting of the Southern AREUEA Association. James R. Webb was appointed the "organizing chairperson" by acclamation. He incorporated ARES in Ohio shortly afterwards. In October of 1985, ARES had its first annual meeting in Denver, Colorado in conjunction with the Financial Management Association (FMA). James R. Webb was elected the first ARES President by acclamation. Webb then nominated Joe Albert as the first President (partial term October-December , 1985) due to his role in forming the Southern AREUEA organization, which was the forerunner of ARES. Webb then became the first full-term President of ARES (January-December 1986). In addition, it was decided at that time that ARES should meet on its own in the future, which it has done.

ARES grew quite rapidly growing to 175 members in a few months. A peer-reviewed journal was established within a year (Journal of Real Estate Research), with three more journals being added by 1998 (Journal of Real Estate Portfolio Management, Journal of Real Estate Literature, and Journal of Real Estate Practice and Education). A fifth journal is planned entitled, Real Estate Strategy. ARES also publishes a newsletter twice a year and an annual research monograph on a different topic each year. Past, present, and future issues of the monograph are shown in Table 3.

Table 3: ARES Monographs: Past, Present and Future

PAST

1994: Essays in Honor of James A. Graaskamp: Appraisal, Market Analysis and Public Policy in Real Estate (481 pages)

1995: Alternative Ideas in Real Estate Investment (189 pages)

1996: Megatrends in Retail Real Estate (co-sponsored by ICSC: 378 pages)

1997: Seniors Housing (sponsored by the National Investment Conference for the Senior Living and Long-Term Care Industries: 248 pages)

1998: Ethics in Real Estate (co-sponsored by the Howard Hughes Corporation: 317 pages)

1999: Essays in Honor of James A. Graaskamp: Ten Years After (co-sponsored by the Wisconsin Real Estate Alumni Association)

2000: Real Estate Education: Past, Present, and Future (co-sponsored by the European Business School: 491 pages)

FORTHCOMING SOON

2001: Appraisal/Valuation Theory (sponsored by the Appraisal Institute)

2002: Financial Engineering and Innovation in Real Estate (sponsored by the Royal Institute of Chartered Surveyors, U.K.)

IN PROCESS

2003: Behavioral Real Estate (needs a sponsor)

2004: Real Estate Market Microstructure (needs a sponsor)

2005: Property Values and Environmental Factors (needs a sponsor)

2006: Indigenous Peoples and Property Issues (needs a sponsor)

2007: Dangerous Visions: The Future of Real Estate Research (needs a sponsor)

One of the innovations of ARES was to establish an Executive Director position. This person's function was/is to keep projects moving forward throughout the year; and it has worked well. Many projects are accomplished throughout the year because of this. Other important innovations include several ideas to promote the involvement of industry members and different types and levels of publications for different audiences.

The ARES currently has over a thousand members from all over the world. These are generally real estate professors at universities and high-level practicing professionals from the total breadth of the real estate industry that are interested in research. As an organization, ARES prides itself on being:

1. Inclusive,
2. Open and friendly,
3. Proactive, and
4. The connecting link between academic real estate, research and practicing professionals in real estate.

Each of ARES' four journals has an extensive editorial board. In addition, the ARES Board of Directors has many real estate industry members. For anyone that wishes to be active, ARES management will find them a job. There are always more things to do than people to do them, as in all volunteer organizations.

In recent years, ARES has adopted a theme of "World Class Water" for its annual meetings. There is no reason that a person cannot learn, network, and be in a pleasant location is their attitude.

ARES has acted as the catalyst for the formation of other real estate societies around the world and the International Real Estate Society (IRES). Currently, in addition to the American Real Estate Society there are the following:

– European Real Estate Society
– Pacific-Rim Real Estate Society
– Asian Real Estate Society
– African Real Estate Society
– Latin American Real Estate Society

In addition, there are currently two groups trying to form a Middle Eastern Real Estate Society.

Anyone desiring further information about ARES (newsletter, member information, meeting information, sample copies of journals) should contact one of the following people:

– James R. Webb, ARES Executive Director at: j.webb@csuohio.edu or

– Theron R. Nelson, ARES Secretary/Treasurer at:
  theron_nelson@und.nodak.edu

Be sure to include your complete mailing address and telephone number, fax, and email address. A complete history of the first decade of ARES is contained in Volume 12, Number 2 of the *Journal of Real Estate Research.* There are numerous articles from the viewpoint of several different key people contained in this volume.

REFERENCES

Nourse, Hugh O., "The Promise of ARES: A Past AREUEA President's Perspective." *Journal of Real Estate Research*, Vol. 12, No. 2, 1996, p.158.

IV

REAL ESTATE EDUCATION IN LATIN AMERICA

Chapter 24

Brazil

Eliane Monetti
Department of Civil Construction, Polytechnic School, University of São Paulo, São Paulo, Brazil

24.1 Introduction

The original purpose of this paper was to discuss Real Estate Education in the whole South American continent. The search started by visiting many South American Universities' web sites, to identify real estate research groups.

As only very few groups could be found, the second stage was involved in attempting to contact them directly.

However, no answers were received from any of the research groups. On the understanding that it was vital to have researchers' or practitioners' points of view about Real Estate Education in their own countries, the search was therefore concentrated on Brazil alone.

Understanding real estate education in Brazil requires a knowledge not only of the evolution of real estate but also of the different macroeconomic environments that the country has gone through, which have had inevitable effects on the current situation.

An important milestone for the beginning of this process took place in the 1960's, when the SFH (*Sistema Financeiro de Habitação* - Housing Financial System) was established. Its main objective was to allow for housing development compatible with increasing demand, driven at least in part by the high population growth rates in the country.

The country developed substantially between 1964 and 1973, when the GDP increased by 120%. Real estate output followed that growth, including the introduction of more modern types of property, like shopping centres, which first appeared on the Brazilian market in that period.

As real estate supply, particularly of housing units, was almost always below demand levels, and access to finance was not restricted, specialised real estate professionals were not essential.

At that time, managerial aspects were hardly ever touched upon in undergraduate programs and, if so, they concerned project management, with the emphasis on building management. The first Brazilian institution to teach real estate issues was the building management discipline of the EPUSP (*Escola Politécnica da Universidade de São Paulo* - Polytechnic School at the University of São Paulo).

However, a period of strong development then began. This fuelled inflationary pressures, which resulted in inflation reaching 100% per year in the early 1990's.

Under those circumstances, investor preferences were concentrated on speculative investments as long as the financial market offered attractive rates, since the government needed to borrow money and had to pay a high interest for it.

In addition, the diminished attractiveness of holding long-term investments (of which investments in real estate are a prime example) even affected housing, in spite of the continuing major shortage of supply. The situation became critical when high inflation rates endangered the maintenance of the financial system that provided funds for both producers and final buyers of housing units. Housing units were also becoming increasingly more expensive.

As a result, by the beginning of the 1990's the country was in deep recession and inflation rose to unprecedented levels.

For those who decided to continue operating in the real estate market, the need to gain real estate knowledge emerged. As a result, in 1985, the first specialised course in this field was offered at EPUSP, where the first group dedicated to real estate research was also assembled.

During that period, many colleges of Civil Engineering offered specialised courses in the area of Appraisal, through agreements with professional bodies.

In spite of the impact of recent economic crises, controlling inflation, which was first achieved in 1994, has helped bring and maintain a new reality to the country, in which stability benefits long-term investments.

New, alternative funding systems also have been introduced, in order to facilitate real estate as a basis for the development of the country.

From the civil construction point of view, firms are under pressure to improve productivity in order to offer more competitive products. They are also trying to design products better adjusted to the needs of buyers, who have not recovered their former purchasing power.

Like the other developing economies, Brazil still has a high level of demand for housing in all market sectors. Limited development during the years of recession has resulted in an even greater housing shortfall.

In 1997, the ratio of dwellings to families was 0.923:1 (GONÇALVES, 1997). This figure is the national average, reflecting express demand to be covered by the production of new units.

From 1995 to 1998, when the market was still moderate, more than 135,000 square metres of office space (in terms Gross Lettable Area – GLA) were sold each year in the City of São Paulo alone (*Bolsa de Imóveis do Estado de São Paulo*, 1999). Sao Paulo has the largest stock of office space in Brazil.

During the same period, many shopping centres were opened to supply retail facilities for the urban population, adding 175,000 square meters (GLA) per year and reaching a total of 3,334,000 square metres by the end of 1998 (ABRASCE, 1998).

Tourist demand (including business-related travel) in the country has also grown extensively. Between 1990 and 1996, investment in hotels, the great majority of which were linked to international chains, totalled more than US$ 442 million (Soteconti-Howarth Consulting apud O Estado de São Paulo, 1996).

This requirement to carry out a variety of real estate projects, together with the increasing propensity for long-term investments, considerably adds to the demand for education and training of real estate professionals.

Recently, the demand for advanced courses in real estate has risen. This is due not only to the necessity for continuing education of professionals in the market, but also to the need to fill gaps in the provision of undergraduate courses.

In Brazilian universities, the supply of courses is still limited although it is being improved, in particular due to the consolidation of real-estate-focussed research groups.

24.2 The Property Profession

The government, professional associations and educational institutions have all been involved in improving professional regulation in different fields, although there is still much to be done.

With a few exceptions, professional qualification is automatic in Brazil, as soon as the relevant undergraduate course has been completed. This link is derived from the former LDB Law (*Lei de Diretrizes e Bases da Educação Nacional*- Law of Guidelines and Bases for National Education), which, although reformulated in 1996, has not yet been finally amended. In its current version, it no longer equates completing an undergraduate course with the award of a professional qualification.

From now on, specific Professional Boards, each of which is related to a different professional field, will grant qualifications. Except in special cases the Boards are linked to government agencies.

This link, required in almost all professions, including those more directly related to the real estate field like civil engineering and architecture, eventually leads to distortions in professional practice in general and in the real estate profession in particular.

As the property professional does not depend on a certificate revalidation, the knowledge development deriving from the university environment is only searched when the professional in case feels like going after it.

However, some professional activities in the real estate field are regulated.

In general, real estate appraisal is exclusively carried out by civil engineers and architects, who are the only professionals qualified to issue reports according to CONFEA (*Conselho Federal de Engenharia, Arquitetura e Agronomia*- Federal Board of Engineering, Architecture and Agronomy), through its CREA's (*Conselhos Regionais* - Regional Boards).

Lawyers, who are responsible for all aspects of Real Estate Law, belong to one of the few professional groups for which licenses are granted by means of a specific examination (Exame de Ordem - equivalent to that of the American Bar Association). This is evaluated by OAB (*Ordem dos Advogados do Brasil*- the Brazilian equivalent of the American Bar Association) an independent body composed exclusively of qualified lawyers. Qualification is granted on a general basis, not related to any specialisation.

It is not necessary for real estate brokers to be university graduates. Brokers are regulated by COFECI (*Conselho Federal de Corretores de Imóveis* -

Federal Board of Real Estate Brokers) and its regional representations – CRECI's. The granting of a licence depends on passing the CRECI Examination.

Another activity that is regulated is that of the Register of Deeds Office, a hereditary government grant, which has been highly criticised in the country.

Other activities, like general real estate consultancy, are usually carried out by professionals, which are accepted by the market. In general: they are not specifically regulated.

24.3 Professional Bodies

In Brazil, real estate professionals are members of one of a number of associations:

– SECOVI - *Sindicato das Empresas de Compra, Venda, Locação e Administração de Imóveis* - Association of Businesses Dealing with the Purchase, Selling, Leasing and Administration of Real Estate;
– IBAPE - Instituto Brasileiro de Avaliações e Perícias- Brazilian Institute of Appraisals;
– FIABCI - Federation Internationale des Administrateurs de Biens et de Conseil Immobiliers - International Real Estate Federation;
– SINDUSCON – *Sindicato da Indústria da Construção Civil* - Civil Construction Industry Association.

24.4 Real Estate Courses at Universities

24.4.1 Undergraduate Programmes

As already mentioned, Brazil is going through a period of reformulation of academic training and professional performance.

In the past, undergraduate courses, especially engineering courses, followed minimum curriculum recommendations, in conformity with the former LDB (Law of Guidelines and Bases for National Education).

After having structured their courses according to LDB recommendations, educational institutions submitted them to the MEC (*Ministério de Educação e Cultura* - Culture and Education Ministry) for analysis. The recognition of the course depended on the approval of its curriculum, structure and institutional facilities.

However, after a course had been recognised by the MEC, its curriculum was analysed by CONFEA/CREA, in order to verify specific professional skills for graduates.

This system is now being analysed under new LDB recommendations, which are leading to evaluation systems for educational institutions and should also lead to the accreditation of courses.

MEC has been working towards fulfilling the provision in Law number 9131 of 1995, which establishes the ENC (*Exame Nacional de Cursos* - National Course Examination). This involves not only the evaluation of the institutional teaching staffs and their facilities but also an examination that must be taken by all undergraduate students.

Civil engineering courses were among the first to be subject to this examination, which has been carried out every year since 1996. The examination is mandatory for almost every undergraduate course in the country.

As a result of the ENC, educational institutions are ranked according to five different levels, from "A" to "E", the "A" being the highest evaluation. When any institution is classified as "D" or "E", it is subjected to a deeper evaluation concerning the topics already analysed. If the poor evaluation is repeated, the MEC may decide to discontinue the institution's accreditation.

This is the main reason why course evaluation has become more important than it used to be.

Real estate-related courses were not formerly subject to the minimum curriculum requirement, and each institution was able to decide on the extent of its own curriculum. As the new LDB does not impose a minimum curriculum for them to follow, the situation may become even worse.

It can be seen that real estate courses at undergraduate level in Brazilian universities have been organised in a diffused and heterogeneous manner, with varying emphasis according to the educational institution concerned. However, the universities' Schools of Civil Engineering have always provided the courses.

Traditionally, real estate issues were the responsibility of the Construction Management professorship, which is why they were first taught in Civil Engineering Schools. Nowadays, real estate courses are taught in the most important Brazilian educational institutions, according to the rating provided by the ENC.

Real estate research is flourishing in such institutions, which are public and can be sponsored by the State or Federal government. Topics related to real estate are generally taught in electives: few schools treat them as mandatory in their curricula.

EPUSP (*Escola Politécnica da Universidade de São Paulo* - The Polytechnic School of the University of São Paulo, São Paulo Campus) through its Department of Civil Construction[1] is the forerunner in introducing management subjects as a mandatory discipline in its Civil Engineering undergraduate program.

The need to study real estate investments, financial systems and other related topics has led to the creation of the first discipline totally related to real estate, which will divide into two new disciplines in 2002.

UNICAMP[2] (*Universidade Estadual de Campinas*- The State University of Campinas, also located in the state of São Paulo), started to offer a real estate curriculum, similar to that available at EPUSP, many years ago.

UFF[3] (*Universidade Federal Fluminense* - The Fluminense Federal University, situated in the State of Rio de Janeiro) covers real estate themes in 3 different mandatory disciplines: Project Management, Economic Evaluation and Decision Processes.

Situated in the city of Porto Alegre, UFRGS[4] (*Universidade Federal do Rio Grande do Sul* - the Federal University of Rio Grande do Sul) has an optional discipline related to Economics in Construction.

At UFSC[5] (*Universidade Federal de Santa Catarina* - The Federal University of Santa Catarina) in the City of Florianópolis, two different optional disciplines concerning Appraisal are offered.

At UFMG[6] (*Universidade Federal de Minas Gerais*- Federal University of Minas Gereais) in Belo Horizonte, there is one, optional discipline in Appraisal.

24.4.2 Postgraduate Courses and Research

Postgraduate courses, both taught and research-related, were subject to evaluation long before undergraduate courses.

The establishment of postgraduate courses is a privilege granted to universities. Evaluation of courses is performed by a government foundation specially created to co-ordinate the further development of graduates – CAPES[7] (*Coordenação de Aperfeiçoamento de Pessoal de Nível Superior* - Development Coordination of High-Level Personnel). The evaluation is based on factors including seniority of the teaching staff, disciplines taught, ongoing research, master's dissertations and doctoral theses (the number of students who have completed the course and time spent in doing so), research papers published in journals, or scientific meetings in which the group participated.

Evaluations take place every other year, by analysis of the annual reports produced by the institution or research group.

The programmes are assigned to major subject areas, which can contain different research groups dedicated to lines of research defined by each group.

The major subject areas are usually established with a link to a related undergraduate course.

Real estate topics are currently found in the major subject areas of Civil Engineering, Architecture, and Production Engineering.

According to the evaluation criteria adopted by CAPES, marks 5 and 6 are assigned to high-quality postgraduate programmes. Some Brazilian universities in this category have Research Groups in real estate-related themes.

The University of São Paulo (Urban Engineering and Civil Construction faculty) offers a postgraduate program in which nine different subjects are strictly related to real estate. Eight of these involve topics, from project management to project finance, which are taught in part by means of business games. Each of these disciplines falls within the responsibility of a professor or researcher linked to the Research Group in Corporate and Development Management. The ninth discipline covers Facilities Management and is linked to the Building Systems Group, in the same faculty.

The Federal University of Rio Grande do Sul has a Construction Management and Economics Group, which offers a course called Economics and Construction Markets.

At the Federal University of Santa Catarina, research in Appraisal and Real Estate Investment is linked to the Appraisal Group, while in Production Engineering such topics are associated with the Management Laboratory in Civil Construction.

At the Fluminense Federal University, the graduate program in Civil Engineering offers courses in Project Management and Economic Evaluation.

As real estate is a new subject area, few research groups have so far been created. Nevertheless, scattered research does take place, sometimes linked to production engineering courses.

24.4.3 Specialisation, Extension Courses and others

As in other educational areas, specialisation and extension courses are now being modified to cater for the need for stricter regulations and clarification concerning the frontiers that divide different types of course.

Originally, there were isolated courses linked to specific fields of knowledge. These so-called extension courses were related neither to the student's background nor professional activity.

As their focus narrowed and they began to cover subjects not taught at undergraduate level, they were renamed "development courses".

As professionals began to seek a wider spectrum of subjects, related to the same core theme, to improve their knowledge, additional related disciplines were added. The courses that resulted were named "specialisation courses". The requirement for qualification was a minimum of 360 hours of didactic activities.

At that time, colleges regarded specialisation courses as desirable qualifications for professors teaching at undergraduate level. Some departments required lengthier courses, usually of 720 hours of didactic activities, including disciplines related to the methodology of teaching and research, characterising the *lato-sensu* (broad sense) of postgraduate courses.

Now, however, postgraduate courses with great emphasis on professional activities, with less rigid requisites than those in courses for academic master's degrees, are required for the award of a so-called technological or "professionalising" master's degree. CAPES is the regulating body for these courses.

Nevertheless, "other" courses, outside federal regulation, can usually be proposed by the institution, with no constraints. They may even be open to undergraduates, depending on institutional criteria.

The oldest of these courses, which started 15 years ago, is the "Specialisation Course in Corporate and Development Management", created by the eponymous research group at the Polytechnic School of the University of São Paulo.

Due to their practical nature, most of the current courses have been organised by a professional body and an educational institution, working together by agreement.

A good example is the specialisation course IAG – Master in Real Estate Management - at the Catholic University of Rio de Janeiro (PUC-Rio[8]). The course is offered through two different university departments, Civil Engineering and Business Administration, working together with SINDUSCON-Rio. The course covers a combination of architectural themes, real estate marketing, investment analysis, real estate law and product management.

Another example is in São Paulo, where the educational institution FAAP (Fundação Armando Álvares Penteado - the Armando Alvares Penteado Foundation)[9] offers 2 different specialisation courses related to real estate. The first one, concerning Appraisal, is offered in partnership with IBAPE. The second course, covering Business in Real Estate, is carried out in partnership with SECOVI.

Santa Cecília University[10], in Santos, also has entered into an agreement with IBAPE to offer a specialisation course in Appraisal.

24.5 Real Estate Research Societies

LARES[11], the Latin American Real Estate Society, is the first association created to encourage and promote real estate research in Latin America.

It was established in São Paulo in October 1998, and held its first seminar in December 2000.

24.6 Real Estate Journals

The only Brazilian journal covering real estate, albeit not exclusively, is *Estudos Econômicos da Construção* (Economic Studies of Civil Construction) a quarterly journal published by SINDUSCON, São Paulo.

Other publications, not however published on a regular basis are available, such as *Caderno Brasileiro de Avaliações* (Brazilian Appraisal Review) published by IBAPE.

NOTES

[1] www.pcc.usp.br
[2] www.unicamp.br
[3] www.uff.br
[4] www.ufrgs.br
[5] www.ufsc.br
[6] www.ufmg.br
[7] www.capes.gov.br
[8] www.puc-rio.br
[9] www.faap.br
[10] www.stcecilia.br
[11] www.lares.org.br

REFERENCES

A ABRASCE e a indústria de shopping centers no Brasil. Dados estatísticos 1998. Boletim informativo. ABRASCE, Rio de Janeiro, 2°semestre de 1998.
Bolsa de Imóveis do Estado de São Paulo. BOLSAIMÓVEIS Web Site. Online. Internet. 15 Jan 1999.
GONÇALVES, R.R. O déficit habitacional brasileiro: distribuição espacial e por faixas de renda domiciliar. Estudos Econômicos da Construção. Sinduscon, São Paulo. V.2, n.4. p127-150 (1997)
O Estado de São Paulo. Caderno de Economia e Negócios. São Paulo. 5 Aug 1996.

Chapter 25

Mexico

Gonzalo Castañeda Ramos
Department of Economics, Universidad de las Américas - Puebla, Cholula, Puebla, Mexico

Joseph B. Lipscomb
Finance and Decision Sciences Department, Texas Christian University, Fort Worth, Texas, USA

25.1 Real Estate Brokerage

In Mexico, real estate brokerage is unregulated. "Currently, Mexico has no formal real estate licensing procedure at the federal, state or local levels." "Individuals representing themselves as real estate agents range from lawyers to taxi drivers to hotel concierges to shoeshine boys."[1] Real estate brokers are free to represent their own interests. Thus, buyers and sellers using the services of a broker cannot rely upon the concepts of agency and fiduciary responsibilities. Professional brokers in Mexico rely on their reputation and relationships of trust that have been cultivated over time. A few real estate franchises from the United States, such as Century 21, ReMax, and Coldwell Banker, have opened offices in Mexico to take advantage of their reputational capital.

Commissions for brokerage services are not regulated. Commissions are negotiable and range from 5 percent on properties in Mexico City to 10 percent on resort properties. Failure to obtain a well-written commission agreement can lead to a re-negotiation at closing. Bringing a lawsuit to collect a commission may take up to 10 years in the court system. Once again, relationship building is paramount to doing business in Mexico.

In addition to brokers, construction specialists, and real estate developers, Mexico has two other professions involved in real estate: appraisers and notarios (notaries public). Real estate appraisers are licensed in Mexico. As a minimum educational requirement, they are required to hold a degree in civil engineering or architecture from a recognized university. Mexico's education requirement for appraisers is more stringent than that of the United States. Consequently, appraisers are among the few professionals who do not have reciprocity under the North American Free Trade Agreement (NAFTA).

Mexicans serve public notice of real estate ownership by recording deeds and liens in the public registry. Notarios are the only agents permitted to make entries in the registry. They examine the registry to verify ownership and prepare and record deeds and mortgage liens. Only lawyers can become notarios. Each notario is appointed for life.

25.2 Real Estate Education

Real estate education in Mexico is almost non-existent. Professional institutes and associations offer a limited amount of training to their members through seminars and presentations at their annual meetings. The educational content of some of these programs is minimal. They usually organize seminars and congresses (1 or 2 days), where politicians related to the industry or bankers gives speeches. From time to time, they organize longer seminars with a more structured content (10 to 20 hours) dealing with issues of appraisal, taxes, credit, and project evaluation. The most notable professional associations are:

- Mexican Chamber of Construction Industries (CMIC);
- Promotores de la Industria de la Vienda (POVIVAC);
- Asociacion Mexicana de Profesionales Inmobiliarios (AMPI);
- Sociedad Norteamericana de Valuadores.

At the undergraduate level, real estate courses are extremely rare. At most you find a few courses on project evaluation, and even those do not focus on real estate if they are taught in schools of business or economics. Only in civil engineering courses are there regular project evaluation courses that use examples from the construction industry. Examples of schools offering real estate project evaluation are:

- Universidad de Las Américas – Puebla (UDLA), in the town of Cholula, state of Puebla;
- Instituto Tecnologico de Estudios Superiores de Monterrey (ITESM), (also known as Monterrey Tech) in the city of Monterrey, state of Nuevo Leon;
- Universidad National Autonoma de México (UNAM), in Mexico City, DF;
- Universidad La Salle (ULSA), in Mexico City, DF;
- Universidad Autonoma de Nuevo Leon (UANL), city of Monterrey, state of Nuevo Leon;
- Universidad Iberoamericana (Ibero), in Mexico City, DF.

The only undergraduate program or degree (licenciatura) completely focused on the management of real estate is in fact a Construction Management program offered at Instituto Tecnologico de la Construccion, which is owned by CMIC. Occasionally, elective courses are offered for college credit in real estate, appraisal, and real estate finance at the undergraduate level, however, they are offered neither frequently nor on a regular basis. These courses can be found on occasion at UDLA. A few architecture departments occasionally offer courses on the marketing of real estate. Two examples are UDLA and ULSA.

At the master's level, project evaluation courses exist in most Finance and MBA programs, but they have little to do with real estate. However, there are some programs in Management of Construction Projects where, among other things, students analyze financial issues in real estate. For instance, there are programs of this nature offered at Ibero, UDLA, ITESM, UNAL and the Instituto Tecnologico de la Construccions. Monterrey Tech also has a masters program in architecture with a mandatory course in project evaluation.

A few universities offer continuing education programs in which they grant certificates or diplomas, called "diplomados." These programs relate to project evaluation and real estate appraisal and typically require between 80 and 100 hours of class time. There are also courses that are as short as 5 to 10 hours. The most well known certificate programs taught on a regular basis are offered by Instituto Tecnologico Autonomo de Mexico (ITAM), Universidad Autonoma del Estado de Mexico (UAEM),Universidad Anahuac, Universidad Inter Continental (UIC), and UNAM.

NOTES

[1] Hunt, Harold and Ari Feldman, "¡Yo Quiero Casa Grande!" *Tierra Grande,* the Real Estate Center Journal, April 1999, Publication 1280.

V

REAL ESTATE EDUCATION IN ASIA

Chapter 26

China

Zhang Hong
Institute of Real Estate Studies, Tsinghua University, Beijing, P. R. China

Liu Hongyu
Institute of Real Estate Studies, Tsinghua University, Beijing, P. R. China

26.1 Introduction

With the development of the national economy as well as the real estate market, the real estate education of China has also matured and greatly progressed. During the years of development, the educational objectives have been continually modified because of changing needs, changes in the external and internal environments, and revised perceptions of related market.

26.2 Real Estate Programmes at Universities and Polytechnics in China

In China, dozens of universities and polytechnics have set up depart-ments, or offer majors, in real estate. They have committed themselves to providing educational programmes in the sector which enable their students to achieve their full potential for academic and personal development within their chosen profession. Table 1 provides an overview of real estate educa-tion in the universities and polytechnics that offer it.

Table 1: Real Estate Education in Major Chinese Universities

University / Polytechnic	Faculty / Department	Major/Institute	Address	Student Number (on this course all years)
Tsinghua University	Construction Management	Institute of Real Estate Studies	Beijing 100084	120
Beijing University	Urban & Environment		Beijing 100871	120
Rebmin University of China	Business School	Land Management	Beijing 100872	120
Fudan University	Economics	Center for Real Estate & Urban Economics	Shanghai 200433	80
Tongji University	Construction Management & Real Estate	Real Estate Management	Shanghai 200092	120
Shanghai University of Finance & Economy	International Investment	Real Estate Management	Shanghai 200433	60
Beijing University of Agriculture	Resource & Environment	Land Planning & Land Use Management	Beijing 100093	90
Shanghai Jiaotong University	Business School	Real Estate Management	Shanghai 200030	100

Source: Yearbook of China Real Estate Market 1996, P899-901, China Plan Press, 1997

The universities and polytechnics mentioned aim to meet the needs of the construction and real estate industry of China by providing a full range of sub-degree and degree programmes, together with postgraduate options. They also serve the professional community by offering a series of lectures of relevance to practice, to satisfy the requirements for continuing professional development. The degree programmes enjoy exemptions of the entry requirements from two professional bodies: the China Institute of Real Estate Appraisers and the China Real Estate Valuers' Association. The key objective is to maintain the high quality of graduate and postgraduate output to meet the needs of the academic domain and the profession, both in China and the world.

Graduates from these courses go into many fields related to the real estate industry, such as the research organisation, financial institution, real estate development companies, real estate investment consultants, and the corporate sector. Most of the graduates, whatever job they take, will attend continuing education programme offered by the professional bodies, which are very helpful for their work.

26.3 Courses and Curriculum Development

In 1998, the Ministry of Education revised all programmes in the level of under-graduate and sub-degree. The courses were updated and restructured into a credit-based format that offers greater flexibility and choice of special modules for undergraduates. In accordance with the requirements of the new modular scheme, the universities and polytechnics have rebuilt the curriculum structure in the field of real estate. The core courses are now as the follows:

– Real Estate Economics

Fundamental knowledge in the field of real estate and real estate market, such as the operation of the real estate market; cycles in the real estate market; the relationship between supply and demand; and the elements related to changes in real estate prices. The course also covers housing and land policy issues, and the impact of local government on real estate markets.

– Real Estate Finance

Finance knowledge in the field of real estate, focusing on: finance theory and real estate; alternative financial instruments; financing and property values; types of housing mortgage loan; basic concepts of real estate securitisation and REITs; loan origination, processing and closing; value, leverage and capital structure; acquisition, development and construction financing; permanent financing of commercial real estate properties; ownership structures for financing and holding real estate.

– Real Estate Development

   Introduction to the real estate development process; developers and their partners; land use system and housing system; real estate market research; project management in real estate development; measurements of return and risk on real estate development; development appraisal; real estate development project finance; real estate marketing; fees and taxes in real estate development; environmental issues in real estate development.

– Real Estate IT

   Introduction to the use of information technology in the field of real estate; prospective changes with developments in both areas; e-commerce in real estate and construction; the network community.

– Real Estate Law

   Laws and regulations governing real estate development and investment, including land administration law; urban planning law; urban real estate administration law; regulations governing urban demolition and resettlements, property rights.

– Real Estate Appraisal

   Fundamentals of real estate appraisal; legal considerations in appraisal; the formal appraisal process; principles and purposes of appraisal; methods of appraisal; the effects of taxation on real estate appraisal; land valuation; commercial real estate appraisal; the appraisal of special types of ownership and interests; case studies in appraisal; appraisal reports; the appraisal system; and standards in appraisal.

– Urban Planning and Land Use

   This course provides a focused summary of the planning curriculum, explores selected urban and land use issues in some depth and offers a bridge to practice for the students.

– Urban Economics

   Major theory and relevant evidence are introduced in the course. A major focus is on the new spatial division of labour and on the role of different types of cities in global and regional economic system.

– Housing Economics And Finance

This course covers mainly a fundamental understanding of housing in its social and economic aspects. Emphasis is placed on the nature of housing problems; the dynamics of the housing market; the history and current status of government attempts at intervention in the market; and the importance of housing in resolving the major public issues of poverty and urban growth and decay.

– Construction Project Management

Construction Project Management covers an overview of alternative technologies, the construction process, and construction procurement management. Topics include the construction industry and the computer-integrated construction; project participants; project delivery methods; project chronology; construction services during design, bidding and procurement; construction and closeout; estimating project costs; project planning and scheduling; controlling project cost, time and quality; job site administration; construction safety and health.

– Property Management

Property Management provides an overview of the field and describes the major functions of property managers. It also details specific practices and problems in the management of various types of property.

– Facility Management

This course is mainly on facility management theory and practice, based on general property management. Many case studies are also provided to inform students about the relevant topics.

– Quality Management

Quality Management is focused on the quality control system in the field of construction management, especially introducing the ISO control system.

– Property Investment

Property Investment provides an introduction to the basic theories of property investment, especially in the field of investment decision-making.

Its major content includes feasibility studies; political restraints; financing; taxation; and investment return.

– Land Management

This course includes a detailed review of the theories of land management. Topics cover the following: relationship between land use controls and real estate development; zoning; development rights transfers; historic designation; real property taxation; and the economic impacts of alternative policies.

– Land Use Planning

This course covers the factors influencing the land use decision-making process, the land use elements of the comprehensive plan as well as the neighbourhood, project and site planning procedures and techniques.

26.4 Real Estate Research in China

The universities and polytechnics are active in conducting research studies, which are carried out by staff members both individually and in specialist research teams. Funding for such projects has been generated from both government and university grants, and by contract from industrial and professional sources. Recent research projects include those in areas such as real estate economics; real estate investment analysis; construction project management; market cycles in real estate; real estate valuation; risk management; housing policy; real estate securitisation; the secondary mortgage market; real estate and socio-economic development; GIS in real estate administration; appraisal techniques; and land management.

During the period 1992 to 2000, the universities and polytechnics enjoyed a sustained growth in research activities with research funding, research output and research studentship all steadily increasing.

26.4.1 Research Activities

The universities and polytechnics have adopted a series of procedures to maintain the high quality of teaching and research. These measures encourage achievement in both the academic and professional fields.

The universities and polytechnics continue to work on teaching and research, inside the university and in the community, in Mainland China and the whole world. They direct their activities towards continual development and progress to improve the standing and contribution of real estate departments.

Another way to develop research activities continues to be the provision and exchange of high quality research papers and reports. This requires the development of computer-based research on demand, and so many universities have input their research interests and results into the World Wide Web for internal or international exchange.

In addition, the universities and polytechnics intend to invite well-known local professionals to work with researchers for part of the year as Visiting Professors. Their role will be to investigate the research from the point of view of the industry and the professional, and to bridge the divide between academic theory and real estate practice.

The universities and polytechnics in China are also beginning some of the preparatory work for the introduction of more self-funding activities, which will help the academic research connect closely with the real needs of practice.

26.4.2 Real Estate Research Societies

The universities and polytechnics continue their links with the real estate industry, the profession and the relevant research societies. The research societies have also been playing a leading role in encouraging all research members to undertake consultancy activities, to organise learning programmes and to participate in the relate scheme, such as Real Estate Appraisal, Real Estate Development, Urban Planning and so on.

Currently, the best-known real estate research societies are as follows:

26.4.2.1 China Real Estate Association (CREA)

China Real Estate Association (CREA), the largest national real estate organisation, is approved by and under the control of the Ministry of Construction.

CREA's major tasks are:

1. Researching real estate theory and policy, providing relevant suggestions related to the development of the real estate industry;
2. Helping the government to produce the real estate industry development plan.
3. Checking the qualification of the enterprises in real estate industry;
4. Collecting the related policies and information of the industry, editing periodicals and reference materials;
5. Holding all kinds of training activities to improve the development of the industry;

6. Making international exchanges.

Individuals, organisations and local real estate associations, who agree with the constitution of China Real Estate Association and have made some degree important influences in the area, can apply for membership of CREA.

CREA publishes several periodicals covering all aspects of the real estate field, among which the following are the most important: *Journal of China Real Estate*; *Journal of China Real Estate Information;* and *Journal of Urban Development.*

The headquarters of CREA is in Beijing, the capital city of People's Republic of China.

26.4.2.2 China Institute of Real Estate Appraisers (CIREA)

The China Institute of Real Estate Appraiser (CIREA) was founded in August 1994 and is the only national real estate appraisers' organisation. It is approved by and subordinated to the Ministry of Construction. CIREA has six committees: Assessment and Registration; Education and Training; Academic; International Exchange; Appraisal Standard; and Supervision.

CIREA plays a very important role in standardising the market behaviour and improving the skills of real estate entities as well as registered appraisers. This is achieved by creating opportunities for the members to exchange all kinds of experiences and receiving further training.

Individuals holding a Real Estate Appraiser Certificate from the Ministry of Construction and the Ministry of Human Resources, who are prepared to recognise the articles and other regulations of CIREA, can apply for membership. Local real estate appraisal organisations can apply for membership as institutional members. Approved real estate appraisal business entities can also apply for membership.

CIREA publishes its own periodical—*The Journal of Real Estate Appraisal,* which is one of the China's best-known journals in the field of real estate appraisal.

The headquarters of CIREA is in Beijing.

26.4.2.3 China Real Estate Valuers' Association (CREVA)

The China Real Estate Valuers' Association (CREVA) was founded in February 1994 and is the only national land valuers' organisation. It is subordinated to the Ministry of Land & Resources.

Analogous to CIREA in the field of general real estate, CREVA plays a very important role in standardising the market behaviour and improving the skills of land valuation companies as well as registered land valuers.

Individuals holding the Land Valuer's Certificate of the Ministry of Land & Resources, who are prepared to recognise the articles and other regulations of CREVA, can apply for membership. Approved land valuation business entities can apply for institutional membership.

CREVA's major tasks are as follows:

1. Academic research into real estate appraisal theory and methodology;
2. Continuing education of land appraisers;
3. Helping government agencies in connection with the assessment and registration of appraisers;
4. Setting appraisal rules and standards;
5. Organising international exchanges.

The headquarters of CREVA is in Beijing.

26.5 Real Estate Journals

There are hundreds of magazines, newspapers and journals covering real estate. The best-known real estate journals are:

26.5.1 Major Journals

– Journal of China Real Estate (Tianjin)
– Journal of Construction (Beijing)
– Journal of Construction Economy (Beijing)
– Journal of Urban Development (Beijing)
– Journal of Urban Planning (Beijing)
– Journal of Urban-Town Construction (Beijing)
– Journal of China Investment Management (Beijing)
– Journal of Investment and Construction (Wuhan)
– Journal of China Real Estate Information (Beijing)
– Journal of China City Finance (Beijing)
– Journal of China Real Estate Finance (Beijing)
– Journal of China Real Estate Appraisal (Beijing)
– Journal of China Real Estate Market (Beijing)
– Journal of China and Overseas Real Estate Times (Shenzhen)
– Journal of House and Real Estate (Shenzhen)
– Journal of Beijing Real Estate (Beijing)
– Journal of Real Estate World (Beijing)

26.5.2 Major Newspapers

– China Construction News (Beijing)

- China Real Estate News (Beijing)
- China Land & Resource News (Beijing)
- Newspaper of Construction (Beijing)

Chapter 27

Hong Kong

K. W. Chau
Department of Real Estate and Construction, The University of Hong Kong, Hong Kong

K. G. McKinnell
Department of Real Estate and Construction, The University of Hong Kong, Hong Kong

27.1 Hong Kong – its importance today, yesterday, tomorrow

The development of real estate education in Hong Kong needs to be perceived within the context of its setting i.e. one of the most dynamic, prosperous and adaptable societies in the world despite having suffered from a degree of uncertainty in the run up to 1997 and its reversion to China and the recent Asian economic crisis.

For much of the last 20 years however Hong Kong's Gross Domestic Product (GDP) growth rate has averaged over 7% per annum and is per capita greater than the UK and Australia. It has a population density of 5,924 persons/sq.km. and 95% of its population of 6.5 million people live in the urban area. It is a densely populated, intensively used urban environment.

At the macro-level, Hong Kong is a significant player in the economic structure of South East Asia and in the international community at large to which its importance lies in its trade, services and communications. It is also of geo-political importance due to its interface between East and West and between capitalism and communism.

One of Hong Kong's major attractions is its most accessible location as the logical base for the rapidly developing business activities in China and at the hub of South East Asia. Since the start of China's open door policy and the economic modernisation programmes of the late 1970's Hong Kong and the mainland have become increasingly more economically interdependent. The two are now each other's largest trading partners. Guangdong province which is Hong Kong's immediate economic and cultural hinterland across the border has a population that is equivalent to most countries in Europe at over 71 million and contains Shenzhen, arguably a Hong Kong concept city and the most prosperous of China's Special Economic Zones. It is estimated that over 2 million people in Guangdong are employed in manufacturing by Hong Kong companies whilst most of the investment in Guangdong is by Hong Kong companies much of it in property. Conversely China is one of the largest investors in Hong Kong with a large proportion of it too in property. In total the six southern Chinese provinces surrounding Hong Kong have a population the size of the United States.

The formal return of Hong Kong to China in 1997 inevitably generated not only a political sea change but also an economic one. For although Hong Kong has played an important role in China's modernisation programme it has been that of a distinct and separate entity acting as a window to the capitalist world on its neighbouring communist giant. This economic perception is changing as Hong Kong and Southern China integrate and the political and physical boundaries become more porous especially through the Hong Kong – Guangzhou axis that embraces the Pearl River Delta area. This is developing as a major economic and technological sub-region in South East Asia and has the fastest economic growth rate in China. Hong Kong's emerging role in this sub-region is as a 'capital city' with international credibility and status which, by slowly moving inside the political net whilst maintaining the two systems one country philosophy, is creating for itself an economic role of even greater dimensions.

It is in this dynamic context that the Universities in Hong Kong have been able to develop their programmes and innovate to produce graduates who are adaptable and oriented to problem solving rather then aiming for technical proficiency in the traditional way of surveying courses which have followed specific branches of the surveying profession.

The changes to which graduates are nowadays subjected during their professional life demand that they themselves be flexible and innovative and what Hong Kong is trying to do is to develop courses that provide an education at both undergraduate and post-graduate level which enable them to hone such talents. The courses developed in Hong Kong are industry benchmarks in terms of the surveying profession in Asia. Many of the major tertiary education institutions in China are adopting the "Hong Kong model" as the way forward for the development of their real estate and construction industries.

27.2 The Profession

Surveyors and surveying have a history in Hong Kong as long as Hong Kong itself. The Hong Kong Government was formed in 1842 and within 12 months the seeds were sown for the surveying profession. By 1843 Alexandar Thomas Gordon was appointed as the first Surveyor – General; the first public land auction took place on the 22nd January 1844. Hong Kong's association with real estate therefore goes back to its foundation.

Over the past 150 years or so the vast majority of qualified surveyors have however been recruited from overseas principally from the United Kingdom. By 1939 the RICS had formally established a foothold with the RICS Hong Kong and China Branch and by the mid 1950's the Hong Kong Government had itself instituted a number of training schemes for local surveyors which was joined by the then War Department of the British Government operating in Hong Kong. Students under these schemes carried out their studies by way of a correspondence course from London which eventually transformed into the College of Estate Management. By the late 1970's this once fledgeling professional body had grown to become the largest branch of the RICS outside of London. However divergent forces were emerging which were having a pull effect from the RICS tradition and in 1978 a working party of the Hong Kong branch of the RICS was convened to examine the possibility of establishing a local institute of surveyors. The conclusion was positive and the shift to independence had begun.

In late 1983 at a special meeting attend by about 150 RICS HK Branch members it was decided by a majority that a local institute of surveyors be created. The Hong Kong Institute of Surveyors was subsequently formed in April 1984 with 85 founder members. In 1988 a set of guidance notes on conduct and discipline for HKIS members was promulgated and in 1990 the

HKIS ordinance was passed by the legislature. This was a milestone in the development of the Institute, followed in 1991 with yet a further initiative with the passing of the Surveyors Registration Ordinance.

27.3 Real Estate Education

27.3.1 Overview

In parallel with the development of the profession the education of surveyors locally was developing with the first home-grown, nurtured General Practice Surveyors emerging in the early 1960's. Like the professional institution, professional education has a pedigree akin to UK though as former colony its development to degree level was hindered and did not begin to flourish until the 1980's.

The first seeds of Hong Kong's real estate education were sown in the 1960's in what was then the Hong Kong Technical College the forerunner to the Hong Kong Polytechnic and latterly the Hong Kong Polytechnic University. These early seeds beyond the U.K. correspondence courses were however at sub-degree level i.e. Higher Diploma; Advanced Higher Diploma and subsequently Professional Diplomas in Land Management/Estate Management. These have now all been phased out but in any event were never fully exempting awards, at best providing Part II exemption only to the RICS professional examinations. This required students to undertake the final part III examination before progressing into the professional competence phase and corporate membership. Many students during this period successfully dual registered on the home-grown Diploma programmes whilst at the same taking the professional examinations.

These courses were a reflection of the UK – centricity of surveying education that pervaded the RICS at that time. Students on the array of diploma courses were steeped in UK practice – green belts, compulsory purchase, planning blight, high street shopping, local authority administration, administrative law etc. all of questionable direct relevance in the local context but considered elements of best practice (to use modern day jargon) at that time.

The development of the profession in Hong Kong was therefore very "British" both in institutional and educational terms all the way to the 1980's when the fledgling Hong Kong Institute of Surveyors was established and local tertiary institutions broke through the UK accreditation barrier and began to offer their own fully accredited degree programmes that were set in the local context.

27.3.2 The First Major Threshold

The first major educational threshold for Hong Kong was the accreditation by the RICS in 1982 of the University of Hong Kong's Quantity Surveying programme "for all those graduating in 1981 and subsequently subject to quinquennial review visits by the Institution". This was the first step on the road to complete convergence with the RICS system and heralded the start of an extremely ambitious period in educational terms in Hong Kong where divergence from this same system also commenced.

The Quantity Surveying programme at Hong Kong University was not a new programme. A degree in Building had in fact been offered in the School of Architecture since the mid 1970's and although called "building" the degree almost from the start became strongly biased towards quantity surveying as it seemed clear that the industry and the community had a particular need for quantity surveying graduates. In 1979 the degree was in fact granted full exemption from the I.Q.S.

Real estate or general practice surveying however remained firmly rooted at what had by then become the Hong Kong Polytechnic in sub-degree partially exempting programmes. The first major breakthrough in real estate education did not occur until in 1987 when the RICS were invited once again by the University of Hong Kong to accredit what has become a landmark programme. By this time a Department of Surveying (now called the Department of Real estate and Construction) had been independently constituted within a separate Faculty of Architecture. With the establishment of this new Department and with the appointment of the first Chair Professor in the discipline in Hong Kong the time was appropriate to review the Department's development and its further contribution to the community. Remember that at that time the Quantity Surveying Degree was still the only fully accredited surveying programme offered by local tertiary institutions. The direction which the course and the Department had taken pointed to a broadening of the provision of surveying courses. The profession locally was also independently like-minded and strongly supported this proposition. However the proposal had a major and significant "twist" to it which marked the beginning of divergence from the RICS tradition for it was a proposal for an undergraduate programme that would allow entry to not only quantity surveying but also to general practice surveying and building surveying. The "twist" was that this was a single programme not three separate programmes. In other words all students were to study exactly the same menu of courses. [The child was beginning to grow and was challenging its colonial parent.] Whilst the RICS accreditation panel were supportive it was felt at that time the programme would not be totally palatable to London and so whilst accreditation was granted and the University and Polytechnic Grants Committee supported the initiative with an intake of 42 students (an increase from 17) the RICS felt that they could only recommend accreditation with the provisio that a certain degree of specialization particularly in the final year project components that defined the traditional quantity surveyor, general practice surveyor and building surveyor be retained. Nevertheless it was a major landmark with a significant number of "firsts" and one that has defined Hong Kong's independent approach to surveying education in general and real estate in particular. It was the first degree programme in general practice surveying in Hong Kong and in a University environment; it was the first fully accredited RICS real estate programme in Hong Kong; it was the first programme accredited by the fledging HKIS; it was the first "common" surveying degree programme of its type anywhere in the Commonwealth countries. This latter marked a conceptual shift in surveying education and one that the University of Hong Kong further developed to its original concept in 1992 when it introduced the first totally common surveying course with no separation whatsoever to cater for any specialism. Graduates decide on completion of the course which area of surveying they wish to enter and take the assessment of professional competence in that area. The course was again fully recognised by RICS and HKIS at this stage of its development.

The support and bravery of the local profession, both RICS HK branch and HKIS for sharing the University's vision of how surveying graduates should be educated for the local context cannot be understated. Given the generally conservative nature of professional bodies world-wide the fact that the industry and the profession locally were prepared to share in such a vision and a fundamental shift in the way that surveyors should be educated is testimony also to the growing independence and divergence of thinking in the way the industry works.

27.3.3 Philosophy & rationale behind the Hong Kong shift

In most tertiary education institutions in Commonwealth countries different surveyors have been trained separately since the day degree programmes were first introduced in UK Polytechnics in the late 1960's. The courses then and today on the whole tend to emphasise the training of technical skills. The University of Hong Kong and the sub-degree programmes offered in the Hong Kong Polytechnic throughout the 1970's and 80's had adopted a similar approach. In the mid 1980's Hong Kong both educationally and professionally recognised that such an approach was outdated and inadequate particularly in the Hong Kong context. Hence the major shift both in education philosophy and course structure.

The broadly based degree was established to reflect a number of initiatives, which recognise the similarities rather than the difference between surveying specialisms. There was a growing belief that education needed to be able to respond to the various forces of change that were enveloping the industry and that if the institution neglected to support such a response the development of the profession would be seriously inhibited as undergraduate education is where many of the major attitudes and perceptions of future entrants to the profession are formed. Hong Kong continues to believe that courses must be designed to reflect the broader base of surveying as a profession and/or real estate and construction as the industry base as a whole rather than specific divisional specialist interests and that they must attract entrants of the highest calibre.

The basic premise underpinning this philosophical shift is that academic institutions cannot teach students all they need to know for their careers; that academic institutions cannot even teach them what they need to know for their first appointment. Once institutions recognise that the jobs that students will take up and the range of their employment possibilities are almost infinitely varied and far from homogeneous then the conceptual shift in terms of teaching and learning can take place. However this does not obviate industry resistance to change. Certainly members of the profession expect students to know everything they themselves know on graduation, plus everything they have learned since! Employers and industry per se need also to understand the shift in concept and what is trying to be achieved and that their conventional expectations may be unrealistic.

The latter part of the 20th century and these early decades of the 21st century are times of rapid change for both the industry and students. Student education cannot be achieved by equipping them with technical knowledge and competencies which at best have a limited life, but by providing them with transferable skills underpinned by sufficient knowledge to exercise those skills. The approach adopted by the Hong Kong University team as long ago as 1987 but reinforced in 1992 was to provide a broadly based course which minimised formal teaching, required students to read for their degree but strongly supported those demands on students by providing a problem based learning environment which helps to provide the skills required for learning throughout the graduates' professional life. A critical element in the success of this approach is the breadth of the curriculum which equips students with insights into the interrelationships of the many facets which make up their field of study.

In the context of this change in philosophy, the aims of such a programme create a very different set of challenges. These are:

1. To enable students to develop their intellectual, analytical and critical abilities and to exercise these abilities within a study of the urban land conversion process.

2. To create a climate in which students can extend these abilities and in which the development of the faculties of independent logical thought and judgement are encouraged.
3. To provide students with a course which focuses on an academic study of the land conversion process and which relates and develops the surveying profession's contribution to the process.
4. To establish an environment within which students feel able to examine critically the established and evolving aspects of the surveying profession within the context of their study of the land conversion process as a whole.
5. To provide on graduation a basis for professional experience in building surveying, general practice surveying and/or quantity surveying to further professional specialisation or higher academic study.

In essence the course seeks to provide students with a framework within which they can establish a sound basis on which to build their careers and from which they are able to initiate, critically examine and adapt to innovations in the land conversion process and the surveying profession.

These are fine words and sentiments embraced by both the University and the profession. But what is the mechanism for delivery of the goods. There are obvious constraints i.e. the course is three years full-time; each academic year is made up of 32 weeks of which at least 2 weeks are set aside for examinations. The answer lies in the course structure. Each year of the course has two major components i.e. the lecture course and what is loosely termed but strictly defined "surveying studio" – a legacy from the Department's origins in the School of Architecture. The lecture course identifies the core academic programme required for undergraduate surveyors and falls into for main bands – land and construction economics, land and construction management, property and construction law with construction technology as the fourth band underpinning all others. The "surveying studio" component provides a teaching and learning environment for application of an interdisciplinary nature over the whole urban land conversion process. Surveying studio is the most significant contribution to integration and develops students initiative and application. The programmes set in the studio are accompanied by seminars and tutorials as appropriate by both teachers and practitioners to lead into and review the work set. The development and progression of the programme is as follows:

Land and Construction Economics proceeds from a first year underpinning course in basic economic theory to a study of land economics, building economics, property development and investment and the associated professional techniques of valuation, development appraisal, construction procurement and project cost control.

Land and Construction Management commence in the first year with a basic study of the urban land conversion process to provide students with an overview of their subject area and also provides students with basic quantitative techniques. The former is significant in laying down the fundamental content of the course so students become familiar with the broad backdrop against which their studies will take place. It then proceeds to examine management theory and techniques and their application to property and construction management. Within this context students will study the procedures adopted by the profession to manage the process.

Property and Construction Law provides students with a basic grounding in and understanding of the legal framework, land law, contract and tort in the first year. The course then progresses to a study of the major areas specifically affecting the urban land conversion process, e.g. landlord and tenant, planning law, building contracts. In the final year it broadens into a study of the changing political and legal situation in Hong Kong in the approach to 1997 and its effect on the urban land conversion process. An objective is to avoid the danger of overlooking basic legal principles whilst concentrating on detailed statutory or contractual provisions.

Construction provides an integrated study in construction technology, structures, materials and services. Such a study provides a fundamental underpinning to many aspect of the other subject of the course. Whilst it is not possible to cover every aspect of construction technology, the objective is to enable students to think technologically so they understand the impact that the technology of construction can have on the surveyors' work and how they will need to be familiar with the technology of the projects they will deal with in practice.

The first year of the course therefore introduces the fundamental academic subjects which underpin the course, including a study of the framework of the urban land conversion process. In this year studio work is designed to develop students' initiatives in studying the urban land conversion process, the major players in the process and their understanding of the role and relevance to the process of the other subjects of the first year. It also allows for coursework in the individual first year subjects.

The second year develops from the fundamental academic subjects of the first year in the four main bands of the course – Land and Construction Economics, Property and Construction Law and Land and Construction Management and Construction. Studio work adopts a case study approach (see later sections) of a real project with students undertaking work on specific components of the project within the context of the project as a whole. The elements are chosen to relate and integrate the content of the taught material and require an element of critical appraisal.

The final year further develops the major areas of land and construction economics, land and construction management and law. The economics area focuses on property investment and development and construction and maintenance economics and the management area on property and maintenance management, and project and construction management. In addition to continuing with conventional property and construction law, the law area also examines the changing legal, administrative and political context of Hong Kong and its effect on property. Project work in the studio will again be within the framework of a case study within which students undertake specific elements. Again, the elements are chosen to relate and integrate the content of the taught material and require the exercise of critical appraisal to a more demanding extent than in the second year.

Students also prepare a dissertation on a topic of their choice from within the body of the course. The dissertation makes a significant contribution to students' ability to demonstrate their individual academic merit.

Such an approach to the academic and professional aspects of a surveying degree course requires that the formally taught material is chosen with great selectivity in order that the course is not overloaded. The syllabuses need to be designed to reflect this and focus upon those aspects of major importance within each subject.

27.3.4 Implementation Problems and Solutions

One of the major problems of implementing such an innovative course was that of convincing the profession and the employers of surveying graduates that the output of a common course met their needs and that graduates would be more adaptable to the changing environment. Although they may not immediately (on graduation) be master of the technical skills, they are capable of picking up the skills quickly. Much informal discussion with the profession was conducted before the course was launched. This seemingly difficult task proved to be easier to accomplish than originally envisaged. Large companies were more readily convinced and more enthusiastic. This can be shown by the fact that most graduates were and are employed by large firms. Smaller firms, while not against the idea in principle, were more concerned about the lead time and resources required for training fresh graduates. This was understandable as small firms, especially consultants, would like to have ready-made personnel who can pick up the work on the first day they join the company so as to reduce short-term costs. Small consultants normally have higher demand for lower cost technically oriented staff produced by technical colleges rather than university graduates who would in the medium term be looking for managerial positions. This, however, does not imply that small companies do not employ graduates but usually those with one or two years experience. Employers in Hong Kong do have a choice of graduates they employ as two of the other universities produce graduates across the range of surveying disciplines with a somewhat stronger technical focus than those of the University of Hong Kong.

Regarding the public sector, staff higher in the hierarchy reacted much more receptively to the philosophy of the course, which seems to contradict the common belief that older people are less open minded about new ideas. However, staff at middle management level whilst not entirely against the idea, were concerned with the extra effort that they would have to spend in training fresh graduates, again something which is understandable. What they did not take into account was the longer term benefit of less supervision in the future.

Another potential problem was the internal one of ensuring that all academic staff understood and agreed with the course philosophy and also worked together towards a common goal. The University of Hong Kong were fortunate in that it was a group of young (average age below 40), intelligent and enthusiastic staff, who all understood and were party to the development of the course. Staff who joined the department after the course was launched, have readily understood and embraced the rationale of the course. This consensus can only be achieved by in-depth debate among members of staff. Such debates were carried out formally before the accreditation visits. One of the benefits of such quality assurance type visits is, that they provide an opportunity to critically examine the course together as a team, which enhances understanding of the objectives and problems faced by each individual. The visits also force staff to review critically the methods adopted to achieve the objectives in a more systematic and formal manner using a holistic approach, and also identifies any problems that may exist and any improvements or adjustments that need to be made.

At a more detailed level, one of the problems of implementing a course of this nature, is to relate the academically rigorous lecture content which is relatively abstract, to real world problems of the urban land conversion process. This, in the past, was achieved by project work in which students were required to solve hypothetical (or real) practical problems. This seemed to work quite well, except that the project-type problems tended to be ad hoc and feedback to the students was often biased to the (1992) views of the staff in setting up the project. To improve this the projects were replaced by case studies. Case studies are completed real life projects or projects in progress. The information and documentation are collected from various organisations concerned with a project. Throughout an academic year, the same project[1] will be used as the basis for simulating real world problems for students to solve. It requires a teamwork approach from the staff, in that the case studies require inputs from a group of staff working closely together.

27.3.5 Parallel Developments at Hong Kong Polytechnic University

Similar developments took place over the 1980's and more particularly the 1990's at the Hong Kong Polytechnic University which is where surveying education locally began and which now counts an alumni of many of the top surveyors in industry in Hong Kong. In many respects the Polytechnic was at the forefront of surveying education across the board and particularly real estate throughout the 1970's and early 1980's. It was inhibited on two fronts. Firstly its belated emergence in the 1990's as a fully-fledged University and secondly a somewhat prejudiced perception by RICS of the then Polytechnic's role in Hong Kong. Many of their graduates from the 1970's now occupy key positions in the industry and as a whole represent an important group of those people contributing to Hong Kong's growth and development. But it wasn't until 1988 that their courses were accredited by RICS despite the considerable historical development within the institution and it wasn't until 1993 that they were accredited at honours level in the areas of Quantity Surveying (currently Construction Economics and Management) Land Management (currently Real Estate) and Building Surveying. The Department of Building and Real estate (formerly Department of Building and Surveying) have produced throughout the 1990's between 100 and 120 surveying students per annum distributed fairly evenly across the three disciplines. They are by far the largest producer of domestically produced surveying graduates but even then only a third of them go into the real estate field. Like the University of Hong Kong it too has deviated from the mainstream in terms of surveying education upholding a generic philosophy that adheres to a focus on the technological, economic, legal and managerial aspects of the Construction and Real Estate Industry. It's mission is to "provide educational programmes in the construction and real estate sectors which enable students to develop their full potential for academic and personal development and to practice and lead within their chosen professional discipline."

The Polytechnic University's philosophy too has meant that their courses have developed in a very particular way with a three year full-time credit based set of programmes with a high degree of commonality particularly in the early years across their portfolio of undergraduate programmes in Building Surveying, Real Estate, Construction Economics and Management, Building Technology and Management and Building Engineering and Management. Though not as studio/project intensive as the programme at Hong Kong University there are still elements of application and integration provided in their Professional Studies components found in all three years of the programme. The programme though more "RICS" conventional than the other domestic producer in that they provide more discrete pathways of surveying specialisms are still a significant departure from the norm again reinforcing Hong Kong's divergent approach. The fact that the two domestic producers of real estate graduates offer different programmes provide a different output which enables the market greater choice in selection of the type of graduate they require for their organisation.

27.3.6 Input/Output

Hong Kong's academic institutions are the principle suppliers of surveying graduates to the market with over 220 surveying students graduating each year from three institutions : The University of Hong Kong, the Hong Kong Polytechnic University and the City University of Hong Kong. However no more than 50 to 55 of these graduates are real estate students with the output from the City University being primarily for the Quantity Surveying and Building Surveying disciplines. This discussion is largely confined to real estate (general practice surveying) hence the focus on the two primary sources i.e. the Hong Kong University and the Hong Kong Polytechnic University. In any event such numbers are small in a population of 6.5 million people and given the importance of the real estate industry here in Hong Kong. Some statistics may help to illustrate this. Out of the total population of some 6.5 million the total labour force is approximately 3 million with some 8% working in the Building and Construction sector i.e. approx. 240,000. About one in ten are employed at a professional and/or managerial level. The Hong Kong Institute of Surveyors currently has approximately 3,000 corporate members of which nearly 1,100 are corporate members of the General Practice Division. The annual domestic new supply of real estate graduates by HKU and HKPU is less than 5% of the current stock of professional members. Over the last 10 years therefore the market in surveying education for overseas academic institutions has grown as their own home markets have declined and Hong Kong has witnessed a proliferation of a variety of courses and methods of study particularly from UK and Australia some of which require extended periods of study overseas though considerably less than the prescriptive 3 years full-time of Hong Kong's domestic institutions. This also has begun to dilute the entry standards as students with Higher Diplomas/Certificates are accepted with up to 2 years advanced standing to take the final year of a fully accredited RICS degree award in those countries.

The entry levels of Hong Kong's domestic institutions have varied between BBB on average for Hong Kong University [Hong Kong A-levels] and CDD to DDD for Hong Kong Polytechnic University. In each of their respective institutions the departments are taking students out of the top 10%

of University applicants and the same applies for the City University candidates for the Building Surveying and Quantity Surveying programmes.

This situation which has developed rapidly over the past five years is a cause for concern for the future. On the domestic supply side the numbers are relatively small with an annual output of no more than 55 but of a high level entry. Government will not allow these numbers to increase. This is now augmented by a similar number of what one might call "imports" from overseas institutions where the levels of entry are much more varied. The large majority of such candidates are those that have not been able to gain entry in the first instance to the domestic institutions. The concern is for a dilution of overall entry standards and this is arguably to some extent reflected in the more recent APC pass rates. The 1999 APC recorded a pass rate of only 18% for General Practice Surveying and 12% for Quantity Surveying. Students from HKU and HPU make up approx 85% of those pass rates for the GP division and 60% for the Q.S. Division. The HKIS has not been slow to react and entry with advanced standing is now under review as well as the initial entry level of students to programmes. HKIS is now formally accrediting all programmes that wish to provide students to the Hong Kong profession independent of RICS and other professional bodies.

27.3.7 What might the future hold?

Institutionally HKIS is now an established fully independent entity within Hong Kong's professional arena. It administers its own affairs; it accredits programmes world-wide for those who wish to enter the local profession. It has a reciprocity agreement with RICS which allows for membership at the corporate level (hence the above statistics). In this respect divergence from RICS has been instrumental in this achievement of independence. However the development of the local profession remains very "British" and the institutional structure still bears a strong resemblance to the UK. On reflection this is to be expected given the cultural provenance of a UK colonial environment. However it too is now developing into one with Chinese characteristics that will determine the direction of surveying education in the future. For what is interesting about Hong Kong's surveying education system is how rapidly it embraced the UK traditions and then has moved on. The move to institutional independence and the support given by the local profession to domestic tertiary institutions plus the desire to maintain and enhance standards in the profession has emboldened local Universities to be slightly more adventurous in pushing the envelope of real estate education beyond the conventional stereotype. The novel nature of Hong Kong's undergraduate programmes are fine examples of this which are being held as models for other jurisdictions none the least being the rapidly expanding markets of mainland China to which Hong Kong has now in a political sense returned. The generalist approach at undergraduate level combined with the ability to respond to change is one that appeals to an industry that is adjusting rapidly to western capitalist practices. This has led to the development of other models at the post-graduate level with fast track conversion programmes designed locally i.e. in Hong Kong to attract new high quality entrants into the profession. This too appeals to the Chinese authorities and new business enterprises who have a good crop of highly educated engineers of all persuasions and architects who find themselves operating in the development industry. This "specialist quick-fix" is an attractive professional development route for already able and qualified people. The model, in a more generalised sense of post-graduate entry only, is one that is now being discussed with some seriousness within HKIS as a means of reinforcing entry standards for the future. This of course will have tremendous implications for real estate education though it would be possible to retain the broader undergraduate programmes which then progress to specialist degrees at post-graduate level perhaps combining elements of APC training which will begin to formalise in a more rigorous manner the corporate level entry whilst maintaining higher entry standards.

A second stream of thought for the future particularly with regard to real estate is pushing the envelope on studio based/project based methods of teaching and learning perhaps fully embracing the problem based approach already adopted at the University of Hong Kong. Hong Kong and China are ideal laboratories to more fully explore this approach given the intensive nature of real estate operations in Hong Kong and the scale of real estate innovation required in economic, financial, political and technological terms to bring China's major cities into the 21st century.

A third and final future theme is the strategic alliance approach to real estate education. The term globalisation is one that is frequently used but infrequently understood and often misconceived. In an era of NAFTA, EMU, ASEAN, CHINA, WTO, currency issues, political instability etc, there is a need to position real estate and construction in the political, economic and social contexts in which they exist and must operate. Without wishing to be provocative much of the prevailing political and economic prescriptions and policy orientations are being built around a philosophical base whereby increased competition is good, protectionism is bad; mobility of capital and labour is good, anything which acts as a barrier to these factors is bad; less government interaction is better than big government and greater transparency is better than less; no industry – stated owned or not - should be exempt from the discipline of competition; bad companies should be allowed to fail and countries who fail to bridge the technology gap should be relegated to a role as a cheap production base.

Though such prescriptions may be arguable they are nevertheless evoking policy responses which will impinge significantly on urban form, the nature and function of cities as well as the nature of real estate and construction investment. There is therefore a growing need for industry professionals to come to terms with how these and other regional dynamics will affect activities in their respective real estate and construction markets and there is concomitantly a growing need for tertiary institutions to provide programmes that provide a global perspective on real estate and construction investment; that enable insights into the structural dynamics of the regions where real estate and construction investment flow; that provides an understanding of the nature and characteristics of different market systems and how they shape urban environments; and that facilitates network development between participants such as aspiring industry leaders, professional executives, government/public sector officers and relevant industry players. Hong Kong and its tertiary institutions have already embarked on this path with HKU and HKPU each offering their own international graduate programmes in real estate and HKU establishing its own China network including the most prestigious Chinese academic institutions offering fully RICS accredited programmes in China.

27.4 Conclusions

It is believed that surveying education in general and real estate education in particular must move in response to the forces which are affecting the profession, and which will have a significant and increasing impact in future years. Essentially, members of the profession have a common interest in the land conversion process and it is upon this, that surveyors need to concentrate their education rather than the acquisition of relatively narrow technical skills as emphasised by the more traditional approach. It is worth emphasising that academic institutions are not 'educating students for the profession or industry', but are educating students for the students sake so that they are equipped to survive in the world of work for 40 years, not two years after graduation.

The development of the profession in the future will require practices, private and public, to be able to offer the type of comprehensive service that clients are demanding. Divisional differences within the profession are breaking down, both within practice and within the institutions themselves. The ability of new entrants to contribute to such changes will depend upon them having a well-developed understanding of the land conversion process against which they can develop their specialist skills. No longer is it appropriate for surveyors to offer only narrowly based technical skills.

To survive in a world in which competition is rising from accountants, brokers, lawyers, bankers, management consultants etc. surveyors must face new challenges. This has resulted in the need for members to identify problems and apply a high level of analytical and critical ability in their solution. This requires entrants to be educated from a stronger intellectual base, so that they can bring to bear on problems an array of analytical tools, and are not restricted in the perspectives they take of the problems to be solved.

As a result of this philosophy, greater demands will be placed on the profession for training graduates in technical skills and professional practice in the period up to Assessment/Test of Professional Competence (A/TPC). The profession is better equipped than an academic environment to do this. This is not to say that professional aspects should be absent from courses. What it means is that professional tasks should not necessarily be practiced on the course to any great extent, but are demonstrated and understood in the context of the land conversion process as a whole.

This approach will produce graduates who, if trained appropriately by the profession up to A/TPC, will result in surveyors capable of coping with change in the future. Surveying will have an appropriate academic base in the same way as its sister professions such as law, architecture and accountancy, for which training after a first degree is seen as extremely important.

Hong Kong's colonial professional heritage has provided a sound base from which institutionally and educationally Hong Kong has been able to map its own future and perhaps more widely influence the future in other jurisdictions particularly China. In doing so it provides the ingredients for a curious recipe. A colonial past influencing a communist present redirecting a socialist market future!

NOTES

[1] Different projects are used as case study material for each year. A relatively simple project will be used in the first year and the complexity of the project increases as students progress to the second and the third years of the course.)"

REFERENCES

Walker, A., Chau, K. W., McKinnell, K. (1997) "Towards a common education in construction and real estate" *Institute of Building Papers* (special edition on Education for Construction Management), 10-19.

Walker, A., Chau, K. W., Lai, W. C., (1995) "Hong Kong in China: Real Estate in the Economy", BHP, Hong Kong.

Hong Kong Monthly Digest of Statistics, Hong Kong Government. Various issues.

Chapter 28

India

Kirit P. Budhbhatti
Budhbhatti & Associates, Gujarat, India

28.1 The property professions

28.1.1 Legal framework

There is no legislation to regulate the professions of valuers, estate agents and real estate developers in India. There are also no regular CPD programmes.

28.1.2 Professional bodies

The "Institution of Surveyors" was established in May 1950. It has the following sub-divisions:

- Land surveying
- Hydrographic surveying
- Cadastral surveying
- Minerals surveying
- Building and quantity surveying
- Valuation surveying

The institute conducts First, Intermediate, Final and Direct Final examinations. The Institution's examinations in Land surveying; Hydrographic surveying; Building and Quantity surveying; and Valuation surveying are recognised by the Government of India for recruitment to superior services and posts.

A second organisation is the "Institution of Valuers", which was established in 1969. The members of this institution are mainly architects or civil, mechanical or electrical engineers practising as valuers of real estate and plant and machinery.

The institute has a syllabus for examinations in real estate valuation. However, this examination is neither recognised by the Government nor held regularly.

There is also an "Association of Real Estate Agents" and a "Builders Association of India".

28.2 Real estate programmes at universities and polytechnics

There is only one programme, offered by Sardar Patel University, Vallabh Vidyanagar – 388 120, Gujarat, which leads to the degree of Master of Valuation (Real Estate). This programme is a full-time residential course with a duration of three semesters. The teaching method is classroom teaching, seminars, site visits and project work. Ranking is carried out using a credit system.

The curriculum includes the following:

First semester
Principles of Economics, Book Keeping and Accountancy, Elementary Surveying, Introduction to Statistics, Principles of Valuation, Building Technology – I, Town Planning, Law – I.

Second semester

Introduction to Computer Applications, Principles of Insurance and Loss Assessment, Law – II, Law – III, Real Estate Management, Principles of Rating, Building Technology – II, Valuation of Real Estate – I, Regional Planning and Urban Land Economics.

Third semester

Environmental Impact Assessment Seminar, Maintenance & Repairs of Buildings and Dilapidations, Building Technology – III, Valuation of Real Estate – II, Report Writing Project.

The Central Board of Direct Taxes (part of the Ministry of Finance of the Government of India) which is the authority responsible for registering valuers, has reduced its experience requirement from ten years to two years for holders of this degree. The Royal Institution of Chartered Surveyors, London has also accredited the course. Candidates must still satisfy the requirements of APC as laid down by the RICS.

As this is the only real estate course in all of India, it is run with the help of a visiting faculty drawn from practical fields such as:

– Former Indian Representative on the International Valuation Standards Committee.
– Former Member, Publication Board, International Property Tax Institute, Canada.
– Former Chairman – Central Valuation Board (established for Property Tax only), West Bengal. (The only such body in whole of India)
– Former Director – Town Planning and Valuation, Maharashtra.
– Former Member (Legislation), Central Board of Direct Taxes, Ministry of Finance, Government of India.
– Former Senior Town Planner, Gujarat.
– Former Estate Manager, Bombay Port Trust.
– Former General Manager- In charge (Finance), Bharat Heavy Electricals Ltd., New Delhi.
– Former Deputy Chief Engineer, Bombay Municipal Corporation, Mumbai
– General Manager – ICICI, Mumbai.
– Former Judge of the Lands Tribunal, Vallabh Vidyanagar
– Principal – College of Architecture, Vallabh Vidyanagar
– Joint Managing Director – Schalafhorst India Ltd., Vadodara.
– Practising valuers and advocates from Surat, Mumbai, Calcutta and academics from educational institutions from Vallabh Vidyanagar.

In the last five years, about 60 graduates have completed this course.

28.3 Real Estate Research

The Institution of Surveyors has been the one that has started real estate research in India. The Institution of Valuers publishes a monthly magazine called *The Indian Valuer*.

The real estate research approaches at Sardar Patel University in India include the following:

1. Investigating the relationship between the level of security offered by real estate investments (in terms of the yield) and other forms of investments including those in the capital market.
2. Discovering the relationship between the security offered by investment in real estate (in terms of yield) and general economic conditions.
3. Trying to eliminate the assumptions made in some of the methods of valuation (e.g. Belting Methods, Hypothetical Layout / Building Method or Residual Method of Valuation etc.).
4. Attempting to create improvements in the methods of valuation for estimating the fair market value of specialised buildings.
5. Trying to eliminate, as far as possible, subjectivity in the comparison of properties for valuation purposes.
6. (1) and (2) above may help in the realistic forecasting of the market values of real estate in the future.

Chapter 29

Indonesia

Connie Susilawati
Faculty of Economics, Petra Christian University, Surabaya, Indonesia

29.1 Introduction

Indonesia is an archipelago country that has 13,677 islands. The major business activities are based on the island of Java. Jakarta and Surabaya, the largest and second-largest cities in Indonesia, are located in the west and east of Java respectively. The business activities in both cities are a good representation of those in the country as a whole.

To support business activities, both the government and private sectors have constructed housing, commercial properties, highways, railways, ports and airports. The above projects are categorised as real estate. Thomsett and Thomsett (1994: p. 253) defined real estate as land and all permanent improvements on it (including building).

In Indonesia, the term "real estate" is applied to housing development only: other, non-residential types are referred to as "property development". Housing development in Surabaya started in the early 1970s. Nowadays, developers construct not only housing development but also other types of property development, such as: mixed-use developments, industrial estates, commercial properties (office buildings and shopping centres), hotels, apartment and condominiums.

Property professionals are in demand, to support real estate and property development. Moreover, property developers require trained, qualified professionals, particularly graduates in the real estate business disciplines. Various institutions now offer real estate courses for both formal and informal education. Formal academic education is provided by higher education institutions, while informal education is mainly organised by the professional bodies. Real estate courses can be categorised as formal courses; continuing education programmes; workshops; training seminars and short courses.

29.2 Major property professions in Indonesia

The major property profession in Indonesia is real estate developer, which have in house marketing, finance, engineering and research staff. Then, the other property professions have grown slowly such as Property Consultant, Property Manager, Broker (real estate agent), Appraiser (valuer), and so on. Although individual professions could not be separated with their companies, there are separate organisations for the individual and institution.

In Indonesia, the licensing of property professionals started with the valuers. The government has introduced supervision of the valuation and accountancy professions by the Ministry of Finance. There are two types of valuers: public and private (Decree of Ministry of Finance no. 57/KMK.017/1996). "Public valuers" are those valuers who work in government departments. Their main duty is the mass appraisal of market values for property taxation purposes. They utilise computer-assisted valuation for mass appraisal, under the Property Tax Act (Act no. 12 of 1994). The information system used for property tax appraisal is called by SISMIOP (Sistem Informasi dan Manajemen Objek Pajak).

"Private valuers" are those who work for appraisal companies which are licensed by the Trade and Industry minister. Private valuers do not just carry out valuation work but also undertake other assignments. They may also be employed as property consultants to carry out feasibility studies, market studies, financial studies and land development appraisals. The work involves comprehensive analysis of the factors that influence land use and values. Potential investment analyses are carried out to identify the marketability of development projects, expected demand, rate of return, and so on.

29.2.1 Legal framework

The laws and regulations in Indonesia follow the Dutch legal system. The most important land law was passed in 1960 (Act 5 of 1960) to co-ordinate procedures for land rights conversion and land administration. The conversion is necessary to administer traditional rights and rights under the Dutch law.

The government has also introduced the Strata Title Act. The Strata Title Legislation in Indonesia is very similar to the Strata Title Management Legislation in Singapore (Suyanto, 1997). However, the Indonesian land rights legislation is binding to the land title (strata). For example, strata building, which is built on freehold land will only transfer to the individual or institution, which could hold the freehold rights. In the land law, the foreigners are prohibited to buy building on freehold land.

In addition to land rights, the government also enforces the property profession licensing regulations. In order to improve the professional standard of Indonesian valuers, the government has stipulated that valuers have to obtain a licence. The licence is granted to valuers who have passed the valuer certification examination (USP = *ujian sertifikasi penilai*). The licensing examination, which began in 1997, is organised by MAPPI (*Masyarakat Profesi Penilai Indonesia* or Indonesian Appraisers Institute), which is recognised by the government.

Before sitting the licensing examination, valuers must undergo basic training and satisfy other requirements under the Decree of Ministry of Finance (no.57/KMK.017/1996)) concerning the valuation profession. The government supervises the valuation profession, together with the accountancy profession, through the Directorate General of the Finance Institute, Ministry of Finance. The government sets the conditions for both professional licensing and permissions to open a branch or start a business.

In addition to the licensing requirement, valuers have to follow the code of conduct for Indonesian Valuers (*kode etik penilai Indonesia* = KEPI) and the standards of practice. The valuers' professional bodies have just revised the Indonesian Valuation Standard (*Standar Penilaian Indonesia* = SPI). The SPI 2000 has been written by a small team (*Tim Penyusun Standar Penilaian Indonesia*) and has been supported by both appraisers' associations (GAPPI and MAPPI). This standard has effectively been in force since 1st January 2001. It refers to the International Valuation Standard, which is published by The International Valuation Standards Committee (IVSC).

At present, real estate brokers and property managers are not subject to licensing requirements. However, the companies concerned have organised in-house training and produced certificates for their staff. The franchise companies, such as Era, Century 21, Vigers, Colliers Jardine, Jones Lang

Lassalle, Ray White, etc., have followed the international standard training and their certificates are valid worldwide.

29.2.2 Professional Bodies

There are separate property organisations for individuals, and companies and institutions. For examples, GAPPI is an association of valuation companies and MAPPI is a professional association of individual valuers. The professional bodies can act as mediators in conflicts between the property professions and the government or the community. Table 1 shows the real estate associations.

Table 1: Real Estate Professional Bodies

No.	Type	Name	Membership
1	Real Estate Developers' Association	REI (Realestat Indonesia)	Developers Companies
2	Low Cost Housing Developers' Association	APERSI (Asosiasi Pembangunan Rumah Sederhana Indonesia)	Developers Companies
3	Association of Indonesian Real Estate Brokerage	AREBI (Asosiasi Real Estate Broker Indonesia)	Brokers Companies
4	Appraiser/ Valuers' Association	- GAPPI (Gabungan Perusahaan Penilai Indonesia) - MAPPI (Masyarakat Profesi Penilai Indonesia) http://www. mappi.org.id - IPPUI (Ikatan Profesi Penilai Indonesia)	Valuers Companies
5	Property Management Association	Asosiasi Properti Manajemen	Property Companies

The professional bodies provide updated information on property development. Members can obtain not only information that is internal to the organisation but also external information, from the government and educational institutions. The property associations are responsible for the continual development of the professionalism of their members.

Each professional body has organised a training programme, which is exclusive to its members. Although some programmes are organised jointly between the associations and the universities, they are not degree courses. The university provides the lecturers and conference facilities, while the professional bodies issue invitations to their members and also support the cost of the training programme. The universities conduct advanced courses, related to very specific topics, while the property profession associations' carry out the introductory and basic training programmes.

Further co-operation between the educational institutions and the professional bodies could be established by way of research. Unfortunately, this possibility has only been discussed between two parties and only a few joint research projects have been conducted.

29.3 Real Estate Programmes at Universities and Polytechnics

In the past, the people who were involved in the property business usually had no specific training in real estate. Most of them had architecture, civil engineering or business qualifications. Later, some professionals went overseas to take formal (degree) courses, or informal training (education). Their courses were taken mainly in the United States of America, the United Kingdom, Malaysia and Australia.

Currently, many institutions offer property courses as additional courses for university graduates in both Engineering and Business. However, these are usually only minor courses or electives. Some institutions present one-day seminars, very intensive training or short courses on a specific topic.

In the formal educational institutions, real estate courses are offered by different departments, e.g. economics and finance or engineering and building. The proposal which is arranged by Tarumanagara University have been submit to the Directorate General of Higher Degrees to start an independent real estate programme as a new faculty has failed. This shows that Indonesian institutions view real estate as a multi-disciplinary course. Table 2 shows the description of real estate programmes in higher education institutions. A sample of non-degree real estate courses is shown in Table 3.

Table 2: Real Estate Programmes at Higher Education Institutions

Institution	Faculty/School	Programme	Duration	Address
Petra Christian University, Surabaya	Faculty of economics School of management (Minor in real estate management)	Bachelor of Economics (undergraduate programme)	8 semesters (4 year course)	http://www.petra.ac.id/ Jl. Siwalankerto 121-131 Surabaya 60236 Phone: (+62-31) 8439040, 8494830, 8494831 Fax: (+62-31) 8436418
	Faculty of postgraduate programmes Master of Engineering (Minor in prop-	Master of Engineering (graduate programme)	5 terms (20 months course)	http://www.petra.ac.id/ Jl. Siwalankerto 121-131 Surabaya 60236 Phone: (+62-31) 8439040, 8494830, 8494831

Institution	Faculty/School	Programme	Duration	Address
	erty manage-ment)			Fax: (+62-31) 8415274
Tarumane-gara University, Jakarta	Faculty of Engineering Urban and regional planning	Bachelor of Engineering (undergraduate programme)	9 semesters (4.5 years course)	http://www.tarumanagara.ac.id/ Jl. Letjen. S. Parman No.1 Jakarta 11440 Phone: (+62-21) 5663124, 5672548 Fax. (+62-21) 5663277

The real estate cycle influences a number of students. In developed countries, when the property market turns down, the more astute practitioners send their staff "back to school", believing that a recession is a good time for training. In Indonesia, the trend is the other way round. The belief is that property graduates have no prospects for the future when the property business is in decline. In practice, not all professionals have suffered during the economic crisis. The valuation profession is required in any situation. In fact, during the crisis the amount of work for valuers has actually increased.

Table 3: Real Estate Non-Degree Programmes

Institution	Programme	Duration	Address
Petra Christian University, Surabaya	Continuing Education Programme – extension class in Introduction to property business, property management, real estate finance, land law, etc.	1 semester for each course	http://www.petra.ac.id Jl. Siwalankerto 121-131 Surabaya 60236 (+62-31) 8439040, 8494830 Fax: (+62-31) 8436418
Sekolah Tinggi Ilmu Administrasi Mandala Indonesia (STIA-MI), Jakarta	Diploma of Valuation Business Administration and Business Property Management (undergraduate programme)	6 semesters (3 year course)	Address: Jakarta Phone: (+62-21) 4213380 Fax: (+62-21) 4228870
	Short course in Valuation and Property Business Management	5 weeks	
Institut Teknologi Properti Indonesia (ITPI), Jakarta	Certified Property Analyst (CPA)		Jl. Imam Bonjol 61, Jakarta 10310 Phone: (+62-21) 3908308, 3908288, 3103707 Fax: (+62-21) 3303987
	Short course in Property Market Research and Analysis or Property Research and Promotion	4 days	

Institution	Programme	Duration	Address
INPRODEV (Indonesia Property Investment and Development Research Centre), Jakarta	Workshop "The difference between Asset Valuation and Business Valuation: a scientific approach"	1 day	http://www.inprodev.com Jl. Rajawali Barat II no. 33, Kalibata, Jakarta Selatan 12750 (+62-21) 7989775 Fax: (+62-21) 7989775

Source: "Undangan Pelatihan..." (2001, p.8), Inprodev Insight (2000, p. 12) and Pusat Studi Properti Indonesia (PSPI, 2000)

As a result of the economic crisis, however, some real estate programmes have been terminated. The Real Estate Indonesian Association (REI) had closed down the joint programmes with Centre of Architectural and Urban Studies (CAUS) that offered a Master's in Real Estate. Programmes that have an international link are more costly, because of the need to invite lecturers from overseas. One of the programmes that are suspended is the cooperation between PT. Surveyor Indonesia and the University of Western Sydney (UWS), who offered a Master of Commerce (Appraisal) course. The lecturers from UWS taught in Jakarta, while in the final term the students had to go to Sydney.

29.4 Real Estate Approaches

Real estate courses and research are composed of interdisciplinary aspects, such as economics, law, regional planning, engineering and architecture. Schulte (1999) mentioned that the basic research approach in Germany is interdisciplinary, unlike in Great Britain, where a surveying approach is used and the USA, where a financial management approach is utilised

Since higher education institutions have no standard curriculum for real estate programmes, their courses have very different basic approaches (see Table 2). The Engineering School at Tarumanagara University offers its programme in the school of urban and regional planning, while Petra Christian University's Construction Management and Property Management course are in the Civil Engineering faculty. Petra Christian University also has an undergraduate programme in the School of Management of its Faculty of Economics.

Since the real estate courses have interdisciplinary aspects, visiting lecturers are invited from other schools or departments. Lecturers from the Civil Engineering and Architecture Department teach the building science courses. The regional planning course is taught by lecturers from the Architecture or Regional Planning Departments. Other courses, such as economics and law, are taught by lecturers from the schools of management and law.

The professional bodies have a very close relationship with the higher education institutions, recognising almost all of their real estate programmes. The universities are authorised to teach the basic training programmes designed by the professional bodies.

At the same time, practitioners have been involved in formal education as guest lecturers or contributors to curriculum review. The university students gain not only theoretical knowledge but also learn about practice in the property business. Real case studies have also been discussed in class and in research for final projects.

29.5 Real Estate Research Societies

Although the real estate approach in Indonesia is interdisciplinary, the dominant issue in research publications is property market research. The published research data provides the "macro" property data demanded by real estate investors. On the other hand, the major academic research is into valuation methodologies and techniques.

It is not easy to carry out property research in Indonesia for several reasons. Firstly, published data is very limited because most property consultants and the in-house research department of developers collect data only for a specific purpose or special project. Not all information has been updated. Secondly, the accuracy of the data very much depends on its source. It is therefore also important to evaluate the accuracy of data by crosschecking with other sources.

Thirdly, most published data do not reflect regional variations. Most property market data is based on the situation in Jakarta. It is very difficult to obtain comprehensive and up-to-date information to show regional effects. For example, the data for property in Surabaya is very limited: the only information is that published by Jones Lang LaSalle and Capricorn Indonesia Consult (CIC). CIC published comprehensive data for the Surabaya market in 1997, but it has not been updated since. Although the property research companies usually have branches in provincial cities, the research staffs there are only responsible for collecting information. It is their headquarters (most of them in Jakarta) that analyse the data and publish the reports.

Property consultants who have published periodical property research data include: Centre for Indonesian Property Study (PSPI), Capricorn Indonesia Consult Inc. (CIC), Investment Property Development (INPRODEV) and Jones Lang LaSalle. The names of journals that publish research reports are listed in the references or in Table 4.

29.6 Real Estate Journals

Since the basic approach to real estate is interdisciplinary, publications can be separated into two main groups. The first group is of general publications, which include some property research items. The second group is of very specific publications, which only discuss a specific theme such as property market performance. Table 4 shows the real estate journals, their publication interval, and dominant articles from their typical content and their publishers.

The property consultants usually publish regular research journals, although some of them only produce periodical bulletins or newsletters. Most of the articles they contain are based on applied research. Academic research is usually published in a variety of subject journals. For example, some real estate articles can be found in architecture, civil engineering or management journals.

One architecture magazine (Info Papan) has changed its name and coverage to become a property magazine, although articles on design and architecture still account for a large proportion of it. As with the other research publications, this magazine places an emphasis on data from Jakarta. Only a very small proportion is devoted to international and regional topics.

Table 4: Real Estate Journals

Name	Publisher	Appears	Typical Content
Jurnal Properti (Property Journal)	Centre for Indonesian Property Study (PSPI) in Association with PSA (Paniangan Simanungkalit and Association)	Annually	Property market performance: housing, office, condominium, apartment, shopping centre, industrial estate, hotels
Properti Indonesia (Indonesian Property magazine)	PT. Totalmegah Medianusa	Monthly	banking and finance, property business, international section, architecture, interior, landscape, profile and book review
Inprodev Insight	INPRODEV (Indonesia Property Investment and Development Research Centre)	Quarterly	property market update, applied research, scientific research, book review
Indonesian Property Market Update	Jones Lang LaSalle	biweekly	special topics, such as: Surabaya property market, Shopping centres in Jakarta, etc.
Property Research Paper Indonesia	Jones Lang LaSalle	monthly	special topics, such as: Jakarta Property outlook, update, Surabaya Property

Name	Publisher	Appears	Typical Content
			outlook, and update.
Dimensi Teknik Arsitektur (Architecture Dimension)	Petra Christian University, accredited by Directorate General of Higher Degree Education	biannual (July and December)	academic papers in Design, Architecture, Regional Planning and Real Estate
Dimensi Teknik Sipil: Jurnal keilmuan dan penerapan teknik sipil (Civil Engineering Dimension: scientific and applied civil engineering journal)	Petra Christian University, accredited by Directorate General of Higher Degree Education	biannual (March and September)	academic papers in Civil Engineering, Structure, Geotechnics, Hydrology, Transportation, Construction Management and Property
Jurnal Manajemen dan Kewirausahaan (Management and Entrepreneur Journal)	Petra Christian University	biannual (March and September)	Academic paper in Management, Hospitality, Finance, Marketing, Real Estate, Information System, Small Business, etc.

REFERENCE

Act 5 of 1960. Undang-Undang Pokok Agraria (land law).

Capricorn Indonesia Consult Inc. (CIC), 1997. *Studi Tentang Prospek Bisnis Properti di Surabaya dan Sekitarnya,* 1997.

Decree of Ministry of Finance no. 57/KMK.017/1996 tentang Jasa Penilai (about Appraisal Profession).

Inprodev Insight. 2000. Indonesia Property Investment and Development Research Center (INPRODEV), 1st edition, December 2000, Jakarta.

Pusat Studi Properti Indonesia (PSPI), 2000. "Prospek Pasar Perumahan dan Bisnis Properti Era Indonesia Baru Tahun 2001", *Jurnal Properti,* 7th ed., December, PSPI (Pusat Studi Properti Indonesia) in association with PSA (Paniangan Simanungkalit and Association)

Schulte, Karl-Werner, 1999. "Property Education in the USA, UK, and Germany – a Comparative Analysis", In *International Real Estate Society Conference 1999,* Co-sponsors: Pacific Rim Real Estate Society (PRRES), Asian Real Estate Society (AsRES), Kuala Lumpur, 26-30 January 1999.

Suyanto, W. 1997. "Hak Milik atas Satuan Rumah Susun". In Seminar on *Management and Legal Aspects of Strata Title,* Petra Christian University, Surabaya, Indonesia, 15 December 1997.

Thomsett, M. C. and Thomsett, J. F. 1994. *Getting Started in Real Estate Investing.* New York: John Wiley & Sons, Inc.

Tim penyusun Standar Penilaian Indonesia, 2000. *Standar Penilaian Indonesia 2000.* GAPPI (Gabungan Perusahaan Penilai Indonesia) dan MAPPI (Masyarakat Profesi Penilai Indonesia). Jakarta.

"Undangan Pelatihan…", 2001. *Properti Indonesia,* no. 1084, January 2001, p. 8.

Chapter 30

Japan

Yuichiro Kawaguchi
Department of Real Estate Science, MEIKAI University, Chiba, Japan

30.1 The Property Profession in Japan

30.1.1 Legal Framework

30.1.1.1 Real Estate Broker licensing requirements

The Japanese government has a licensing law, which regulates practitioners in the real estate business. A licence is required in order to conduct real estate brokerage. Each real estate sales office must have at least one licensed broker per five employees. The licensed brokers are responsible for 1) the explanation of the material considerations of the real estate for sale, and 2) the completion of documents used in the sales and leases negotiated by people in their firm.

Anyone interested in obtaining a brokerage licence must apply to take the brokerage licence examination. The topics covered in the examination are: Law of Real Property; Landlord and Tenant Law; Land Use Regulation; Taxation; and Brokerage Law. There are fifty questions in the examination, which is set once a year. Each year around 200,000 candidates sit the examination, which has an average pass rate of about 14%.

30.1.1.2 Real Estate Appraisal licence requirements

Many types of appraisal may only be carried out by government-licensed real estate appraisers. These include: Land price surveys of land commissioned by local government authorities (The authorities periodically open to public the land prices as standard land prices); appraisals of reference land prices for inheritance taxation purposes by the Tax Administration Agency (The agency asks the government-licensed real estate appraisers to determine the land prices); and appraisals of reference land for property taxation purposes by local governments (cities or towns or villages). Of course, the licensed appraisers also carry out valuations for sale and purchase, mortgages, leases, and litigation purposes.

Anyone interested in obtaining an appraiser's licence must apply to take the relevant licence examination. The examination consists of three tiers. Candidates who have graduated from universities are exempted from the first tier examination requirement. The topics of the second tier examination are: Business and Contract Law; Law of Administration of Real Property; Economics; Accountancy; and Real Estate Appraisal Methods. On average, about 10 percent of candidates are successful. The final tier of the examination covers solely appraisal practice. The successful candidates interested in taking the final examination are required to have a two years experimental experience.

30.1.2 Professional Bodies

30.1.2.1 Real Estate Brokers

There are about 120,000 real estate brokerage firms. Any firm wishing to undertake real estate sale and brokerage must deposit a guarantee in court. The amount of the deposit required is 10 million yen for the firm's headquarters plus 5 million yen for each branch. However, if the firm is an associate member of the real estate brokers' association that is approved by government authority, the amount of the deposit required is reduced to 600,000 yen for the headquarters and 300,000 yen for each branch. For this reason, all brokerage firms are members of one of the two associations: *Zentaku-Ren* (National Association of Real Estate Brokers - NAREB) or *Zennichi-Ren* (All-Japanese Real Estate Federation - AJREF). NAREB has about 110,000 associate members, while AJREF has about 10,000. NAREB provides educational programmes, publishes materials, and promotes professionalism amongst its members. NAREB has educational links with the National Association of REALTORS (NAR) in the USA.

30.1.2.2 Real Estate Appraisal

There are two professional bodies authorised to carry out real estate appraisal, "The Japanese Association of Real Estate Appraisers (JAREA)" and "The Japan Real Estate Institute (JREI)".

JAREA is only one professional body authorised to carry out real estate appraisal for the official purposes of taxation, land price reference, and land purchase by the government. The government, through the Ministry of Construction and Transportation (former National Land Agency - Land Price Research Division, Land Bureau) has given members of the Association monopoly powers to carry out real estate appraisal in Japan. The Real Estate Appraisal Association has about 5,000 members. Members of the association engage in:

1. General consultancy for real estate appraisal,
2. Study of, and research into, the theory of real estate appraisal for the purpose of consolidating real estate appraisal systems,
3. Investigation of the actual conditions of real estate, collecting and collation of domestic and foreign reference literature and materials,
4. Organising seminars for the advancement and improvement of member's professional skills, publishing the results of studies and research, and administration works for members,
5. Contacts with foreign real estate appraisal organisations and participation in international conventions,
6. Directing the training of assistant licensed real estate appraisers (as the only government approved and certified practical administrative body)
7. Carrying out land price surveys on behalf of central government and regional public bodies

Major work commissioned by central government and regional public bodies includes:

1. Publication of land prices, based on land price surveys of the land commissioned by central government under the National Land Use Planning Act.

2. Land-price surveys of the land commissioned by local government authorities under the National Land Use Planning Act.
3. Detailed research of specific monitored areas. These areas are designated in accordance with the National Land Use Planning Act. Designation may be continued or discontinued. Research is carried out into land price change (fluctuation) in the monitored areas.
4. Inheritance tax appraisals: Appraisals of the land for inheritance taxation purposes as required by the Tax Administration Agency.
5. Appraisals for property taxes: Appraisals of the reference land for property taxation purposes, by the authority.

JREI (The Japan Real Estate Institute) is another professional body which carries out real estate appraisal. The JREI is not an association but a foundation as an independent, self-funded, non-profit research organisation. Ministry of Finance, Ministry of Construction and Transportation, and Ministry Home Affairs, however, heavily influences the JREI.

JREI provides three main services:

1. Appraisal: JREI is the biggest real estate appraisal organisation, with 53 regional offices. This network enables JREI to utilise the nation-wide "institutional" valuation procedure,
2. JREI provides interdisciplinary consultancy services,
3. Research: JREI carries out a number of periodical surveys of real estate values, rents, and investment returns and provides the "Urban Land Price Index", "Office and Apartment Rent Index", and "National Wooden House Construction Costs", etc. The institution has over 500 employees.

There are several real estate appraisal organisations as well as JREI. The JREI, however, has been at a monopoly position in Japanese real estate appraisal business. Recently, some organisations have challenged to change this situation.

30.1.2.3 Real Estate Development
There are many professional bodies for real estate development in Japan. The top three are: "The Real Estate Companies Association"; "The Urban Developers' Association of Japan"; and "The Japan High-Rise Condominiums Association". These bodies are all involved in promoting an understanding of real estate practices. They also act as lobbyists.

30.1.2.4 Real Estate Management

There are a small number of professional bodies for real estate management. They provide educational programmes, publish materials, and promote professionalism among property managers.

30.1.2.5 Real Estate Counselling

"The Japanese Society of Real Estate Counsellors" provides several services: 1).Development and publicity of the real estate counsellor system, 2).Training sessions for real estate counsellors, 3).Collection of data, materials and conducting research studies concerning real estate consultancy activities, 4).Consolidation of joint facilities for real estate consultancy activities, 5).Sustaining and improving ethical standards of members, 6).Other activities necessary for the achieving of the objectives of the subject Society.

30.1.2.6 Real Estate Securities and Syndication

"The Japanese Real Estate Securities and Syndication Organisation" provides published materials and promotes professionalism in the marketing real estate securities and syndication shares.

30.2 Real Estate Programmes at Universities and Polytechnics in Japan

There are several real estate-related programmes at universities in Japan. Nearly all courses are provided in departments of Architecture, departments of (Urban) Economics, and departments of Law. These programs are not independent real estate programmes, but are rather real estate "related" programmes in the respective departments.

Meikai University, however, offers both undergraduate and postgraduate real estate programmes. So far, there is no real estate MBA course in Japan. Since 2000, some of the universities have been developing plans to found real estate MBA courses, in particular real estate finance and investment courses. In the near future, US-style MBA courses for real estate business will be established in Japan.

30.2.1 Degree Specialisation

Two universities, Meikai University and Nasu University, offer courses leading to the award of a Bachelor of Real Estate Science degree. Meikai University and Nihon University offer Master's and Doctorate degrees in Real Estate Science.

30.2.2 Programme description and core curriculum

There might be two kind of real education styles, "Continental" style and "USA" style. The Continental style is like a Germany educational style or a French educational style. The Continent mainly focuses "Academic" – in other words "Ivory Tower". The USA style mainly focuses "Business Improvement." UK real education style might be located at the middle ladder between these two education systems. Historically, the Continent (through UK) has heavily influenced real estate education in many Asian countries. However, since 1980s, Asian real estate education styles have been shifted from the Continent to the US. Asian real education style might be located at the middle ladder between the Continent and the US as well as UK real education style.

Japanese real estate education program is also an mixture of the Continent and the US. The Japanese real estate programs at Universities tend to be more comparable with those in the UK. In order to assist foreigners in understanding the Japanese programme, the following comparative course outlines of real estate education in the UK and Japan are provided.

Table1 shows a comparison between the core curricula of the real estate courses at the Department of Land Economy, Cambridge University and the Department of Real Estate Science, Meikai University.

Table1 . Course Outlines: Real Estate Education in UK and Japan

University of Cambridge, State University in UK	University of Meikai, Private University in Japan
Department of Land Economy (1996-7, University of Cambridge, State University in UK) All papers: 17 papers in three years: one paper = around 30 lectures one lecture = 60 minutes Requirements: 14 papers in three years	Faculty of Real Estate Sciences (1999, University of Meikai, Private University in Japan) All subjects: 100 subjects in three years: one subject = around 14 lectures one lecture = 90 minutes Requirements: 48 subjects in three years
Economics	Microeconomics Macroeconomics
Public Law	Constitutional Law Administrative Law Development Administration Law Tax Law
Accounting and Data Evaluation	Bookkeeping Accounting Real Estate Accounting Mathematical Analysis

University of Cambridge, State University in UK	University of Meikai, Private University in Japan
	Statistical Analysis
	Information Processing
Land, Environment and Structural Change	Regional Ecology
	Environmental Law
Land and Environmental Economics	Land Economics I II
Finance and Investment Analysis	Real Estate Finance
	Public Finance
	Real Estate Financial Law
Regional Economics	Regional Planning
	Regional Management
Law of Real Property	Property Law
	Real Estate Law
	Condominium Ownership Law
	Real Estate Taxation
	Real Rights Granted by Way of Security Law
	History of Land Law
	Comparative Real Estate Law
Private Law	Law of Contract and Tort
	Commercial Code
	Family Law
	Law of Succession
	Civil Procedure Law I II
	Company Law
	Business Administration
The Built Environment	Urban Design and Development
	Basic Building Technology
	Infrastructure Facility Planning
Land Markets and Public Policy	Real Estate Market Analysis
	Urban Economics
	Asset Economics
	Public Economics
	Land Economic History in Western Countries
	Land Economic History in Japan
Law and Economics	not included
Landlord and Tenant Law	Landlord and Tenant Law
Land Use Planning	City Planning
	Housing Planning
	Real Estate Administration Planning
	Urban Law
	Urban Development Project
	Urban Renewal Planning
Valuation Theory and Practice	Real Estate Appraisal I, II
Agriculture, Forestry and Rural Development	not included
Land Policy and Development Economics	Economic Policy
	Real Estate Administration
	Land Policy Act
	City Protection from Disasters

University of Cambridge, State University in UK	University of Meikai, Private University in Japan
(Construction & Management: not included)	Architectural Structure Planning
	Structural Mechanics I II
	Architectural Materials I II
	Architectural Equipment
	Architectural Execution
	Architectural History
	Architecture Planning
	Real Estate Management
	Collective Housing Management
	Space Design
	Project Management
	Residential Land Development
	Surveying
	Land Registration
	Land Surveying
	Applied Surveying
	Urban History
	Geographical Information System and Computer Aided Design
	International Real Estate

30.2.3 Faculty and Student numbers

The Faculty of Real Estate Sciences at Meikai University is unusual in Japan, because of its distinctive interdisciplinary nature. Its four primary disciplines are law, economics, architecture/civil engineering and planning/administration. Its main focus is to understanding interactions among space, life, business and environment. Its teaching programme comprises a four-year full-time undergraduate course, a two-year full-time Master's degree course, by instruction and research, and a Doctorate (three years full-time) by research.

The students: The Faculty (Meikai University) is responsible for the teaching and supervision of around 1,600 undergraduate and postgraduate students. The balance of numbers is heavily weighted towards undergraduate students.

Table 2: Numbers of Students in the Faculty of Real Estate Sciences, Meikai University, Japan (1999)

	Day-time students	Evening students	Total
1st year	325	133	458
2nd year	284	136	420

	Day-time students	Evening students	Total
3rd year	221	116	337
4th year	211	129	340
Master's degree (2 years)	30	-	30
Doctorate (3 years)	A few	-	A few
(Total)	1,071	514	1,585

All undergraduate students are full-time students only. The difference of the daytime courses and the evening courses is just difference in time for providing lectures.

The teaching staff: The multidisciplinary nature of the subject is reflected in the range of expertise of the teaching staff, now numbering over 80 (including part-time staff at 50%) which includes specialists in law, economics, architecture/civil engineering and planning/administration.

30.2.4 Teaching Methods

There are a variety of approaches. The methods chosen by lecturers generally depend to some extent upon the numbers of students taking the seminar, and their own preferences.

30.2.5 Ranking

There is no ranking system for evaluating university departments in Japan. In general, the status of Japanese universities depends on their "brand name" (the so-called Old and Big scale) and the *Hensa-chi Score*. Students orient on those before entering a university. The Hensa-chi Score is a kind of normalisation score for ranking student's "intelligence". When high school students take an examination, they get their Hensa-chi-score from the examination result. The Hensa-chi Score is defined as "fifty (50) plus score deviation (each student's score – sample mean of scores) divided by standard deviation of scores." For example, if a high school student has the Hensa-chi score of more than sixty (60), he/she may be able to pass a Class A University entrance examination and may hope to enter the Class A University. If he/she has below forty (40) score, he/she cannot pass the Class A University examination and must be going Class D or Class F University.

Interestingly, the Hensa-chi score of their candidates who take their "entrance" examination decides Class ladders of Japanese University. This means that students' achievements result from university education is never accounted in raking the university ladders. In other words, Japanese University ranking is not depend on "ex post" achievements of their students but depend on their "ex ante" capabilities. As the result, many university professors do not study hard and do not provide attractive lectures to their students in Japan, because they have never been evaluated from the ex post achievements of their students.

If a student, who has over 60 hensa-shi score, wants to learn real estate science, he may not enter university real estate courses because these courses are provided by under the Class C universities.

30.3 Real Estate Research in Japan

30.3.1 Research Approaches

Real estate research is not independent as an interdisciplinary research methodology. There are a variety of approaches, with those chosen generally depending on the original background of the researchers concerned, e.g. law, economics, architecture/civil engineering or planning/administration.

30.3.2 Real Estate Research Societies

There are two academic societies for real estate research: "The Japanese Real Estate Association (JRES)" and "The Japanese Association of Real Estate Financial Engineering (JAREFE)." The multidisciplinary nature of the research, in both societies, is reflected in the range of expertise of the associate members, who include specialists in law, economics, architecture/civil engineering and planning/administration.

JRES provides opportunities for cultural exchange among professors, government officials, real estate businesses and politicians. For example, the authors of papers in their bulletin, *The Japanese Journal of Real Estate Sciences* include a politician (a speech note), government officials, developers and appraisers, as well as professors. The association has about 800 members.

JAREFE is similar to the American Real Estate and Urban Economic Association (ARUEA) and the American Real Estate Association (ARES). The multidisciplinary nature of the subject is reflected in the range of expertise of the association's members, now numbering over 300. They include specialists in real estate economics; real estate finance and investment; financial engineering; real estate portfolio analysis; housing; urban economics; law; and economics.

30.3.3 Real Estate Journal

There are two real estate journals in Japan, published by JAREFE and JRES (as mentioned above, JRES's Journal is styled as a bulletin). Papers on real estate issues also appear in other journals, e.g. those published by the Applied Regional Science Conference (ARSC); the Japanese Association of Urban Housing Sciences (JAUHS), and the Japanese Association of Financial Econometrics and Engineering (JAFEE).

Chapter 31

Korea

Jinu Kim
School of the Built Environment, University of New South Wales, Sydney, Australia

Joo-Hyun Cho
Department of Real Estate, Konkuk University, Seoul, Korea

31.1 Property Profession

In Korea the real estate industry is classified, in accordance with the Standard of Industry Classification, into two categories, real estate lease and supply and real estate related services.

Real estate lease and supply is sub-divided into real estate investment and real estate development. This sector was opened to foreigner investors in 1998.

Real estate related services are sub-divided into real estate brokerage, real estate appraisal, real estate management and other real estate related services.

These classifications are illustrated below in Table 1.

Table 1: Real Estate Industry Classification

70 **Real estate industry**	701 Real estate lease and supply	7011 Real estate investment
		7012 Real estate development
	702 Real estate related services	70201 Real estate brokerage
		70202 Real estate appraisal
		70203 Real estate management
		70209 Other real estate services

New areas are emerging in the real estate industry, such as real estate information technology, real estate trust, real estate finance, and real estate insurance. University graduates with real estate majors have a variety of employment opportunities. Construction companies, financial institutions, appraisal firms, brokerage firms, and real estate consultants employ approximately 50% of graduates. There are increasing demands for graduates from shopping chains developers for site analysts.

Table 2: Number of firms and employees in Real Estate Industry in 1996

	Number of Firms	**Number of Employee**	**Employees per firm**
Real estate industry	52,660	239,574	4.5
Real estate investment and development	2,005	27,936	13.9
Real estate related services	50,655	211,638	4.2

The total amount of output from the real estate industry in Korea was about 11.7 trillion won (U\$9.8 billion) in 1996. As Table 2 shows, the number of real estate firms was 52,660, and the total number of employees was 239,574 in 1996.

31.2 Legal Framework

There are various development regulations and taxation laws to control real estate business. Also, there are licensing requirements for certified real estate brokers, certified real estate appraisers, and certified housing managers. Educational qualifications are not included in the licensing requirements for those licences. There are no exemptions for licence examinations based on the tertiary qualifications.

In the past, real estate brokers were strictly limited their business activities to real estate brokerage. However, after the Korean economic crisis in 1997, this limitation was loosening and they can extend their business into real estate consultancy and real estate investment consultation. These trends have also occurred with certified real estate appraisers. However, only certified real estate appraisers normally employed the appraisal firms are allowed to conduct public appraisal business. Certified housing managers are restricted to multi-family housing complex management. The legal regulations and laws in the real estate industry are shown in Table 3.

Table 3: Regulations in Real Estate Industry

	Regulations	Business Contents
Real estate investment	Income Tax Act Corporate Tax Act Fire Service Act Housing Construction Promotion Act Rental Housing Act Housing Lease Protection Act	Leasing, lease contract, rent collection, maintenance and repair, security, cleaning, technology, management, legal issues.
Real estate development	Housing Construction Promotion Act Housing Site Development Promotion Act	Development risk, design, construction, disposal.
Real estate brokerage	Real Estate Brokerage Act (license of broker)	Sale or leasing agency for land and building
Real estate appraisal	Public Notice of Values and Appraisal of Lands, etc. Act (license of appraiser)	Real estate appraisal, appraisal for mortgage or taxation.
Real estate management	Enforcement Decree of Multi-family Housing Management	Multi-family housing management by owners or companies employ certified housing manager. Management of other building types and land is not regulated.
Real estate trust	Trust Act Trust Business Act	Trust business of real estate development.

Certified real estate brokers must pass the examination conducted by the Minister of Construction and Transportation (MOCT) (this is delegated to Governor or Mayor). The applicants must be over 20 years old. They must pass the first and second written examinations. The first examination covers subject areas, such as introduction of real estate studies including real estate appraisal and real estate brokerage in the civil laws. The second examination includes subject areas, such as Real Estate Brokerage Act, practice of real estate brokerage, public notice acts in real estate, taxation in real estate, and real estate brokerage in public laws.

Certified real estate appraisers must pass the first and second written examinations conducted by MOCT and have professional experience. The first examination covers subject areas, such as civil laws (property rights), principles of economics, regulations in real estate, and accounting. The second examination includes subject areas, such as valuation and appraisal, appraisal theory, and appraisal practice. Applicants who have more than five years appraisal experience can be exempted from the first examination. After passing the first and second examinations, they need a certain period of professional practice to become a certified real estate appraiser.

31.3 Professional Institutions

There are two compulsory professional institutions, namely, the National Association of Real Estate Brokers (NAREB) and Korea Association of Property Appraisers (KAPA). Companies involved in real estate brokerage and real estate appraisal should be a member their respective institution. An individual who obtains a licence can be a member of the institution. These institutions also provide professional indemnity insurance for brokerage and appraisal businesses. However, the government has a plan to allow dual professional institutions in order to encourage market competition. There are non-compulsory professional institutions for housing managers, real estate consultants, and building management.

31.4 Tertiary Education of Real Estate

Real estate education in the university sector was initiated by the Konkuk University postgraduate programs (evening class) in 1970. By 1999, there were eight universities (Konkuk University, Kangnam University, Chunju University, Kangwon University, Daeku University, Hansung University, and Kyungju University) offering undergraduate programs. Six advanced colleges (two-year programs) have real estate programs. Konkuk University, Kangnam University, and Chunju University have postgraduate and research programs. Over 10 universities have evening class postgraduate programs for students currently employed in the real estate industry.

31.4.1 Program description

In the university sector, the structure of real estate programs consists of general and major subjects. The general subjects are general laws, government administration, economics, and management. After finishing the general subjects, students undertake the major subjects. The major subject areas are real estate laws, real estate economics and management, real estate technology, and etc. Real estate departments are in located in different colleges depending on the university, for example, in the college of politics at the Konkuk University and in college of social science at other universities. The awarded degree is also varies, with titles such as Bachelor of Government Administration, Bachelor of Law, and Bachelor of Business Management.

Full-time (day class) postgraduate programs focus on research and a theoretical approach whilst evening class postgraduate programs focus on practical studies. However, because there are many students from other than a real estate background in the postgraduate program, general subjects such as law, economics, management, and information technology are included in postgraduate programs.

The programs can vary amongst universities depending on their Parent College and background of the faculties. In Konkuk University the department of real estate is in the college of politics. Historically the program focused on the areas of urban development, general laws, and related systems. However, the program has recently moved into the areas of real estate economics, real estate investment, real estate finance, real estate market analysis, econometrics, and information technology.

Other universities have the following specialisation:

– The Hansung University is trying to gain a specialisation in real estate appraisal, real estate macro economic analysis, and real estate marketing.
– The Kangwon University is focusing on real estate appraisal, real estate laws, and real estate policies.
– The Kangnam University is trying to gain a specialisation in housing policy and real estate laws.
– The Chunju University is focusing on real estate laws and real estate finance.
– The Daeku University has a close link with the regional development department and focuses on the area of regional development.

Most of the advanced colleges offer two-year programs that provide studies for the examination of certified real estate brokers or certified housing managers.

31.4.2 Core curriculum

There are small differences in curriculum content between universities, but in the main all universities focus on the areas of real estate public laws, real estate investment, real estate policy, real estate appraisal, real estate market analysis, and law subjects. Previously, real estate appraisal and laws were the most important subjects in real estate education, but more recently, real estate investment and market analysis have become the focus for real estate studies in universities.

Table 4: Curriculum of real estate education in Konkuk University

Subject	Year	Content
Real estate public laws (I)	2	Land and building regulations for real estate usage
Surveying technology	2	Land surveying and surveying technology
Microeconomics	2	Price theory, real estate market, policy
Real estate private laws (I)	2	Property right, real estate title
Real estate public laws (II)	2	Real estate related Building Code
Real estate information technology	2	Information technology in real estate investment and development
Real estate introduction	3	Principles and practice of real estate studies
Real estate private laws (II)	3	Contract laws, bond
Theory of real estate appraisal	3	Introduction of appraisal, feasibility analysis
Financial management	3	Corporate investment decision making, finance
Real estate economics	3	Land use, real estate market, value, investment
Public notice in real estate	3	Land title, surveying
Practice of real estate appraisal	3	Case studies of real estate appraisal
Regional planning	3	Industrial planning, urban space development
Urban planning	3	History of urban plan, urban growth, planning method
Real estate investment	3	Investment decision making, investment efficiency
Real estate business	3	Theory of real estate business
Real estate taxation	3	Theory and system of real estate taxation
Real estate laws	4	Analysis of real estate laws in practice
Real estate market analysis	4	Development, market analysis, feasibility study
Real estate finance	4	Investment, development, securitisation
Real estate development	4	Development process, regulations, feasibility

Subject	Year	Content
		study
Land policy	4	Land use, development system, taxation
Housing policy	4	Housing problem, housing taxation, housing mortgage

31.4.3 Students number

Each university normally accepts 40 or 80 students per year in real estate department, and the total number of students is estimated at 1200 to 1400. Each advanced college normally accepts from 40 to 120 students per year, and total number of students is around 800 to 1000. Full-time (day class) postgraduate students are estimated at less than one hundred, and there are several hundred evening class postgraduate students.

31.5 Real Estate Research and Journals

Academic research in real estate focuses on housing policy, land policy, real estate market analysis, and appraisal, whilst industrial research mainly focuses on real estate appraisal and consulting areas. Research topics vary depending upon the conditions and performances of the real estate market in Korea. In the past during rapid economic development, most of the academic concerns were given to the introduction of new real estate systems and to the rationalisation of existing legal systems. A typical topic area was, for example, compensation to landowners whose real estate was to be used for public projects such as roads, parks, and industrial complexes. Other areas of concern were the recapture of windfall profits and suppression of real estate speculation. The most popular real estate approach was therefore a legal and institutional one. Most of the research results were reflected in existing and new laws.

Because the real estate market responded in different directions or showed various undesirable side effects from such reforms, economic and market approach gains power during the 1990s. Globalisation and localisation trends also gave more justification on market approaches. Many early 1990s' research topics dealt with the negative side effects of various regulations covering demand, supply and prices. Recently, after the IMF's special bailout financing, many academic papers dealt with real estate financing and securitisation of real estate. In addition to this, other newly emerging areas for research topics includes consumer protection, environmentally sound and sustainable development (ESSD), building management, and real estate consulting.

The field is covered by the following real estate journals

- Journal of Korea Real Estate Analysis Association (KREAA)
- Housing Studies Review
- Journal of Korea Planners Association (KPA)
- Real Estate Research (by Korea Appraisal Board)

31.6 Conclusions

There is clearly a very large potential for growth in the numbers of property professionals in Korea undertaking full time and part time studies. Indeed, given the scale and levels of activity in the Korean property sector the educational infra structure is remarkably under developed. By comparison the Royal Institution of Chartered Surveyors (which is the premier property institution in the UK) has 83,000 chartered surveyor members, 3,000 technical surveyors subscription and 21,000 students and trainees are working towards full membership.

Chapter 32

Malaysia

Ismail Omar
Centre for Land Administration Studies (CLAS), University Technology of Malaysia, Johor Bahru, Malaysia.

32.1 Introduction

Malaysia was administered under the British Colonial administration until its independence in 1957. Since independence, Malaysia has developed economically, politically and socially. Land has been cleared for settlement and development of the country. Highways, ports and airports have been built. Since then, property professionals have been in high demand, to support the economic development and real estate activities. The property professions involved are land surveying, land development, land administration and so on. At the same time, real estate activities require professionals who were trained at and have graduated from higher education institutions. As a result, real estate courses are offered at various tertiary and higher education institutions in the country.

32.2 The Property Profession

In Malaysia, the property profession is generally recognised under the umbrella of the surveying profession. Generally, property people are professionals involved in the valuation of land and buildings, or known as general practice surveyors, quantity surveyors, land surveyors, land and development consultants, architects, property managers, estate agents, land administrators and so on. With the clamour for land and economic development of the country after independence in 1957, the Valuation Section was introduced as a section of the Ministry of Finance, Malaysia. The main objective was to manage valuation work for taxation purposes.

In Malaysia, the two main functions of a general practice surveyor are:

a) To value land and buildings for various purposes. In the public services sector, valuers are employed by the Valuation and Property Services Department, Ministry of Finance. Their main objective is to assist and advise the Federal Government, State Government, Local Authorities, and Statutory Authorities on matters pertaining to the valuation of landed property. The public valuers are required to estimate open market value for stamp duty, estate duty, real property gain tax, annual rents, alienation and premiums and rates. Other than for taxation purposes, public valuers also assist in civil suits as expert witnesses in the Court of Law. Public valuers also advise on land matters pertaining to capital issues committee (CIC) and housing loans, insurances and rentals.

b) In the private sector, valuers provide services in the form of valuation, property and project management and estate agency. Private valuers are required to advise on open market value for loan collateral purposes. Other than that, they are also required to manage, and undertake the marketing of, projects, as well as collecting rents and co-ordinating the maintenance of buildings after completion. Private valuers are also engaged in consultancy, such as carrying out feasibility studies, financial studies and development appraisals to ascertain the expected demand, future return, expected value and marketability of development projects. In this context, the work involves a multi-disciplinary environment pertaining to land, and socio-economic factors influencing land use and values.

32.2.1   Legal Framework

Since the main function of general practice surveying is to offer advice on the value of land and buildings, factors affecting value, such as economic and legal considerations must be fully reflected. In this context, there are various land-related laws that must be taken into account in order to undertake a general practice surveyor's task. The Federal Constitution stipulates various provisions pertaining to laws related to the administration, valuation and development of landed property. There are also various acts of parliament, enactment, bye-laws and ordinances related to land and buildings. More importantly, a National Land Code was established in 1960 (Act 134 of 1960) to co-ordinate procedures for land administration and development. In 1960, the real estate profession was upgraded with the introduction of the Land Acquisition Act (Act 34 1960) which has widened the scope of the general practice surveyor in valuing land for compensation and development purposes. The amount of compensation must be assessed according to the principle of just compensation, as stipulated in the Federal Constitution. Apart from valuation for compensation purposes, a general practice surveyor is also responsible for the valuation of land and building for taxation purposes, such as for rating under the Local Government Act (1976).

32.2.2   Professional Bodies

The general practice surveyor as a profession was first officially recognised with the introduction of the Surveyor Registration Act in 1966. This Act, which came into force with the purpose of controlling property professionals who were part of the surveying profession, introduced the Institute of Surveyors Malaysia (ISM). In 1981, the government passed the Valuers, Appraisers and Estate Agents Act. This Act set up the Board of Valuers, Appraisers and Estate Agents to govern the valuation profession, while on the professional side, the Institution of Surveyors Malaysia continues to represent the profession. In the private sector, the property profession is co-ordinated by the Association of Private Sector Valuers (PEPS). In the public sector, valuers are organised under the Association of Valuers in the Public Sector (PENILAISAMA). There is also an association of estate agents in the private sector, which is known as the Malaysian Real Estate Agents (MREA).

Generally, to become a registered valuer, a property or project manager, or an estate agent, it is a requirement to have passed a four- or five-year degree course at an academic institution. The real estate programmes are multi-disciplinary courses, which include financial, economic, legal, commercial, social and public interest aspects of land use, development and management.

Prior to registration with the Board of Valuers, Appraisers and Estate Agents, a would-be-valuer needs to undergo about two years' work experience before sitting for the Test of Professional Competency (TPC).

32.3 Real Estate Programmes at Universities

During the British Colonial administration, valuers were educated in the United Kingdom. In addition, some professionally qualified valuers were brought from the United Kingdom to Malaysia. After independence in 1957, there was a need for programmes to train and educate local valuation officers as well as other property-related courses. In 1976, the University Technology of Malaysia or UTM (formerly the National Technical Institute) was offering courses in Valuation and Property Management, with the opening of the Property Management and Valuation Department in the Faculty of Surveying at its campus in Kuala Lumpur. At the same time, valuers were also trained at various universities and polytechnics in the UK, Canada, New Zealand and Australia.

With the expansion and the needs of local valuation trainees, the University Technology MARA or UiTM (formerly known as Institute Technology MARA) has also begun to offer courses related to surveying, property management and town and country planning. At present, the University of Malaya, the University Putra Malaysia and the University Science of Malaysia are also offering property-related courses. These universities are also offering courses at postgraduate level, such as Master's and Ph.D. degrees in real estate.

Most of the property courses in Malaysia cover subjects such as:

– Principles of valuation of land and buildings
– Valuation Methodologies
– Building and Construction Technology
– Advanced Valuation
– Statutory Valuation
– Statistical Analysis for Valuation
– Urban Land Economy
– Land Law
– Project and Construction Management
– Estate Agency – Principles and Practice
– Property Management
– Facility Management
– Town and Country Planning

32.4 Real Estate Research

Most of the research on real estate in Malaysia investigates the issues, problems and solutions related to current valuation methodologies and techniques, land and development administration and the use of computers in the real estate world. Recently, many researchers have been considering the dynamics of the property market in the country and the institutions that affect property and land development activities. This includes the research on indigenous land such as the Malay Reservation Land issues and problems in the country. The present trends in real estate research are to look into property-related problems with the use of quantitative as well as qualitative analysis. These include the conceptual and potential applications of geographic and land information technology in the real estate professions. This can be seen from initiatives undertaken by various government departments to utilise computerisation systems such as at the National Land Information System (NALIS).

32.5 Real Estate Journals

The *Valuation and Property Services Journal* is published by the National Valuation Training Center (INSPEN), under the Valuation and Property Services Department, Ministry of Finance, Malaysia. *The Surveyor* is a property magazine published privately in Malaysia.

REFERENCES

Ismail Omar (1992, 1997), Penilaian Harta Tanah, Dewan Bahasa dan Pustaka, Kuala Lumpur.
Directory of Members (1988), Institution of Surveyors Malaysia.

Chapter 33

Taiwan

Yao-Min Chiang
Department of Finance, National Chengchi University, Taiwan

Chin-Oh Chang
Department of Land Economics, National Chengchi University, Taiwan

33.1 Introduction

In the past, Taiwan's real estate market was highly affected by the government's land policy. However, following the economic liberalisation, the real estate market is now mainly driven by market conditions. Our past real estate education focused on making land policy, but now we have to change our focus to train students to be able to meet the challenges of a dynamic market.

Despite the growing popularity of real estate programmes, and more and more fresh Ph.D.s devoting themselves to real estate education, the way Taiwan's real estate education adjusts to face the environmental change is worthy of study.

In this article, we investigate a survey of real estate academics in Taiwan to obtain information on their teaching and research. Survey questionnaires were sent to individual academics and real estate related departments based on the directory of the Chinese Society of Housing Studies (Taiwan). 36 effective respondents answered the questionnaire and became our analysis base. The Chinese Society of Housing Studies is the largest real estate association in Taiwan and contains almost all real estate academics and many employees of the government and industrial companies. The sample is acceptably representative.

The survey results show that the focus of real estate education has been switching from policy orientation to market orientation. We are glad to see there are more and more Ph.D.s with modern real estate knowledge to join the field. New programmes and new research centres have been established. Researchers continue to carry out fine research and to participate actively in international conferences.

33.2 Respondents' background

In this article, we aim to gain an understanding of real estate education in the higher education system. 50 questionnaires were sent to real estate academics and researchers on March 20, 1999. 36 effective responses were collected.

Table 1: Respondents' academic degree
This table shows respondents' academic degree. Survey questionnaires are sent to real estate academics and researchers.

Degree	Number of respondents	Percentage
Ph.D.	27	75%
Master	8	22%
Bachelor	1	3%
Total	36	100%

Of the 36 respondents, 26 were male and 10 female. We could find no evidence to show gender difference in terms of the questions we asked. Most academics have a doctoral degree (27/36). 8 out of 36 have a Master's degree (see Table 1). Our academics are well trained. Table 2 shows that most of real estate academics in Taiwan are young. Respondents with less than 10 years' experience account for 79% of the total. In particular, we see that 15 fresh Ph.D.s have joined real estate education in Taiwan over the past three years.

Table 2: Academic experience

Survey questionnaires are sent to real estate academics and researchers to ask them how long they have been working in academic institutions. 7 respondents work for government, research institutions or private companies and did not answer this question.

Experience	Number of respondents	Percentage
1~3 years	15	52%
4~6 years	2	7%
7~10 years	6	21%
11~15 years	1	3%
16~20 years	4	14%
20~25 years	1	3%
Total	29	100%

From Table 3, we see that most real estate academics/researchers were awarded their degrees from the United States. 21 out of 36 were educated in the U.S.A. Local graduates account for 36.11% of all respondents. Local universities provide a large portion of academics/researchers. However, most of these local graduates specialize in land economics and urban planning. On the other hand, graduates from the U.S.A. are mostly well versed in real estate finance, investment, and economics. These fresh Ph.D. are believed to be the major driving force to lead Taiwan's real estate education past the threshold of the 21st century.

Table 4 shows that the major strengths of real estate faculties are in teaching urban planning (10 out of 36), economics (5 out of 36), and finance (6 out of 36). As we know, those academics with a major in finance joined real estate education during the past three years. Their theses are about REITs, mortgage-backed securities, real estate investment, and real options.

Table 3: Countries in which respondents earned their degree

Survey questionnaires are sent to real estate academics and researchers to ask them where they were awarded their highest academic degree.

Country	Number of respondents	Percentage
Taiwan	13	36%
U.S.A.	21	58%
Germany	1	3%
Great Britain	1	3%
Total	36	100%

12 respondents rank as associate professors, and 7 of them are professors. The ranking of assistant professor is new and resulted from a change in national rules in 1997. Assistant professors have seven years to be promoted to a higher rank, or they may lose their jobs. We expect them to play active roles in Taiwan's real estate education system.

Table 4: Respondents' academic background

This table shows respondents' academic background.

Departmental affiliation	Number of respondents	Percentage
Finance	6	17%
Economics	5	14%
Land Management	2	5%
Land Economics	2	5%
Architecture	3	9%
Engineering	1	3%
Urban Planning	10	28%
Landscape	2	5%
Others*	5	14%
Total	36	100%

Government, private companies, or research institutions.

Table 5: Respondents' academic ranking

Ranking	Number of respondents	Percentage
Instructor	7	19%
Assistant Professor	4	12%
Associate Professor	12	33%
Professor	7	19%
Others*	6	17%
Total	36	100%

Includes government employees, researchers, etc.

33.3 Real Estate Education

33.3.1 Institutions and enrolment

In Taiwan's higher education system, universities play a key role in real estate education. Private universities outnumber the public universities, and are avid providers of real estate related programmes. Several different types of university department provide real estate education in Taiwan. (see Table 6) Typical departments include land economics (National Chengchi University and National Taipei University), and land management (Fengchia University and Chang Jung Christian University). The finance and economics departments in several universities also provide real estate courses. Leader University recently created a new department of real estate management. National Chengchi University is establishing a Master's programme in its business school and National Taiwan University is establishing a new department, also in its business school. They will provide courses in real estate economics, law, development, management, financing, investment, and marketing. These integrated programmes are designed to meet the needs of the market.

Most programmes in universities confer Master's degrees, while some of them award Doctorates. Among them, the Department of Land Economics in the National Chengchi University, and the Graduate Institute of Building and Planning in the National Taiwan University are the most important. They generate a large number of Ph.D.s to teach in universities and especially in colleges of technology.

The college of technology is an important type of higher education institution in Taiwan. Upon completion of middle school (with altogether nine years of school education) students are provided with a five-year programme in which the final two years are considered to be part of higher education[1]. Over the past decade, the better-equipped among these colleges have been upgraded to polytechnics. Most of these colleges provide real estate programmes. For example, there are real estate management departments in National Pingtung Institute of Commerce, Kung Shan Institute of Technology, Nankai College Technology and Commerce, Ging-Chung Business College, and Sze-Hai Institute of Technology and Commerce. However, the purpose of these programmes is mainly for job orientation.

Table 6: Real estate programmes in Taiwan

This table shows current and forthcoming real estate programmes in Taiwan's higher education system.

Panel A. University

| School | Department | Degree conferred | | |
		Bachelor	Master	Doctor
National Taiwan University	Graduate Institute of Building and Planning		x	x
National Chengchi University	Land Economics	x	x	x
National Taipei University	Urban Planning		x	x
National Taipei University	Land Economics	x	x	

School	Department	Degree conferred		
		Bachelor	Master	Doctor
National Chung-Kung University	Urban Planning	x	x	x
Chinese Culture University	Land Resource	x	x	
Fengchia University	Urban Planning	x	x	
Fengchia University	Land Management	x	x	
Leader University	Real Estate Management	x		
Chang Jung Christian University	Land Management	x	x	

Panel B. Polytechnics and colleges of technology

School	Department	Degree conferred		
		Bachelor	Master	Doctor
National Pingtung Institute of Commerce	Real Estate Management	x		
Kung Shan Institute of Technology	Real Estate Management	x		
Nankai College Technology and Commerce	Real Estate Management	x		
Ging-Chung Business College	Real Estate Management	x		
Sze-Hai Institute of Technology	Real Estate Management	x		

Panel C. Forthcoming programmes

School	Department	Degree conferred		
		Bachelor	Master	Doctor
National Chengchi University	Graduate Institute of Real Estate Management		x	x
National Taiwan University	Real Estate Management	x	x	

To enrol at universities, for all bachelor-, Master's and Doctoral levels, students have to take an entrance examination. However, a new admission procedure has been adopted. Students can now apply to individual departments, who then take account of teachers' recommendations and undertake interviews to process the application. This new admission process is becoming an important way for departments to find suitable students.

There are also some continuing education programmes. For example, the Center for Public and Business Administration Education at the National Chengchi University provides a 72-hour programme for the real estate professionals. The programme is focused on the training of professional brokers. On February 3, 1999, a law was passed, which requires brokers to have a licence. The licence must be renewed every four years. Therefore, some private institutes have started providing courses for brokers to get their licenses. The Banking Institute[2] provides programmes about mortgage financing to bankers. They also teach courses related to mortgage-backed securities. Bankers in Taiwan are enthusiastic to set up local secondary mortgage markets. Several other associations also provide short-term programmes to teach subjects such as land law, land economics, development, and investment.

33.3.2 Curriculum

Table 7 lists popular course subjects and their credit hours, with the average number of students enrolled.

Table 7: Popular courses in real estate programmes
This table shows average numbers of students in popular real estate courses. These courses may have different titles with the same contents. Based on the opinion of questionnaire respondents.

Subject	Credits	Average student number	
		Bachelor	Master
Real Estate Economics	2	38	10
Land Economics	2	50	9
Urban Economics	3	60	7
Spatial Economics	3	10	3
Real Estate Investment	3	80	9
Real Estate Finance	3	80	9
Seminar on Real Estate Issues	3	10	3
Methods of Urban and Regional Analysis	2	22	10
Real Estate Marketing	3	50	10
Market Analysis	3	20	10
Environment Planning	3	31	8
Urban Planning	3	60	10
Geographic Information Systems	3	20	15
Land Use and Transportation	3	45	15
Planning Analysis Methods	2	45	10
Econometrics	3	30	12
Law	3	50	10

The most popular course is real estate economics, which is viewed as the basic course in a real estate programme. Real estate investment and finance have become more and more popular. As mentioned, several fresh Ph.D.s have just earned their degrees in finance from universities in the United States and have come back to Taiwan to teach in universities.

The average number of students is 50 at undergraduate (bachelor) level and 10 for a Master's course. The most popular textbooks used in these courses include Chin-Oh Chang's "Real Estate Investment and Decision Making" (in Chinese), Brueggeman and Fisher's "Real Estate Finance and Investment", and Mills & Hamilton's "Urban Economics". Most instructors use English edition textbooks.

We mentioned that there are several junior colleges that provide real estate programmes. A good example of these is the courses designed at the Gung Shan Institute of Technology. Real estate courses are mainly divided into three groups: management (including land development, appraisal, administration, marketing, etc.); investment (including market analysis, tax, financing, etc.); and law.

33.3.3 Teaching

Respondents were asked to indicate the amount of time they spent on teaching, the number and titles of courses, and the number of students registered. Of 36 respondents, 32 were involved in teaching. The average number of teaching hours is 10.42 hours per week. The number of courses taught is 3 to 5 per week. After adding to these figures the time spent in preparing teaching materials, we can see that the teaching load is heavy. Although teaching time accounts for a large portion of the total time of the average Taiwan real estate lecturer, they are also active in research. We will discuss research issues in a later section.

33.3.4 Teaching methods and supportive materials

Table 8 contains a list of teaching methods. Typical academic methods for instruction involve combinations of class lectures with students being asked to prepare short papers and assignments, to make oral presentations, to participate actively in case and academic paper discussions, and to undertake tests and homework. Instructors especially view homework and tests as the most effective ways of encouraging students to study. From the survey results, we understand that instructors try to teach students to achieve the learning goals of communication, teamwork, personal accountability and knowledge as described by Butler, Guntermann, and Wolverton (1999).

Popular textbooks have already been mentioned. We understand that most textbooks are written in English and that there is a lack of local textbooks. To develop teaching materials related to the local environment and specific local issues is an urgent task for real estate academics in Taiwan. The newly established "Taiwan Real Estate Research Center" in the National Chengchi University views this task as its objective.

Table 8: Methods for instruction

Teaching method	Ranking
Lecture using board	1
Homework/test	2
Term papers	3
Case study	4
Transparencies	5
Discussing articles in magazines and newspapers	6
Academic papers	7
Discussing current issues	8
Field trip	9
Guest speech	10
Movie	11
Simulation	12
Web application	13

33.4 Research

From the survey, we find that respondents believe that the content of teaching should be influenced by their research. There are few respondents who teach courses without having research interest in the subject(s) concerned. Also, from data not shown here, we can discern a link between postgraduate teaching and research interest.

Researchers usually get their financial support from the government's National Science Council. Funds may sometimes be available from other departments of the government and from industry. An objective of the newly established Taiwan Real Estate Research Center is to raise funds to support academic research.

33.4.1 Research topics

Table 9 shows that the most favoured research topics are development, economics issues, and econometric methods. A few respondents are researching investment and financial analysis, and a few are researching marketing. However, this result does not mean that these topics are less important: a review of respondents' backgrounds shows that there is a lack of researchers being trained in these areas. The survey results also show that research topics focus not only on the residential real estate market, but also on commercial and other market segments. Papers submitted to the annual conferences of the Chinese Society of Housing Studies show that there are more and more papers investigating issues regarding industrial parks, shopping centres, and office buildings.

Table 9: Respondents' research and teaching interest

This table shows the teaching and research interests of respondents. Ranking is in terms of number of people who have research or teaching interest in the subject.

	Research	Teaching	Both	Total	Ranking
Real Estate Economics	3		14	17	2
Market Analysis	3	1	5	9	6
Finance/Investment	2	1	10	13	5
Leasing	1			1	15
Marketing		1	4	5	12
Development	6	2	10	18	1
Appraisal	4	1	7	12	6
Management	3		3	6	10
Laws	2	3	2	7	8
Tax	1	2	4	7	8
Econometrics/ research tools	8	1	6	15	3
Information system	4		2	6	10
Land policy	2		6	8	7
Architecture	2		2	4	13
Engineering	1	1	1	3	14
Urban planning	5		10	15	3

33.4.2   Publication

We asked respondents about their activities in terms of producing academic books, academic articles, research reports or monographs, presenting papers at academic conferences, and writing articles for newspaper or magazines. In Taiwan, there may not be a pressure to secure tenure, but academics recognise that a strong record of successful research is important in faculty evaluations.

The most important academic conference is the annual conference held by the Chinese Society of Housing Studies. Each year more than 60 papers are submitted, of which usually 40 will be accepted for presentation to the conference. The annual conferences of the Chinese Finance Association (Taiwan) also include a real estate session. Popular topics include housing price, investment analysis and development analysis. At the latest meeting, there were several papers discussing the application of real options model.

Two local professional journals are the Journal of Housing Studies and the Quarterly Journal of the Taiwan Land Bank. Each issue may have 4-6 papers. Taiwan also has a contribution to the newly published Journal of the Asian Real Estate Society, both in terms of editing and submitting papers.

In 1998, Taiwan hosted the third Annual Asian Real Estate Society meeting. Professor John Quigley and many other participants voiced the opinion that this was one of the best-run international conferences. This meeting inspired our researchers to work harder in order to have better results for presentation at other international conferences.

33.4.3 International activities

Taiwan's real estate researchers are becoming more active in attending international academic conferences. For example, Taiwan had the second largest group attending the joint international conference of the American Real Estate and Urban Economics Association and the Asian Real Estate Society held in Maui, Hawaii from May 5-7, 1999. Increasing numbers of research topics cover not only local, but also international issues. Most of our researchers were awarded their degrees at universities in the U.S.A. and Europe. We may expect they will continue to be involved in a range of international professional activities such as publishing articles, membership of editorial boards or reviewing articles for international journals, working collaboratively with academics from other countries, and travelling abroad to study or to do research.

33.5 Prospects

Facing a changing environment of the real estate market, real estate education in Taiwan has been adjusting to meet the new challenge. Real estate education in Taiwan is adapting by making the following changes:

1. more and more scholars with modern knowledge are joining real estate education;
2. creating integrated real estate programmes;
3. establishing real estate research centres;
4. developing local textbooks;
5. developing new teaching methods, computer software, and web instruction;
6. diversifying research topics; and
7. continuing to be involved in international academic activities.

NOTES

[1] Japan has a similar system, see Amano(1997) and Teichler (1997).

[2] As a foundation operating under the jurisdiction of the Ministry of Finance, the Institute is for the purpose of nurturing and training bank personnel and thereby facilitating the modernization of the ROC banking industry.

REFERENCES:

Amano, Ikuo, "Structural changes in Japan's higher education system - from a planning to a market model", Higher Education, 34, 1997, p125-139.

Benzing, Cynthia, and Christ, Paul, "A survey of teaching methods among economics faculty", Journal of Economic Education, Spring 1997, p182-188.

Bulter, Jay Q., Guntermann, Karl L., and Wolverton, Mimi, "Integrating the real estate curriculum", Journal of Real Estate Practice and Education, Vol. 1, Number 1, 1998, p51-66.

Chang, Chin-Oh, "Real Estate Market in Taipei", working paper, Department of Land Economics, National Chengchi University.

Colliers Jardine Commercial Agency, "Taipei's Office Market in 1998", Space Journal, Vol. 114, March 15, 1999, p46-48.

Gregorowicz, Philip and Hegji, Charles E., "Economics in the MBA curriculum: some preliminary survey results", Journal of Economic Education, Winter 1998, p81-87.

Lin, Tengou, "Higher technological education in Taiwan", Technology Journal, 1995, p281-289 (in Chinese).

Teichler, Ulrich, "Higher education in Japan: a view from outside", Higher Education, 34, 1997, p275-298.

The Economist, "Management Education", March 2nd, 1991, p5-26.

VI

REAL ESTATE EDUCATION IN
THE PACIFIC RIM

Chapter 34

Australia

Graeme Newell
Property Group, University of Western Sydney, Richmond, Australia

Angelo Karantonis
University of Technology, Sydney, Australia

James R. Webb
Department of Finance, James J. Nance College of Business, Cleveland State University, Cleveland, USA

34.1 Introduction

Property education and research in Australia at the university level has undergone a major transformation in the last 25 years. From an original focus on basic domestic professional education in the valuation area, it has been significantly expanded to encompass all aspects of property education and research at an international level.

Regarding terminology, there are some fundamental differences between Australia and the U.S. "Property" is the terminology used in Australia instead of "real estate", with "real estate" tending to refer to the buying and selling of real estate and "property" generally referring to real estate as an investment (e.g.: office, retail, industrial). Similarly, "valuation" is used instead of "appraisal", reflecting the U.K. background to property in Australia. The terms "property" and "valuation" will be used throughout this study.

This study will highlight a number of significant factors contributing to the development of property education and research in Australia. In particular, the significant role of the Pacific Rim Real Estate Society (PRRES) will be identified as the major catalyst to recent developments in property education and research in Australia.

34.2 The Property Environment in Australia

Australia is one of the major countries in the South-East Asian region. With a population of nearly 20 million, Australia has proven to be a significant regional economic force, both in terms of its physical resources and its economic/financial role in the Pacific Rim region.

Comprising seven states, the cities of Sydney and Melbourne are the major financial, cultural and population centres, comprising populations of 4.4 million and 3.2 million respectively. Canberra is the centre of government for Australia. Exhibit 1 provides a geographic profile of Australia, with the key cities identified.

Both Sydney and Melbourne are truly international and multi-cultural cities, with the CBDs being the most significant financial centres in Australia and the preferred location of head offices of globally significant corporations. For example, Sydney is the preferred location for the regional headquarters of many international corporations including BT, Digital, IBM, Amex and Microsoft, with over 60% of all regional headquarters in Australia located in Sydney. Sydney is also the location of the Australian Stock Exchange, Reserve Bank of Australia and Australia's only Futures Exchange (Newell and Herborn, 1999).

At December 1998, the Sydney CBD accounted for over 4.8 million m^2 of office space or 35% of total Australian office space, well ahead of its next competitor, Melbourne (3.9 million m^2 or 28% of total Australian office space) (Newell and Herborn, 1999). Exhibit 2 provides an overview of the Sydney CBD at December 1999 (Jones Lang LaSalle, 2000a).

Institutional investors have all sectors of the property market represented in their property portfolios. At June 1999, an average institutional property portfolio comprised CBD office (44% of portfolio), non-CBD office (9%), retail (39%) and industrial (8%) (Property Council of Australia, 1999). Other property sectors also included in institutional portfolios are hotel/leisure, agricultural and international property. The investment performance analysis of the various Australian property sectors over 1985-1999 is also shown in Exhibit 2 (Property Council of Australia, 1999).

Given the internationalisation of property in recent years, the leading real estate agencies in Sydney are Jones Lang LaSalle, Colliers Jardine and Knight Frank. Joint ventures of local companies with international players (e.g. Stanton Hillier Parker, CB Richard Ellis) are also key players for commercial property agency.

Freehold ownership is the most common form of tenure, with Torrens title being the state government land titling system. Current office leases are typically from five to ten years, with open market rent review every two years. Lease structures have changed significantly in the last 20 years, where previously much longer leases and rent reviews on an annual basis to CPI and every three years to market were the norm.

The dynamics of the Australian commercial property investment markets have also changed considerably over the last 20 years. This change has been characterised by the emergence of foreign investors, significant growth in funds under institutional management, development of new property investment vehicles (via listed property trusts) and recent government legislation regarding superannuation (pension) funds. All of these forces have had and will continue to have a significant effect on property investment in all sectors of the Australian property markets.

Total funds under management accounted for AUS$559 billion in December 1999. Leading Australian (and international) players in the investment management sector (including property) are AMP, Colonial, Bankers Trust, Lend Lease, Commonwealth Property. A major catalyst to the further development of this institutional managed funds sector has been the recent introduction of compulsory superannuation in Australia. The level of superannuation funds of AUS$320 billion in 1998 is expected to increase to over AUS$1,300 billion by 2008. This significant increase in the superannuation fund asset base will need to be invested nationally and internationally across the principal asset classes, including property.

A fundamental change has also occurred in recent years regarding the role of direct property in institutional portfolios in Australia. In 1985, direct property accounted for an average of 18% in institutional portfolios, with some institutions having up to 30% of their portfolios in property. In 1999, direct property only accounted for 6% (on average) in institutional portfolios. Over this same period, the level of indirect property (via property trusts) in institutional portfolios increased significantly. This trend sees property trusts taking on increased investment significance, now representing over 50% of current institutional property exposure, compared to only 10% in 1985.

Being generally equivalent to U.S. REITs, property trusts have been the most successful indirect property vehicle in Australia over the last 10 years. Key factors in this success have been their advantageous investment attributes (e.g. tax exempt status), strong institutional acceptance and strong investment performance in recent years. This has seen property trusts having over AUS $30 billion in assets in 1999, a significant increase from only AUS$2.6 billion in 1986. The property trust sector accounts for 5% of the total Australian stock market capitalisation.

This change in the levels of direct and indirect property in institutional portfolios has seen a closer alignment of the property and capital markets. This has had a significant impact on property education programs in Australia for degree and post-graduate levels.

34.3 The Property Professions in Australia

The Australian Property Institute (API) is the leading professional association for property professionals. Originally established in 1926 as the Commonwealth Institute of Valuers, this organisation has expanded from a valuation base to encompass all activities in the property professions. The API currently has over 7000 members throughout Australia.

Membership to the API is now by degree entry via one of the eight API accredited property degrees (see Exhibit 3), or via a partially qualifying degree (e.g.: economics, law, engineering) with five years professional experience. API members with valuation expertise are called a "Certified Practising Valuer". The API has reciprocal membership arrangements with equivalent property associations in the U.K., New Zealand, Hong Kong and Singapore.

The API also has a quarterly professional journal (**Australian Property Journal**) and an active Continuing Professional Development (CPD) Program, with members required to complete 12 hours per year of CPD from seminars, presentations and property activities. University academics actively contribute to the development and delivery of this CPD program, presenting regular industry seminars in key areas of property.

The requirements for valuation licensing vary from state to state. Some states have no licensing requirements (e.g. Victoria), while some other states (e.g.: NSW) require government registration for individual valuers.

For property companies, the Property Council of Australia (PCA, and previously called BOMA) is the major professional body. The leading property investment, finance, development and management companies, such as

Lend Lease, Westfield and AMP are members of PCA. The primary function of the PCA is advocacy on behalf of its members at all levels of government. PCA also publishes a monthly professional journal **(Property Australia)** and the benchmark direct property performance indices for Australian commercial property since 1985 on a quarterly basis (Newell and Webb, 1994). The PCA property indices currently include a performance portfolio of 693 properties valued at AUS$42 billion (Property Council of Australia, 1999), with the PCA indices being equivalent to the NCREIF indices in the U.S..

34.4 Property Education Programs in Universities

Specific property degrees have been offered in Australian universities for over 25 years. While initially targeted to the valuation profession, these property courses expanded considerably in the 1980s to offer the full spectrum of property activities, including valuation, property investment, property finance, property development, property management and property market analysis. Completion of these property degrees is the entry point into the property industry and for API membership.

Exhibit 3 lists the major university providers of property education in Australia. Most of these 3-year degree programs are offered from business schools, enabling the inclusion of general business subjects in the degree. The major difference with an Australian degree to the U.S. system is that the undergraduate degree is not necessarily general, but can be very vocation specific (e.g.: property). Students get the opportunity to do property subjects from day one of their degree! Similarly, there is only one private university in Australia; the other 35 universities are all state universities. Degree fees are approximately AUS$4K per year.

Current government policy has seen a significant reduction in government funding for universities in the last five years. This has resulted in significant increases in student fees, class sizes and staff workloads, with very limited staff growth.

Exhibit 4 shows a typical property degree program in Australia. Property degrees are generally three years of full-time study over two 14-week semesters per year (February-June, July-November). Students typically take four subjects per semester of three hours each. A range of electives is offered in the later stages of most degrees to enable specialist property or business subjects to be taken. Opportunities are also available for students to do these property degrees on a part-time or correspondence basis. Web-based property degrees are currently being developed.

With the closer alignment of property and the capital markets, this is now reflected in all property degree programs, with more emphasis on property investment, property finance and asset management.

Student intake into these property degrees varies considerably across universities. With most of the property employment concentration being in Sydney and Melbourne, these areas tend to have the largest student intakes. For example, the University of Western Sydney and the University of Technology Sydney took 100 and 75 new students, respectively, into their property degrees in February 2000. Property course intakes in the other states tend to be smaller, with students often doing joint degrees over 4 years in order to obtain career flexibility.

Typically the top students are now seeking careers in the institutional investment area, with only 20% of graduates going into valuation. Employment prospects for most students are strong, with currently 95% of graduates having jobs within three months of degree completion. Often students have jobs before completing their degrees. Strong interaction with the property industry throughout their degree is a key factor in employment opportunities.

Property academics are appointed at the levels of Professor (U.S.$64K), Associate Professor (U.S.$49-54K), Senior Lecturer (U.S.$41-47K), Lecturer (U.S.$33-40K) and Associate Lecturer (US$23-32K). These salaries are fixed and compare very unfavourably to the private sector. Property staffing profiles are shown in Exhibit 3. Depending on course size, some of the property departments comprise up to ten property academics. These are also supplemented by part-time property professionals as needed. Staff typically teaches ten hours per week. Promotion is dependent upon quality teaching, research and administrative contributions.

Most property subjects are presented as three hours per week, comprising two lectures and one tutorial. Assessment focuses on major assignments and final exams. Students undertake a project/dissertation in their final semester and examine a specific aspect of property. Student performance is strongly recognised by the property industry by providing a number of scholarships (e.g.: PCA, Jones Lang LaSalle, Colliers Jardine, Knight Frank) and prizes (e.g.: API, Urban Development Institute of Australia, leading property companies). Work experience is also a key feature in most property degrees, and is usually undertaken by most students.

Course rankings are available on an annual basis from the Graduate Careers Council of Australia, which surveys all university graduates on ten criteria regarding teaching quality and overall student satisfaction with their property education.

34.5 Post-Graduate Property Education in Australia

With entry into the property professions available via an approved undergraduate property degree, the demand for post-graduate programs has increased significantly in the last five years. This reflects the need for specialist skills (e.g.: property investment, finance, development), as well as those professionals with related degrees seeking property expertise. All of the previously mentioned universities offer Masters programs by coursework, generally as two-year part-time programs in property, or in the specific niche areas of valuation, property investment and finance, and property development. Typical course fees are AUS$8-10K. Recent developments in educating property professionals are discussed in Boyd (2000).

A non-university provider (the Property Council of Australia) is now offering a two-year part-time Graduate Diploma in Property Investment and Finance, similar to the equivalent stockmarket investment course offered by the Australian Securities Institute.

Off-shore Masters programs have also become popular in the last five years as sources of additional income. The previously mentioned universities offer Masters degrees in various areas of property in Singapore, Malaysia, Indonesia, Thailand and China. The downturn in some South-East Asian countries has had a temporary impact on current student demand, but they are expected to recover in the near future.

Property research degrees at both Masters and Ph.D. levels are becoming more popular, but with small cohorts. Areas of research interest are property trusts, valuation of contaminated land, international property, property finance, property cycles, market dynamics and corporate real estate.

34.6 Property Research in Australia

34.6.1 Property research environment

Most of the leading institutional investors (e.g.: AMP, Commonwealth Property, Lend Lease) and commercial agencies (e.g.: Jones Lang LaSalle, Colliers Jardine) have property research teams. Their property research activities have mainly been for internal purposes, market reports or for local professional journals. Only a few practitioners (e.g.: Adrian Harrington, David Parker) have sought to have their research published in leading U.S. or U.K. property research journals, such as the **Journal of Real Estate Research** (U.S.) or the **Journal of Property Research** (U.K.).

While the breadth of property data available is not as extensive as in the U.S., key data sources have proven to be very productive property research opportunities. These include:

– Listed property trust data (equivalent to REITs) from the Australian stock exchange and sector-specific indexes (e.g.: Warburg Dillon Read) (Warburg Dillon Read, 2000).

- Direct property performance indices from the Property Council of Australia, detailing sector specific and geographic property indices since 1985 (Property Council of Australia, 1999; Newell and Webb, 1994). These direct property indices are equivalent to the NCREIF property indices.
- Residential property databases held by various state valuation departments and commercial agencies (e.g. RP Data); with this data often available in electronic spreadsheet format.
- Property market data from leading commercial agencies (Jones Lang LaSalle, 2000a, b) for both Australian and Pacific Rim property markets.

34.6.2 Role of PRRES

As such, most of the published property research in Australia is obtained from the university sector. In recent years, the establishment of the Pacific Rim Real Estate Society (PRRES) has been a major catalyst to this expanded property research profile and international property networks for property academics in Australia.

After initially being established as the Australasian Real Estate Educators Association, under John Baen's guidance in 1990, the Pacific Rim Real Estate Society (PRRES) was established in 1994 to promote property research and education and to provide a formal focus for property researchers, educators and practising professionals in the Pacific Rim region. PRRES includes members from Australia, New Zealand, Papua New Guinea, Fiji, Hong Kong, China, Malaysia, Singapore, Thailand, Indonesia and Korea.

PRRES is recognised as comprising the property research and property education leaders in the Pacific Rim region. The PRRES Board, with Directors currently from Australia, New Zealand, Singapore, Thailand, Fiji and Malaysia, provides the strategic direction for PRRES. Exhibit 5 gives the current PRRES officers and board of directors.

The objectives of PRRES are:

- to promote property research and education in the Pacific Rim;
- to promote local and international networking opportunities for PRRES members;
- to encourage the dissemination of relevant property research results to property practitioners;
- to encourage the personal development of emerging property researchers and educators;
- to provide and promote research publication opportunities for PRRES members;

- to provide a supportive and independent environment for the discussion of property research and education issues; and
- to expand the recognition of property as a formal academic discipline with its own body of knowledge.

There are numerous benefits from being a member of PRRES, including:

a) Annual Conference

PRRES conducts an annual 3-day conference in January focusing on key issues in property research, practice and education. Six previous conferences have been held in Melbourne, Brisbane, Palmerston North, Perth, Kuala Lumpur and Sydney. The 2001 conference is to be held in Fiji. Keynote speakers at recent conferences have been international property leaders, including Steve Pyhrr (U.S.), Patric Hendershott (U.S.), Jim Webb (U.S.), Austin Jaffe (U.S.), Gerald Brown (Singapore), Andrew Baum (U.K.), Neil Crosby (U.K.) and David Parker (Australia).

The conference provides an excellent opportunity for the supportive exchange of the latest property research and ideas, and the discussion of key property issues. Parallel sessions and panel sessions on all aspects of property valuation, property investment and finance, property management, property markets, property development and property education are regular features of the PRRES conference. Exhibit 6 gives details of the 24 sessions from the 2000 PRRES conference in Sydney.

PRRES members are also regular participants at the conferences held by all of the other regional real estate societies throughout the world.

b) Property Journals

First published in 1989, the **Australian Land Economics Review** (ALER) is the PRRES journal, providing the major refereed property journal for research by PRRES members. ALER is published twice yearly and is recognised as the leading refereed property journal in the Pacific Rim region. Exhibit 7 gives details of the Editorial Board of ALER. From January 2000, ALER has been re-named the **Pacific Rim Property Research Journal** to more fully reflect its stature and research agenda in the region.

PRRES also provides an electronic journal, **Property Issues**, that offers an electronic forum for the discussion and debate of the latest property issues for property practitioners, researchers and educators. The electronic journal editor is John MacFarlane (j.macfarlane@uws.edu.au).

c) Newsletter

PRRES members receive an informative newsletter twice yearly. This

10-page newsletter provides PRRES conference details and feedback, regional updates, forthcoming international property conference details, member profiles and news/updates.

d) Property Awards

To recognise outstanding leadership and achievement in property research and education, the "PRRES Achievement Award" has been instituted. This award consists of a plaque and is presented at the PRRES conference. Previous recipients of this prestigious award have been Bill Cleghorn (1996), Tony Walker (1997), Graeme Newell and Tom Whipple (1998), Patrick Rowland (1999) and Maurice Squirrell (2000). Full award citations and photos of these award recipients are available at the PRRES website (www.bf.rmit.edu.au/PRRES).

A range of alternative PRRES membership categories are available, including:

- academic;
- professional;
- institutional; and
- student.

Membership fees are kept to a minimum (currently AUS$55 for academics) to encourage broad representation and participation in the PRRES membership. Further details regarding any of the above can be obtained from the PRRES website (www.bf.rmit.edu.au/PRRES).

This website also has links to the other regional real estate society (ie: ARES, ERES, AsRES and IRES) webpages.

Amongst the various regional real estate societies, PRRES has a number of "firsts", including:

- 1st female president (1997-98): Sandy Bond (New Zealand)
- 1st conference proceedings on CD: Kuala Lumpur (1999)
- 1st "refereed" papers section in conference: Palmerston North (1997)
- 1st "Hall of Fame" website for PRRES Achievement Award
- 1st "New Researcher" awards (sponsored by professional institutes)
- first conference proceedings on PRRES website: Perth (1998).

34.7 Future Development in Property Research in Australia

Funding for property research in Australia has been very limited. The major development in this area is the establishment of the Property Research Council of Australia (PRCA) in January 2000, representing research interests from the Property Council of Australia and PRRES.

As well as providing an effective marketing vehicle for PRRES research into the institutional property arena, the PRCA is expected to develop along similar lines to the Real Estate Research Institute (RERI) in the U.S., representing a consolidated pool of property research funding from various institutional sources, available for competitive bidding to address priority research areas in the property sector in Australia.

CONCLUSION

Property education and research in Australia have made considerable progress in recent years. PRRES has been a key player in expanding the local research agenda into a truly international research agenda via strong linkages into the other regional real estate societies.

Much still needs to be done. The key players in PRRES and the universities offering property education in Australia are strongly committed to further developing this agenda, in order to ensure property education and research in Australia are competitive at an international level and that graduates are prepared for exciting and fulfilling careers in the rapidly expanding property industry in Australia.

REFERENCES

Boyd, T., Educating the Property Professional of Tomorrow, in PRRES "Property Into the Next Millennium" Monograph, 2000, 45-62.

Jones Lang LaSalle, Real Estate Digest – Australia, Sydney: Jones Lang LaSalle, 2000a.

Jones Lang LaSalle, Asia Pacific Property Digest, Sydney: Jones Lang LaSalle, 2000b.

Newell, G., The Pacific Rim Real Estate Society, in "PRRES" Property Into the Next Millennium" Monograph, 2000, xiii-xvi.

Newell, G. and P. Herborn, Sydney Property Market, in "Cities in the Pacific Rim: Planning Systems and Property Markets", London: E and FN Spon, 1999, 203-224.

Newell, G. and J. Webb, Institutional Real Estate Performance Benchmarks: an International Prospective, Journal of Real Estate Literature, 1994, 2:2, 215-226.

Property Council of Australia, Investment Performance Index: June 1999, Sydney: Property Council of Australia, 1999.

Squirrell, M., The History of the Pacific Rim Real Estate Society, in PRRES "Property Into the Next Millennium" Monograph, 2000, xvii-xix.

Warburg Dillon Read, WDR Listed Property Trust Indices, Sydney: Warburg Dillon Read,
  2000.

APPENDIX

Exhibit 1: Location of major cities in Australia

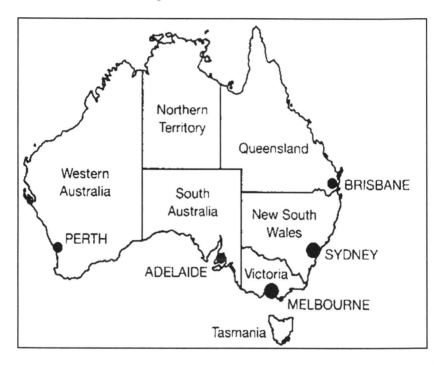

Exhibit 2: Sydney CBD Office Profile: December 1999

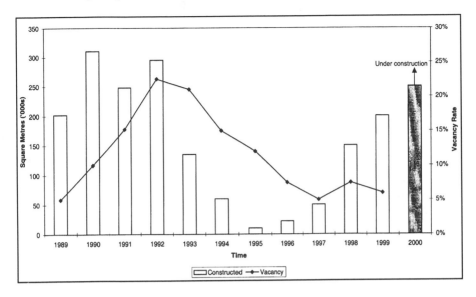

Exhibit 2 cont'd: Australian Property Performance Analysis: 1985 - 1999

Asset	Average annual total return (in %)	Risk (in %)
Total property return	10.00	7.36
CBD Office	7.97	9.51
Non-CBD Office	8.86	8.07
Retail	13.82	4.08
Industrial	11.33	6.35
Stocks	14.84	16.89
Bonds	12.26	6.91

Exhibit 3: Major University Providers of Property Education

– Curtin University of Technology (Perth)
 (Website: www.curtin.edu.au)
 Property staff: 1 professor, 1 senior lecturer, 3 lecturers
 Degree name: Bachelor of Commerce (Property)
– Queensland University of Technology (Brisbane)
 (Website: www.qut.edu.au)

Property staff: 1 professor, 3 lecturers
Degree name: Bachelor of Applied Science (Property Economics)
- Royal Melbourne Institute of Technology (Melbourne)
  (Website: www.rmit.edu.au)
  Property staff: 2 senior lecturers, 4 lecturers
  Degree name: Bachelor of Business (Property)
- University of Queensland (Brisbane)
  (Website: www.uq.edu.au)
  Property staff: 2 lecturers
  Degree name: Bachelor of Business (Property Studies)
- University of South Australia (Adelaide)
  (Website: www.unisa.edu.au)
  Property staff: 2 senior lecturers, 5 lecturers
  Degree name: Bachelor of Business (Property)
- University of Technology Sydney
  (Website: www.uts.edu.au)
  Property staff: 1 associate professor, 1 adjunct professor, 1 senior lecturer, 4 lecturers
  Degree name: Bachelor of Land Economics
- University of Western Sydney
  (Website: www.hawkesbury.uws.edu.au)
  Property staff: 1 professor, 1 associate professor, 2 senior lecturers, 6 lecturers
  Degree name: Bachelor of Commerce (Property Economics)
- University of New South Wales (Sydney)
  (Website: www.unsw.edu.au)
  Degree name: Bachelor of Building (with property electives)

Exhibit 4: Typical Property Degree Program in Australia

Semester 1	Semester 3	Semester 5
Introduction to Property	Commercial Valuation	Management & Organisa-tional Behaviour
Principles of Economics	Theory of Value	
Business Law	Building	Local Planning
Introduction to Planning	Finance & Accounting	Elective
		Elective

Semester 2	Semester 4	Semester 6
Principles of Valuation	Planning & Environmental Law	Property Development
Quantitative Methods		Project Work
Information Systems	Property Investment	Elective
Land Law	Urban & Regional Economics	Elective
	Elective	

Property Electives:

Commercial Property ManagementCompulsory Acquisition & Litigation	Property Portfolio & Asset Management
	Rural Valuation
Valuation of Special Premises	Property Finance & Tax
	Investments
	Commercial Leases

Exhibit 5: Pacific Rim Real Estate Society Officers And Board Of Directors: 2000

PRESIDENT	**EXECUTIVE DIRECTOR**
John Loh	Graeme Newell
CH Williams Talhar Wong, Malaysia	*University of Western Sydney*

PRESIDENT-ELECT	**PAST-PRESIDENT**
Patrick Rowland	Angelo Karantonis
Curtin University of Technology	*University of Technology Sydney*

SECRETARY	**TREASURER**
Patrick Rowland	Geoff Page
Curtin University of Technology	*University of South Australia*

DIRECTORS	
John Flaherty	Pachara Pacharavanich
RMIT University	*Thammasat University, Thailand*
Sandy Bond	Spike Boydell
Curtin University of Technology	*University of South Pacific, Fiji*
Yu Shi Ming	David Parker
National University of Singapore	*Suncorp Metway*

Exhibit 6: Sessions at 2000 PRRES Conference

1. Property Trusts
2. Land Title Issues
3. Residential Property
4. China Property Markets
5. Valuation
6. Commercial Property Markets
7. Property Education
8. Residential Property Market Analysis
9. Property Trusts

10. Real Estate Investment
11. Property Law/Issues
12. Residential Property Market Analysis
13. Corporate Real Estate
14. Investment Decision Making/Retail Property
15. Taxation and Property
16. Information Technology/Simulation
17. Corporate Real Estate/Facilities Management
18. Valuation Theory and Practice
19. Residential Property/Agency
20. Commercial Property Markets
21. Indigenous Land Tenure/Rights
22. Property Trusts
23. Residential Housing Policy/Issues
24. Rural Property

Exhibit 7: Editorial Board Of "Pacific Rim Property Research Journal": 2000

Editor:	Mervyn Fiedler (email: mervyn.fiedler@uts.edu.au)
Editorial Chairman:	Angelo Karantonis

Board Members

Andrew Baum	Peter Rossini
University of Reading	*University of South Australia*
Anthony Walker	Patrick Rowland
University of Hong Kong	*Curtin University of Technology*
James R. Webb	Ric Small
Cleveland State University	*University of Technology Sydney*
Graeme Newell	Geoff Page
University of Western Sydney	*University of South Australia*
Terry Boyd	John Flaherty
Queensland University of Technology	*RMIT University*
David Parker	Helen Gilbert
Suncorp-Metway	*University of Technology Sydney*
Adrian Harrington	Hera Antoniades
Paladin Australia	*University of Technology Sydney*

Chapter 35

New Zealand

Rodney L Jefferies
Recently retired Senior Lecturer in Property, The University of Auckland, Auckland, New Zealand

35.1 The property professions

The real estate professions in New Zealand are referred to as the property professions, as the term real estate is both traditionally and effectively reserved for agency or brokerage.

There have traditionally been separate and distinctly different professional property cadres consisting of separate professional Institutes:

- Valuation – The New Zealand Institute of Valuers (NZIV), established 1939. Membership as at June 1999 was just over 2000.

– Property Management (now Land Economy) – formerly known as the Property Management Institute (PMI), which had been formed in 1977 and incorporated in 1978. In 1995 the name was changed to the Property & Land Economy Institute of New Zealand Incorporated (PLEINZ). Membership as at June 1999 was just over 1,300; and
– Real Estate – The Real Estate Institute of New Zealand (REINZ), formed in the early 1900's following the voluntary merge of various land agents and auctioneers groups which had been operating as self-governing bodies on a regional basis. A contributing factor for amalgamation was the passing of the La0nd Agents Act of 1912. The National Dominion Estate Agents and Land Auctioneers Association of New Zealand was formed in July 1915. Its name was later changed to the Real Estate Institute of New Zealand, which was incorporated in 1928. Membership as at February 2000 includes both individual licensees (540); licensed companies (800) in 670 Branch Offices; and also 13,500 salespersons.

Two of these Institutes, NZIV (incorporating the Plant & Machinery Valuers' Institute of New Zealand) and PLEINZ, agreed in 1999 to merge to form the New Zealand Property Institute (NZPI), which at time of writing (February 2000) is still in its transitional phase. Due to common membership, the total membership after the merger is likely to be over 2600.

Only two of the Institutes have Statutory Incorporation and Registration (licensing) – Valuation being under the Valuers' Act 1948 which also established the Valuers' Registration Board (VRB) and – Real Estate being under the Real Estate Agents Act 1976 which also established the Real Estate Agents' Licensing Board (REALB). The third, PLEINZ has its own non-statutory professional Licensing Board. All these licensing Boards require applicants for registration to have minimum academic qualifications together with minimum post-graduate professional experience, character references and a *viva-voce* examination before being registered or licensed.

Continuing registration and maintenance of membership of PLEINZ and NZIV (PINZ) requires certain minimum Continuing Professional Development (CPD) hours per year of continuing education, approved study, research or attendance at professional conferences, seminars etc. The REINZ have a voluntary CPD scheme for certain members who are members of the College of Salespersons who get access to a closed member Internet site for the Institutes' Services.

There have traditionally been separate and distinctly different educational programs for *property* and *real estate (agency)*.

35.2 Real estate programs at universities

35.2.1 Overview

In academia, courses offered are in 'property' or 'property studies', except for the real estate (agency) profession where a specific 'real estate' course is offered. Up until the 1980's property education was offered through three Universities at undergraduate Diploma level or through the professions' own professional examinations, taught through Polytechnics and correspondence Schools. During the 1980's as each University upgraded it programs to specialist undergraduate degree programs the professional examinations were phased out. Now, Property education is offered only at Universities.

In New Zealand specialist degree programs are offered at undergraduate level for secondary school (high school) leavers, and on graduation these degrees are accepted by the various property and real estate cadres, subject to applicants having passed certain subjects, to satisfying their academic requirements for membership.

Graduates may proceed to Post-Graduate Diploma; Masters Degree; and to Doctorate level in property studies at each of three Universities.

Real Estate (agency) education is offered through lectures at Polytechnics or by correspondence. Massey University now offers a specialised undergraduate Real Estate major in its Business degree at its expanding Albany Campus, situated on the North Shore, Auckland.

The three Universities in New Zealand offering property studies and real estate programs are:

- The University of Auckland, – Department of Property, Faculty of Architecture, Property, Planning, and Fine Arts, Auckland City Campus, North Island, New Zealand.
- Lincoln University, – Property Studies Group, Department of Accounting, Finance and Property Studies, Applied Management and Computing Division, Lincoln Campus, Canterbury, South Island, New Zealand.
- Massey University, – Property Studies Group, Department of Finance, Banking and Property, College of Business, Turitea Campus, Palmerston North and Albany Campus (for Real Estate), North Shore (Auckland), North Island, New Zealand.

A summary of the degree and diplomas programs offered, student numbers expressed as equivalent full time students (EFTS), recent graduate numbers, and specialist full-time property or real estate faculty staff at each of the three Universities follow.

Within New Zealand the University courses are not ranked, and apart from accreditation of various university degree courses by Institutions inside and outside New Zealand, no international ranking is carried out. However, The University of Auckland is part of Universitas 21.

See later under polytechnic education for the role of the New Zealand Qualifications Authority (NZQA) who have no jurisdiction over the Universities' courses.

35.2.2   The University of Auckland, – Department of Property

35.2.2.1 Degree specialisation & program description

The Department offers a specialist undergraduate property degree, Bachelor of Property (BProp). One of the features of the BProp is that it can be taken conjointly with other undergraduate degrees in other faculties: Arts (BA), Engineering (BE), Commerce (BCom), Law (LLB); Science (BSc) by sharing of common core papers that extends the normal full-time degree program by another year's study. Exceptional qualifying students are able to complete two degrees in eight Semesters (four years) in most cases.

Post-graduate property degree programs include the following:

– Bachelor of Property (Honours) (BProp (Hons)), requiring BProp graduates to undertake additional papers, a research project and complete a Dissertation.
– Master of Property (MProp), requiring BProp or equivalent degree graduates to undertake additional papers in research methods and complete a Thesis.
– Postgraduate Diploma in Property (PGDipProp), requiring BProp graduates or others with approved qualifications to undertake advanced papers. Designed to be taken part-time for people employed in property and if successful candidates for graduation may transfer credits to complete a MProp.
– Doctor of Philosophy (PhD), requires a bachelor's degree with Honours or equivalent and is by research over a minimum of four Semesters (two years) and completion of an independently supervised research based thesis.

35.2.2.2 Curriculum

The core undergraduate subjects are common with degrees from other faculties:

Statistics for Commerce; Accounting Information; Law, Commerce & Government; Microeconomics; and Macroeconomics.

Specialist subjects taught in the Property Department include:

Valuation; Construction; Property Marketing, Property Management; Land Use Planning & Controls; Property Finance & Investment; Property Economics; Property Law; Property Development; Facilities Management; Plant & Machinery Valuation;

Special and applied papers include:

Property Project; Applied Valuation; Maori Land Issues;

Post-graduate papers offered include advanced studies in:

Property Marketing; Property Finance & Investment; Valuation; Property Management; Property Management; Property Development and other specialist topics.

35.2.2.3 Faculty

The Department's normal full staffing complement consists of a Professor (as Head of Department) and six Senior Lecturers or Lecturers supplemented by a number of part-time staff and visiting lecturers drawn from the property industry, plus support staff.

35.2.2.4 Number of equivalent full-time students (EFTS) per year

Over the 1997 – 1999 period the number of EFTS has averaged approximately 135.

35.2.2.5 Number of graduates per year

The average number of graduates over the period 1997-1999 from the various degree and diploma programs is:

Program	Average Number of graduates
BProp	40
BProp(Hons)	nil
MProp	1
PGDipProp	2
PhD	nil

35.2.2.6 Accreditation

The BProp degree is accredited by the VRB; the Malaysian Board of Valuers, Appraisers and Estate Agents; and the Singapore Institute of Surveyors and Valuers for the purpose of registration and practice as a valuer. It is also recognised by REINZ, NZIV and PLEINZ (NZPI).

35.2.2.7 Teaching methods

The principal teaching method is by lectures supplemented by tutorials and field trips. Assessment is partly internally by assignments, tests and also final examinations.

The Department also runs compulsory Skills Workshops in Computer software applications and voluntary workshops in public speaking, presentations, and job interviews.

A Buddy Programme is offered to all students that enables them to spent several days with different experienced property professionals in conjunction with the NZIV, PLEINZ and REINZ.

35.2.3 Lincoln University, – Property Studies Group

35.2.3.1 Degree specialisation & program description

The Property Studies Group offers both rural and urban undergraduate degree qualifications. Rural valuation and farm management is through a sub-option in the Bachelor of Commerce (Agriculture) (Valuation and Farm Management option) (BComAg (VFM)) which equips graduates for a career in rural valuation and farm management. Urban valuation and property management through the specialist property degree, an option in the Bachelor of Commerce (Valuation and Property Management) (BCom (VPM)), which equips graduates for a career in urban valuation, real estate and property management

Post-graduate property degree and diploma programs include the following:

– Master of Property Studies (MPropStud), is structured as a professional Masters degree for the senior property consultant, adviser or investor concentrating on urban property. Offered part-time and also extramurally through centres in Auckland, Wellington and Christchurch. Participants are required to have two years professional property experience and to have a tertiary qualification. The course extends over two semesters full-time (a minimum of two years part-time) consisting of papers and a major empirically based research project and report (dissertation).
– Master of Commerce and Management (MCM) is also available majoring in property subjects. A two-year research based masters comprising either a thesis or examination and thesis.
– Post Graduate Diplomas in Property Studies. These enable existing commerce based degree holders to take further study in the property area and where appropriate, subjects can be completed to attain recognition by the property professions.

35.2.3.2 Curriculum

The Commerce degree common core subjects consist of:

Computing; Principles of Economics; Business Financial Administration; Introduction to Business Finance; Elements of Mathematics; and Statistics.

The compulsory Valuation and Property Management core subjects consist of:

Introduction to Real Estate; Principles of Urban Property Management; Principles of Urban Valuation; Valuation of Investment Property; Real Estate Planning Law; Property, Investment & Development; Property Market Portfolio Analysis; Statutory Valuations (Urban); Applied Property Studies.

Additional subjects required to meet prerequisites for professional recognition consist of:

Introduction to Legal Structures, or Environment of Business; Building Construction and Services; Building Administration and Services; Real Estate Marketing and Management; Introduction to Rural Property; Land Engineering; Law of Business Organisations.

Post-graduate papers offered include advanced studies in:

Property Investment Analysis; Property Market Analysis; Property and Project Development; Evaluation of Market Traded Securities; Property Portfolio Analysis; and Property Management and Analysis.

35.2.3.3 Faculty

The Property Studies Group's normal full staffing complement consists of a Professor (as Head of the Group) and four Senior Lecturers or Lecturers supplemented by part-time staff and lecturers drawn from the Department, plus support staff.

35.2.3.4 Number of equivalent full-time students (EFTS) per year

Over the 1997 – 1999 period the number of EFTS has averaged approximately 80.

35.2.3.5 Number of graduates per year

The average number of property graduates over the period 1997-1999 from the various degree and diploma programs is:

Program	Average Number of graduates
BCom(VPM)	22
BCom(VFM)	20
PGDip	1
MPropStud	5
PhD	nil

35.2.3.6 Accreditation

The BComAg (VFM) degree is accredited by the Farm Management Registration Board and recognised by the New Zealand Institute of Farm Management. The BCom (VPM) degree is accredited by the VRB and recognised by REINZ, NZIV and PLEINZ (NZPI).

35.2.3.7 Teaching methods

The principal teaching method is by lectures supplemented by field trips and case studies. Assessment is partly internally by case study assignments, tests and final examinations.

The MPropStud program uses multi-media and audio-conferencing, includes case studies, practical assignments, group work and student networking; team development and regular facilitator contact.

35.2.4 Massey University, – Property Studies Group

35.2.4.1 Degree specialisation & program description

The Department offers two specialist undergraduate property degrees, Bachelor of Business Studies (BBS) in Valuation and Property Management BBS(VPM) from its Turitea Campus and a BBS with a Real Estate Major from its Albany Campus.

It also offers a property specialisation in its undergraduate agricultural Bachelor of Applied Science degree in Rural Valuation and Farm Management.

It also offers four undergraduate Diploma Courses in Business Studies specialising in Property Management; Rural Valuation; Real Estate; or Urban Valuation. Successful students can cross-credit subjects to a BBS degree.

Post-graduate property degree programs include the following:

– Bachelor of Business Studies (Honours) BBS (Hons) based on papers, a research project and dissertation.
– Diploma in Business and Administration (DipBusAdmin) (Endorsed Property Studies) for graduates who have previous tertiary experience in property being one year's full-time or part-time study over a number of years, based on papers and research project.
– Master of Management (MMgt) (Property Studies) for graduates of the DipBusAdmin or of equivalent status being either full or part-time study based on papers and reported research.

- Master of Business Studies (MBS)(Property Studies) for BBS or BBS (Hons) graduates or equivalent, based on papers including research methods and reported research.
- Master of Philosophy (MPhil) and Doctor of Philosophy (PhD) consisting of independent supervised research and research report or thesis.

35.2.4.2 Curriculum
The core undergraduate subjects are:

Introductory Accounting; Intro Bus Communications; Fundamentals of Finance & Property; Intro Organisation & Management; Intro Business Law; Principles of Marketing; Intro Business Statistics; and Principles of Economics.

Specialist subjects taught by the Property Studies group for the property Studies and Real Estate Majors are:

- *Property Studies (Valuation and Property Management)*: Law of Property; Real Estate Valuation and Management; Applied Valuation; Property Structures; Planning Studies; Land Economics; Property Management & Development; Advanced Valuation; Building Technology; and electives: Property Practicum; Business Finance; and other business course subjects.
- *Real Estate Major*: The Real Estate Process; Real Estate Appraisal; Property Structures; Law of Property; Property Management & Development; Real Estate Investments; Real Estate Business Practice; Planning Studies for Real Estate; Planning Studies; plus electives from other business course subjects.

The DipBusStud courses require selected papers from the degree courses and additional papers, where appropriate, from agriculture or business papers

The BApplSc course is primarily based on papers from agricultural science plus rural valuation papers and some business papers.

Specialist post-graduate papers offered by the Property Studies Group include advanced studies in:

Rural Valuation; Urban Valuation; Property Finance; Public Sector Housing Management; Property Portfolio Management Analysis; Property & Banking Administration; Property & Taxation; Property & Advanced Accounting; Property Structures and Environmental Performance; Research Topics; and Thesis.

35.2.4.3 Faculty
The Property Studies Group's normal full staffing complement consists of a Professor (as Head of the Group) and six Senior Lecturers or Lecturers

supplemented by part-time staff and lecturers drawn from the Department, plus support staff based at the Turitea Campus. In addition there are two Senior Lecturers plus part-time staff and support staff based at the Albany Campus.

35.2.4.4 Number of equivalent full-time students (EFTS) per year

Over the 1997 – 1999 period the number of EFTS has averaged approximately 160.

35.2.4.5 Number of graduates per year

The average number of graduates over the period 1997-1999 from the various property studies degree and diploma programs is:

Program	Average Number of graduates
BBS (VPM)	40
BBS (Real Estate)	20
BApplSc	20
Diplomas	40
BBS (Hons) and MMgt and MBS	4
PhD	nil

35.2.4.6 Accreditation

The BBS (VPM) and BApplSc degrees are accredited by the VRB and recognised by NZIV and PLEINZ (NZPI).

The DipBusAdmin endorsed in Real Estate are accredited by the REALB and the REINZ

35.2.4.7 Teaching methods

The principal teaching method is by lectures supplemented by tutorials and field trips. Assessment is partly internally by assignments, tests and also final examinations.

The Property Studies Practicum requires students to obtain practical work during vacations.

BBS and DipBusStud courses are available extramurally by correspondence learning from the Centre for Extramural Studies at the Turitea Campus.

The BBS Real Estate Major, DipBusStud - Real Estate and extramural teaching are supplemented by Residential Courses

One of the recent innovations is that Massey commenced web-based teaching in 1999 The Property Group is developing teaching resources for a number of property courses for both internal and extramural students that will become available over the Internet.

35.2.4.8 Property Foundation

The Massey University Property Foundation receives membership subscription from a broad representation of the property industry. It was established to: *facilitate the research development and promotion of teaching and principles to the management and valuation of both real and personal property.*

35.3 Real estate programs at polytechnics

The New Zealand Qualifications Authority (NZQA) controls non-University education and vocational training in New Zealand. The NZQA administers qualifications and provides assurances about qualifications quality, oversees the examination system, and develops the National Qualifications Framework (NQF) and to approve non-university degrees. The NFQ is a means whereby national qualifications have a high credibility both throughout New Zealand and overseas. To date the Universities in New Zealand have strongly rejected advances to bring their qualifications under the NZQA.

The NZQA accredit education providers, both public and private, including the polytechnics. It also develops prescriptions, and issue results and certificates and diplomas in conjunction with Industry Training Organisations (ITOs). The Real Estate Service Sector sub-field ITO comes under the umbrella of the REINZ. Most industries, including REINZ have moved to National Certificates and National Diplomas on the NQF. The ITOs contract Education Providers to provide the units (courses) on their behalf who with the ITO conduct examinations. The ITOs are responsible for the quality assurance and monitoring of the assessments and the development of the qualifications.

Real Estate (agency) courses are provided under the Service Sector/Real Estate category at both levels:

1. *National Certificate in Real Estate*, with strands in Business Sales, Commercial/Industrial Sales, Residential Sales, Rural Sales, Commercial/Industrial Property Management, and Residential Property Management. This qualification provides individuals to become fully licensed as individuals and qualify for Associate membership of the REINZ.

   The National Certificate is in Four Parts:

   - Part 1: Salesperson's Course: consisting of eight units required to obtaining a Certificate of Approval from the REALB, prior to starting a career in real estate.

   - Part 2: Advanced Core: consisting of six units

- Part 3: Specialist Options: consisting of units the above strands.

- Part 4: Elective Units:

2. National Diploma in Real Estate.
   The Diploma is in Six Parts covering various units in:
   Management; Appraisal; Law; Finance; Business Administration; and
   Business Planning.

The accredited Education Providers for the Real Estate sub-field are:

- The Open Polytechnic of New Zealand, Lower Hutt;
- UNITEC Institute of Technology, Mt Albert, Auckland; and
- TAFE College New Zealand Ltd., Milford, North Shore, Auckland

The above structure are new in New Zealand and were introduced into Real Estate (Agency) Education in 1996, and from 1997 to date 161 have achieved the National Certificate in Real Estate and 12 have achieved the Diploma in Real Estate. Many people also complete part one of the Diploma, needed to operate as a Branch Manager in Real Estate, who need to work under a Licensee, the owner of the agency business.

35.4 Real Estate Research

Property and real estate research is fostered at each of the Universities and most academic appointments are for both research and teaching. Property Faculty staff are expected to do research and present papers at International conferences and submit papers for publication. Senior faculty staff frequently undertakes joint research with academics in Australia, USA and UK in specialist areas and their research results culminate in papers presented at international academic conferences and published in refereed journals.

New Zealand property academics are particularly conscious of their need to undertake quality research and encourage study to PhD level. Although PhD programs have been offered in new Zealand for some years and a number of (mainly academic staff) have been enrolled, as at the date of writing no PhDs have been awarded in property or real estate disciplines. A number of masters students in property have gone overseas to complete their postgraduate work, primarily in Australia and the United Kingdom.

35.5 Real Estate Research Societies

The NZIV and the three NZ property Universities in 1989 instituted the Australasian Real Estate Educators' Conference (AREEC) a bi-annual forum principally for academics in New Zealand and Australia. In 1993 this was expanded to include countries around the Pacific Ocean with the formation of the Pacific Rim Real Estate Society (PRRES) to provide a formal focus for property researchers, educators and practitioners in the Pacific-Rim Region. It is affiliated with the International Real Estate Society (IRES). PRRES now runs annual conferences, which generally alternate between Australia and New Zealand and other Pacific Rim countries. Though this is the primary forum for presentation of real estate research in the South Pacific, New Zealand academics frequently attend other academic conferences in the USA run by AREUEA, ARES and IRES, and in Europe by ERES and the Cutting Edge RICS Property Research Conferences.

While PRRES is the main international real estate research society to which New Zealand academics contribute the three property teaching Universities have research activities and research programs, generally in conjunction with post-graduate research or faculty staff research.

The Auckland University Department of Property has the Auckland University Real Estate Research Unit, which has published papers and monographs over a wide range of property subjects.

Massey University has the Massey University Real Estate Analysis Unit (MUREAU) that provides property information to the property industry, the land-based professions and the public. Regular publications include a home mortgage affordability index; a farm mortgage affordability index (discontinued); quarterly real estate market outlook analyses for Residential and Commercial markets in Auckland, Wellington and Christchurch; and quarterly NZ Residential Rental Market analysis.

35.6 Real Estate Journals

Each of the property and real estate institutes has official professional journals:

NZIV: *The New Zealand Valuers' Journal*, published four monthly by NZIV, Wellington, New Zealand, being a primarily professionally orientated journal with articles, reviews, valuation court case reports and professional directory.

PLEINZ: *The Property Business*, a magazine style publication, published six times a year by AGM Publishing Ltd., Auckland, New Zealand, being also marketed through bookshops and containing news and short informative articles, advertising and market reviews, products and services.

REINZ: *The Real Estate Journal*, published bi-monthly by the REINZ, Auckland, New Zealand, being a primarily professionally orientated journal with news, short articles, reviews, Licensing Board case reports and limited advertising.

None of these are refereed academic journals (except for a refereed section in the New Zealand Valuers' Journal, published by the NZIV). The NZ Valuers' Journal is the only specialist valuation journal in New Zealand and its referee panel represents an international spectrum of professional and academic persons who moderate articles in the refereed section of the Journal.

The new NZPI will be reviewing the merged NZIV and PLEINZ publications and a new journal may well emerge in time.

The main referred academic journal in the South Pacific is the official journal of PRRES, being the *Australian Land Economics Review*, published six monthly by the Faculty of Design, Architecture and Building at the University of Technology, Sydney, Australia.

The *PRRES Property Issues Journal* is an electronic journal launched in November 1997. The journal is published twice annually under the PRRES Web site. The journal actively encourages debate of the key property issues.

New Zealand property academics have published in a wide range of international refereed journals, particularly those published in the United Kingdom and United States.

REFERENCES:

The web sites for the three New Zealand Universities offering property programs are:
  The University of Auckland, – Department of Property:
     http://www.property.auckland.ac.nz/
  Lincoln University, – Property Studies Group:
     http://www.lincoln.ac.nz/amac/groups/propgrp.htm
  Massey University, – Property Studies Group:
  http://www.property-group.massey.ac.nz/
The web sites for the Polytechnics offering real estate programs are:
  The Open Polytechnic of New Zealand, – http://www.topnz.ac.nz
     UNITEC, – http://www.unitec.ac.nz
The web sites for the property and real estate institutes are:
  NZIV: http://www.nziv.org.nz/ (to become NZPI)
  PLEINZ: http://www.pleinz.org.nz/ (to become NZPI)
  REINZ: http://www.reinz.org.nz/
  NZPI   http://www.propertyinstitute.org.nz/

The web site for the Pacific Rim Real Estate Society is:
   PRRES: http://www.bf.rmit.edu.au/Property/PRRES/
The web site for the New Zealand Qualifications Authority is:
   NZQA: http://www.nzqa.govtnz.nz/

VII

REAL ESTATE EDUCATION IN AFRICA

Chapter 36

Africa

Valmond Ghyoot
Department of Business Management, University of South Africa, Pretoria, South Africa

36.1 Introduction

The African continent is second in size only to Asia. It houses 54 independent countries, with an estimated population of 700 million people (MBendi, 1999) and literally hundreds of languages and dialects. Generalising about real estate education on the continent is hazardous. Because of differing economic and land tenure systems, even the concepts of real estate and of the property industry[1] as a business are unfamiliar in some countries.

In researching this review, The World of Learning 1998 was used to identify those tertiary institutions on the continent and surrounding islands that were likely to offer real estate, land economics or property education. A total of 153 institutions were approached. Those that responded are reflected here, together with other institutions about which published information was available. In general, the Arabic, Portuguese and French speaking countries either reported no relevant courses or did not respond. The discussion is therefore limited to the English speaking countries south of the Sahara and by the available information.

36.2 Real Estate Profession and Education

Professionals in the property industry are usually affiliated with their local statutory and professional bodies, and sometimes with international bodies such as the Royal Institution of Chartered Surveyors (RICS), the Commonwealth Association of Surveying and Land Economy (CASLE), or the International Federation of Surveyors (FIG). Apart from the African Real Estate Society, there are no professional bodies that cater for the entire continent. In the construction industry, the Africa Association of Quantity Surveyors was formed recently (Quantity surveyors stride together, 1999). It includes members from Botswana, Ghana, Kenya, Namibia, Nigeria, Tanzania, Uganda and South Africa. Other statutory and professional bodies will hopefully follow suit. AfRES is working towards a similar integration of real estate professionals across the continent.

Despite being the second most populous, Africa is the least urbanised continent, contributing only one percent of worldwide industrial production. Not surprisingly, agriculture, fisheries and related education and research are well represented on this continent comprised mainly of developing countries. In Sudan, for example, the University of Gezira has a faculty dedicated to Economics and Rural Development (The World of Learning 1998, p. 1394). Best (1996a) also mentions the emphasis on vocational and agricultural education in Africa.

Many African academics were trained in American or European universities. When combined with local influences and legal systems, the result is a wide variety of terminology, analysis methods and philosophies. Epley (1996, p. 232-233) describes several possible teaching paradigms for real estate curriculums, namely development, land economics, analysis and decision-making, systems or management approach, employer needs approach and licensing requirements. All these paradigms are encountered in Africa.

The countries discussed here are Kenya, Tanzania, Nigeria, Ghana, South Africa, Zambia and Zimbabwe. In every instance, the discussion progresses from general characteristics, through the property market and professions, and ends with tertiary education, research and publications. Contact details of people and institutions are provided in the appendix.

36.3 Kenya

36.3.1 General

Kenya forms part of the East African Region and lies on the Indian Ocean coast. Although possibly best known for its wildlife and the Masai Mara game reservation, it is also the most highly industrialised country in East Africa (Garst, 1996b). Before attaining independence in 1963, Kenya was a British colony. The current population numbers about 30 million people, who speak mainly Swahili (national language) and English (official language for communication). The capital city is Nairobi (MBendi, 1999).

Major industries include oil, chemicals, lubricants and mining on a limited scale. Agricultural produce processing and export are also important. Tourism is the largest foreign exchange earner (Garst, 1996b).

The Kenyan property market is well established and relatively sophisticated in operation and financial structures. Because insurance funds may not be invested outside Kenya, real estate is an important investment medium, with institutional portfolio weightings of 25 percent and higher. Some institutions hold 70 percent of their investments in real estate. Investment trading and thus liquidity is low (Knight Frank, 1998, p. 6).

36.3.2 Property profession

The real estate profession is governed by statutory registration in terms of two Acts, one for Valuers (referred to as appraisers in the US) and one for Estate Agents. After graduation, a prospective valuer has to complete two years' apprenticeship and then sit for a professional examination, conducted by the Institution of Surveyors of Kenya (Valuers and Estate Management Chapter). The valuer may then be registered by the statutory Valuers Registration Board. Estate agents are not required to pass a qualifying examination, but must have a diploma in any field, as evidence of literacy. Apart from the statutory Estate Agents Registration Board, there is no professional association similar to the Institute of Realtors in the United States. Estate agents may however become members of the Institution of Surveyors of Kenya.

36.3.3 Real estate programs at tertiary institutions

Real estate education in Kenya started in 1956 when the Royal Technical College of East Africa trained candidates for the examinations of the Royal Institution of Chartered Surveyors (RICS). The college later became University College, Nairobi, part of the University of East Africa, and finally the University of Nairobi. From 1967 it introduced degree programmes in land economics, building economics and architecture. Town planning is available at post graduate level.

The Department of Land Development at the University of Nairobi offers a B.A. degree in Land Economics, a taught[3] M.A. in Valuation and Property Management and a taught M.A. in Housing Administration. The PhD program requires research and a dissertation. A certificate programme in estate agency for industry-required training is also available. The syllabus for the B.A. in Land Economics is given in Table 1. The program prepares graduates to work in fields such as estate management, valuation, development and land administration.

Table 1: Syllabus for the B.A. in Land Economics, Department of Land Development, University of Nairobi, Kenya

The B.A. is a four year degree in land economics. At graduate level, the student may complete an M.A. in Valuation and Property Management, or in Housing Administration, both through coursework. The PhD is earned through research. The syllabus for the undergraduate programme is as follows:

Year 1: First Semester
Physical environment
Elements of descriptive statistics
Introduction to microeconomics
Introduction to mathematics for economists
Introduction to architectural design in building construction
Elements of mathematics for theory of structures for land economists
Elements of law
Environmental building services
Communication skills

Year 3: First Semester
Introduction to computing
Introduction to management II
Land economics I
Applied valuation
Elements of urban and regional planning I
Local government law
Law of real property I

Year 1: Second Semester
Planning for building services
Elements of inferential statistics
Introduction to macroeconomics
African economic problems
Building construction technology
Elements of theory of structures
Law of contract
Fundamentals of development
Science and technology

Year 3: Second Semester
Elements of organizational theory
Elements of agricultural economics & management
Land economics II
Agricultural forestry valuation
Elements of urban and regional planning II
Administrative law
Principles of land information systems

Year 2: First Semester	Year 4: First Semester
Introduction to land surveying	Investment appraisal I
Microeconomic theory	Housing policy studies I
Introduction to valuation	Estate management I
Building finishes and fixtures	Building maintenance technology I
Law of tort	Land taxation
Elements of theory of structures II	Research project
Elements of agriculture & forestry I	
Year 2: Second Semester	Year 4: Second Semester
Elements of commercial law	Investment appraisal II
Investment approach to valuation	Housing policy studies II
Macroeconomic theory	Estate management II
Building materials	Building maintenance technology II
Law of real property I	Land policy studies
Elements of agriculture & forestry II	Research project.
Introduction to management I	

Source: Syagga (1999)

The Department has 14 academic staff members, of which eight hold PhD's. Half are female. Six staff members hold Masters degrees and are pursuing their PhD's. Many of the faculty members were educated in Britain. About 30 students are accepted for the B.A. degree each year. Currently there are approximately 120 students enrolled for the four year B.A. curriculum, with four masters and two PhD candidates. Evening classes and distance education are under consideration.

36.3.4 Research and publications

Most real estate research in Kenya is done by students and staff at academic institutions. Local and international real estate consultancy, valuation and brokerage firms such as Knight Frank compile statistics on market indicators, including rental, vacancies and capitalisation rates.

The Kenya Surveyor is published quarterly by the Institution of Surveyors of Kenya. Keitu Enterprises Ltd. publishes a trade journal that focuses on property development: The Building and Real Estate Guide.

36.4 Tanzania

36.4.1 General

The republic of Tanzania is located in East Africa, on the Indian ocean and is Kenya's southern neighbour. Tanzania is home to Kilimanjaro, the highest peak in Africa and also the Serengeti Game Reserve, known for the annual wildebeest migration. The population numbers almost 30 million and the dominant languages are Swahili and English. The historic capital is Dar Es Salaam. Prominent industries include agriculture, mining and oil. (MBendi, 1999).

36.4.2 Property profession

Until recently, because of its socialist economy, all real estate transactions in Tanzania were carried out by the state. Even now, land is vested in the President, but statutory and customary title is recognised and commercial exploitation by the private sector is encouraged. Until 1975, there was only one real estate firm in the country. Now there are 20 registered firms, who are active in real estate valuation, development, management, feasibility and investment analyses.

Land economy surveyors and land surveyors are registered in terms of the Professional Surveyors (Registration) Act of 1977. The Act established a National Council of Professional Surveyors (NCPS) to serve as a registration board for valuers and surveyors. The Tanzania Institution of Valuers and Estate Agents (TIVEA) was established to protect the interests of the Land Economy, Surveying and Estate Agency professions and to uphold professional conduct. TIVEA recommends registration and deregistration of professionals and firms to the NCPS.

36.4.3 Real estate programs at tertiary institutions

Before 1972, real estate professionals were trained in the U.K. and in Kenya. The Ardhi Institute started training real estate professionals in 1972. It also provided courses in Land Surveying, Urban and Rural Planning, Architecture, Quantity Surveying and Environmental Engineering. In 1988 the diploma in Land Management and Valuation was accredited by CASLE. The diploma was also accredited by the National Council of Professional Surveyors (NCPS). In 1996, Ardhi Institute became a college of the University of Dar Es Salaam and the diploma courses were converted into four year degrees. The BSc in Land Management and Valuation is offered by the University College of Lands and Architectural Studies (UCLAS). The syllabus is given in Table 2. Core courses in the degree are Economics, Land and Urban Economics, Property Valuation, Property Management and Development, Construction, Law, Mathematics and Computing, Taxation and Land Administration. Students must also complete industrial training every year, semester projects and a dissertation. Teaching methods include lectures, tutorials, project work and industrial training. The UCLAS enrolls tutorials, project work and industrial training. The UCLAS enrolls about 30 students per annum for the four year degree.

Table 2 - Syllabus for the BSc in Land Management,
Department of Land Management and Valuation, University College of Lands and Architectural Studies, University of Dar Es Salaam, Tanzania.

This four year BSc course has a specific theme to be mastered in each of the eight semesters. The core courses are Economics, Land and Urban Economics, Property Valuation, Property Management and Development, Construction, Law, Mathematics and Computing, Taxation and Land Administration.

Year 1: First semester: General studies
Mathematics and computing
Principles of economics
Environmental studies
Development studies I
Statistics
Communication skills I
Semester project

Year 3: First semester: Property development and management
Maintenance of built environment
Property management I
Urban economics
Property finance
Semester project

Year 1: Second semester: Introduction to land economy surveying
Construction and architectural studies
Land information system
Principles of management
Introduction to valuation
Elements of law
Communication skills II
Development studies II
Semester project

Year 3: Second semester: Asset and business valuation
Applied valuation
Special valuations
Business valuation
Semester project

Year 2: First semester: Land resources management
Construction
Land economics
Principles of valuation
Property law I
Semester project

Year 4: First semester: Professional practice
Computer applications
Property management II
Valuation casework
Land administration II
Semester project

Year 2: Second semester: Land administration
Property taxation
Planning law
Land Administration I
Property law II
Semester project

Year 4: Second semester: Dissertation
Dissertation

Source: Department of Land Management and Valuation (1997)

36.4.4 Research and publications

Commercial real estate research in Tanzania is currently limited by the small volume of market activity. Student research is conducted mainly in the areas of market valuation, construction cost, rents, return on investment, demand and accessibility.

Apart from articles on property by local newspapers and publications by individual firms, the Tanzania Institution of Valuers and Estate Agents publishes a newsletter and the University College of Lands and Architectural Studies publishes The Journal of Building and Land Development three times per year.

36.5 Nigeria

36.5.1 General

The Federal Republic of Nigeria is located on the Atlantic coast of West Africa. Formerly a British colony, it became independent in 1960. The federal capital is Abuja and the commercial capital, Lagos. Although English is the official language, it is not widely understood outside major urban areas (Garst, 1996c). Nigeria is the most populous country in Africa, with an estimated 100 million people. Exports are mainly crude oil and cocoa (MBendi, 1999).

36.5.2 Property profession

The first Estate Surveyors and Valuers in Nigeria became active in the mid 1950's. Currently the profession is regulated by both the Nigerian Institution of Estate Surveyors and Valuers (NIEVS) and The Estate Surveyors and Valuers Registration Board. The Registration Board was established in terms of the Estate Surveyors and Valuers (Registration, etc.) Act, 1975. The Institution sets the educational standard for membership, organises National Conferences, seminars, workshops and professional examinations for prospective surveyors. It also administers the continuing professional development (CPD) program, in terms of which members earn CPD credits. In 1994, the Institution had 1300 members, 1750 probationers and 2 000 student registrations (Nwankwo, 1995, p. 5).

36.5.3 Real estate programmes at tertiary institutions

Table 3 - Syllabus for the B.Tech. (Estate Management)
Department of Estate Management, Federal University of Technology, Minna, Nigeria

Level 1: First semester
Principles of estate management I
Accounting I
Principles of management
Architectural graphics I
General mathematics II
Building construction technology I
Freehand sketching I
Nature of environmental science
Writing and use of English
People and culture of Nigeria
Introduction to technical drawing

Level 1: Second semester
Principles of estate management II
Accounting I
Basic elements of planning
Architectural graphics II
General mathematics II
Building construction technology II
Freehand sketching II
Reading and oral work
Urban development planning
Principles of drafting

Level 2: First semester
Valuation I
Land economics I
Principles of economics I
Building construction and materials
Land surveying and site materials
Architectural design II
Site selection and planning
Statistical methods I
General agriculture

Level 3: Second semester
Valuation IV
Law of contract and tort II
National and rating taxation II
Principles of town and country planning
Economic theory II
Arbitration and awards
Building services (plumbing)
Building and development economics II
Construction Management

Level 4: First semester
Principles of property management
Estate and development finance
Comparative land policy
Elements of land law I
Housing policy and concepts
Urban renewal techniques
Project planning and control
Research methods I
Management and planning
Environmental perception
Rural development planning

Level 4: Second semester
Valuation V
Estate and development finance
Land economics III
Elements of a land laws II
Building maintenance
Management of building projects
Elements of estate management
Advanced project management

Level 2: Second semester	Level 5: First semester
Valuation II	Applied valuation I
Land economics II	Feasibility and viability studies I
Principles of economics II	Applied property management
Building construction and materials II	Project dissertation I
Land surveying and site analysis I	Land use and resources development I
Statistical methods II	Public health engineering
Introduction to computers	Applied town planning I
Natural resources and environmental planning	Regional development planning
Logic and history (philosophy)	
Level 3: First semester	**Level 5: Second semester**
Valuation III	Applied valuation II
Law of contract and tort I	Feasibility and viability studies II
National rating taxation I	Professional practice and code of conduct
Principles of town and country planning	Project dissertation II
Economic theory I	Land use resources development II
Arbitration and awards	Applied town planning II
Building services (electrical)	Advanced housing studies
Computer applications	Environmental impact assessment
Tendering and estimating	
Building and development economics I	

The five level B.Tech. (Estate Management) course covers the disciplines of property management, property valuation, building construction, land surveying, town planning, land law, land economics, property development and finance; Source: Oyegbile (1999)

In 1957, the Nigerian College of Arts Science and Technology, Enugu, introduced the syllabus of the RICS up to intermediate level. That course eventually grew into the estate management department of the University of Nigeria. Currently there are 11 universities presenting degree courses and 15 polytechnics presenting diploma courses (Nwanko, 1995, p. 4-5). Details are available on one institution, the Federal University of Technology, at Minna.

The Department of Estate Management, Federal University of Technology, Minna, Nigeria, has a five level B.Tech. (Estate Management) program. It aims to educate students comprehensively in the disciplines of property management, property valuation, building construction, land surveying, town planning, land law, land economics, property development and finance. It is taught through lectures, tutorials and practicals. Details are given in Table 3. Student numbers increased from 44 in 1992 to 301 at present. There are approximately 60 students in each of the five years (levels).

36.5.4 Research and publications

The Nigerian Institution of Estate Surveyors and Valuers (NIEVS) publishes a quarterly magazine: The Estate Surveyor and Valuer. The contact details are provided in the appendix.

36.6 Ghana

Located in West Africa on the Atlantic Ocean, Ghana was formerly the British colony of Gold Coast. It gained independence in 1957, the first African country to do so. The capital is Accra. Ghana was initially governed on a Socialist basis, but became a multiparty democracy in 1992. It is the largest producer of cacao in the world, and earns most of its export earnings from this source (Garst 1996a).

The Department of Land Economy at the University of Science and Technology (UST), Kumasi, offers a BSc (Land Economy). Details about the syllabus are given in Table 4. The programme has a more rural emphasis than the others described here. Another distinctive characteristic is the industry attachment programme for third and fourth year students, which enables them to gain practical experience while studying. Student research projects are selected by their employers, which enhances the practical orientation. UST's Land Economy degree is accredited inter alia by the South African Council for Valuers.

Table 4 - Syllabus for the four year B.Sc. (Land Economy)
Department of Land Economy and Estate Management, University of Science and Technology, Kumasi, Ghana

Year 1	Year 3
General principles of law	Law relating to estate management I
Customary land law	Law relating to estate management II
Building construction I	Valuation I
Principles of land surveying	Valuation II
Principles of land surveying - photo interpretation	Land appraisal I
	Land appraisal II
Post 'O' level mathematics	Building construction IV
Post 'O' level mathematics (continued)	Building construction V
Computer programming	Principles of accounting I
Computer programming (continued)	Principles of accounting II
Principles and practice of arable crop production	Fundamentals of planning I
	Fundamentals of planning II
Introduction to animal production	Research methods
Principles of economics	Research methods (continued)
Principles of economics (continued)	
Principles of forestry	

Year 2	Year 4
Law: Contract and torts	Law relating to estate management III
Law of real property	Law relating to estate management IV
Mathematics of finance	Advanced valuation I
Elements of central and local government	Advanced valuation II
Building construction II	Land use planning and administration I
Building construction III	Land use planning and administration II
Land use and resources I	Property management I
Land use and resources II	Property management II
Theory of land values I	Rating and taxation I
Theory of land values (continued)	Rating and taxation II
Computer programming I	Project work (2 semesters)
Computer programming II	
Introductory statistics	
Experimental design and analysis	
Agricultural economics	

Source: Hammond (1993)

36.7 South Africa

36.7.1 General

Known as much for its former president, Nelson Mandela as for its wild-life, South Africa has excellent business and educational infrastructure. It currently dominates the southern economies. Independent from Britain since 1961, English is the business language and is widely understood. Johannesburg, the largest city, is the central point of the most economically productive province. South Africa's exports have traditionally been dominated by minerals, but have recently become more diversified. The population is almost 40 million people.

Three noteworthy aspects of this new democracy's current property market are land restitution, liberalisation of the economy and decentralisation of commercial development. Land restitution is an ambitious attempt to restore land expropriated (compulsorily purchased) in the past under racially discriminatory laws. The volume of work is daunting, with about 40 000 claims to be settled. This has created a significant source of business for the valuation profession. Liberalisation of the economy has enabled life companies and pension fund asset managers to invest offshore since 1995 (Kriel, 1999, p. 223). Combined with more short term investment objectives, this will reduce their dominance of local real estate investment as they liquidate some assets. State organs have also started selling surplus real estate. In the coming years, asset divestment by these two investor classes will create opportunities for acquiring and securitising portfolios of investment class property. Decentralisation of commercial development, a global phenomenon, is being exacerbated by crime levels in South Africa's major city centres. For several years, centralised office and retail rentals have been decreasing and vacancies increasing. The effect on property values has been severe. In the present climate, central city investment should be evaluated carefully.

36.7.2 Property profession

The profession is governed by three Acts: The Estate Agents Act is intended to maintain and promote the integrity of estate agents, through the Estate Agency Affairs Board (statutory body). The Valuers' Act establishes the South African Council for Valuers (statutory body), which regulates the affairs of valuers. The Administration of Estates Act regulates the administration of deceased estates and the appointment of appraisers to value such assets. The terms "valuer" and "appraiser" therefore have specific meanings in South Africa.

Approximately 27 000 estate agents and 8 500 firms are registered with the Estate Agency Affairs Board. The South African Council for Valuers has more than 2 000 registered Valuers, Associate Valuers and Valuers in Training. The number of registered appraisers is not known.

A proposed new act (currently in draft bill form) aims to create a SA Council for the Built Environment. This Council will coordinate the current separate legislation for architects, construction managers, engineers, landscape architects, valuers, and quantity surveyors.

The South African Council for Valuers accredits several academic programs as entry-level examinations into the valuation profession. Accreditation usually means that graduates are exempted from theoretical examinations, but still have to complete a practical workshop and examination, and gain a minimum of three years' appropriate practical experience. Programs currently accredited include those at the universities of South Africa, Natal, Pretoria, Queensland (Australia), Copperbelt (Zambia), UST Kumasi (Ghana), the Diplomas and BTech degrees in valuation of the various Technikons (Polytechnics) in South Africa, the diploma of the Institute of Bankers in South Africa, and the examinations of the RICS (General Practice Division or Rural Practice Division) and the Incorporated Society of Valuers and Auctioneers (General Practice Division). Membership of the New Zealand Institute of Valuers is also recognised (South African Council for Valuers, n.d.).

Estate agents are professionally organised into the Institute of Realtors, and Valuers may join the Institute of Valuers. These professional organisations exist independently of their statutory counterparts, but have statutory registration as a minimum entrance requirement. Both organisations regularly organise continuing professional development seminars and workshops for their members. Appraisers have no professional body.

The SA Property Owners Association combines the services of the Urban Land Institute (ULI) and the Building Owners and Managers Association (BOMA) in the US into a single entity. SAPOA runs several training programs geared to the needs of industry and has a National Property Education Committee that produces teaching materials for tertiary institutions. The role of SAPOA is being taken over by the Property Council of South Africa (PROCSA), which aims to act as an umbrella body that represents all interests in the property and construction industries. Member bodies include the SA Institute of Black Property Practitioners, SA Council of Shopping Centres, Commercial and Industrial Brokers Association, SA Association of Quantity Surveyors, Institute of SA Architects and the Association of Black Architects.

36.7.3 Real estate programs at tertiary institutions

Several tertiary institutions in South Africa have real estate courses. Less detail on individual institutions will be provided than for the other countries.

Tertiary institutions that offer a one or two course service package (Black, Carn, Diaz & Rabianski, 1996, p. 189) include the Rand Afrikaans University, University of the Witwatersrand and University of Stellenbosch. A four course major concentration is available at the University of South Africa. Comprehensive programs are available from Wits Technikon, Natal Technikon, Technikon SA and Cape Technikon. The University of Pretoria offers a taught masters program. Comprehensive undergraduate and post graduate programs are planned by the University of the Witwatersrand, the University of Natal and the University of Cape Town. The individual programs will be described briefly.

Rand Afrikaans University includes a property management course as part of the Honours BCom degree (the BCom is a three year business management degree and the honours degree requires a fourth year of study). Other undergraduate papers and informal courses have been available in the past.

The Department of Business Management at Stellenbosch University includes a real estate finance and investment course at undergraduate level and a valuation course at postgraduate level. There are approximately 30 undergraduate and 20 postgraduate students per annum (Doppegieter, 1999).

At the University of the Witwatersrand, the Department of Business Economics includes papers in local authority taxation and in property finance and investment as part of the BCom degree (Department of Construction Economics and Management, 1999).

The Department of Business Management at the University of South Africa has four real estate papers. Undergraduate papers include real estate (overview), real estate investment analysis and real estate valuation. The introductory paper is accredited by the Estate Agency Affairs Board and graduates may register as estate agents. The BCom degree, when it includes the introductory real estate paper and the real estate valuation paper, is accredited by the South African Council for Valuers (SACV). At postgraduate level, a paper in real estate valuation, investment and development is available. The Department draws approximately 300 real estate students per annum. The focus of real estate teaching in the Department will in future become more finance oriented.

At the four universities discussed thus far, real estate courses are available as electives in a business degree, and have a management decision-making emphasis. The duration of study is three years and includes subjects such as accounting, commercial law, management, marketing, human resources, operations management, finance and quantitative techniques. A fourth (honours) year allows the student to specialise and earn a second degree. Masters (MCom) and doctoral (DCom) studies require the completion of a dissertation or thesis on an approved topic, which could be in real estate.

Technikons (Polytechnics) have real estate courses designed to meet industry and licensing requirements. All technikons in South Africa have the same real estate syllabus for their national qualifications, for example a National Certificate or National Diploma. In real estate, the South African Council for Valuers accredits their two year and three year property valuation diplomas and four year BTech degree in property valuation. The largest is Technikon SA, with approximately 800 real estate students per annum. It employs distance education and is currently the only technikon that offers the BTech degree in addition to the diplomas. MTech and DTech research-based degrees are also available. Cape Technikon, Technikon Natal (Durban) and Technikon Witwatersrand (Johannesburg) present the certificate and diploma courses (South African Property Owners Association, n.d.; Kruger, 1999). The syllabus for the BTech degree is given in Table 5.

Judged in terms of customer orientation, the technikon courses are well-structured. Inspection of Table 5 will show that after the first year of study, a student earns a National Certificate; after two years, a National Higher Certificate; after three years, a National Diploma; and after four years, the BTech degree. Thereafter the student may complete masters and doctoral studies. This structure provides several exit points for the student, and also fits logically into the proposed National Qualifications Framework (NQF). The purpose of the NQF is to categorise all education and training into a standardised hierarchy that allows students to move between institutions, with full credit for previous education and even experience. Contact details of the South African Qualifications Authority, which administers the NQF, are provided in the appendix.

Table 5: Curriculum for the National Certificate, National Higher Certificate, National Diploma and B Tech: Real Estate, available from various Technikons in South Africa

This four year degree allows specialisation in property marketing, valuation or property practice. At graduate level, the student may complete a masters (MTech) or doctorate (DTech) in real estate through research. The subjects comprising the undergraduate curriculum are as follows:

Year 1: National Certificate: Real Estate	Year 3: National Diploma: Real Estate (Property Marketing / Property Valuation / Property Practice)
Property Economics and Finance I	
Property Valuation I	
Property Marketing I	Property Economics and Finance III
Property Practice I	Property Marketing III, or
	Property Valuation III, or
	Property Practice III.
	And any two of the following:
	Financial Accounting I
	Principles of Information Systems
	Property Marketing II
	Property Valuation II
	Property Practice II
Year 2: National Higher Certificate: Real Estate (Property Marketing / Property Valuation / Property Practice)	**Year 4: B Tech: Real Estate (Property Marketing / Property Valuation / Property Practice)**
Property Economics and Finance II	Property Economics and Finance IV
Principles of Property Law	Property Marketing IV, or
	Property Valuation IV, or
Any one of the following combinations:	Property Practice IV.
Property Marketing II and Law on Property Marketing	Research Methodology
	Advanced Strategic Management IV
Property Valuation II and Law on Property Valuation	
Property Practice II and Law on Property Practice	

Source: Kruger (1999)

A comprehensive real estate program in the form of a BSc degree is planned by the Department of Construction Economics and Management at the University of the Witwatersrand. The Department also has a postgraduate diploma in property development and management (Schloss, 1999; Department of Construction Economics and Management, 1999).

At the University of Natal, the BSc Property Economics and MSc Building Economics are accredited by the South African Council for Valuers. A proposed new BSc in Property Development includes courses in Construction Technology (3yrs), Design Appraisal 1, Construction Contracts, Project Planning, Construction Materials, Property Studies, Economics, Accounting, Finance, Commercial Law, Urban Development, Language, Business Administration, Environmental Management and various construction oriented topics (South African Council for Valuers, n.d.; White, 1999).

The University of Pretoria has a taught MSc Building Management (Real Estate) program, which is accredited by the SACV. It is intended for graduates in the construction industry, for example, architects, quantity surveyors, engineers and building managers. Graduate students who do not have a degree in construction management or quantity surveying may be required to complete additional undergraduate courses (South African Property Owners Association, n.d.; Department of Quantity Surveying and Construction management, n.d.).

At the University of Cape Town, the Department of Construction Economics and Management has in the past presented real estate courses and plan to introduce several comprehensive real estate courses. This includes a B.Sc. Property Studies, a Postgraduate Diploma in Property Studies, a B.Sc. (Honours) in Property Studies and a taught M.Sc. in Property Studies or in Housing Development. The degrees M.Sc., M.Phil. and Ph.D. may also be earned through research. Syllabus details for the first four years of study (B.Sc. and B.Sc. Honours degrees) are given in Table 6. The curriculum blends construction, real estate and business subjects.

The syllabus for the taught M.Sc. (Property Studies) at the University of Cape Town includes such topics as urban land economics, property law, property finance, property valuation, property development, facilities planning (elective), property portfolio management (elective) and a dissertation. It is taught in eight cycles, of which each has the following format: preparatory reading (20 hours); contact block week (40 hours); assignment period (120 hours). The cycle is repeated eight times, for a minimum of two years' part time study. The prerequisite is an appropriate four year degree (Department of Construction Economics and Management, 1999a; 1999b; n.d.).

Most tertiary institutions provide informal training in addition to their formal courses. Some are custom-developed for individual clients, others have a broad community orientation or continuing professional development (CPD) focus. The Cape Technikon, for example, has a successful property development and investment course, run in the evenings. The University of Pretoria, in conjunction with SAPOA, presents several certificate courses.

Table 6: Curriculum for the B.Sc. and B.Sc. (Honours) in Property Studies

Department of Construction Economics and Management, University of Cape Town
The B.Sc. is a three-year degree and includes construction, real estate and business subjects.
The B.Sc. (Honours) degree requires a fourth year of study. Masters (M.Sc.) studies may be
completed through coursework or the completion of a dissertation. The PhD is available by
research. The subjects comprising the undergraduate curriculum and honours are as follows:

Year 1	Year 3
Thinking About Business	Construction Management 1
Property Information Systems	Cost Engineering
Property Studies 1A	Property Studies 3A
Property Studies 1B	Property Studies 3B
Construction Studies	Property and Contract Law
Practical Training	Practical Training
Microeconomics	Business Law 2
Macroeconomics	Professional Communication
Statistics 101	
Statistics 100	Plus two of the following:
	Business Accounting
	Managerial Accounting & Finance 1
	Marketing 1
	Finance 2
	Labour Law
	Construction Costing
	Economics 203
	Economics 204
	Business Statistics
	Research & Survey Statistics

Year 2	Year 4 (Honours degree)
Financial Accounting 1A	Housing Development & Management
Business Finance	Advanced Property Studies A
Human Resource Management	Advanced Property Studies B
Measurement & Design Appraisal 1	Property Law
Property Studies 2A	Practical Training
Property Studies 2B	Research Report
Practical Training	
Business Law 1	
Plus two of the following:	Plus any four of the following:
Business Accounting	Business Accounting
Labour Law	Managerial Accounting & Finance 1
Business Statistics	Marketing 1
Economics 203	Finance 2 (Counts as two)
Economics 204	Labour Law
Marketing 1	Construction Management 2 (Counts as two)

Construction Costing
Economics 203
Economics 204
Business Statistics
Research & Survey Statistics
Any other approved elective

Source: Department of Construction Economics and Management (1999b)

The University of Cape Town's Graduate School of Business has been offering a property development programme almost every year since 1969. It covers property investment, development, marketing and management.

Many tertiary institutions have recently started to adopt distance teaching methods, combining techniques such as direct broadcasts, tape or video recordings of lectures and web-based material with contact lectures and tutorials. Paper-based correspondence style teaching still predominates, however. The University of South Africa (UNISA), the largest tertiary institution in the country, has about 110 000 students and has taught on a distance education basis since 1946. It is the oldest Open University in the world (Distance learning, 1995). Nelson Mandela is among its distinguished graduates. The largest technikon, Technikon SA (TSA), has about 84 000 students and has been in operation since 1984 (Feite oor TSA, 1999).

There are few qualified real estate academics in South Africa. Most have degrees in associated disciplines such as construction, or in entirely different fields. Many institutions rely on outside lecturers, drawn from industry or from other academic institutions.

36.7.4 Research and publications

Research by South African academics covers the entire spectrum of real estate topics encountered in the international journals. However, the small number of real estate academics restricts their contribution to the field.

In commercial research, Rode and Associates is the most prominent firm, specialising in property market statistics, trends and forecasts. It publishes the following: Rode's SA Property Trends, Rode's Report on the SA Property Market, Rode's Report Online, Rode's Outgoings for Offices, Rode's Address List and Rode's New Office Developments Online. Contact details are provided in the appendix.

The internal research divisions of pension funds and insurance companies (Old Mutual, Sanlam, Liberty Life and others) and financial institutions (ABSA, Nedcor, First National, Standard and others) prepare market research mostly for internal use. Local and international consulting, brokerage and valuation firms such as JHI, Knight Frank and CB Richard Ellis perform contract and internal research. Several other firms publish market related information, although they do not have research divisions.

The South African Property Information Exchange (SAPIX) is administered in conjunction with the Investment Property Databank (IPD) in Britain. In December 1998, the SAPIX data bank included 1508 properties, with a total value of over thirty billion rand (five billion US$). This is equivalent to half the institutionally owned property in South Africa (SAPIX/IPD digest, n.d.). Subscribers to the SAPIX service benefit from benchmarking of their properties against the others in the data bank. Contact details are provided in the appendix.

South Africa has no accredited real estate journals--academics have to publish in business and other journals. The South African Valuer, published by the South African Institute of Valuers, serves the valuation community and trade journals such as The Property Professional serve estate agents. SAPOA members receive SAPOA News, SAPOA Property SA Update and an annual Property Register with contact details of members. SAPOA also tracks and publishes office vacancy levels across the country.

36.8 Zambia

Zambia has been independent from Britain since 1964. With a population of about 9 million people, this landlocked country exports mainly minerals, but a diversification program is under way. English is the business language (Snaden, 1996).

Table 7 - Syllabus for the B.Sc. (Land Economy)

Department of Planning and Land Economy, Copperbelt University, Zambia
The core subjects for the five year B.Sc. (Land Economy) degree includes valuation of interests in land, evaluation of land resources and investment, land use planning, property development and management, housing, law and taxation, land use policy, agricultural and industrial development. The syllabus is as follows:

Year 1	Year 4
Studio projects	Land taxation and finance
The built environment	Zambian land law
The economic environment	Land use control
The physical environment	Valuation II
The social environment	
Communication skills	
Mathematics and statistics	

Year 2	Year 5
Studio projects	Special project
Construction and services	Housing economics and policies
Land economics	Comparative land policies
Land surveying	Property management
Principles of law and government	Land management law
Quantitative studies	Advanced valuation

Year 3
Building construction and economics
Resource management
Planning theory and practice I
Law of contract and tort
Valuation I

Source: Department of Planning and Land Economy (1994)

The Department of Planning and Land Economy in the School of Environmental Studies, Copperbelt University, offers a BSc degree in Land Economy. The program includes 16 weeks' practical training, continuous assessment and annual examinations. It is accredited inter alia by the South African Council for Valuers. Core subjects for the five year curriculum include valuation of interests in land, evaluation of land resources and investment, land use planning, property development and management, housing, law and taxation, land use policy, agricultural and industrial development. The syllabus is given in Table 7.

36.9 Zimbabwe

Independent from Britain since 1980, the Republic of Zimbabwe is South Africa's northern neighbour. Landlocked, it spawned the ancient civilization that created the Zimbabwe ruins. The population is 12 million and English is widely understood. Major industries are manufacturing, mining and agriculture. Exports are mainly tobacco and minerals (Best 1996b).

The property market is well established, but currently suffers from the effects of high inflation and lending rates. This has caused operating costs to escalate faster than rental levels, and negative returns on some properties. Institutions have been selling under performing properties and switching investment to the higher yielding money market (Knight Frank, 1999, p. 3).

The real estate profession[6] is regulated in terms of the Valuer's Act and the Estate Agents Act. A correspondence course and entrance examination is administered by the Real Estate Institute of Zimbabwe.

Harare Polytechnic has been presenting a four year Higher National Diploma in Valuation and Estate Management since 1993. The Department of Rural and Urban Planning at the University of Zimbabwe plans to introduce a four year BSc (Honours) in Land Economy. The proposed syllabus covers the theory and methodology of estate management, valuation, urban and rural planning and development, and property research. More detail is provided in Table 8.

Table 8: Proposed broad syllabus for the BSc (Honours) in Land Economy

Department of Rural and Urban Planning, University of Zimbabwe
The proposed BSc (Hons) is a four year honours degree in land economics. The syllabus covers estate management, valuation (appraisal), planning and development, and property research.

Year 1	Year 3
Introduction to planning	Valuation 2
Quantitative techniques	Law 2 (property and contracts)
Economics principles	Principles and practice of planning law
Environmental systems analysis	Building technology 2
	Property development
Year 2	**Year 4**
Valuation 1	Valuation 3
Urban land use planning	Property investment appraisal
Law 1 (general and commercial)	Property management and marketing
Building technology 1	Urban planning
Real estate economics	Dissertation

Source: Chimbetete (1999)

36.10 Conclusion

This review is based on a survey of 153 educational institutions and on published information. It is clear that a wide range of real estate educational opportunities are available to students in Africa and, through distance education, elsewhere. Most programmes reviewed are multidisciplinary in nature, with land economics and physical development topics receiving most attention. The new financial instruments and securities are currently addressed mostly in postgraduate courses. As African real estate markets are liberalised, a change in emphasis is expected.

All the countries surveyed were in the past subject to British administration, and the British influence on education is strong. The prominent professional institutions are all based in Europe. Academic and professional associations originating in the US, Africa and elsewhere are underrepresented.

The continent is hopefully emerging from its slumber, and references to an African Renaissance are frequently encountered. Judging by the available educational programs, real estate practitioners are well positioned to assist in

Africa's upliftment. This will require closer cooperation between educational and professional institutions. With the support of the International Real Estate Society, the African Real Estate Society will spread the message of real estate as a worthwhile economic activity and assist in integrating the industry throughout the continent.

END NOTES

[1] For purposes of this discussion, real estate and property are used interchangeably, and are defined as immovable property (land and improvements) and interests in immovable property. The property industry includes estate agency (property brokerage), valuation (appraisal), property investment, property development, property finance and services provided by the public sector. The construction industry and its related professions of architecture, quantity surveying and engineering are excluded, except where real estate courses are offered in such faculties.

[2] Except where indicated otherwise, the information on the property profession and on real estate education in Kenya was kindly provided by Prof PM Syagga, Dean of the Faculty of Architecture, Design and Development of the University of Nairobi.

[3] As referred to here, a taught masters or doctoral program combines examinations in various courses with a dissertation of reduced scope. A research based program requires that the student write a comprehensive dissertation (thesis) on an agreed topic.

[4] Except where indicated otherwise, the information on the property profession and on real estate education in Tanzania was kindly provided by Prof JM Lusugga Kironde, of the University College of Lands and Architectural Studies at the University of Dar Es Salaam.

[5] Except where indicated otherwise, the information on the property profession and on real estate education in Nigeria was kindly provided by Mr SO Oyegbile, Head of the Department of Estate Management, Federal University of Technology Minna, Nigeria.

[6] Information on the real estate profession and on real estate education in Zimbabwe was kindly provided by Mr I Chimbetete, Chairman, Land Economy, in the Department of Rural and Urban Planning at the University of Zimbabwe, and by Mr Jim Gibbons of Knight Frank in Harare.

REFERENCES

Best, A.C.G., Africa, Grolier Multimedia Encyclopedia, 1996a.

Best, A.C.G., Zimbabwe, Grolier Multimedia Encyclopedia, 1996b.

Black, R.T., Carn, N.G., Diaz, J. and Rabianski, J.S., The Role of the American Real Estate Society in Defining and Promulgating the Study of Real Property, The Journal of Real Estate Research, 1996, 12:2, 183-193.

Chimbetete, I., Personal correspondence, May 21, 1999.

Department of Construction Economics and Management, University of Cape Town, Advertisement, Mail & Guardian, May 7 to 13, 1999a.

Department of Construction Economics and Management, University of Cape Town, Web page at www.uct.ac.za/depts/cons/, 1999b.

Department of Construction Economics and Management, University of Cape Town, Promotional leaflet, n.d.

Department of Construction Economics and Management, University of the Witwatersrand, Web page at www.wits.ac.za, 1999.

Department of Land Management and Valuation, Curriculum for the BSc degree in Land Management and Valuation, first edition, Dar Es Salaam: University College of Lands and Architectural Studies, January 1997.

Department of Planning and Land Economy, Syllabus for B.Sc. (Land Economy), Copperbelt University, Zambia. 1994.

Department of Quantity Surveying and Construction management, University of Pretoria, Promotional leaflet , n.d.

Distance learning: Faraway thoughts, Economist, 7th-13th January, 1995.

Doppegieter, J., Personal correspondence, 1999.

Epley, D.R., The Current Body of Knowledge Paradigms Used in Real Estate Education and Issues in Need of Further Research, The Journal of Real Estate Research, 1996, 12:2, 229-236.

Feite oor TSA. Rapport: Persoonlike Finansies, October 3, 1999, 10.

Garst, R.D., Ghana, Grolier Multimedia Encyclopedia, 1996a.

Garst, R.D., Kenya, Grolier Multimedia Encyclopedia, 1996b.

Garst, R.D., Nigeria, Grolier Multimedia Encyclopedia, 1996c.

Gibbons, J., Personal correspondence, 1999.

Hammond, D.N.A. Syllabus for B.Sc. (Land Economy) degree programme, Department of Land Economy and Estate Management, University of Science and Technology, Kumasi, Ghana, Correspondence dated July 8, 1993.

Kironde, J.M.L., Personal correspondence, 1999.

Knight Frank, Kenya property report, Nairobi: Knight Frank, May 1998.

Knight Frank, Property report, Harare: Knight Frank, April 1999.

Kriel, D., Asset Management in South Africa, in J. Reuvid and I Priestner, editors, Doing business in South Africa, 222-225, fourth edition, London: Kogan Page, 1999.

Kruger, A., Personal correspondence, 1999.

MBendi, Web site located at www.MBendi.co.za, 1999.

Nwankwo, P.C., Property Management Practice in Nigeria, Nigeria: Pelin, 1995.

Oyegbile, S.O., Personal correspondence, May 12, 1999.

Quantity surveyors stride together, The Property Professional, August/September 1999, 43.

SAPIX/IPD digest, Property SA Update, Sandton: SAPOA. n.d., 3.

Schloss, R., Interview, 1999.

Snaden, J.N., Zambia, Grolier Multimedia Encyclopedia, 1996.

South African Council for Valuers, Information Document, Pretoria: SACV, n.d.

South African Property Owners Association, A Guide to Property Education in South Africa, Sandton: SAPOA, n.d.

Syagga, P.M., Personal correspondence, March 30, 1999.

The World of Learning 1998, forty-eighth edition, London: Europa Publications, 1998.

White, M., Personal correspondence, October 7, 1999.

APPENDIX

Contact details:

Kenya	
Prof P M Syagga Dean Faculty of Architecture, Design and Development University of Nairobi P.O. Box 30197 Nairobi	Mr N Nzioki Chairman Department of Land Development University of Nairobi P.O. Box 30197 Nairobi
Institution of Surveyors of Kenya P.O. Box 71460 Nairobi	Keitu Enterprises Ltd. P.O. Box 11028 Nairobi
Mr F Reynolds Knight Frank P.O. Box 39773 Nairobi	

Tanzania	
Prof J M L Kironde Department of Land Management and Valuation College of Lands and Architectural Studies P.O. Box 35176 Dar Es Salaam	Mr F Komu Secretary General Tanzania Institution of Valuers and Estate Agents c/o University College of Lands and Architectural Studies University of Dar Es Salaam P.O. Box 35176 Dar Es Salaam

Nigeria	
Mr S O Oyegbile Head Department of Estate Management Federal University of Technology, Minna PMB 65, Minna Niger State	Nigerian Institution of Estate Surveyors and Valuers Flat 2B, Old Dolphin Scheme Ikoyi Lagos, Nigeria

Ghana	
Dr D N A Hammond Head Department of Land Economy University of Science and Technology, Kumasi	Dr S O Asiama Department of Land Economy University of Science and Technology, Kumasi

Souh Africa

Adv G Van Zyl Registrar South African Council for Valuers P.O. Box 114 0161 Menlyn	Mr A Harrison Chairman Estate Agents Board Private Bag X10 Benmore
Mr CH Hablutzel General Secretary South African Institute of Valuers P.O. Box 18041 7824 Wynberg	Prof R Schloss Department of Construction Economics and Management University of the Witwatersrand Private Bag 3 2050 Wits
Prof C E Cloete Department of Building Management University of Pretoria 0002 Pretoria	Mr M White School of Civil Engineering, Surveying and Construction P.O. Box University of Natal 4041 Durban
Prof V Ghyoot Department of Business Management University of South Africa P.O. Box 392 0003 Pretoria	Mr A Kruger School of Real Estate and Economics Technikon SA Private Bag X6 1710 Florida
Prof J Doppegieter Department of Business Management University of Stellenbosch Private Bag X1 7602 Matieland	Prof P Bowen Department of Construction Economics and Management University of Cape Town Private Bag 7001 Rondebosch
Rode & Associates P.O. Box 1566 Bellville 7535 South Africa	South African Property Information Exchange Hunt's End Office Park 36 Wierda Road West Wierda Valley 2146 Sandton
JHI Professional Services P.O. Box 2100 2121 Parklands	Richard Ellis Africa P.O. Box 783670 2146 Sandton
Knight Frank SA P.O. Box 781945 2146 Sandton	South African Qualifications Authority Private Bag X06 0145 Waterkloof
South African Property Owners Association P.O. Box 78544 2146 Sandton	The Property Professional P.O. Box 3695 2115 Northcliff

Zambia

Department of Planning and Land Economy
Copperbelt University
PO Box 21692
Kitwe

Zimbabwe

Mr I Chimbetete
Chairman, Land Economy
Department of Rural and Urban Planning
University of Zimbabwe
P.O. Box MP 167
Mount Pleasant
Harare
Zimbabwe

Mr G Tanner, Secretary
Real Estate Institute of Zimbabwe/Estate
Agents Council
P.O. Box HG 898
Highlands
Harare

Mr J Gibbons
Knight Frank
P.O. Box 3526
Harare

Contributors

Alastair S. Adair

Alastair Adair is Head of the School of the Built Environment and Professor of Property Investment at the University of Ulster. He holds degrees in geography, land management (Ph.D., University of Reading) and education. He is a Fellow of the Royal Institution of Chartered Surveyors (FRICS), the Irish Auctioneers and Valuers Institute (FIAVI) and the Royal Geographical Society (FRGS). He is also Senior Vice President of the Irish Auctioneers and Valuers Institute.

Alastair Adair has played a leading role in the development of real estate education in the University of Ulster at both undergraduate and postgraduate levels, specialising in financial aspects of development and investment appraisal. His areas of research interest comprise the financing of urban regeneration and the comparative study of European valuation practice. He has an extensive publication record, is a member of the editorial boards of a number of journals and is market review editor for the Journal of Property Research. His contribution to research and teaching was recognised in 1999 by the presentation of the European Real Estate Society Achievement Award for an outstanding contribution to real estate research in Europe.

Maurizio d'Amato

Maurizio d'Amato is Researcher (assistant professor) in the Faculty of Engineering at the Polytechnic of Bari, Italy, where he teaches real estate and valuation. He completed his undergraduate work in economics at the

University of Bari and then worked for several banks (Bank of Rome, Bank of Salento, Micos - Mediobanca) in real estate finance before entering the doctoral programme in Planning, specialising in evaluation methods, at the Polytechnic of Bari. After completing this programme, he served as a contract professor in Real Estate Valuation for three years. During this time he has received research grants from the Italian Council of Research for projects undertaken at the University of Florida and the University of Alicante (SP) in the summers of 1997, 1998, 1999 and 2000. He received the faculty appointment of Researcher at the Polytechnic of Bari in 1999.

Alain Bechade

Alain Bechade, Doctor of Law, is Professor at the ICH in Paris and Course Director at the University of Paris 1 (Pantheon-Sorbonne). Alain is a Fellow of the Royal Institution of Chartered Surveyors and a past president of RICS Europe and RICS France. He is a member of the French institute of property expertise.

Alain Bechade has published numerous papers and articles concerning the law of property and real estate economics. He is the author of the books "La promotion immobilière" (Property Development) and "connaissance et pratique du marché immobilier" (Knowledge and Practice of the Real Estate Market).

After two years in the legal department at St. Gobain, he was Directeur Général of Bourdais from 1976 to 1985. He then became President and Director-General (P.D.G.) of Ferinel Industries (commercial property developers) until 1994. From then he took control of Interconstruction (commercial and residential developers as P.D.G.). He sold Interconstruction on 1 January 2001 and became P.D.G. of Auguste Thouard, one of the leading commercial property advisers in France and Europe.

Stanisław Belniak

Stanisław Belniak holds a Doctorate in economics, specialising in the economics of real estate and investment. Since 1972 he has been a faculty member of the University of Economics in Cracow where he has held lectures and seminars on the functioning of the real estate market, financing investment in real estate, and real estate management.

Since 1995, Stanisław Belniak has been a professor at the Małopolska Higher School of Economics in Tarnów, where he heads the Real Estate Management department. He is a licensed real estate valuer and an expert on real estate transactions and board member of the European Real Estate Society.

In the professional area, his main interest has been in the functioning of the real estate market. Consequently, his habilitation thesis focused on the development of the real estate market in Poland compared with the developed countries.

Stanisław Belniak has authored and co-authored more than 60 publications and has taken part in over 80 research projects commissioned by various enterprises and institutions. The results of his work have been implemented by his clients.

Elizabeth Brown

Elizabeth Brown is a former lecturer in Valuation and Property Management at the University of Ulster. She has extensive experience in property management and consulting in Belfast.

Kirit Budhbhatti

Kirit Budhbhatti is Honorary Advisor to the Centre For Valuation Studies at the Institute of Science & Technology For Advanced Studies & Research. This is the only institute in India that offers real estate education and the only institute in the world to offer an academic course on the valuation of plant and machinery. Kirit Budhbhatti holds degrees in Electrical Engineering (Sardar Patel University) and Valuation Surveying (Institution of Surveyors -India). He is a Fellow of the Institution of Surveyors (India) and a Senior Member of the American Society of Appraisers. He is a Former President of the Institution of Surveyors. He is a pioneer in the development of education in both real estate and plant and machinery valuation in India. Kirit Budhbhatti carries the professional banner in the second generation and has a wide and varied experience in the practical field of valuation for large industrial groups.

Gonzalo Castañeda

Gonzalo Castañeda has a Ph.D. in Economics from Cornell University where he was also awarded his Master's degree. He has two bachelor degrees, in Economics and in Applied Mathematics, both from the Instituto Tecnológico Autónomo de México. Currently, Gonzalo Castañeda is a national researcher level II and head of the Economics Department at the Universidad de las Américas-Puebla. He has acted as a consultant for Bancomer, a leading bank in Mexico, for the Ministry of Trade and Industry (SECOFI) and for the Ministry of Finance in the State of Puebla.

Gonzalo Castañeda has published three books on issues related to financial systems, corporate governance and real estate finance. He has several papers in scientific journals from Mexico, Chile, Europe and the United States. Currently, he has grants from the Mexican Agency for Science and Technology (CONACYT), the University of California and the Inter-American Development Bank to do research on internal capital markets, business groups and the Mexican banking system.

Chin-Oh Chang

Chin-Oh Chang is Professor in the Department of Land Economics, National Chengchi University, Taipei, Taiwan. He was awarded his Architecture Master's degree at MIT, USA in 1980 and a Ph.D. in City and Regional Planning at the University of Pennsylvania, USA in 1986. He has been Director of Taiwan Real Estate Research Center in National Chengchi University since its establishment in 1998. He was President of the Asian Real Estate Society in 1997-98. Chin-Oh Chang has concentrated his research in areas related to housing and land policy, real estate investment and financial analysis, urban economics and planning. He has published more than 40 peer-reviewed papers, in Chinese and English, in the housing and real estate field.

Kwong Wing Chau

Kwong Wing Chau is Chair Professor in the Department of Real Estate and Construction at the University of Hong Kong. He has taught at both undergraduate and postgraduate levels at the University of Hong Kong since 1987. He has been Associate Dean of the Faculty of Architecture at the University of Hong Kong since 1991.

Kwong Wing Chau was the past president of the International Real Estate Society (2000-01) and first president of the Asian Real Estate Society (1996-97). He was the recipient of the 1999 International Real Estate Society Achievement Award and the 1999 The University of Hong Kong Outstanding Young Researcher Award.

Kwong Wing Chau is the executive co-editor of the International Real Estate Review (the official Journal of the Asian Real Estate Society) and is also a member of the editorial boards of a number of peer-reviewed real estate journals.

Yao-Min Chiang

Yao-Min Chiang, Ph.D. is assistant professor of finance at National Chengchi University, Taiwan. He currently serves as the director of the CNCCU-SINYI Center for Real Estate at Chengchi University. The mission of the newly established centre is to conduct real estate related research and to educate real estate professionals. The ultimate goal of the centre is to provide a wide range of information for developing Taiwan's real estate market.

He was awarded an MBA at Chengchi University in 1990 and a Ph.D. in finance from the University of Iowa in 1996. The title of his dissertation is "Balloon mortgages as an alternate choice": the dissertation advisor is Professor J. Sa-Aadu. He became a member of the faculty of YanZe University immediately after graduation. He has been an assistant professor of finance at Chengchi University since 1997. His major research topics are mortgage-backed securities and shopping centre development.

Joo Hyun Cho

Joo-Hyun Cho is currently professor of real estate finance and market analysis in the Department of Real Estate Studies at Konkuk University, Seoul, Korea. He was awarded a B.S. in Architectural Engineering and Master of City Planning by Seoul National University, Korea. He received his Ph.D. in Urban and Regional Planning at MIT, USA.

He previously worked as a Research Fellow at the Korea Research Institute for Human Settlements. He is now Vice President of both the Korean Association of Housing Policy Studies and the Korea Real Estate Analysis Association. He also serves as a Board Member of the Korea Planners Association, the Korea Regional Science Association and the Korea Facility Management Association.

Joo-Hyun Cho has written several books including the recent (2000) "Real Estate Principles and Practices", published by Konkuk University Press.

His professional activities in the public area include Commissioner, Committee on Green-belt Reform, Central Committee on Land Appraisal, Committee on Real Estate Brokerage Examination, Sub-committee on Compensation, and Committee on SOC Development at the Ministry of Construction & Transportation (MOCT). He is Housing Advisor to the Korea National Housing Corporation (KNHC), and Advisor on Management

National Housing Corporation (KNHC), and Advisor on Management of Land owned by the state at Ministry of Finance & Economy.

Henn Elmet

Henn Elmet is currently Rector of the Estonian Agricultural University (1998) and the Professor of the Institute of Land Surveying (1993). His main fields of research are the economics of land utilisation, the economic evaluation of land, land valuation for tax purposes (mass valuation) and property appraisal for mortgage security. In these fields of research Professor Elmet has published more than a dozen articles in Estonian and European scientific publications.

He is a member of the Academic Council to the President of the Republic of Estonia; Chairman of the Land Evaluation Licensing Commission of the Estonian Ministry of Environment; a member of the Board of the Estonian Union of Real Estate Appraisers; a member of the Accreditation Commission of Real Estate Appraisers to the Estonian Banks' Union, a member of the Research and Development Council to the Prime Minister of the Republic of Estonia; and a member of the Consulting Council of the Estonian Ministry of Foreign Affairs.

Philippe Favarger

Philippe Favarger was awarded his Ph.D. in Economics by the University of Geneva. For the past twelve years he has been involved in research as well as teaching in the fields of housing, construction and real estate economics.

During the 1990's, students in Architecture at the University of Geneva attended his course in Real Estate Economics. Today, he teaches Real Estate Appraisal to professionals - mainly architects - in a postgraduate programme for which he is responsible at the Swiss Federal Institute of Technology in Lausanne.

His research concerns the functioning of real estate markets, the construction of real estate price indices, and methodologies of real estate valuation. His work has been published in various articles and reports. Apart from his academic activities, he also works as a financial consultant for real estate projects.

Nick French

Nick French is the Acacia Senior Lecturer in Land Management in the Department of Land Management and Development at the University of Reading in England. He is Course Director of the MSc Land Management degree and teaches extensively in the areas of appraisal, valuation and corporate real estate.

In 2000, Nick French was awarded the Jonathan Edwards Consulting Fellowship in Corporate Real Estate. In this role, he works closely with his colleagues at Jonathan Edwards Consulting in writing papers, presenting conference papers and developing a research agenda for the corporate real estate market.

Nick French is the Editor of the Journal of Property Investment & Finance, the award-winning academic international journal of the real estate industry. He also writes regularly for other professional and academic journals.

Nick French is a member of the RICS Appraisal and Valuation Standards Board as well as being a member of the joint RICS/Investment Property Forum on Calculation of Worth. He was a founder member of the European Real Estate Society and held the post of an Executive Director until 1997.

Daniel Gat

Daniel Gat is an associate professor in the Faculty of Architecture and Town Planning, and Director of the Center for Urban and Regional Studies at Technion, the Israel Institute of Technology, Haifa, Israel.

He was awarded a Bachelor of Architecture degree at Technion in 1960; Master of City Planning, Yale University, New Haven, Connecticut, USA, 1967; and a Master's degree and Ph.D. in Administrative Sciences, Yale University, 1969, 1971. His teaching philosophy is that "Urban planners who understand real estate markets make better plans and contribute value to consumers and producers, while upgrading the interface between built and natural space". Courses he is currently teaching include: Real Estate Development—Introduction; Real Estate Economics—Special Topics; Spatial and Visual Thinking; Urban Planning Studio with special emphasis on Sustainable Development.

Valmond Ghyoot

Valmond Ghyoot is Professor of Real Estate in the Department of Business Management at the University of South Africa, a distance teaching institution. He has a Doctorate in business, majoring in real estate, a Master's majoring in project management, and degrees in business and in construction. He is an active consultant and is licensed as a valuer and as an appraiser. An eclectic mix of research interests has produced work in multicultural sensitivity; computer based training, computer modelling and programming; public sector real estate policy; feasibility analysis; retail market analysis; trade area demarcation and project management.

Professional affiliations include the Southern African Institute of Management Scientists; American and Pacific Rim Real Estate Societies, and the African Real Estate Society, where he is also a director.

Stanley Hamilton

Stanley Hamilton is the Philip H. White Professor of Urban Land Economics at the Faculty of Commerce, University of British Columbia. Professor Hamilton's current research interests include real estate valuations and investment, portfolio analysis, and real estate brokerage. He is currently chair of the Faculty Pension Plan and serves as a trustee with one of Canada's major REITS. He has served as an advisor to various public and private organisations.

Martin Hoesli

Martin Hoesli holds a Doctorate in business administration from the University of Geneva. He is Professor of real estate investment and finance at the University of Geneva and Professor of finance at the University of Aberdeen. He has written four books and numerous academic articles in journals such as Real Estate Economics, the Journal of Real Estate Finance and Economics, the Journal of Housing Economics, and the Journal of Property Research and Urban Studies. He is on the editorial boards of Real Estate Economics, the Journal of Property Research and the Journal of Property Investment & Finance. He also has extensive practical experience, most notably in real estate index construction. In 2000, Martin Hoesli was conference chair for the Bordeaux 7th Annual Conference of the European Real Estate Society.

Rodney L Jefferies

Rod Jefferies recently retired from the Department of Property, the University of Auckland, New Zealand where he specialised in the teaching of property valuation and research for over 25 years. He is a Past-President of the New Zealand Institute of Valuers, a founder and Past Vice-President of the New Zealand Property Management Institute, and a Life Member of the (now merged) New Zealand Property Institute. He was the author of the New Zealand standard texts: "Urban Valuation in New Zealand" – Vols I & II. He is now a commercial & industrial real estate manager and consultant with L J Hooker - Commercial, North Shore, Auckland, NZ.

Hanna Kaleva

Hanna Kaleva (MSc, Econ) completed her Master's degree at Turku School of Economics and Business Administration in 1989. Since 1997, she has worked as research manager at KTI (Institute for Real Estate Economics) Finland. Previously she worked as a researcher in several research projects at KTI. In 1990-1994 she worked in the money market department of the Turku Savings Bank.

Hanna's recent publications and research projects include: Property securitisation (two publications in Finnish, in 1995 and 1996, jointly with Ari Lahti, Asko Miettilä and Olli Olkkonen); Finland and the global real estate market (1998); real estate services market, the usage of office space in the future (a publication in Finnish in 2000, jointly with Jaana Heikkilä and Olli Olkkonen) and Corporate Real Estate Strategies (published in 2001, jointly with Olli Olkkonen).

Angelo Karantonis

Angelo Karantonis is Associate Professor and Program Director of the Property Program at the University of Technology, Sydney; he is also a Director of the UTS Property Research Unit. In addition, he chairs the editorial board of the Pacific Rim Property Research Journal and is an editorial board member of two other journals. He has published extensively in several property areas, particularly in international property investment.

Angelo Karantonis is the Executive Director of the Pacific Rim Real Estate Society (PRRES), having previously served as President, and is a member of the Board of the International Real Estate Society (IRES). In 2000, he

was conference chair for the Sydney 6th Annual Conference of the Pacific
Rim Real Estate Society.

Yuichiro Kawaguchi

Yuichiro Kawaguchi is Professor of Real Estate Science, at Meikai University in Japan. He is also a Visiting Professor at Tokyo, Kyoto, and Keio Universities. He was awarded a Doctorate of Engineering (Civil Engineering) from Tokyo University.

He has developed "Real Estate Financial Engineering" and established the "Japan Association of Real Estate Financial Engineering" (JAREFE) in 2000. He has written many books on real estate in Japan, including "Introduction to Real Estate Financial Engineering (2001)", "Real Estate Financial Engineering (2001)", "Japan Real Estate Investment Trust (2001)". He is the director of the Asian Real Estate Society (1999-2001) and the vice president of JAREFE.

Jinu Kim

Jinu Kim joined the Faculty of the Built Environment at the University of New South Wales, in 1991. Prior to that he had wide international experience of architectural design, project management and property development in several countries including Korea, the UK, Libya, and Australia for more than 15 years. More recently he has undertaken numerous research activities in the property development process, property and construction market analysis, facility management, and property asset management. In 1996 he completed a thesis "Effects of locational obsolescence in investment appraisal of industrial buildings" for his Ph.D. Jinu Kim is the visiting research fellow at the Construction and Economy Research Institute of Korea (CERIK) and was the visiting research fellow at the Seoul National University, Department of Architecture in 1998. His teaching areas are property development and management, property investment analysis, and construction project management.

Paul P. Kohnstamm

Paul P. Kohnstamm has been part-time professor of real estate at the University of Amsterdam and chairman of the board of the Centre for Investment and Real Estate (SBV) since 1989. SBV is responsible for the organisation of the most important post-graduate course in Real Estate Studies in the Netherlands. He holds a degree in economics (BSc, University of Groningen and MSc, University of Rotterdam) and is a Fellow of the Royal Institution of Chartered Surveyors (FRICS).

After 7 years in travel and tourism he joined the Wilma-group in 1974. He served nearly 20 years as property manager, marketing director and vice-president strategy and external affairs.

Since 1992 he has been advisor to the board of the Dutch Association of Property Developers and Investors (NEPROM) and the Dutch Property Federation (ROZ). He is a non-executive member of the boards of directors of several companies and runs his own consulting firm.

Paul P. Kohnstamm was President of the European Real Estate Society (1998/1999) and received the ERES achievement award in 2001.

Kaisa Leiwo

Kaisa Leiwo works as a development manager in the Finnish Real Estate Training and Education Institute. Her work is related especially to real estate economics, real estate management and real estate education.

Joe Lipscomb

Joseph B. Lipscomb is Professor of Finance and Real Estate in the Neeley School of Business at Texas Christian University in Fort Worth, Texas.

He has published articles in many real estate academic and professional journals including Journal of Real Estate Research, Journal of Real Estate Portfolio Management, Journal of Real Estate Literature, and the Appraisal Journal. His areas of expertise include real estate valuation and the Mexican mortgage market.

He is currently the President of the American Real Estate Society (2001/2002) and the Director of the Center for Financial Studies at Texas Christian University. He served as Chairman of the Finance and Decision Sciences Department in the Neeley School from 1993 - 2001.

Liu Hongyu

Liu Hongyu's career has always been in the field of real estate and construction. After completing his undergraduate (BSc in Civil Engineering,

1985) and graduate (MSc in Management Engineering, 1988) work at Tsinghua University (THU), he went to Hong Kong Polytechnic University for two years joint research on land management. After returning to Beijing, he joined the work on land use system reform in mainland China. In October 1992, the Institute of Real Estate Studies at THU, the first on-campus real estate research organisation, was founded with his efforts. During the past decade, the Institute has retained its position as one of the leading real estate groups in China.

Liu Hongyu was promoted to Full Professor in 1996, when he began to serve as the director of the Institute of Real Estate Studies at THU. The major interests of his research are focused on real estate economics, real estate development, real estate finance and investment and construction project management. In 2000, he was recruited from the Department of Civil Engineering to head the Department of Construction and Real Estate at THU as its founding Head. He has since successfully established a real estate concentration within the Department.

He has served as Director of the Asian Real Estate Society (AsRES) since its founding in 1996, and was its President in 1999/2000. In 2000, he was a chairman for the Beijing 5th Annual Meeting of AsRES.

Jens Lunde

Jens Lunde was awarded a Master's in Economics from the University of Copenhagen in 1973. He was research assistant at the Danish Building Research Institute from 1974 to 1980. He then worked as an economist in the department for planning of housing policy in the Danish Ministry of Housing until the end of 1984. Since then he has been associate professor at the Department of Finance at the Copenhagen Business School.

His main research field is Housing/Real Estate Economics and Finance. During the years he has written on a wide range of subjects - mostly in Danish - in books and journals.

His teaching experience includes several finance and economics courses. In particular, each year he teaches a one-semester course at Master's level in housing economics and finance at the Copenhagen Business School.

He has also participated in housing economic and policy working groups and committees and has carried out consultancy work for authorities and organisations. He has given courses in housing economics and finance for special groups. He is considered by Danish journalists to be an expert in housing economics.

Stellan Lundström

Stellan Lundström is Professor in Real Estate Economics in the Department of Real Estate and Construction Management, at the Royal Institute of Technology (KTH) in Stockholm, Sweden. His special fields of interest are investment, valuation, property management and brokerage. His positions at KTH are: Director of the Executive programme in Real Estate Economics and Director of KTHs International Master's Programme in Real Estate Management. Since 1980 he has published about 200 books, articles and papers in the field of real estate economics.

Stellan Lundström was President of the International Real Estate Society (1997-98).

Graham McIntosh

Graham McIntosh, Director of Business Programs, Faculty of Commerce, University of British Columbia, has been involved with design, development and teaching of innovative real estate education programmes since 1988.

He has taught numerous courses in real estate, including mortgage finance, real estate investment analysis and appraisal, and real property development.

Keith McKinnell

Keith McKinnell has been head of the Department of Real Estate and Construction, at the University of Hong Kong since 1992. He is the driving force for the development of the professionally accredited undergraduate and postgraduate programmes in his department. He has been teaching at both undergraduate and postgraduate levels at The University of Hong Kong since 1985.

He is a Chartered Surveyor and currently the Chairman of the Surveying Courses Board of the Hong Kong Institute of Surveyors. The Board is responsible for accrediting local and non-local real estate courses. He has also served on the accreditation panel for the Royal Institution of Chartered Surveyors.

Recently, he has been appointed by the Hong Kong Special Administrative Government to serve on the Town Planning Board.

Alfons Metzger

Its current owner, Alfons Metzger founded the MRG Metzger Real Estate Group in 1971 as an international construction enterprise. In 1978, it was expanded to focus on the fields of the real estate management and agency. In the 1980's, Alfons Metzger began to channel his vast experience into specialised international real estate consulting. Today, the MRG is rated as a top enterprise not only in Austria but internationally, through its partnership with King Sturge Corfac International throughout the world.

Alfons Metzger is a member of The Royal Institution of Chartered Surveyors and The Counselors of Real Estate.

In 1998, Alfons Metzger founded the Austrian Institute of Property Valuation and Valuation Standards and in 1999 the Austrian Association of Chartered Surveyors. Both organisations focus on education and know-how in order to get highly qualified specialists into the fields of property valuation and consulting work. He also was the 1997-98 FIABCI world president.

Eliane Monetti

Eliane Monetti concluded a Civil Engineering Course at the Escola Politécnica of the University of São Paulo, Brazil, in 1978. In 1991 she was awarded the degree of Master in Civil Engineering and in 1996, Doctor in Civil Construction and Urban Engineering, both at the Escola Politécnica.

Since she started working in the Civil Construction Department of the Escola Politécnica (1989), she has worked in the Management and Real Estate Group, dealing with business administration in civil engineering and real estate.

At undergraduate level, she teaches financial and economic planning for ventures in construction and real estate. She has also co-ordinated undergraduate activities in the Department of Civil Construction since 1999.

She is assistant professor in two different disciplines at graduate level and supervises much research. In MBA courses, she is responsible for two disciplines and she has been one of the two co-ordinators of the Course since 1994. She acts as a consultant in real estate, specialising in financial and economic planning.

Ingrid Nappi-Choulet

Ingrid Nappi-Choulet, was awarded her Ph.D. in Economics by the University of Paris XII. She is currently associate professor in property studies at ESSEC, where she has been in charge of the real estate chair since 1995. She has recently been elected as an Academic Fellow of the ULI (Urban Land Institute) and member of the ERES Executive Board (European Real Estate Society).

She has written numerous articles about commercial property markets and office markets analysis. She is also the author of two recent books: "Les bureaux, analyse d'une crise" (Offices: analysis of a crisis, Paris, ADEF, 1997) and "Marketing et stratégie de l'immobilier" (Property marketing and strategy, Paris, Dunod, 1999. Her current research interests center on the real estate cycles and on office property markets.

Graeme Newell

Graeme Newell is Professor of Property Investment at the University of Western Sydney in Sydney, Australia. He has been actively involved in real estate education and research for over 25 years.

He has published extensively in the leading USA and UK real estate journals, including the Journal of Real Estate Research, Journal of Real Estate Portfolio Management and Journal of Property Research.

Graeme Newell has been actively involved in the Pacific Rim Real Estate Society (PRRES) and the International Real Estate Society (IRES).He has served as President of both PRRES and IRES and is currently Executive Director of IRES.

In 1998, the Pacific Rim Real Estate Society (PRRES) acknowledged Graeme Newell as recipient of the PRRES Achievement Award. In the same year he received the IRES achievement Award.

Olli Olkkonen

Olli Olkkonen is a managing director of KTI, Finland. He is a MSc and graduated from Turku Business School, where he majored in international economics and business administration, in 1988. His licentiate thesis on real estate economics was approved in 1997.

Before taking over management of KTI (Finnish Institute for Real Estate Economics), Olli was a researcher and subsequently research director there. KTI was founded in 1993 to service the real estate business by producing benchmarking and research services for the Finnish market. KTI maintains extensive databases on the Finnish real estate market. Olli Olkkonen has been actively involved in developing several information and expert services for the real estate sector. He has also been instrumental in developing continuing education for real estate executives and managers in Finland. His academic research interests include: the dynamics of the real estate market; cycles; corporate real estate; and real estate investment.

Olli Olkkonen is a past President of the European Real Estate Society (ERES) and a member of the ULI Europe Policy and Practice Committee.

Ismail Omar

Ismail Omar has been a senior lecturer in property at the Universiti Teknologi Malaysia since 1983. He gained his first degree in estate management from Heriot-Watt University, Scotland in 1986. He then pursued his studies, reading for a Master's degree in property at the University of South Australia before completing his Ph.D. in land economy at Aberdeen University, Scotland.

Ismail Omar has written many articles and books on land and property development. He is active in research in land and property related fields. His interests are in land and property management and development.

Zeynep Önder

Zeynep Önder received her B.S. and M.B.A. degrees from the Middle East Technical University, Ankara, Turkey and an M.S. degree in Finance and Ph.D. degree in Housing from Cornell University. She was one of the recipients of the U.S. Department of Housing and Urban Development Dissertation Grant in 1994.

Currently, she is an Assistant Professor in the Department of Management at Bilkent University. She teaches corporate finance and investment analysis in the undergraduate programme and real estate finance and investment at graduate level. Her research interests include public policies related to housing and mortgage markets, real estate finance and investment, and issues relevant to individual and institutional investors and regulators in real estate and financial markets. Her articles have been published in several journals, including the Journal of Housing Economics, Applied Economics, and Russian and Eastern European Finance and Trade.

Scarlett Palmer

Scarlett Palmer is the Research Manager in the Department of Land Management and Development at the University of Reading. She also runs the departmental web pages. Her background is in Information Science and before coming to Reading she worked at City University, London and the University of Cambridge. She is currently carrying out research in the area of inclusive environments and her most recent work concerns issues surrounding access to the built environment for people with disabilities.

Stephen E. Roulac

Stephen E. Roulac is CEO of the Roulac Group, Inc., a strategy and financial economics consultancy, with offices in San Francisco and Hong Kong. He is a Distinguished Professor of Global Property Strategy at the University of Ulster in Belfast.

A leading academic, he is a recipient of the James A. Graaskamp Award for iconoclastic thinking that advances real estate paradigms, the Warner Bloomberg Award for promoting a vision of the future established on principles of social justice, and past president of the American Real Estate Society (ARES). He was recognized by the Fisher Center at UC Berkeley as one of the 100 individuals who had most significant influences on the real estate industry in the 20th century. Author of the forthcoming "Renaissance of Place and Space" which documents the story of strategic geography, he has written over 350 articles and numerous books.

Much in demand as a professional speaker, he has delivered keynote presentations and training sessions to some 500 organisations. He hosts the national weekly radio show "Location Matters: The Stephen Roulac Conversation", broadcast on National Public Radio. His credentials include B.A., Pomona; M.B.A., Harvard; J.D. Berkeley; and Ph.D. in strategy and finance from Stanford and the AICP, CMC and CPA designations.

Kaarel Sahk

Kaarel Sahk is lecturer in real estate appraisal at the Institute of Land Surveying at the Estonian Agricultural University. His main fields of research are real estate appraisal and techniques, planning solutions and restrictions and construction economics. His "masterworks" topic at the Tartu University, *Real Estate Appraisal in the Emergency Market*, will be published in January 2002. Kaarel Sahk has been involved in real estate appraisal since 1992. He is a certified real estate appraiser (2000) and chartered civil engineer (1999). Kaarel Sahk is a member of the Court of Honour of the Estonian Society of Real Estate Appraisers and is the founder of the Estonian Society of Cost Estimators. He has taken part in the consultancy work on governmental housing policy - Housing 2010 (1999).

Karl-Werner Schulte

Karl-Werner Schulte was appointed to the professorship of the Chair of Business Administration, in particular Investment and Finance, at the European Business School (ebs) in Oestrich-Winkel near Frankfurt, Germany in 1986. Since 1990 he has been academic head and, since 1992, managing director of the ebs Real Estate Academy. In 1994 he established the endowed Chair of Real Estate at the European Business School. Among his special honours are to be elected president of the German Society of Property Researchers, president of the European Real Estate Society (ERES) as well as the presidency of the International Real Estate Society (IRES) and his nomination as an Honorary Member of the Royal Institution of Chartered Surveyors (HonRICS). He received the Service Award from the International Real Estate Society in 1999 and the Achievement Award from the European Real Estate Society in 2001.

He has published books in German on Real Estate Economics Volumes I & II, Real Estate Development, Corporate Real Estate Management, Real Estate Investment, Facilities Management, Real Estate Marketing and Real Estate Banking and Finance.

As a member of numerous advisory and editorial boards of renowned real estate companies and journals, Karl-Werner Schulte links the practical and theoretical aspects of real estate economics.

Halbert C. Smith

Halbert C. Smith earned a D.B.A. from the University of Illinois (1962), an M.B.A from Indiana University (1959) and a B.S. from Purdue University (1956).

He is a member of the Appraisal Institute (MAI), a Counselor of Real Estate (CRE) and a member of the Italian Association of Real Estate Counsellors (AICI).

In 1998, he was presented with the "Real Estate Pioneer Award" by the ARES in recognition of his work, throughout his career, in educating and encouraging graduate and undergraduate students, conducting and publishing real estate research, and working with professional and academic real estate organisations. In 1985 he was the first recipient of the George Bloom Award of the American Real Estate and Urban Economics Association for "outstanding contributions to real estate research and analysis and to the work of AREUEA".

Since 1971, Halbert C. Smith has been Professor of Real Estate and Urban Analysis at the Warrington College of Business Administration and Graduate School of Business, University of Florida (he entered phased retirement in 1996). From 1983 to the present he has been a member of the Board of Directors and Officer of both the Homer Hoyt Institute and the Homer Hoyt Advanced Studies Institute. Since 1983 he has been a faculty member and from 1986 to 1988 Dean of the Weimer School of Advanced Studies in Real Estate and Land Economics of the Homer Hoyt Advanced Studies Institute. From 1962 to 1971 he was Professor of Real Estate and Urban Analysis at Ohio State University. As well as being member of the editorial board of several real estate journals, Halbert C. Smith was a member of the board of Directors of the Counselors of Real Estate (1996-2000).

He was President of the American Real Estate and Urban Economics Association in 1970 (1st VP in 1969, 2nd VP in 1967, Secretary-Treasurer 1964-1967).

Halbert C. Smith has published several books and numerous articles on real estate topics.

Maruška Šubic Kovac

Maruška Šubic Kovac is an assistant professor of municipal economics at the University of Ljubljana and a deputy director of the Municipal Economics Institute of Ljubljana, Slovenia. She is the author of several articles and books in the field of real estate valuation, land policy, land use and development and municipal economics, including Housing Construction and Protection of Agriculture Land (1989) and Building Land Valuation (1997).

Maruška Šubic Kovac is a sworn-in expert in civil engineering and a sworn-in real estate appraiser, registered at the Ministry of Justice of the Republic of Slovenia. She is a holder of the Broker's Certificate of Slovenian Real Estate Exchange, and the Real Estate Appraiser Certificate of the Agency of the Republic of Slovenia for the Reconstruction and Privatisation of Companies, acquired at the ASA (American Society of Appraisers) seminar. Maruška Šubic Kovac is a member of the European Real Estate Society and the European Faculty of Land Use and Development of Strasbourg. More recently, she has been involved in the projects of re-establishing individual and mass real estate appraisal in Slovenia.

Connie Susilawati

Connie Susilawati was awarded her bachelor's degree in Civil Engineering from Petra Christian University, Surabaya, Indonesia in 1992 and Master of Commerce in Property from Curtin University of Technology, Perth, Western Australia in 1996. She lectures on the following courses: Introductory to Building and Property Management in the Real Estate Management School; Organisation & Human Resources Management and Operational Research courses in Civil Engineering; and also Real Estate Finance, Property Management and Appraisal on the Postgraduate Program in Construction Management. She has carried out research on property market, valuation methodology, building quality, property management, construction engineering and construction management. She is currently acting as Deputy Director of the postgraduate programme in Petra Christian University and coordinator of property courses.

Paloma Taltavull de La Paz

Paloma Taltavull de La Paz is a Doctor of economics from Alicante University. She is senior lecturer in the Department of Applied Economics and her speciality is the Spanish Economy, sectorial economics and urban economics. She began teaching real estate economics in Architectural and Economics Degrees at Alicante University in 1995 and, since 1998, she has also taught real estate markets on doctoral courses. Jointly with eleven other Spanish Universities, she began the first Real Estate undergraduate courses in Spain, in 1997.

Research subjects in her background are housing economics, real estate markets and also the Spanish economy, where she has numerous publications, both books and articles in specialised reviews. She has undertaken research in projects with the local Government and Ministry, analysing housing markets in Spain.

In 2001, Paloma Taltavull de La Paz was conference chair for the Alicante 8th Annual Conference of the European Real Estate Society.

Nikolai Trifonov

Nikolai Trifonov has been the Head of Valuation Department in the Belarusian State University since 2000. He was the founder and, since 1996, has been the President of the Belarusian Society of Valuers and also, since 1994, of the Belarusian Real Estate Guild.

He has worked in professional international organisations as the Chairman of the Co-ordination Council for Valuation in the C.I.S. since 2000, as well as the Director at Large, responsible for Central and Eastern European Relations of the European Real Estate Society, since 1998. He is a member of the editorial board of the Accounting and Analysis journal, Minsk, Belarus, the Valuation Question journal, Moscow, Russia, and the Property Management journal, Vilnius, Lithuania. He is an Honorary Member of the Association of Kyrgyzian Appraisers, OKO, of the Portuguese Association of Valuers of Fixed Assets, AAPOR, as well as of East-European Union of Experts, Germany, OSV. He was the American Biographical Institute International Man of the Year in 1999.

He studied mathematics in the Belarusian State University, graduated in 1975 with an Honours Diploma and a Ph.D. degree in 1987. His career included positions as a Lecturer in Mathematics and Economics, Co-Chairman of the Minsk Exchange, Member of the Council of the Belarusbank, Minsk.

Sotiris Tsolacos

Sotiris Tsolacos received his first degree from the University of Athens and his Master's and Ph.D. from the University of Reading. Dr. Tsolacos is currently the UK Forecasting Manager at Jones Lang LaSalle in London and visiting lecturer at the University of Reading. He was previously a lecturer at the Centre for Spatial and Real Estate Economics at the University of Reading where he taught macroeconomics, property market economics and quantitative analysis of real estate markets.

Sotiris Tsolacos has carried out extensive quantitative research on real estate markets. His articles have appeared in major UK and international property research journals. He regularly presents research papers at international conferences, contributes to practitioners' journals and lectures in European academic real estate centres.

Sotiris Tsolacos is on the editorial board of the Journal of Property Research and sits on the Board of Directors of the European Real Estate Society, of which he was President for 2000-2001.

James R. Webb

James R. Webb is Professor of Finance and Director of the Center for the Study of Real Estate Brokerage/Agency and Markets at Cleveland State University, U.S.A.

He was awarded a Ph.D. in Finance from the University of Illinois, as well as an MBA in Finance and a B.S. in Management and Production, both from Northern Illinois University.

Since 1991, he has been Professor and Director of the Center for the Study of Real Estate Brokerage and Markets, Department of Finance at James J. Nance College of Business, Cleveland State University. From 1989 to 1991, he was Professor and Chairman of the Department of Finance in the James J. Nance College of Business. In addition, he has published over one hundred articles on various aspects of real estate investment in academic journals.

James R. Webb has also served as a consultant in many capacities, e.g. for pension funds on asset allocation, for the Ohio State University Research Foundation, for mass appraisal firms, numerous County appraisal divisions and as an expert witness on real estate valuation and capitalisation rates.

In addition, he was the recipient of the first ARES James A. Graaskamp Award (1990), Executive Director of the American Real Estate Society for 15 years (1987-2001) and the first full-time President of the American Real Estate Society (1986). He was a founder (1987), President (1993) and is an executive director (1992-present) of the American Real Estate Society Foundation. Currently he is Director of Development for ARES.

James R. Webb is on the editorial boards of: the Journal of Real Estate Research, the Journal of Real Estate Portfolio Management, the Journal of Real Estate Literature (international and case studies sections); Real Estate Capital Markets Report, Journal of Housing Research, the Journal of Property Investment and Finance (U.K.), Journal of Property Research (U.K.), Journal of Real Estate Education and Practice, The Journal of the Asian Real Estate Society and Australian Land Economics Review.

In addition, James R. Webb also serves as Chairman of the Board and CEO of the National Bureau of Real Estate Research (NBRER).

Brendan Williams

Brendan Williams is currently Faculty Research Fellow and Lecturer in Urban Economics at Dublin Institute of Technology and consultant to public and private clients.

Previous experience includes academic and professional practice in the areas of property appraisal, planning and development. He initially studied Environmental Economics at the Dublin Institute of Technology and subsequently obtained his MA and Ph.D. at the University of Dublin Trinity College. He is a Fellow of the Royal Institution of Chartered Surveyors, the Society of Chartered Surveyors in Ireland and the Irish Auctioneers and Valuers Institute.

Zhang Hong

Zhang Hong is a lecturer at the Institute of Real Estate Studies at the School of Civil Engineering and Hydraulics of Tsinghua University. Zhang Hong received her B.E. and M.E. from Renmin University of China (formerly the 'People's University of China') and a Ph.D. in economics from the Renmin University of China and The Hong Kong Polytechnic University in 1998. Since June 1998, she has served at Tsinghua University. Her research interests include real estate finance, housing and urban economics, and quantitative policy analysis.

She has published around 35 research papers, in both English and Chinese, in prestigious real estate journals and has translated two books during the last three years. Zhang Hong has served as a China Certificated Real Estate Appraiser, a Member of the Expert Committee of the Beijing Association of Real Estate Development, and as Member of China Institute of Construction Management Research (Hong Kong) since May 1997.

Subject Index